CASE AND COURT PREPARATION IN CRIMINAL LAW

CASE AND COURT PREPARATION IN CRIMINAL LAW

First Edition

Leona Harrison

cognella
SAN DIEGO

Bassim Hamadeh, CEO and Publisher
Gem Rabanera, Senior Project Editor
Samantha Hansen, Production Editor
Jessica Delia, Graphic Design Associate
JoHannah McDonald, Licensing Coordinator
Stephanie Adams, Senior Marketing Program Manager
Natalie Piccotti, Director of Marketing
Kassie Graves, Senior Vice President, Editorial
Alia Bales, Director, Project Editorial and Production

Printed in the United States of America.

Contents

WEB-BASED RESOURCES: ACCESSING QR CODES AND LINKS

The author has selected some supporting web-based content for further engagement with the learning material that appears in this text, which can be accessed through QR codes or web links. These codes are intended for use by those who have purchased print copies of the book. You may scan them using a QR code reading app on your cell phone, which will take you to each website. You can also search for the link using a web browser search engine. Readers who have purchased a digital copy of the book can simply click on the hyperlinks beneath each QR code.

Cognella maintains no responsibility for the content nor availability of third-party links. However, Cognella makes every effort to keep its texts current. Broken links may be reported to studentreviews@cognella.com. Please include the book's title, author, and 7-digit SKU reference number (found below the barcode on the back cover of the book) in the body of your message.

Please check with your professor to confirm whether your class will access this content independently or collectively.

cognella®
SAN DIEGO

Chapter 1

Introduction to the Criminal Justice System

Introduction: Understanding the Roles of the Various People in the Criminal Justice System

This chapter will discuss who is involved in the criminal justice system and each person's purpose and provide an overview of the types of crimes involved in the criminal justice system.

Chapter Objectives

In this chapter students will learn:

- The basic constitutional rights that the defendant is afforded during a criminal trial
- How the US Supreme Court interprets those constitutional rights and applies them to each defendant's case
- The role of the individuals involved in the criminal justice system: the judge, the prosecutor, the defense attorney, the defendant, the victim, the witness, and the jury
- The different types of witnesses involved in the criminal justice system
- The role of the individuals involved in the criminal justice system who are outside of the courtroom: the magistrate, the court clerk, the probation officers, the parole officers, the court referral officers, and victim service officers
- The role of other individuals in the criminal courtroom: the bailiff and the court reporter
- Ethical dilemmas of each individual involved in the criminal justice system
- The three main categories of criminal offenses
- What constitutes an inchoate crime

Key Terms

Key terms and professional terminology that are used in this chapter include:

- **Constitutional amendments**
- **Due process**
- **Ex parte**
- **Precedent**
- **Magistrates**
- **Prosecutors**
- **Court clerk**
- **Criminal defense attorney**
- **The defendant**
- **The victim**
- **Victimless crimes**
- **Fact/lay witness**
- **Character witness**
- **Expert witness**
- **Jury**
- **Ethical dilemma**
- **Bailiff**
- **The court reporter**
- **Probation/parole officers**
- **Inchoate crimes**
- **Victim service officers**
- **Court referral officer**
- **Specialized courts**
- **Probation/parole officers**

What Is the Criminal Justice System?

The criminal justice system is a complex system that is designed to protect society by punishing wrongdoers. The system is grounded by the US Constitution and its **amendments**, which were written to protect the rights of the people. The Constitution and amendments are consistent, while the interpretation of them has fluctuated over the years. The US Supreme Court is the guiding body that interprets the Constitution and its applicability to the people.

The Constitutional Basis

The criminal justice system relies on the Fourth, Fifth, Sixth, Eighth, and Fourteenth Amendments to protect the rights of the people and states.

The Fourth Amendment

The right of the people to be secure in their persons, houses, papers, and effects, against unreasonable searches and seizures, shall not be violated, and no Warrants shall issue, but upon probable cause, supported by Oath or affirmation, and particularly describing the place to be searched, and the persons or things to be seized.

The Fifth Amendment

No person shall be held to answer for a capital, or otherwise infamous crime, unless on a presentment or indictment of a Grand Jury, except in cases arising in the land or naval forces, or in the Militia, when in actual service in time of War or public danger; nor shall any person be subject for the same offense to be twice put in jeopardy of life or limb; nor shall be compelled in any criminal case to be a witness against himself, nor be deprived of life, liberty, or property, without **due process of law**; nor shall private property be taken for public use, without just compensation.

The Sixth Amendment

In all criminal prosecutions, the accused shall enjoy the right to a speedy and public trial, by an impartial jury of the State and district wherein the crime shall have been committed, which district shall have been previously ascertained by law, and to be informed of the nature and cause of the accusation; to be confronted with the witnesses against him; to have compulsory process for obtaining witnesses in his favor, and to have the Assistance of Counsel for his defense.

The Eighth Amendment

Excessive bail shall not be required, nor excessive fines imposed, nor cruel and unusual punishments inflicted.

The Fourteenth Amendment, Due Process Clause

All persons born or naturalized in the United States, and subject to the jurisdiction thereof, are citizens of the United States and of the State wherein they reside. No State shall make or enforce any law which shall abridge the privileges or immunities of citizens of the United States; nor shall any State deprive any person of life, liberty, or property, without due process of law; nor deny to any person within its jurisdiction the equal protection of the laws.

The above amendments are included in the Bill of Rights, also known as the first ten amendments. Those amendments were drafted to limit the power of the federal government. The state governments were free to draft their own state constitutions to protect the people in each state. The Fourteenth Amendment is the mechanism that has allowed the US Supreme Court to limit the power of the states through the Due Process Clause.

The US Supreme Court's Role

As the ultimate decision-maker, the Supreme Court's purpose is to ensure the American people receive equal justice under the law. The Court does this through its interpretation of the applicability of the amendments to fact patterns. This establishes a legal precedent. A **precedent** is a ruling by a higher court that is binding on all lower courts. Precedents are important because they give people consistency and security in knowing how laws will apply to future scenarios. This is why it is important that lower courts defer to precedent of the Supreme Court when possible.

Courts cannot always follow precedent when the fact pattern differs from the previously established precedent. This is known as a distinguishing case. Distinguishing cases will result in new case law for that particular set of facts. Because most criminal cases involve different sets of facts, the courts are routinely tasked with making new decisions. These new decisions can be appealed and then the US Supreme Court can establish a new precedent.

The Supreme Court can also overrule itself. Reversing precedent is unusual but will happen if the Court believes that its past reasoning was flawed. This can also happen because of changes in the Court composition over time. Politics should not be a factor in the Supreme Court's decisions, but arguably, since the justices are nominated by the president of the United States and accepted by the US Senate, some argue that politics are involved. The Supreme Court justices are nonpolitical individuals who are appointed for life. This appointment for life is thought to dissuade the influences of politics on the Court's decisions. The justices can use reasoning based in academia rather than what is popular with the public at the time.

Parties Involved in the Criminal Justice System

The criminal justice system is a complex legal system that necessitates many checks and balances from many individuals with many different purposes. Below, those individual parties and how they combine with each other to form the American criminal justice system will be discussed.

The Judge

Judges are also lawyers in the criminal justice system. They are responsible for ensuring that parties follow the established rules and maintain order. They are also responsible for moving the cases along in a timely fashion. With thousands of criminal cases in each small jurisdiction in each state, it is possible for criminal courts to get backlogged. Judges are tasked with keeping the cases moving forward and giving the parties an opportunity to be heard. Judges have pretrial responsibilities and posttrial responsibilities.

For simplicity's sake, we will consider all action prior to trial. The judge's first contact with the criminal justice system is when they issue warrants for seizure or arrest. This is known as an ex parte procedure, where only one side is heard. At this point in the process, the defendant does not know that he or she is subject to the impending search or arrest. The judges listen to the facts of each situation as sworn by a law enforcement officer. Then the judge makes the legal determination of whether to issue the requested warrant. If the warrant is allowed, the judge may also be involved in setting the bond amount for that warrant. The judge will weigh several factors, including but not limited to the criminal history of the accused, the type of crime, the possibility of flight, and the safety of the community.

A judge is involved in the criminal justice system when he or she precedes over a pretrial hearing. Early proceedings, such as initial appearances, can be **ex parte**, while later pretrial proceedings can be adversarial in nature. An adversarial proceeding is a proceeding in which both parties are heard. The courtroom is a safe location where both sides can appear and discuss their differences. The judge must maintain order and courtroom decorum at all times, disallowing unprofessional behavior from both sides. The judges preside over court filings and motions relative to a case that will ultimately be resolved by either guilty plea, dismissal, or trial.

The judges' roles continue if the case is set for trial. A bench trial is a trial by judge. There is no jury; the judge makes decisions of law and fact and pronounces a verdict. The judge acts as a referee between the parties when objections are made during trial. The judge must determine which pieces of evidence will be admissible and what procedures will be allowable during the trial. One may think that this should not be necessary if the attorneys trying the case follow the rules. The need for a referee arises when the parties disagree on the application of certain rules to certain facts. This is when the judge must be the ultimate decision-maker.

A state rule of criminal procedure reads as follows: Evidence that a witness has been convicted of a crime shall be admitted, if the crime was punishable by death or imprisonment in excess of one year under the law under which the witness was convicted, and the evidence that an accused has been convicted of such a crime shall be admitted if the court determines that the probative value of admitting this evidence outweighs its prejudicial effect to the accused. The prosecutor seeks to enter a conviction of a defense witness who was convicted of a drug crime that carried greater than a one-year sentence. The defense attorney objects that the conviction for a drug crime does not bear on the witness's credibility or truthfulness and therefore should not be admitted just to make the witness look bad. The judge will need to balance the conviction, facts, and law, and make a ruling. Once done, the attorneys must accept that ruling for the duration of the trial.

In a jury trial, the judge must maintain order in and outside of the courtroom. The juries are usually the responsibility of the judge they are assigned to. This means that any needs of theirs that arise during the trial will be addressed by the judge. For example, if a jury is selected, and during the trial of the case a juror falls ill, the judge will need to seek medical care for that juror and monitor the situation. Keeping up with a jury could also mean that the judge organizes coffee and snacks to be available to the jury during deliberations, provides a computer or other like equipment for the jury to view certain pieces of evidence admitted, or arranges for escorts to and from the courthouse for the jurors. The judge must answer questions of the jury and give them instructions at the close of the case. After all, the jurors are not schooled in the law and will look to the judge to guide the application of the facts heard in the trial to that law he instructs.

Judges are also responsible for posttrial issues involving certain aspects of the case. The trial judge is still responsible for a number of days after the trial has concluded to make rulings relative to new filings by the attorneys. Some jurisdictions call for the juries to pronounce sentence upon the defendants, but others leave that responsibility to the judge. Sentencing hearings can be complex and give great discretion to judges because of wide sentencing ranges proscribed for different crimes.

Judges in appellate courts have the responsibility of reviewing decisions and actions of attorneys and judges in lower courts. Those judges rely on the record and possibly oral arguments from appellate counsel rather than live testimony. Those judges must consider whether the case appealed followed precedent or can be factually distinguished from the predicate.

Ethical Dilemmas

US Supreme Court Justices are sworn to a constitutional oath and a judicial oath. A combined version reads as follows:

> "I, __________, do solemnly swear (or affirm) that I will administer justice without respect to persons, and do equal right to the poor and to the rich, and that I will faithfully and impartially discharge and perform all the duties incumbent upon me as __________ under the Constitution and laws of the United States; and that I will support and defend the Constitution of the United States against all enemies, foreign and domestic; that I will bear true faith and allegiance to the same; that I take this obligation freely, without any mental reservation or purpose of evasion; and that I will well and faithfully discharge the duties of the office on which I am about to enter. So help me God."[1]

Lower judges in the federal and state criminal justice systems take a similar oath. However, judges are human and can be overcome by emotion from time to time. Judges could encounter situations wherein they are conflicted about how justice will be served.

> Judge Johnny is a state judge and sworn to uphold the laws of the state. Judge Johnny also has a moral reservation about the state's use of the death penalty as a punishment. He impanels a jury, asking whether all potential jurors can set aside his or her personal opinion on the death penalty and render a sentence based on the law and the evidence. However, Judge Johnny has never been able to do what he is asking the jurors to do. The government convicts the defendant, and the jury recommends a sentence of death. Judge Johnny is in a state that allows judicial override of jury verdicts, and he does just that. Judge Johnny sentences the defendant to life imprisonment without the possibility of parole. Are Judge Johnny's actions unethical?

The Magistrate

Magistrates are sometimes lawyers and sometimes non-lawyers who have been trained in certain aspects of criminal procedure. Many state statutes and rules give magistrates the authority to issue search warrants and arrest warrants, and to proceed over nonadversarial proceedings, such as an initial appearance. Magistrates can set bonds and determine other conditions of release. Most state statutes limit the discretion of magistrates to the statutory bond schedule giving only judges the ability to increase or

1. https://www.supremecourt.gov/about/oath/oathsofoffice.aspx.

decrease the bond amount. While making decisions to take someone's liberty or invade one's privacy with a search, the magistrate's role is a limited one in the criminal justice system.

Ethical Dilemmas

Magistrates are not immune from ethical dilemmas while trying to remain neutral parties in the criminal justice system. Magistrates have great discretion in initial matters of warrants and bonds. They interact with law enforcement on a daily basis and can hear the same criminal's name again and again. A magistrate could let emotion dictate the amount of a bond or issuance of a warrant.

> Margie Magistrate is dating a police officer in a neighboring jurisdiction. She hears him constantly complaining that the magistrate in his jurisdiction will not give high bonds on domestic violence cases. Margie likes the law enforcement officers in her jurisdiction and does not want them to complain about her. Therefore, she sets every bond on domestic violence cases as high as legally possible. Are Margie's actions unethical?

The Prosecutor

The **prosecutor** is a lawyer who represents the government in a criminal proceeding against individuals accused of crimes. The position of prosecutor falls under the executive branch of government. Prosecutors are the seekers of justice and not bound to represent any one person. Sometimes referred to as "the victim's lawyer" because the prosecutor is the voice of the victim in the criminal proceeding, he or she is not technically the victim's lawyer. The prosecutor has a duty to seek justice even if it is not beneficial to the victim of the crime. The prosecutor is not bound to act at the direction of the victim, although may ask for input from the victim.

A prosecutor's office is a political office because the prosecutor is usually an elected position. The attorney general's office is an appointed position but is still a political office by nature. Because prosecutors are elected, they are accountable to the people whom they serve. This accountability can carry great weight. The prosecutor must do what he or she believes is right under the law that he or she was sworn to follow. The right thing may not be the popular thing, and some good prosecutors could run afoul of public opinion for certain actions. For example: There have been a lot of shootings in Smallville. The police have been unable to make arrests because victims of and witnesses to the shootings will not come forward and give statements. Instead, they take the law into their own hands by retaliatory shootings. One day, Investigator Lockemup is able to secure a video of a shooting wherein the victim was shot in his car and sustained serious injuries. The victim cannot identify the shooter and there are no witnesses who came forward. Investigator Lockemup believes that the video depicts Sam Shooter as the one doing the shooting. The video is of very poor quality, and the prosecutor cannot be certain. Investigator Lockemup tells the prosecutor that he knows Sam is the shooter because that is what his informants on the street say. Investigator Lockemup asks the prosecutor for a warrant for Sam's arrest, but the prosecutor declines. A rumor is spread in the community that the police have a video of the shooting but still won't do anything to stop the shootings in the area. This is an example of the right decision (not bringing charges without enough evidence) being unpopular.

Prosecutors are heavily connected with law enforcement officers with the goal of crime control. Law enforcement officers are the first responders, the front line on the war on crime. The prosecutors are the secondary actors and seek accountability for the charged crimes. Law enforcement officers and prosecutors are in constant communication about ongoing investigations as well as charged crimes pending trial.

Prosecutorial discretion is the power of a prosecutor to weigh the facts, circumstances, and community morals and values in making charging decisions. That same prosecutorial discretion continues throughout the criminal case until the case is resolved. Prosecutors may offer plea agreements or reduce cases as they see fit. However, in making charging decisions and in case resolution, it is important that a prosecutor use the power of discretion equally and fairly. If a prosecutor does not, this is called an abuse of prosecutorial discretion. Prosecutors can be sued in civil court for failing to exercise prosecutorial discretion in a just manner. This is called selective prosecution. The Fourteenth Amendment's Due Process Clause also applies to selective prosecution. The US Supreme Court in *Oyler v. Boles* said the conscious exercise of some selectivity in enforcement of a state habitual criminal statute is not in itself a violation of the federal Constitution. A policy of selective enforcement does not violate the Equal Protection Clause of the Fourteenth Amendment where the selection is not deliberately based upon an unjustifiable standard such as race, religion, or other arbitrary classification.

Prosecutors can also decide not to prosecute when the case may be clearly chargeable. This is a use of prosecutorial discretion. For example: A state has a statute making adultery a criminal offense prosecutable for up to three years in the penitentiary. Sally suspects her husband, Alan, of cheating and hires a private investigator to follow Alan. The private investigator follows Alan to a cheap motel. Alan goes to the door of the motel, is greeted by a woman resembling his secretary, and they disappear inside. Alan neglects to close the curtains all the way and the investigator is able to walk up to the window and view inside. The investigator records Alan and the woman in sexual acts and gives the recording to Sally. Sally files a complaint that Alan has cheated on her and wants to prosecute him to the fullest extent of the law. She gives the recording to the prosecutor along with their marriage certificate. The prosecutor declines to prosecute Alan for adultery although the case can be proven and is a violation of the law. This is not a problem unless the prosecutor prosecutes many others for the crime of adultery and Alan happens to be a good friend of the prosecutor.

Prosecutors present evidence to grand juries in states mandating the use of grand juries for felony prosecutions. They also present evidence in juvenile proceedings and other civil proceedings such as condemnation of property cases.

A prosecutor's duty during the trial of a case is to prove the case to the jury beyond a reasonable doubt. This could be during a bench trial or jury trial; the burden is the same in all criminal trials. This involves securing subpoenas for witnesses, records, documents, or other physical evidence in the case. The prosecutor generally has one opportunity to try the case and must be ready.

Prosecutors handle certain issues after the criminal case is resolved, such as complaints of the defendant about his or her trial counsel. Prosecutors also represent other prosecutors in appellate cases. Appellate representation is usually done by the attorney general's office. Prosecutors can also be taxed with handling public policy decisions such as local taxation.

Ethical Dilemmas

Prosecutors also swear an oath of office with slight variations depending on the jurisdiction. Most oaths include a promise to be truthful, honorable, fair, and courteous. The oath usually includes a statement that the attorney will support the US Constitution and the constitution of the state in faithfully preforming the duties of the office. In performing the official duties of the office of the prosecutor, the prosecutor must assist the court in seeking the truth. This is the duty even if the criminal defendant's counsel is neglectful in his or her duties. A prosecutor must zealously represent the citizens of the jurisdiction but also safeguard the rights of the accused. Therefore, the prosecutor should never focus on the win, but rather seek justice, even if that means a loss.

Paul Prosecutor is assigned a case of child sexual abuse for prosecution. In reading the file, he learns that the victim, Vicki, alleges that the defendant, David, was her mother's boyfriend. Vicki was initially interviewed at a child advocacy center and disclosed that the abuse began when she was four years old and continued for several months until her mother broke up with David. Vicki's mother states that one day she walked in on David and Vicki in bed together and Vicki did not have on clothes. Vicki's mother said that David explained that Vicki wet the bed and he had just taken off her clothes. Vicki's mother didn't think anything about it until Vicki made a disclosure a few days later. Vicki is now seven because the case has been continued multiple times due to a worldwide pandemic. Paul Prosecutor meets with Vicki to prepare for her courtroom testimony. During this meeting, Vicki tells Paul that she can't remember anything that happened with Paul and doesn't want to talk about it anymore. Paul decides that he cannot try this case because he will lose without Vicki's testimony proving the elements of the crime. Paul decides to bluff the defense attorney and offers David a deal to plead guilty and receive probation. David pleads guilty and is given five years supervised probation. During those five years, David is caught with a controlled substance at a traffic stop. This new charge violates David's probation, and he goes to prison on the original charge of sexual abuse. Was Paul Prosecutor's failure to disclose that a witness could not testify unethical?

The Court Clerk

The **clerk of court** is usually an elected position and falls under the umbrella of the administrative offices of courts in the judicial branch of government. The clerk of court is responsible for the court's nonjudicial day-to-day operations, things such as issuing subpoenas, summons, orders, processes, or writs as directed by state statute. The clerk of court could also be responsible for matters such as marriage certificates and passport applications.

The clerk's office is also a place that receives money for payment of court costs and fines. It maintains the court record and distributes the collections to other officers who may share in receipts of those collections based on a state statute or local law.

The most important function of the clerk of court is being the custodian of the records for the court. All lawsuits and criminal actions that are brought before a judge for a proceeding must be initiated in the clerk's office. This is where an action is "filed" in and given a proper style name and case number. The clerk's office receives all motions and filings on the cases and is the central hub between all parties. The clerk keeps records of all jurors summonsed and witnesses called. In fact, the clerk is the authority that sends jury summons inviting jurors in for duty. If there is a need to prove a prior conviction, the clerk of court could provide a certified copy or give testimony concerning a prior record.

The clerk's office is a neutral office that is not on the side of either party. It is an administrative office yet still an elected position in most jurisdictions. Most clerks of court are not attorneys, and some may be elected or appointed to the position with little or no legal training.

Ethical Dilemmas

At first glance it seems that the keeper of the record may not have any ethical dilemmas; however, most offices can face ethical dilemmas. The clerk's office is the keeper of the records and usually receives all moneys paid into the court system. These can be very large amounts of money taken in on a daily basis for payment of fines or costs, or in payments for cases like garnishment and child support. Anytime you have someone responsible for handling lots of money, there is a potential for unethical behavior.

The clerk's office is also responsible for subpoenaing potential jurors and witnesses for trials. If the clerk has an emotional attachment to a case, he or she could fail to subpoena certain persons in hopes that doing so would help or hurt the case.

> Claudia works in the clerk's office. She is well known and liked in the small town. Each month, she summons potential jurors for jury trials. Each month, several people call into Claudia's office and ask to be excused from service for varying reasons. Claudia is elected by the people and has incentive to keep the community members happy. She usually excuses the jurors and removes their names from the judge's list. Claudia does not have the legal authority to excuse jurors; that is the judge's function. Claudia has worked with the judge for a number of years and knows that he usually excuse potential jurors for any excuse because he is also in an elected position. Claudia figures that they will be excused anyway and doesn't see the harm in saving them a trip to the courthouse. Is Claudia's behavior unethical?

The Criminal Defense Attorney

A **criminal defense attorney** is tasked with assisting a criminal defendant through the criminal justice system. The attorney serves the defendant and has a duty to act on the defendant's behalf. The criminal defense attorney is unlike a prosecutor in that he or she must have consent from the defendant to proceed. The criminal defense attorney merely advises the criminal defendant, with the criminal defendant making the ultimate decision on issues rather than the attorney.

Criminal defense attorneys are either retained or appointed. If the defendant can afford an attorney, he or she can hire an attorney of his or her choosing. If the defendant knows that there is a pending investigation, he or she may hire the attorney before charges are even brought. If the criminal defendant is indigent and cannot afford an attorney, one will be appointed for him or her. This right is grounded in the Sixth Amendment to the US Constitution. This right attaches at a "critical" stage of the proceeding and not necessarily when the criminal defendant wants an attorney. For example, a criminal defendant is under investigation for a murder. The law enforcement officers are interviewing him and read him the Miranda warnings. He requests an attorney at that time. He will not be provided a free attorney at that stage in the proceeding because an interrogation has not been determined to be a critical stage in the criminal proceeding. Law enforcement will, however, not be able to continue questioning of the defendant after he requests an attorney. If the criminal defendant is at the critical stage of the trial and the right to counsel has attached, the court will appoint a competent attorney at the expense of the government. Some jurisdictions have a public defender's office with a group of attorneys available to assist criminal defendants. These offices are also funded by the government.

With either a public defender or specially appointed defender, there are certain duties undertaken. The first duty of a criminal defense attorney is to assess the charge leveled against the defendant. In doing that, the attorney must collect as much information as possible. This could involve visiting the crime scene and talking with witnesses. The criminal defense attorney could also request additional information from the prosecutor. This is known as the discovery process. The criminal defense attorney should keep the defendant updated about the information received and discuss challenges to evidence gathered. The defense attorney also must be capable of analyzing the evidence and charges against the criminal defendant so as to advise the defendant of the best way to proceed with the case. The criminal defense attorney must communicate with the prosecutor's office and seek out potential offers for lowering or dismissing the charges. Perhaps the attorney could offer information on other cases, codefendant testimony, or other incentives to the prosecutor's office to obtain a good plea offer for his client. The criminal defense attorney must take all this information to the client and relay any offers made by the prosecutor. The attorney can advise the client as to what is reasonable and may be in his or her best interest, but ultimately, the decision is for the defendant. The attorney must also file motions or subpoenas that would assist his client in the case. The attorney must be present and represent his client to the best of his abilities in all court proceedings. Keeping up with the case and communication of the progression of the case with the client is very important. Lastly, the criminal defense attorney should be available to handle stressful situations for the defendant and offer the defendant emotional reassurance throughout the criminal justice prosecution.

Ethical Dilemmas

In some cases, defense attorneys may find themselves in an ethical dilemma when representing a criminal defendant. This situation can arise if the defendant tells the defense attorney different versions of a story. For example, the defendant is charged with robbery of a gas station clerk. The clerk says that the defendant cut himself when reaching through the broken safety class to get cartons of cigarettes. The defendant tells his attorney that he is not guilty as charged because he was not at the scene of the crime but was with his girlfriend at the time of the crime. The defense attorney and the defendant begin working toward an alibi defense based on the client's representations that he was not there. Then, the prosecutor gives the defense attorney the discovery in the case, and it included a lab report putting the defendant's DNA/blood on the safety glass at the store. The defense attorney confronts the defendant with the lab report, and the defendant says he was in the store in the past and cut himself on the safety glass when he reached through to pay for gas. This is the defense that the defendant sticks with and wants the defense attorney to assert to the judge and jury. The attorney knows that the second story was only in response to the DNA lab report and may be fabricated, but how can the attorney be sure which version is true?

The US Supreme Court has discussed the issue of ethical representation in many cases. In *Nix v. Whiteside*, the Supreme Court held that a criminal defendant has no right to the assistance of counsel in giving false testimony and that lawyers who refuse to give such assistance or who threaten to disclose the future perjury of the client have not denied the client effective assistance of counsel under the Sixth Amendment to the US Constitution. The American Bar Association has also drafted rules of conduct that state an attorney cannot assist a client in committing perjury. The caveat to the rule is that it only applies in situations where the lawyer knows the testimony to be false.

> The defendant is charged with murder of his wife. He tells his attorney that he did kill his wife because he was sick of her attitude and had had enough. He tells his attorney that he intends to testify that he killed her in self-defense because he is a small man, and he thinks the jury will believe that his wife attacked him. The attorney cannot call the defendant to the witness stand or elicit false testimony from the defendant. The attorney should notify the court of the defendant's intentions, and if the defendant intends continue with this false statement, the court can allow him to testify and tell his story without the assistance of counsel. Of course, he will be subject to cross-examination by the prosecutor. Likewise, the jury may believe it odd that the defense attorney does not question the defendant at all or support his position of self-defense.

The Criminal Defendant

The criminal **defendant** is the person who is accused of a crime. The defendant does not have to do or say anything in response to charges filed against him or her. It is the government's burden of proof to establish that the defendant committed the crime beyond a reasonable doubt. The defendant does have the responsibility to appear in court when required and to obey the orders of the court. The defendant can contribute and assist his attorney in any way that he wishes during the trial and can even assist in the presentment of his case.

A criminal defendant may also represent himself at trial. This is called a pro se defense. The constitutional right to represent oneself at trial is guaranteed by the Sixth Amendment. However, not every criminal defendant will be allowed to proceed without counsel. Only criminal defendants who are competent and intelligent can waive the right to counsel. The court can also appoint standby counsel to assist the criminal defendant, if needed during the trial.

The defendant may also testify as a witness in his own case, if he or she chooses. This will be the defendant's sole decision to make. He or she may consult with council, but the council cannot prevent the defendant from testifying. If the defendant chooses not to testify or present a defense, it cannot be subject to comment by the government. This is a well-established constitutional right: the Fifth Amendment's right to silence.

The defendant should also assist in the trial of his or her case. After all, the defendant is the only one who has something to lose should the outcome of the trial be unfavorable. This includes suggesting witnesses to call or not call in the defense, documents to present, or arguments to make.

Ethical Dilemmas

Criminal defendants may be faced with the biggest of ethical dilemmas because they are the only individuals involved in the criminal justice system with something to lose. This can be a big incentive to act in a manner inconsistent with one's usual character. Criminal defendants can become desperate, and desperate people can do desperate things. Criminal defendants can lie, ask others to lie, hide evidence, destroy evidence, and involve others in their misdirection of the facts. To some extent this can be understandable with a criminal defendant rather than any other individual in the criminal justice system. Certainly, no matter the reason for these actions, they are still unethical.

Chatman has pled guilty to possession of controlled substances and is pending sentencing. His attorney has told him that the judge usually orders everyone drug tested at sentencing and the result will affect sentencing. Chatman is addicted to cocaine and knows he will test positive for it at sentencing. He decides to borrow some urine from his mother and try to trick the drug test. He knows that the probation officer will be watching him closely while he urinates to ensure that he does not swap the urine. Chatman fills a small bottle of hand sanitizer with urine and tapes it to his chest. He runs a piece of aquarium tubing down and tapes it to his penis. He has a small stopper of wax at the end of the tube that he hopes to dislodge without notice. He "urinates" in a cup while the probation officer watches. He hands the cup to the probation officer, and the probation officer notices that the urine is room temperature. The probation officer confronts Chatman and asks him to lift his shirt, revealing the bottle and tube taped to his body. The probation officer reports this to the judge, and Chatman receives a harsher sentence for his attempted deception on the court. What do you think about Chatman's actions?

The Victim

Most criminal cases have a **victim**, with the exception of **victimless crimes** against the community as a whole. The victim is oftentimes a witness in the case as well. The victim may be afforded special treatment by those in the criminal justice system, depending on the situation. The victim may be given a special place to sit in the courtroom, an escort to and from the courtroom, or additional attention. Some jurisdictions employ victim service officers to assist the victims of crime through the criminal justice system. The victim service officer can offer information to the victim about social services available in the area. This could include counseling opportunities, housing options, restitution recovery, or other social services.

Ethical Dilemmas

Most crimes have a victim who has suffered an injury or a monetary loss or both. These cases are often initiated by the victim via a police incident report. In that regard, if the victim had not made the report, the defendant would not be involved in the criminal justice system. After the victim initiates the case, the government takes over, investigating and prosecuting the offender. The victim loses control of the case and the government takes over. In some circumstances, the victim changes his or her mind about prosecuting the offender. This is more common in cases where the victim and defendant have some type of relationship. The victim may have forgiven the offender and is not seeking any further punishment. However, the government still believed the defendant should be prosecuted. This can be an ethical dilemma for the victim.

> Amy is a victim of domestic violence. Jeff is the perpetrator. Amy and Jeff are married and have been in an on again, off again relationship for years. They have two children. On this night, Amy calls 911 screaming that Jeff has slapped her in the face. The police respond. Amy has a red mark on her left cheek and is crying. Jeff is irate and when asked "what happened" by the police officer, Jeff says, "She wouldn't shut up, so I warned her that if she didn't shut up, I was going to slap her mouth shut. She didn't shut up and I am a man of my word." The officer took Jeff to jail for domestic violence. Several months later, the case is set for trial. Amy and Jeff are back together, and everything seems fine between them. Jeff has apologized to Amy and Amy has forgiven him. Amy wants to tell the truth, but she knows that the truth will convict Jeff, and he may lose his job with a conviction. Amy claims spousal privilege and refuses to testify. Without Amy's testimony, Jeff is acquitted of the domestic violence charges. Was Amy's behavior ethical?

The Witness

Every criminal prosecution will involve witnesses. The prosecution must have a witness in order to prove a case beyond a reasonable doubt. In certain types of offenses, the prosecution need not have more than one witness in order to prove the case as long as that one witness can give testimony on each and every element of the crime. For example, Ed is on his way home from his office, which is just three blocks from his home. He is approached by a man he has seen in the streets before. That man brandishes a gun and demands that Ed give him money and his watch. Ed does so. The man runs off. Ed immediately reports the incident to the police and the next day identifies his robber from a photo lineup. At trial, Ed can give testimony about each and every element of the crime, and the jury will be able to convict the defendant based solely on Ed's testimony, if they believe Ed is a credible witness.

Most criminal cases involve several witnesses. These witnesses could be victim witnesses, fact witnesses, character witness, or expert witnesses. Both the prosecution and the defense can call witnesses to testify what they know about the circumstance. The witnesses offer testimony under oath, which means that the witness will swear or affirm to tell the truth.

1. Victim witnesses are fact witnesses who were the victim of the crime. These witnesses are the ones who were affected by the defendants actions directly. These witnesses will be allowed to testify about the facts of the crime, what they saw or heard during the crime, and how it affected their lives. The victim witness will not be allowed to give opinion testimony.
2. **Fact witnesses** are witnesses who saw something related to the crime at issue. The witness will tell facts about what he or she saw, heard, or felt. This testimony will be factual. The witness will not be able to give an opinion about what they thought about the situation; the witness may only describe the situation to the judge or jury so that the finder of the fact will be able to reach the truth. Fact witnesses are often called lay witnesses. Fact witnesses are the most common type of witnesses called in a trial.
3. **Character witnesses** are individuals who knew the defendant, victim, or other people involved in the criminal case. Character witnesses are not usually witnesses who saw the crime or have any information about the facts of the case. Instead, the character witness gives testimony about the type of person the defendant, victim, or other witness was before the crime occurred. This type of witness must first be qualified by the court, and a foundation for their knowledge base must be established by the attorney offering their testimony.
4. **Expert witnesses** are specialists or experts in a field, people who are educated beyond the average person in a particular area. It is not required that the expert witness have a college degree or any formal education, but rather the expert witness must have a specialized knowledge in the area testified about. For example, a pathologist may have multiple degrees and a doctorate degree and testify that in his opinion the cause of death of the victim was a gunshot wound to the head, while a mechanic with no formal education may testify that in his opinion the brake line of the vehicle was intentionally cut. The key to an expert witness's testimony is that

they are relaying an opinion. They do not necessarily know any facts about the crime charged, but they are testifying relative to a specialized area relevant to one of the facts in the crime charged.

The judge can also call witnesses. These individuals are called the court's witnesses. This is unusual but can occur. For example, if a prosecutor has an eyewitness subpoenaed and now that witness has become hostile, the prosecutor could ask the court to call that person as a witness. That person could still be questioned by the prosecutor and defense attorney, but on cross-examination rather than direct examination. An attorney is said to be vouching for a witness's credibility when calling a witness to the stand. If an attorney feels that a witness will be less than honest when called to testify, the attorney may ask the court to call the person as a Court's witness. This will give the attorney the ability to cross-examine the witness.

All witnesses, as well as any person in the courtroom, could be punished for contempt of court by the judge for conduct unbecoming in the courtroom. This gives the judge broad latitude to determine what he or she believes is inappropriate behavior. This could be talking when being told to remain silent, being physically aggressive, or exhibiting disrespectful attitudes. Witnesses can be found in contempt for failing to answer questions posed. The defendant is the only individual who has the right to remain silent. The judge can impose monetary sanctions or imprisonment for an unlimited time.

Ethical Dilemmas

Being a witness is often a very difficult position to be in. The witness may not have an interest in the case yet is involved by virtue of the circumstance surrounding the crime. There are some social stigmas attached to being a witness. Some people may refer to a witness as a snitch or with some other negative connotation. Witnesses could receive direct threats not to testify or experience an implied indirect threat. These situations can cause a witness to be reluctant or uncooperative. The witness may have to balance doing the right thing (by telling what he or she saw) with the potential for adverse consequences if they do.

Witnesses could also be subjected to bribery attempts. Some defendants or defendant's families may reach out to witnesses and offer money or other things of value to entice the witness to "forget" what they saw. In some cases, the witness could be offered a sum of money to change his or her story to benefit the defendant. This is a riskier position for the witness because the witness may have already given a version of events to law enforcement officers. If the witness changes his or her story at the trial, he or she could be charged with hindering prosecution, giving false information to a law enforcement officer, or other similar charge.

Jeremy was out playing basketball with friends when he sees a car slowly drive by the courts. Jeremy recognizes the two teenagers in the car. All of a sudden, shots are fired from the car and two of Jeremy's friends are killed. Jeremy runs home. The next day, the police come to Jeremy's house to get a statement from him. Jeremy is scared because he knows the teenage shooter and that he has a reputation for violence. Jeremy knows that if he says he saw the shooting, he will be in danger. Jeremy also knows that all his friends will think he is a snitch if he gives a statement to the police. At first, Jeremy tells the police that he was not out there playing basketball and see a shooting. Then the police officer confronts Jeremy with video showing the courts and Jeremy running away just after shots were fired. Jeremy tells the officer that he was there but did not see who was in the car that drove by. Is Jeremy's decision for self-preservation a violation of his ethical obligation to the community to report crime? Why or why not?

The Jury

The **jury** is known as the finders of the truth. The jury must determine what the true facts of the case are. The jury listens to evidence during the trial as presented from the witness stand. They determine which pieces of evidence they will give much weight and which pieces of evidence they will give little weight. They decide which witnesses they believe are telling the truth and which witnesses are lying. They listen to the law as given them by the judge and apply that law to the facts of the case. They listen to the attorney's arguments and then they deliberate among themselves to make a decision. During jury deliberations, they will select a foreperson who will lead the deliberations and mediate the group should disagreements occur. If the jury has questions during the deliberations, they may inquire with the judge and then be sent back into deliberations. Ultimately, the jury will reach a verdict in the case and find the defendant guilty or not guilty. If the verdict is not guilty, this is the end of the juror's service. If the finding is guilty, this could be the end of the juror's service unless there is a need for the jury's involvement in the sentencing phase. Some state statutes mandate juries to determine the sentence and some state statutes mandate the judge to determine the sentence. If the case moves into a sentencing phase, the jury will then listen to witnesses testifying about the punishment for the defendant. The jury will then again retire to deliberate and return a verdict about the appropriate punishment in the case.

In some instances, the jury cannot reach a verdict. This is called a hung jury. A hung jury occurs when there is not a unanimous agreement among all jurors. This could occur if the vote is 10–1 or 5–5. Anything less than unanimous is a hung jury. Depending on the case, juries may not be able to reach a unanimous verdict. Sometimes, they will relate to the judge that they cannot reach a verdict. The judge will then reinstruct the jury to go back to deliberations with an open mind and try to consider the opinions of fellow jurors and reach a verdict. Judges and parties put a lot of effort into a jury trial and many tax dollars are spent to have a jury trial. It is not in anyone's best interest to retry a case. However, sometimes this must happen.

Ethical Dilemmas

When juries are impaneled, they are sworn to find the true facts and render a fair verdict based on the facts and law presented to them. Juries are not immune to ethical dilemmas. An **ethical dilemma** could present to the group as a whole or to an individual juror. An ethical dilemma could present to the entire group in a case where the facts clearly show a defendant has violated the law, but the jury does not want to convict because of some emotional issue in the facts. This is known as jury nullification.

Jurors could also face ethical dilemmas as individuals. When a jury is impaneled, they are directed not to have any contact with the parties or witnesses to the case, not to discuss the case with anyone, or not to do any independent investigation into the facts presented in the case. If a juror felt compelled to drive to a crime scene or do internet searches of relevant issues in the case, the juror would be violating the oath. Juror tampering could also occur if a defendant or representative of the defendant approached an individual juror to talk about the case. There could be an offer of money or just a plea for mercy.

Adam is on trial for rape in the second degree. In this jurisdiction this means that the rape is due to the difference in age between the parties and no other element. The victim must be less than sixteen years old and the defendant must be eighteen years old or older. Adam was eighteen years old and Lovelace was thirteen years old. Lovelace's family was very upset when they found out that their daughter, Lovelace, had slept with several boys and wanted someone prosecuted. When Investigator Lockemup went to interview the boys who allegedly had sexual intercourse with Lovelace, Adam was the only boy to confess. He admitted that she came on to him, and he knew she had had sex with several of his friends in the past. Adam said he did not know her age but thought she was sixteen. At the trial, Lovelace testifies that she did have sex with Adam. Lovelace's mannerisms on the witness stand include disrespectful language, rude come backs to the attorneys, and a general sour attitude. Adam takes the witness stand and pleads his case telling the jury that he is truly sorry for his actions. The jury knows that if they convict Adam of this crime, he will be a registered sex offender for the rest of his life. The jury does not convict Adam, although the evidence is clearly there to convict. What do you think about the jury's nullification of the law in this case?

Other Individuals Directly Related to the Criminal Justice System

Bailiffs

A **bailiff** is an individual who assists the judge in managing the people in the courtroom. The bailiff could be a sworn law enforcement officer or not. The bailiff's duties could include escorting witnesses to and from the courtroom, escorting jurors to and from the courtroom, and notifying the parties of their responsibilities and duties while in the courtroom, such as taking off hats off, turning off cell phones, and not talking when court is in session. The bailiff could pass exhibits back and forth between parties, witnesses, or jurors so the parties do not have to directly interact. The bailiff is in charge of maintaining general order in the courtroom.

Court Reporters

The **court reporter** is the official keeper of the record. Jurisdictions have different rules regarding when proceedings must be taken down on the record for official use in a future proceeding or appeal. If the proceeding is taken on the record, the court reporter uses a special machine that allows for typing words phonetically and fast. The machine has letter combinations and is similar to a keyboard. Most higher courts have court reporters to take down all pretrial and trial proceedings. This is necessary in the case of an appeal to a higher court.

The court reporter takes down every word spoken by all parties and may use some type of video or audio recording to review at a later time. It can be difficult to spell unusual names or specialized terms, and the recording helps the accuracy of the transcript. The court reporter may also find it difficult to take down testimony when parties talk over each other, which can happen in an adversarial environment. The witness may begin to answer a question before the attorney finishes the question or vice versa. The court reporter will also take down the objections, which are by nature interruptions. The court reporter is also the person who marks, usually with stickers or cards, the physical evidence admitted in a trial. As a courtesy, many attorneys premark evidence to speed the flow of the trial, but ultimately the court reporter must maintain the list of every piece of evidence marked, whether it is admitted into evidence or not.

The court reporter is also the individual who maintains the physical evidence admitted at trial. For example, if a murder case has two thousand photographs and three hundred pieces of physical evidence admitted in the trial, the court reporter will need to transport that evidence to and from the courtroom or somehow maintain that evidence for the parties to use during the trial. The court reporter also must maintain that evidence indefinitely after the conclusion of the trial.

Court Referral Officers

Court referral officers are non-law enforcement officers who accept defendants into various programs at the direction of the court. These court officials may be employed by a governmental, nonprofit, or profit agency. The court referral officer may meet with the defendant referred and determine what level of services the defendant may need. Court referral officers are utilized in jurisdictions using nontraditional court settings, which may be known as deferment programs. These programs may defer the defendant's criminal charges for some period of time, conditioned on the defendant completing some recommended program. This usually takes place before a plea of guilt or sentencing in the case. Examples of various nontraditional courts include veterans court, gun court, drug court, and domestic violence court. Jurisdictions establish these courts as an alternative to the traditional system where defendants either plead guilty or have a trial. The defendants first must qualify for a **specialized court**. Criteria is in place and the judge, bailiff, judicial assistant, or panel of people will determine whether the defendant meets the criteria for the group, For example, a drug court program may accept individuals with no felony convictions who are in possession of certain types of drugs; the program, however, may not accept an individual with a lengthy arrest record with a charge of distribution of drugs. Second, in these specialized courts the defendants must agree to do certain things and pay certain fees. These things can include specific counseling groups, work programs, or regular drug testing. Third, if the defendant completes the required actions, the case against him or her maybe dismissed. For example, if a criminal defendant qualifies for veteran's court and completes all the requisite requirements, that defendant's case will be dismissed.

Probation Officers

A **probation officer** is a law enforcement officer who is responsible for keeping up with criminal defendants after they have been sentenced, if the sentence includes a term of probation. The probation officer will access the charges against the criminal defendant and meet with the defendant, after which the probation officer will determine a plan for hopeful success on probation. That plan can include things such as checking in each week, random drug testing, obtaining a job or GED, attending regular drug or alcohol counseling, or anything that the probation officer deems helpful for the defendant's success in the community.

The probation officer may also interact with the defendant before he or she is sentenced by the court. Probation officers are often responsible for providing the court with a presentence investigation report. This report can contain the family, social, and criminal history of the defendant, what other pending charges may be against the defendant, a statement of the crime itself, a defendant's statement about the crime, and other information that will be helpful to the court when sentencing the defendant. The report may also contain the probation officer's recommendations toward sentencing.

A probation officer may conduct home visits to the defendant's residence to verify he or she is in compliance. These visits could be scheduled or random. Although the probation officer is a sworn law enforcement officer, the Fourth Amendment protections do not apply to probationers in regard to search and seizure. The probationer is treated as if he is incarcerated but to a lesser degree. In other words, just as a corrections officer would be able to search the inmate's belongings, therefore the probation officer will be able to search the probationer's belongings. The probation officer may also question the probationer while he or she is detained without the Miranda warning being given.

If the criminal defendant fails to comply with the terms of his or her probation, the probation officer will alert the sentencing court. The probation officer also has the discretion to not notify the court for certain infractions. For example, if the defendant fails to appear to meet with the probation officer at the scheduled time, the probation officer may choose to give the defendant another chance rather than notify the court. If the court is notified that the defendant is delinquent in his responsibilities, the court may sanction the defendant or revoke the defendant's probation outright. Sanctions can include ordering the defendant to serve a certain number of days in jail. An outright revocation of the defendant's probation means that the defendant's probation is ended, and he or she will be ordered to serve the sentence imposed. For example, the defendant may have received a ten-year sentence with a two-year probationary term. If during the two years, the defendant violates the terms of his or her probation, the defendant will be ordered to serve the ten-year sentence.

Parole Officers

Parole officers are similar to probation officers in that they have many administrative responsibilities surrounding the criminal defendant. If a criminal defendant receives early release, he or she will be placed on parole. This is a transitional position from prison to complete release wherein the defendant is prepared for complete release back into society. Defendants released on parole may have served a number of years of incarceration and the world may have changed dramatically. The parolee needs to have a life plan in place to be successful in the free world. This plan can include job skills training, housing arrangements, and reconnection of past relationships with family and friends. The parolee is supported by the parole officer during this journey from incarceration to freedom.

The parole officer's duties can include scheduled or random home visits to the parolee's residence. The parole officer's position is similar to the probation officer's position in that the Fourth Amendment will not apply to searches of the parolee's belongings or person. Also, the Fifth Amendment right to remain silent does not apply to parolees. The parole officer may be required to visit the parolee's place of employment to make sure the transition is going well. The parole officer may administer scheduled or random drug tests. The parole officer may insist that the parolee attend counseling for mental health issues, alcohol or substance abuse, or any other need the parolee has.

If the parolee cannot make the transition and comply with the parole plan, the parole officer can ask that the parolee be reincarcerated. The parole officer will notify the parole board that the parolee has failed to comply with the conditions of parole and a hearing will be conducted. At the hearing, the parole board has the discretion to revoke the parolee's parole and order him or her to serve the remainder of his sentence. The parole board could also allow the parolee to remain on parole with greater supervision and other conditions in hopes for success.

Ethical dilemmas can impact all individuals involved in the criminal justice system. It is important that each individual recognizes the potential for an ethical dilemma, accesses the situation from all viewpoints, and makes a decision that is based on ethical standards. There must be a balancing of rights of all parties, a reaction that is grounded in reason rather than emotion and a decision based on acceptable standards in the profession.

The Types of Criminal Offenses in the Criminal Justice System

There are many types of criminal offenses in America. These are enacted by statute and outline what elements constitute commission of the crime in the relevant jurisdiction. An overview of criminal offenses can be broken down into three different types: crimes against persons, crimes against property, and crimes against the community.

1. Crimes against persons involve personal injury to the victim. These crimes include murder, manslaughter, assault, robbery, sexual offenses, child abuse, and kidnapping.
2. Crimes against property involve taking, destroying, or interfering with a property right. These crimes include burglary, theft of property, fraudulent use of a debit/credit card, breaking and entering a vehicle, and criminal mischief.
3. Crimes against the community are sometimes called victimless crimes. These crimes involve the general disregard for community standards without affecting an individual person but rather the community at large. These crimes include drug offenses, possession of illegal firearms, possession of child pornography or obscene materials, possession of explosive devices, failure to register as a sex offender, and driving under the influence.

Along with these main categories of criminal offenses, there can also be inchoate crimes of most of these offenses. An **inchoate crime** is a crime that hasn't been completed. There are three types of inchoate crimes: attempt, conspiracy, and solicitation.

Attempt—These crimes are charged under an attempt statute and may lower the class of the offense or may carry the same punishment as the stated charge. After all, should the defendant get the benefit of getting caught? For example, Abby goes into a bank to rob the bank but is caught in the process and never takes any money. She could be charged with robbery of the bank in a state having a statute where the crime encompasses an attempt.

Conspiracy—These are crimes that are plans for committing a crime that exist between two or more persons. In the law it is thought that there must be a "meeting of the minds" in order for a conspiracy to exist. Several people may conspire to commit a single crime, and each conspirator need make one substantial step toward accomplishing the unlawful act. A conspirator may also withdraw from the conspiracy before the crime is complete, to negate culpability—for example, conspiracy to manufacture a controlled substance. The conspirators agree that they will manufacture methamphetamine and each buys ingredients to manufacture the controlled substance. It is not necessary that the methamphetamine actually is made, but that they made substantial steps toward the manufacture of it.

Solicitation—This crime also involves two or more persons. The solicitor must intend that another person will engage in the conduct constituting a crime, and "solicits, requests, commands or importunes" the person to commit the crime. It is not necessary that the person commit the crime. The classic example of solicitation is solicitation to commit murder: "Will you kill my husband?" It matters not whether the person kills the husband; what matters is that the wife wanted her husband dead and asked someone she thought would do it.

Rules to Remember

Below is a list of rules to remember from this chapter.

- The criminal justice system is grounded in the US Constitution and its amendments.
- The Fourth Amendment to the US Constitution protects individuals against unreasonable arrest, search, or seizure by government officials.
- The Fifth Amendment to the US Constitution affords criminal defendants the right to remain silent.
- The Sixth Amendment to the US Constitution gives the criminal defendant the right to confront his or her accuser.
- The Eighth Amendment to the US Constitution protects criminal defendants against excessive imprisonment or fines, or cruel and unusual punishment.
- The Fourteenth Amendment to the US Constitution's Due Process Clause ensures that the rights afforded individuals through the federal government are also applicable to the state government.
- The US Supreme Court is the highest court and ultimate authority on the application of the constitutional amendments. Their rulings are known as precedent.
- The judge is the finder of the law in the trial against the defendant. If the case is not a jury trial but rather a bench trial, the judge is also the finder of the fact.
- The jury is the finder of the facts in a jury trial.
- A magistrate can be a non-lawyer or lawyer and makes neutral decisions for issuing warrants or setting bail.
- The prosecutor is the government attorney whose primary role is to investigate and prosecute criminal suspects on behalf of the people.
- Prosecutors have a wide variety of discretion in bringing charges and in which charges are brought. However, the prosecutor must act fairly and use that discretion evenly across all sexes, races, and groups of persons.
- The clerk of court is an administrative position that maintains the records of the court, along with other duties.

- The criminal defense attorney serves the defendant and is responsible for ensuring the defendant receives a fair trial. The defense attorney also advises the defendant concerning pretrial issues, such as plea offers.
- The criminal defendant is the person accused of a crime; this person has no duty to present evidence of his or her innocence.
- The victim is the person who is affected by the defendant's criminal action.
- There are several types of witnesses: the victim witness, the fact/lay witness, the character witness, and the expert witness.
- The bailiff maintains order in the courtroom and assists the parties and witnesses during court proceedings.
- The court reporter must keep the official record of what was said in the criminal proceeding. The reporter also maintains a record of evidence marked and admitted during trial.
- Probation and parole officers are both responsible for keeping up with defendants who have been convicted and sentenced for the crime.
- Criminal defendants lose some constitutional rights to privacy and the right to silence while on probation or parole.
- Specialized courts can be an alternative to traditional punishment for certain qualifying individuals.
- There are three main categories of criminal offenses: crimes against persons, crimes against property, and crimes against the community.
- Inchoate crimes are actions that have criminal liability, although the crime may not be complete.

End of Chapter Comprehension and Application

Directions: Use what you have learned in this chapter to help you respond completely and correctly to each question or prompt below.

1. Outline the constitutional amendments that form the basis of the criminal justice system and explain the right afforded to the individual by that amendment.
2. Explain the US Supreme Court's role in interpreting the constitutional amendments. What do you think about the United States' role in setting precedent? Do you think the Supreme Court should overrule itself?
3. How does the judge's responsibility change in a jury trial versus a bench trial?
4. What do you think about magistrates, non-lawyers, issuing arrest warrants and setting bail?
5. What are the duties of a prosecutor? How do they differ from the duties of a criminal defense attorney?
6. Do you believe prosecutorial discretion is a good or bad thing? Explain in detail.
7. What are some duties and responsibilities of the clerk of court, and why are they important to the

criminal justice system?

8. What are some ethical dilemmas of criminal defense attorneys? How can they be overcome?
9. What is a court's witness and do you think it should be allowed? Why or why not?
10. Crime victims do not have any specific constitutional rights. Why do you think that is?
11. Explain the differences in witnesses who can be called in a criminal case. What testimony is allowed or disallowed for each?
12. What is a hung jury and when could it occur?
13. What are the duties and responsibilities of the bailiff?
14. In what cases is it necessary to have a transcript? Who is responsible for taking down testimony during a trial?
15. What Constitutional rights do probationers lose as a result of being on probation? What do you think about this loss of constitutional rights?
16. What similarities do you see between the duties of probation officers and parole officers?
17. Do you think parole is a necessary component of the criminal justice system? Why or why not?
18. Who do you think is the most important person(s) in the criminal justice system? Why?
19. How are specialized courts different than traditional courts?
20. Do you think it is fair that a defendant who enters a specialized court may have his or her case dismissed, where other defendants may not qualify for the same treatment? Explain your position.

References

Fourteenth Amendment, https://constitution.congress.gov/constitution/amendment-14/.
Oyler v. Boles, 368 US 448 (1962).
Nix v. Whiteside, 475 US 157 (1986).

Chapter 2

Meeting Your Suspect

Introduction: Making Contact with the Suspect

Every crime has a suspect; otherwise, it would simply be an accident. There is an important distinction between a crime and an accident. An accident may still have consequences in the legal system, but the consequences may lie on the civil side of the courts. Civil **torts** encompass situations like personal injury, destruction of property, and wrongful death. In those cases, someone may be "at fault" for the occurrence, but not criminally liable. It is important to have a good grasp on the difference in civil and criminal law when determining whether you have a suspect.

Chapter Objectives

In this chapter students will learn:

- How to determine if there has been a crime
- To develop probable cause for the legal seizure of a person
- The rules of engagement
- How to properly detain a suspect
- To follow identification procedures outlined by the US Supreme Court

Key Terms

Key terms used in this chapter include:

- **Civil court**
- **Criminal court**
- **Torts**

- **Seizure**
- **Precharge identification**
- **Postcharge identification**
- **Lineup**
- **Showup**

Civil versus Criminal Actions

Civil cases usually involve disputes between individuals organizations, businesses, or corporations. The remedy sought is usually monetary compensation for losses suffered. The complaining party could ask for specific performance from the defending party, such as removing a structure over a property line. A Criminal case involves a governmental body (state federal or municipal) prosecuting an individual for a violation of a criminal law. The remedy can be loss of liberty (incarceration) or probation or fines. Let's look at a few examples of civil actions and criminal actions to get a grasp of the differences.

> Bailey is a new driver without much experience on the road. One day Bailey is driving on an unfamiliar road taking a friend home from school and engaged in conversation with her friend about the drama at school that day. Bailey runs a stop sign and hits another car. The driver of the other car sustains injuries and both cars are damaged. Should Bailey be arrested and punished through the criminal justice system for her actions? No. This is a standard traffic accident and will be handled through the **civil courts**.
>
> In contrast, a driver's criminal actions could turn a traffic infraction into a more serious criminal offense. See the below example.
>
> Bailey is a new driver without much experience on the road. One day Bailey is driving a friend home from a party, in the friend's car. Both Bailey and her friend have been drinking at the party. Bailey runs off the road and hits a tree. This causes serious injury to her friend. The friend's parents want to press charges. Should Bailey be arrested and punished through the criminal justice system for her actions? Yes, as long as her intoxication can be proven to have impaired her driving.

Compare the below examples of fact versus opinion:

Example 1: Tonya has a two-year-old child and is a stay-at-home mom. Her friend Christina also has a two-year-old child but works full time. Tonya makes an agreement with Christina wherein Tonya keeps Christina's child for her during the day for pay. One day, Tonya puts both the children down for a nap in the outdoor hammock and falls asleep herself in the adjoining hammock. When Tonya awakes, Christina's child is dead at the bottom of Tonya's swimming pool. Should Tonya be arrested for her actions and punished through the criminal justice system? No. Although taking a nap outdoors while attending young children near a pool isn't responsible, it is not criminal. Tonya can be sued for torts through the civil courts.

Example 2: Tonya has a two-year-old child and is a stay-at-home mom. Her friend Christina also has a two-year-old child but works full time. Tonya makes an agreement with Christina wherein Tonya keeps Christina's child for her during the day for pay. One day, Tonya puts both the children down for a nap in the outdoor hammock. Tonya is upset about how the children have been acting and decides that she needs a hit of methamphetamine to give her some energy. She gets in her car to go to a house where she regularly gets methamphetamine and does a hit as soon as she gets it. She drives herself home and finds Christina's child dead at the bottom of the pool. Should Tonya be arrested for her actions and punished through the criminal justice system? Yes. Tonya's involvement in illegal activities is what caused her to leave the children unattended and therefore caused the death of Christina's child.

Encounters with the Suspect

In this chapter, you will think about the various encounters with suspects. You will be challenged to think about how probable cause can be developed to seize a suspect. These encounters could be initiated by the suspect, the victim of a crime, or a witness to a crime. The witness may be the law enforcement officer him or herself. You will be challenged to think about what a law enforcement officer should do when contact is made with a suspect. Students will apply case law to fact patterns and learn how the courts have interpreted the US Constitution.

Encounters with suspects usually occur in two ways:

1. The suspect is caught red-handed.
2. The suspect is developed through investigation.

1. Caught Red-handed

One way that a police officer comes in contact with a suspect is when the police officer catches the suspect during the crime. This can occur in two ways:

- The police officer witnessing the crime
- A witness calling the police for assistance
- When a police officer identifies a suspect because he witnessed the crime himself, it is important for the officer to access the totality of the circumstances. The officer should consider such things as the following:

The Seriousness of the Crime

Most state statutes allow for warrantless arrests when a police officer witnesses a crime firsthand, no matter the seriousness of the offense. For example, an officer witnesses a driver swerving through traffic, stops the vehicle, and ultimately determines that the driver is driving under the influence of alcohol or a controlled substance. The officer may make a warrantless arrest of the individual based on his finding probable cause that the suspect is operating a vehicle while under the influence.

Whether the Suspect or Others Could Need Emergency Care

When an officer witnesses a crime in progress, the officer must also access the need for emergency care to others on scene. The officer must make a quick assessment of the situation and the seriousness of the crime committed. If it is determined that others are in need of medical care, the officer could decide to render the aid or wait until emergency medical personnel to arrive and abandon further contact with the suspect.

The Degree to Which Evidence Could Be Altered or Destroyed

An officer who witnesses a crime often diverts the original plan of the suspect. The suspect, being caught red-handed, must now make a hasty plan for escape, which could entail disposal or destruction of the property. For example, a burglar who is caught red-handed with stolen merchandise could decide to discard the property in hopes of a speedier getaway. In that situation, the officer must decide whether to pursue the property or the suspect. The totality of the circumstances must be quickly accessed by the officer. For example, if the property is great in value and set on fire, the officer may opt to try to save the property rather than pursue the suspect. On the other hand, if the property discarded can remain in its place safely until the suspect is apprehended, the officer will likely pursue the suspect.

2. Developed as a Suspect

Another way that a police officer comes in contact with a suspect is when the suspect is developed as such as part of an ongoing investigation.

Witnesses

The most common way suspects can be identified is through eyewitnesses. An eyewitness is a person who has personally seen something or can give a firsthand description of it. The witness may have seen the actual crime. The witness may have seen occurrences before or after the crime. The witness may not have seen the crime but heard something relevant to the crime. This person is called an ear witness.

Silent Witnesses

Silent witnesses are usually not people, but rather devices. Silent witness theory or rule of law states that photographic evidence produced by a device is as reliable as a live witness. Silent witness theory negates the need for a live witness to verify what is being viewed in a photograph or video representation. There are rules of evidence that must be satisfied to render the client witness reliable, such as a witness to verify that the recording device was functioning properly. With the advent of lower-priced recording devices, many businesses and even residences have cameras that record events all day long. These become invaluable to an investigator in developing a suspect.

Louise owns a lake house that she visits on long weekends and in the summer. She has installed cameras surrounding the house to monitor activity when she is away. The cameras are set to send her notifications when a person is on camera. She received notifications one day and viewed her cameras. She saw a man she did not recognize breaking into her lake house. She immediately called the police. Since the lake house is in a rural area of the county, it took a while for them to respond; the suspect was gone by the time they arrived. Louise shared all the video images of the break-in with the police. Investigator Lockemup posted the video on the police department's social media site asking for the public to call in if they could identify the individual on video. That same day, an anonymous call revealed the name of the suspect on video. Lockemup looked him up in the driver's license database, and it was, in fact, Tom Thief. Lockemup made contact with Tom and showed him the video. Tom admitted it was him. Lockemup arrested Tom for burglary of the dwelling.

- Was the identification valid? Why or why not?
- Was the arrest valid? Why or why not?
- What will Investigator Lockemup need to solidify his case using the silent witness?

The Usual Suspects

Often an investigator can develop a suspect because suspects tend to be repetitive in their crimes. This is called modus operandi. Modus operandi (MO) is the working habits typically employed by criminals. This is not always a reliable source for suspects, but it is a good starting place if the case is cold. The MO of drug and property crimes tend to become repetitive to the person committing them. Individuals also tend to stay in the same general area when committing these crimes because it is comfortable. These crimes also depend on a market of buyers and sellers. Investigators working these types of crimes will benefit from networking with officers from surrounding jurisdictions. Also, networking pawn shops, metal recycle yards, and the like will often lead to a suspect for a property crime. The usual suspects tend to unload stolen property in a predictable manner.

The Karma school has had a series of thefts of exterior wiring from their air-conditioning units. These large industrial units have a lot of copper wire inside, and it has all been stripped, rendering the units useless. Investigator Lockemup is called to the scene and immediately connects this theft to another he has at the Dharma school across town. The Dharma school had video cameras that captured images of Scott Catchings breaking the units and removing the copper. Lockemup traveled to several scrap metal recyclers asking whether Scott Catchings had brought in any items recently. Metal Again had video of Scott Catchings bring a truckload of copper wire on the same day as the school's theft.

Should Lockemup make an arrest of Scott Catchings for theft of the copper wire from the Karma school? Should Lockemup make an arrest of Scott Catchings for theft of the copper wire from the Dharma school? What could Lockemup do to strengthen his case against Scott Catchings?

Anonymous Tips

Anonymous tips can develop a suspect. An investigator must be cautious with these types of tips because they could be unreliable. Think about the game of telephone that we played as children. Everyone sat in a circle, and someone started the game by telling a short story. Then each person whispered the story around the circle until everyone had passed the story around. The last person told the story aloud. The story was often completely different at the end. This may be what an investigator gets from an anonymous tip. If an investigator wants to use an anonymous tip, it's important that the tip be independently verified through other evidence.

The US Supreme Court in *Illinois v. Gates* adopted a totality of the circumstances test. In this case, a copy of an anonymous letter informing the police of the defendants' alleged drug trafficking activities and details as to an alleged imminent transaction was attached to the affidavit, which contained corroborating data collected by the police in an independent investigation. The question was whether the anonymous letter contained enough information to meet the two-pronged Aguilar-Spinelli test. This test required the affiant to reveal his informant's "basis of knowledge" and provide sufficient facts to establish the informant's "veracity" or the "reliability" of the informant's report.

The Court held that probable cause determinations were not susceptible to the rigid, technical methodology that had been read into Fourth Amendment jurisprudence. The Court held that the elements of an informant's veracity and knowledge should be understood simply as issues that could illuminate the commonsense inquiry of whether there was probable cause to issue a search warrant. The Court held that this approach comported with the standard of proof for a warrant, which required only the "probability," and not a prima facie showing, of criminal activity. The Court held that although relating to innocent activities, the informant's recitation of detailed facts, when corroborated by observation by police officers, afforded probable cause to believe that respondents had drugs in their possession. In doing this, the Supreme Court stated that "probable cause is a fluid concept—turning on the assessment of probabilities in particular factual contexts—not readily, or even usefully, reduced to a neat set of legal rules. Informants' tips doubtless come in many shapes and sizes from many different types of persons. Informants' tips, like all other clues and evidence coming to a policeman on the scene, may vary greatly in their value and reliability. Rigid legal rules are ill-suited to an area of such diversity. 'One simple rule will not cover every situation.'. . . Probable cause requires only a probability or substantial chance of criminal activity, not an actual showing of such activity. By hypothesis, therefore, innocent behavior frequently will provide the basis for a showing of probable cause."

This ruling allowed for anonymous tips to be the starting point for a probable cause determination. The tip must be corroborated through independent investigation.

Investigator Lockemup received an anonymous tip that a large shipment of cocaine was being delivered by FedEx to 3820 Rycroff Road. His anonymous caller said that the package would be delivered on May 5 and that the address was abandoned. Lockemup checks with his contact at the power company and is told that the address has not had power in several years. Lockemup checks with the tax accessor's office and learns that the owner of the residence passed away several years ago and the property is now contested by the heirs. On May 5, Lockemup travels to 3820 Rycroff Road and watches the residence. After a few hours, a FedEx truck pulls up and a delivery is left on the front porch of the residence. As soon as the truck pulls away, a man appears from the bushes and retrieves the package. He begins to walk back toward the side of the house with the package in hand. Lockemup exits his vehicle, chases the man with the package, and ultimately seizes the package. He opens the package to find a large amount of cocaine.

- Were Investigator Lockemup's actions legal? Why or why not?

Physical Evidence Left at the Scene

Often a suspect is developed because of the physical evidence left at the crime scene. Forensic investigators are trained to collect fingerprints, DNA, and trace evidence from a crime scene. However, as often as these items are used to identify suspects on television shows, in reality it is much more difficult to gather this evidence. One reason is that small jurisdictions do not have a forensic team that collects evidence from crime scenes. In small jurisdictions, there may be only one or two investigators who work the case from start to finish. Another reason that this evidence isn't collected is that it is often not left. Outside of sex crimes, criminals do not usually leave their DNA at a scene. Occasionally a suspect caught in the act of burglary by a homeowner may run off quickly and leave a hat or shoe, but that is rare. Fingerprints are another piece of evidence that can be difficult to collect. A fingerprint is just the moisture left by a finger, and depending on weather conditions and how porous the surface is, it can dissipate quickly.

Tangible objects, such as cell phones or keys, can be accidentally left at a crime scene. Depending on the sophistication of the criminal, this could be useful. Often the home screen of the mobile device will give away its owner. Also, these devices can be traced back to the owner through internet sites. However, a sophisticated criminal will not have any personal information on a mobile device and will have prepaid, as not to leave a billing history.

Seizure of a Suspect

Once a suspect has been identified, the investigator needs to make contact with the suspect. There are important Fourth Amendment considerations for **seizure** of a suspect. First, you must know what a seizure is. A person is legally seized when his or her movement is restricted. In order to seize a person, the Supreme Court requires that the officer have reasonable suspicion. "According to the Maricopa County, Arizona, website, 'reasonable suspicion' has been defined by the US Supreme Court as 'the sort of common-sense conclusion about human behavior upon which practical people . . . are entitled to rely.' Further, it has defined reasonable suspicion as requiring only something more than an 'unarticulated hunch.' It requires facts or circumstances that give rise to more than a bare, imaginary, or purely conjectural suspicion." In *Terry v. Ohio*, the court recognized that a limited stop and frisk of an individual could be conducted without a warrant based on less than probable cause. The stop must be based on a reasonable, individualized suspicion based on articulable facts, and the frisk is limited to a pat-down for weapons. An anonymous tip that a person is carrying a gun is not, by itself, sufficient to justify a stop and frisk. Keep in mind that there are instances where reasonable suspicion is not required in order to make contact with a suspect. These would be incidences where there isn't a legal seizure. For example, if a suspect is standing around the crime scene and the law enforcement officer approaches the suspect, there is not a seizure. The law enforcement officer has not restricted the suspect's movement. However, if the suspect walks off when the law enforcement officer approaches and the officer beckons him back, there is a seizure and there must be reasonable suspicion.

As a marked police car in which several police officers were riding approached a street corner in Detroit, Michigan, a man standing at the corner turned and began to run. The police officer driving the car followed the man around the corner, briefly accelerating to catch up with him, and then drove alongside him for a short distance. While the car was alongside, the officers observed the man discard a number of packets from one of his pockets. One of the police officers got out of the car to examine the packets, which were found to contain pills, and the man shortly stopped running. Suspecting that the pills were illegal drugs, as was later proven to be the case, the police officer arrested the man. A subsequent search of the man at the stationhouse turned up additional illegal drugs. The man was charged with knowingly and intentionally possessing the drugs in violation of Michigan law. At a preliminary hearing before a magistrate, the man moved to dismiss the charges on the ground that the conduct of the police prior to his disposal of the packets constituted an unlawful seizure of his person within the meaning of the Fourth Amendment. The magistrate granted the motion and dismissed the complaint, ruling that the police's pursuit implicated Fourth Amendment protections and could not be justified under the circumstances of the case. The Michigan trial court upheld the magistrate's order of dismissal, and the Court of Appeals of Michigan affirmed (157 Mich App 181, 403 NW2d 74). On certiorari, the US Supreme Court reversed and remanded. It was held that under the circumstances, the conduct of the police officers in pursuing the man did not amount to a seizure within the meaning of the Fourth Amendment, since such conduct would not have communicated to a reasonable person that he was not at liberty to ignore the presence of the police and go about his business.[1]

Police Tactics Used to Make Contact with a Suspect

When the police witness the crime or the suspect is still on scene, making contact with the suspect is relatively simple. Making contact with suspects who have fled the area can be more challenging. Officers may need to get creative. There is no restriction on the amount of trickery that can be used to lure a suspect in, beyond that of common sense. The officer should remember that whatever tactic is used, it could be subjected to jury scrutiny at a trial.

The following are examples of trickery used to lure a suspect in for contact:

- Calling a suspect and telling him that he has won a lottery and is needed at a certain address to collect his winnings.

1. *Michigan v Chesternut*, 486 US 567 (1988)

- Creating a fake social media post alerting a suspect to an event that may be of interest to him to appear at.
- Collaborating with a family member or friend of the suspect to trick him into a meeting.
- Leaving the suspect a flyer on his door alerting him that his government benefits will be cut off unless he verifies his address with the local tax accessor.

Confirming Identity

When making contact with a suspect, the first thing the law enforcement officer must think about is confirming the identity of a suspect. In *Hiibel v. Sixth Judicial District Court of Nevada*, the Supreme Court has ruled that a suspect had been lawfully arrested and prosecuted for refusing to give his name during a police stop. The Court reasoned that a state statute can require a suspect to disclose his or her name in the course of a brief stop, if the detention was based on reasonable suspicion of a crime. Bear in mind that this case was in Nevada, a state that has a specific stop and identify statute. This case does not apply to states that do not. Therefore, if state law requires a suspect to identify himself/herself to an officer, refusing to answer a request for one's name during a stop could lead to an arrest.

Most officers are not satisfied with the suspect's confirmation of his or her identity and want further proof that the person is who he or she says they are. Most law enforcement officers have access to a database accessed by their phone or laptop computer. If the officer does not have access to a database of identifiers, the officer can call into central dispatch to assist in the identification process.

Suspects who have arrest warrants outstanding could give the wrong name or date of birth. This is a criminal offense in every state and could carry substantial jail time depending on the individual state statute.

Officer Safety

Officer safety is at the forefront of any discussion surrounding contact with suspects. An officer must always prioritize safety over anything else. Law enforcement officers often develop a good sixth sense when dealing with the public on a regular basis. That sense can alert the officer to a hidden danger or to when an incident is about to escalate into a dangerous situation. The Supreme Court has interpreted the US Constitution to give law enforcement officers, prosecutors, judges, and others in the criminal justice network parameters under which to act. Most of those parameters involve how to admit evidence into a criminal trial. These parameters should never be followed at the detriment of personal safety.

Documenting the Contact

Every contact with a suspect must be documented. Two reasons that documentation of the contact with a suspect is so important are evidentiary value and protection of the officer.

Evidentiary Value

Any statement of the suspect could be used against him or her at a trial. When contact is made with a suspect soon after the crime occurs, the suspect may be caught off guard by the police contact. After all, most suspects do not expect to be caught. The initial statements a suspect makes sticks with him or her forever. Whether it is the truth or a lie, it is an important part of the investigatory file. The common mistake officers make is that they fail to document initial statements that aren't confessions. For example, if a suspect is questioned about a crime and he says he knows nothing about it, he was not there, the officer may not see the importance in preserving that statement. However, that could become very relevant if DNA found at the scene matches the suspect. His statement that he was not there is obviously a lie.

There is also evidentiary value in the lack of a statement. All suspects have the right to remain silent, and that right cannot be commented on at trial. A mistrial would ensue if it were said that "the suspect did not even make a statement." However, the lack of a suspect statement may be relevant and could be referred to in an indirect way. For example, in a murder trial the suspect initially refused to give a statement to law enforcement. After securing an attorney, the defense asserted at trial is self-defense. The responding officer's bodycam shows the defendant at the scene of the crime walking around the yard and then being detained by the officers. He does not make any spontaneous statements to the officers. He complies with their commands and don't seem at all upset. A juror seeing that bodycam footage of the defendant could believe that someone who just had killed another in self-defense would be explaining himself to the officer and upset about what just happened. This could discount the self-defense claim.

The body language of a suspect may have evidentiary value. It is human nature to expect people to act a certain way in a certain situation. When that expectation is not met, an investigator must ask whether this is because of dishonesty or another reason. Nervousness is often displayed in body language. Nervousness could be due to guilt or some other reason. It is important to document this so that the jury can later see what the officer saw.

Protection of the Officer

Avoiding civil liability is always in the back of an officer's mind. Civil liability is the person's degree of risk of being sued for one's actions. Some argue that the worry associated with being sued hampers the otherwise effective operation of law enforcement agencies.

Unfortunately, there is increasing police scrutiny in the media. Occasional bad conduct is highlighted, questioning the entire force.

The following are some ways to avoid civil liability:

- Know the law.
- Know your department's standard operating procedures.
- Stay current with continued education and changes in the law.
- Refrain from getting involved in situations that do not involve you.

Incidental Seizure of a Suspect

When the police officer witnesses the crime, the circumstances dictate what is done first. The priorities are as follows:

1. Handle any emergency situation.
2. Secure the suspect.
3. Investigate.

1. Handling the Emergency Situation

The first priority with any police response is to handle the emergency caused by the crime. Most emergencies involve a risk of harm to individuals or property. Crimes against persons, such as assaults, rapes, or robberies, could leave the victim injured. In those cases, the first priority is to give immediate assistance to the victim or anyone injured at the scene, including the suspect.

For example, if an officer arrives on the scene of a shooting and the victim is alive but injured and the suspect has just fled the scene, the victim's well-being should be the officer's focus. The first priority will be to call for immediate medical assistance and stay with the victim until assistance arrives. The officer can radio for backup to assist with capturing the fleeing suspect, but that must be the second priority.

2. Securing the Suspect

When the officer is called to a crime scene, often the suspect is still at the scene, while other times the suspect is apprehended in close proximity to the scene. In this case, the suspect must be secured. This detention can occur for a brief period without a formal arrest.

These scenarios are analogous to a so-called "Terry stop" (see *Terry v. Ohio*). Under the Fourth Amendment, the US Supreme Court has held that a policeman who lacks probable cause but whose "observations lead him reasonably to suspect" that a particular person has committed, is committing, or is about to commit a crime, may detain that person briefly in order to "investigate the circumstances that provoke suspicion" (*United States v. Brignoni-Ponce*). "The stop and inquiry must be 'reasonably related in scope to the justification for their initiation.'" Typically, this means that the officer may ask the detainee a moderate number of questions to determine his identity and to try to obtain information confirming or dispelling the officer's suspicions. But the detainee is not obliged to respond. And, unless the detainee's answers provide the officer with probable cause to arrest him, he must then be released (*Berkemer v. McCarty*).

3. Investigating

Having an eyewitness that saw the suspect commit the crime or some act associated with the crime can be a powerful tool for an investigator. The US Supreme Court and state courts across the country have established strict guidelines regarding police identification procedures. The rules and procedures are divided into two main categories: **precharge** identification and **postcharge** identification.

Precharge Identifications

Whether the precharge identification is a showup or a lineup, the law enforcement officer needs to properly instruct the witness before the identification is made. The officer should give the witness clear instructions: the witness should take his or her time in viewing the individuals in the lineup, the witness should not confer with any other witness about the individuals in the lineup, and it is okay for the witness not to be able to identify anyone in the lineup. If a series of photo packs is used with the witness, the witness should be instructed that he or she will view a series of photo packs and that the suspect may or may not be in any grouping.

Lineup

Usually, a photo **lineup** involves placing the suspect into a group of other similar-looking individuals who had no involvement in the crime. This was traditionally done in person with five to six people lining up against a wall. The group would be asked to face forward and may be asked to then turn to the right and left side. The eyewitness would be positioned behind a screen or glass so the individuals in the lineup would not see the witness, but the witness would see the individuals in the lineup.

Photo lineups usually are compiled of six to eight photos of individuals for a witness to view during an identification process. These photos could be pulled from any available database; however, they need to be similar in nature. For example, an officer cannot use a booking photo of the suspect and driver's license photos of the other individuals in the lineup. Most police departments have computer programs that will generate photo lineups based on the filters selected by the officer. For example, an officer may have a suspect who is five foot ten, 175 pounds, with blond hair, blue eyes, and a beard. The officer can input those criteria and the computer will randomly select individuals with similar characteristics. However, an officer cannot rely solely on the computer-generated photo lineups, as there is no comparison to the human eye to ascertain similarities. Also, there are situations where the computer-generated method may not be available—for example, if the suspect is a fourteen-year-old juvenile. Most computer-generated lineup programs are not equipped to produce juvenile lineups. In this scenario, the officer must get creative by using social media pictures, school yearbook pictures, or any other source of juvenile photos.

The photo lineup, often called a photo pack, also must contain similar images of individuals. With modern technology and the popularity of social media, it is easy to obtain similar pictures of individuals. One issue arises when the suspect has unique characteristics—for example, the witness describes the suspect as having face tattoos. In this case, the officer cannot produce a picture of the suspect with face tattoos along with five other pictures of individuals matching the description of the suspect, minus the face tattoos. It may be challenging to find several pictures of similarly described individuals with face tattoos.

The officer will need to get creative and perhaps even use photo enhancements to produce similar photos to show an eyewitness.

Problems with Lineups

To get an understanding of the rules for police lineups, specifically problems with lineups, right to an attorney, freedom from suggestion, and freedom from substantial likelihood of misidentification, please see this website.

Read at: https://tinyurl.com/2kzrdbyd

Showups: To read the definition of a **showup**, please see this website.

Read at: https://legal-dictionary.thefreedictionary.com/Show-Up

In *Kirby v. Illinois*, the defendant had been arrested in connection with an unrelated criminal offense and was taken to the police station. The victim of a robbery was at the police station and identified defendant as the robber. At the time of the identification, no lawyer was present, the defendant had not asked for legal assistance, and the defendant had not been advised of any right to the presence of counsel. After the identification, the defendant was indicted for the robbery and was arrested. At trial, the victim testified as to the police station identification and also made an in-court identification of defendant. The court reasoned that the showup had occurred prior to the suspects being charged in the case and the suspects did not have the right to counsel being present. The court also stated that it will not apply an absolute constitutional guarantee to a routine police investigation. It is only when charges have been brought by the government and the government has committed itself to prosecute that counsel will be required. The Sixth Amendment right to counsel only applies to criminal prosecutions. This makes a distinction between investigative proceedings and adversarial proceedings.

Investigator Lockemup gets called out to a shooting in an occupied vehicle scene. Upon his arrival, he finds a newer model Acura has been shot into. Other officers on scene brief him as to the following facts: Mary was driving down Pot Street when another car approaches from a side street. The other car has two men inside and both start shooting at Mary's car. Inside the car with Mary is her Aunt Jane and Mary's two small children, ages three and eight. One of the bullets breaks the back passenger window causing glass to embed in the eight-year-old's hand. Mary speeds away and there are no further injuries. At the scene, Lockemup finds 40 caliber and 9mm bullets. Mary thinks she knows one of the shooters by the street name of "Little D." She shows one of the patrolmen a picture of Little D on Facebook on her phone. The patrolman forwards the picture of Little D to Lockemup and Lockemup knows Little D as Donald Ragland. Lockemup travels to Dontavios Ragland's house and sees the car that Mary described him driving parked out front. Lockemup calls a tow company to tow the vehicle to the police impound lot and plans to get a search warrant for the vehicle. Later that day, Lockemup meets with both Mary and Aunt Jane at his office. He asks Mary about the identification she made of Little D, and Mary replies that she does not know him but has seen him around. Lockemup asks Aunt Jane if she can identify either shooter, and she says, "I don't know any of these young boys who run in the streets."

- Is there probable cause to arrest Little D for shooting into an occupied vehicle? Why or why not?
- Should Lockemup show Mary a confirmatory picture of Dontavious Ragland?
- Should Lockemup show Mary a lineup with a picture of Dontavious Ragland in it? Why or why not?
- Should Lockemup show Aunt Jane a lineup with a picture of Dontavious Ragland in it? Why or why not?

Postcharge Identifications

When a lineup or showup is preformed after a "critical stage," the Sixth Amendment's right to counsel is triggered. This is usually after a post indictment or equivalent formal proceeding. The US Supreme Court stated in *United States v. Wade* that the Sixth Amendment right to counsel applies to any critical stage as well as trial. In Wade, the federally insured bank in Eustace, Texas, was robbed on September 21, 1964. A man with a small strip of tape on each side of his face entered the bank, pointed a pistol at the cashier and the vice president, the only persons in the bank at the time, and forced them to fill a pillowcase with the bank's money. The man then drove away with an accomplice who had been waiting in a stolen car outside the bank. On March 23, 1965, an indictment was returned against the respondent, Wade, and two others for conspiring to rob the bank, and against Wade and the accomplice for the robbery itself. Wade was arrested on April 2, and counsel was appointed to represent him on April 26. Fifteen days later an FBI agent, without notice to Wade's lawyer, arranged to have the two bank employees observe a lineup made up of Wade and five or six other prisoners and conducted in a courtroom of the local county courthouse. Each person in the line wore strips of tape such as allegedly worn by the robber, and upon direction each said something like "put the money in the bag," the words allegedly uttered by the robber. Both bank employees identified Wade in the lineup as the bank robber. At trial, the two employees, when asked on direct examination if the robber was in the courtroom, pointed to Wade.

If the defendant is identified in a post-indictment lineup and the defendant was not afforded the right to an attorney at that lineup procedure, the testimony about that lineup procedure cannot be used at the trial. The question becomes what to do with the same witness's in-court identification of the defendant. The witness's in-court identification is not automatically excluded if the right to counsel was violated at the lineup procedure. The prosecution must show that the witness's in-court identification does not rely on the prior lineup identification. The judge must conduct a hearing to determine whether the in-court identification was "purged of the primary taint" (*Wong Sun v. United States*).

The question that must be asked is whether the in-court identification is tainted by the out-of-court identification. If it is, then it must be excluded. This is a severe blow to the prosecution of the accused, as it should be. This is a remedy used to deter bad police conduct and limit infringements on the rights of the accused. However, if the in-court identification can be separated from the out-of-court identification, it may be admissible.

Relevant factors to consider in determining whether the in-court identification should be admitted are:

- the extent of the prior opportunities to view the suspect,
- differences in the witness's description of the suspect prior to the lineup compared to the suspects true description,
- the certainty of the witness's identification,
- the lapse of time between the witness's opportunity to view the suspect and the lineup, and
- the degree of suggestibility of the lineup.

This is critical to the government's case against the defendant. If the in-court identification is found to be tainted by the lineup procedure, the entire identification could be suppressed and disallowed into evidence. Often, cases are made with a single witness, and if this witness's identification is suppressed, the case against the suspect may be dismissed entirely.

As with most constitutional rights, the right to have an attorney present at a postindictment lineup can be waived. The waiver must be made knowingly and intelligently. This waiver has the same legal analysis as in any other waiver of attorney, and the courts often reference the Miranda decision when discussing waiver of attorneys at lineups. This means that the suspect must be informed of his rights and waive those rights voluntarily. Voluntary waivers will be discussed in depth in the Miranda chapter, but suffice it to say that the suspect must be of sound mind and not under any duress at the time of the waiver.

Exceptions

Photo Lineups

There are exceptions to the postindictment lineup requirements. There is no right to counsel at a post-indictment photo lineup. The Wade exclusionary rule only applies to in-person identification procedures (*United States v. Ash*). The rationale is that the suspect's rights cannot be violated if he or she is not present.

Photo lineups are usually attacked for two reasons: lack of similarity of the suspects in the lineup or suggestibility used during the viewing process. A common sense rationale is applied to determine whether the suspects in the photo pack appear to be similar, and this will be left to the judge's discretion. The suggestibility of the presentment of the photo lineup is generally done through cross-examination of the witness or police officer. For example, a defense attorney may ask the eyewitness if the police officer indicated any particular person in the photo pack or suggested that any particular picture was more relevant that another.

Photo lineups can also be slightly suggestive, such as the image, below. This image shows six white males of similar hair color, facial structure, and eye color. What is different?

Image 2.1

Catriona Havard and Martin Thirkettle, "Six White Males Lineup," https://timesofmalta.com/articles/view/20190507/life-features/police-photo-lineups-background-colours-can-skew-identification.709291. Copyright © 2019 by Times of Malta.

One is smiling. Also, the picture of the smiling suspect is tilted slightly. This would not be an issue unless he is the suspect. If he is the suspect, the defense will certainly argue that the eye naturally goes to the photo that is different and thus creates suggestibility.

More unusual, but still possible, is a video identification. All the same rules apply to video identifications as do photo identifications. In *United States v. Amrine*, a lineup was conducted at approximately 3:10 p.m. on March 29, 1982. The lineup participants consisted of Amrine, three persons from the detention unit, and a law enforcement officer. Each person in the lineup was a Black male of approximately the same height, size, and age. During the lineup, each of the participants was required to face the witnesses, then turn from side to side and to speak two times, each time saying, "this is a robbery." Hall and Parker were the only witnesses at the lineup, and they were not told that the defendant would be in the lineup. Hall and Parker viewed the lineup at the same time but were seated at separate tables ten to fourteen feet apart. The two witnesses did not speak to each other during the lineup, and it was not possible for either witness to see what the other was writing on their identification card. Each made a positive identification of Amrine as one of the robbers of the credit union.

On March 30, 1982, Amrine was formally charged with the robbery. Thereafter, a videotape of the lineup conducted on March 29 was shown to witnesses Calfas and Pierce, two other employees of the credit union. As in the actual lineup, the two witnesses were seated apart and did not speak to each other during the viewing of the videotape. They were not told Amrine would be in the lineup, and they did not know who Parker and Hall had identified in the actual lineup. Both Calfas and Pierce identified Amrine as one of the robbers. All four of these witnesses testified at trial and made in-court identifications of Amrine. The government was also allowed to introduce evidence of the out-of-court identifications (*United States v. Amrine*).

The Application of the Sixth Amendment Right to Counsel in Lineup Procedures Is Charge Specific

In *United States ex rel. Hall v. Lane*, the defendant was awaiting trial on one offense and asked to participate in a lineup for an unrelated offense. The defendant requested counsel, but his request was denied. The defendant was identified in the lineup and convicted. Prior to trial, the defendant's request to suppress the lineup identification as a violation of his Sixth Amendment rights was denied. On appeal, the court affirmed and held that at the time of the lineup, the appellant was still a genuine suspect, and the state was seeking to determine whether to prosecute him. At the time of the lineup, the defendant had no Sixth Amendment right to counsel. The defendant failed to show that at the time of the lineup the government had crossed the constitutionally significant divide from fact finder to adversary. The court further held that the fact that the defendant was in custody for an unrelated offense at the time of the lineup had no bearing because the government had not committed itself to prosecute him for the unrelated offense at the time of the lineup.

Other Forms of Identification During a Lineup

It does not violate a person's privilege against self-incrimination to compel that person to stand in a lineup, to produce a fingerprint, to utter specified words, or to put on a specific clothing item. These acts have been held to be nontestimonial and thus not within the privilege of self-incrimination (*United States v. Wade*). For example, in *United States v. Wade*, Wade was ordered to say, "put the money in the bag" during the lineup proceeding and the Supreme Court found that to be a permissible identification procedure.

Documentation of Lineup Procedures

As with everything in law enforcement, documentation of the lineup procedures is necessary. The question becomes how to document the various lineup procedures. When a photo pack is created, it is usually printed and made part of the original police file. It is often customary for the law enforcement officer to ask the witness to document on the photo pack itself the person chosen. This is usually done by circling a picture and/or having the witness sign their name next to the picture. The police officer then retains the witness's indication in the original case file. The law enforcement officer could also have the witness write a brief statement to accompany the photo pack. This statement could include such details as the date the witness was shown the photo pack, the certainty in which the witness is convinced he or she is the suspect, and a general statement about how no one has suggested any particular person in the photo pack.

Another way to document the photo identification procedure is to video-record the procedure. This may seem the easiest method, but remember, it will be the most scrutinized. There is a fine line between a witness taking too long to identify a suspect and a witness looking unsure of the decision. While this is the most thorough way to document an identification procedure, this can leave a lot of room for attorney argument at a later date.

In-person lineups are less common ways to identify suspects because it is difficult to find individuals who look similar, especially in smaller jurisdictions and especially if the suspect has any unique characteristics (e.g., green hair). Although they are less common, they give the witness a more accurate look at the suspect than a one-dimensional photo. The in-person lineup can be recorded, but the same problems exist as discussed above when an identification procedure is recorded. The most common way that an in-person identification procedure is documented is in writing. The police officer makes a written report of the procedure, indicating the time, place, procedure used, and persons present. This method should also include the names and other identifying information of the individuals in the lineup. This is less important in the photo lineup because the personal characteristics can be easily viewed in the photo. The officer should always keep in mind that any procedures will be subjected to judicial scrutiny at a later date. For example, the police officer documents the names and dates of birth of the individuals in the in-person lineup at the time of the lineup. Then once judicial procedures are initiated, the information is given to the defendant's attorney. The attorney requests driver's license photos of all of the individuals in the lineup. The driver's license photos do not reflect how the individuals looked at the time of the in-person lineup (beards, piercings, hair styles, etc.), and the defense files a motion to exclude the identification based on suggestibility violating the defendant's due process rights. The burden will be on the government to prove the lineup was proper.

The same documentation is necessary for a showup procedure. Showups are usually done just after a crime has occurred and everything is moving at a fast pace. The showup is usually documented in a written form as part of the incident report and includes things such as, time, place, persons present, and the particulars of how the showup occurred. Again, the law enforcement officer's actions will be subjected to judicial scrutiny at a later date. For example, showups usually occur because the suspect has been captured a short time after the crime. The suspect is usually in some type of custody or detention pending the witness's ability or inability to identify the suspect. This means that the identification could be made while the suspect is in handcuffs, in the back of a patrol car, or detained in an interview room with glass viewing. In all these scenarios, the mere position of the suspect makes him or her look more guilty than not. This will surely be brought up by a defense attorney arguing for suppression of the identification. These are things the officer should consider during a showup procedure. Again, it will be the government's burden to show the procedure is constitutionally sound.

Rules to Remember

Below is a list of rules to remember from this chapter.

- An officer must be able to differentiate between criminal and civil matters in order to be most efficient with department time and resources. Criminal matters will violate criminal statutes and have an identifiable suspect. Civil wrongs will be instances where a victim has been wronged, but it does not rise to a criminal act.
- When a crime occurs and a suspect is caught by law enforcement, law enforcement must consider certain things before focusing on apprehending the suspect. Those things are the seriousness of the crime, whether emergency care is needed by anyone on scene, and to what degree would evidence be immediately destroyed.
- Anonymous tips can aid law enforcement in developing a suspect, but they must be verified by other independent information.
- If law enforcement is relying on technological evidence, such as surveillance footage, that silent witness must still be reliable. It is important to secure the technology and gain names of the witnesses who are accustomed to using that surveillance equipment and can testify later that it is reliable.
- Physical evidence at a scene, such as DNA, fingerprints, and trace evidence, can help law enforcement officers develop a suspect. Therefore, investigators should always visit the physical scene.
- Law enforcement officers may use trickery to make contact with a suspect who is intentionally evading law enforcement.
- Showup identifications are done in the field and close in time to the crime.
- If a suspect is not immediately identified, the investigator must develop a suspect from sources such as other law enforcement agencies, informants, surveillance technology, or latent witnesses.
- Precharge identification procedures do not require the presence of an attorney.
- Postcharge, in-person lineup procedures require the suspect be provided with an attorney.
- The Sixth Amendment right to counsel at a postcharge, in-person lineup is case specific.
- Photo lineup identification procedures, whether precharge or postcharge, do not require the presence of an attorney.
- All identification procedures should be thoroughly documented with an eye on the trial of the case.
- The remedy for a constitutional violation during the identification is that the pretrial identification could be suppressed. If the pretrial identification is suppressed, the judge must conduct a

hearing to determine whether the pretrial identification taints all subsequent identifications. If so, the case against the suspect could be dismissed if there is only one eyewitness.

End of Chapter Comprehension and Application

Directions: Use what you have learned in this chapter to help you respond completely and correctly to each question or prompt below.

1. Tom is driving in an area he is not familiar with and runs a stop sign because he didn't notice it. He slams into a pedestrian crossing the street and causes serious injuries to the pedestrian. What should an officer do when called to this scene?
2. If a police officer witnesses a crime occur, what three things should the officer consider before pursuing the suspect?
3. What is modus operandi? How can the modus operandi be used by an officer to identify a suspect? Give an example.
4. What is the Supreme Court's definition of a seizure? Give an example.
5. Can an anonymous tip be used to seize a person? Give an example of an anonymous tip being used to properly seize a suspect.
6. Can a police officer lie to a suspect in order to get the suspect to do something? Give an example of the use of police trickery.
7. How does the cooperation of the public or other police agencies help in identifying and arresting suspects? How is public cooperation and cooperation from police agencies different in the identification process?
8. How are individuals selected for an in-person lineup? How should the lineup be conducted? What are the legal requirements for due process during a lineup procedure?
9. What is the procedure used to make a photo pack for identification purposes? What are the legal requirements for the photo pack to be constitutionally sound?
10. What is the difference in a preindictment lineup and a postindictment lineup?
11. Suppose you have information that a robbery has occurred at a convenience store wherein the clerk was injured during the robbery. The clerk can give a description of the individual who robbed her and thinks she could identify him if she saw him again. What steps could be taken by law enforcement to secure a suspect? How could an identification be made?
12. Suppose there were ten cars broken into in a residential area of town last night. All the victims were asleep when their cars were broken into; therefore, none of the victims can provide any identification information for a suspect. What steps could be taken by law enforcement to secure an identification? What sources of information could be used to develop a suspect?
13. Investigator Lockemup is called in to investigate a drive-by shooting. He finds one eyewitness who says she thinks she can identify the shooter because she has seen him in the

neighborhood. She describes him as a Black male with a pigmentation disorder making his lips white. Lockemup knows that Rod, who was just released from jail on gun charges, has a pigmentation disorder and lives close to where the shooting occurred. Lockemup puts a picture of Rod in a photo lineup to show the eyewitness. Lockemup uses a database to search for Black males with Rod's general height, weight, and hair and eye color. The other five pictures Lockemup uses look similar to the picture of Rod, except they do not have the pigmentation issue around their mouths. How can Lockemup make a proper photo lineup to show the eyewitness?

14. A report comes in of an attempted rape at a service station near the interstate. The service station is also a truck stop with shower stalls available. The clerk reports to law enforcement that a customer came into the store at approximately 2:00 a.m. and asked if the showers were available. She said that they were, but she needed to clean them because they had not been cleaned since the last use. When she went into the shower stall, the suspect followed her into the stall and locked the door behind him. He asked her how much sex would cost and started to undress. She refused and tried to leave the stall. He physically assaulted her and tried to unbutton her pants. She was able to get out of the stall and call the police. The police were able to stop him just as he was pulling his big rig out of the back lot. The police placed the suspect in the back of a patrol car and drove him to the front of the store, where the clerk was obtaining medical attention for the scratches on her arms. The officer parked the car in front of the clerk and asked her if the man in the back seat was the man who had assaulted her. She said he was. What is this type of identification called? Was this identification procedure performed in the proper manner? Why or why not?
15. A report comes in from child protection services that a six-year-old child has disclosed sexual abuse at the hands of her paw paw. The child does not know the terms "paternal grandfather" or "maternal grandfather," so at the direction of law enforcement, the child protection services worker shows the child a picture of each of her grandfathers and asks, "Which one did something to you that you didn't like?" The pictures do not look similar, and in fact the grandfathers are of different races. The child picks out her paternal grandfather, saying that he is the one who did it. What is this identification process called? Is it proper? Why or why not?
16. Investigator Lockemup is called in by a neighboring agency to assist in a murder investigation. He is paired up with Investigator Newbee. Newbee has prepared three photo packs with six photos each to present to an eyewitness of a murder. Newbee tells Lockemup that he plans to bring the eyewitness into the interview and present the photo packs to her one at a time. Newbee also tells Lockemup that he plans to videotape the lineup procedure. Newbee sets up a video camera and brings the eyewitness into the room. He shows her the first photo pack. She looks and appears to carefully consider the pictures of the individuals. She says, "I think it's him" and points to the person in the third photo. Newbee asks how sure she is, and she says, "Ninety percent." Then Newbee shows her the second photo pack and she carefully considers the

pictures. She points to the individual in the second picture and says, "This is him." Newbee asks how sure she is and she says "Ninety-nine percent sure." Newbee then shows her the third photo pack and she does not indicate anyone. Newbee has her sign and initial the second photo pack and tells Lockemup that he plans to obtain a warrant for that individual's arrest. What newbie mistake(s) has Newbee made?

17. Anthony Hoptins has been arrested for murder. He has been assigned counsel and there have been multiple preliminary hearings on matters related to the murder. A reluctant eyewitness has just come forward and reported seeing the murder. The police want to be certain that the eyewitness can identify Hoptins and place his photo along with five others in a photo pack. The photo pack is shown to the eyewitness, who picks out Anthony Hoptins with one hundred percent certainty. Will this identification be useful to the prosecutor at trial? Why or why not?
18. When Frances, the assistant principal, opened up Ridgemont High School in the morning, she immediately noticed that the school had had a break-in overnight. There was vulgar writing spray painted on the walls and smashed vending machines in the lobby. She called the police immediately. While waiting on the police, she went into the technology department closet and checked to see if the school's surveillance system had captured anyone's image on the school's cameras. She watched the ten hours of video footage in fast motion. At about the recorded time of 2:00 a.m., she noticed three figures appear on camera wearing large Easter bunny masks and black clothing. The figures quickly approached the cameras and sprayed them with paint, obscuring any later view. Frances remembered that there was one other camera that was not connected to the DVR system. This camera was the first tester camera that was installed in the school before the multicamera system was installed the previous year. When they installed the multisystem, the installers had just tucked the original camera into an air-conditioning vent but left it connected to a power source. Frances went to that vent in the main lobby and found the older camera there. She ejected the SD card from the camera and took it back to her computer to see if it showed anything. Jackpot. After the students thought they had covered all the cameras with paint, they took off their bunny masks and proceeded to vandalize the school. Frances turned this SD card over to the police and wants to prosecute all three students identified on the video. Under what theory will the suspects be identified? Will this be sufficient to sustain a conviction for the vandalism of the school? Why or why not?
19. Joy is a law student at the University of Whatchamacallit. She is in her second year and hopes to be a criminal defense attorney one day. She is on a tight budget and lives in a lower-income part of town. One day, while she is in class, her apartment is broken into. She comes home to find her television and computer missing. She calls the police and files a report, but she doesn't have any confidence that the police will solve the case. She decides to try to solve it herself. She talks to her closest neighbor, who is an elderly woman. The woman says that he saw a man carrying a television out of Joy's apartment but didn't think anything about it. She said he was a white male, approximately six foot tall, not skinny and not fat, and had a tattoo on his neck. Joy's neighbor

thinks she will be able to recognize him if she ever sees him again. Joy goes to the four pawn shops in the area and finds her television for sale on a shelf. Joy demands to see the manager and tells him that this is her television. She wants to know who brought it in. The manager is resistant and tells her that he cannot disclose this information to her. Joy tells the manager that she will call the police and they can compare the serial numbers of her television and all the other electronic items in his shop, if that is the way he wants to go, or he can give her the television back and tell her who sold it. The manager decides he does not want the police to come inventory his shop, so he gives Joy her television and the name of the person who pawned the television. Joy is in law school with a police officer named Dennis who works for a neighboring jurisdiction. Joy calls Dennis and asks for a favor. Joy asks Dennis for a driver's license picture of the person who pawned her television. The driver's license picture reveals that the man has a tattoo on his neck and fits the general description that Joy's neighbor gave her. Joy remembers a class she had in law school about identification procedures and decides to find photos of five other white males on the internet. Joy presents her six-person photo pack to her neighbor, who then identifies the man whose name Joy got from the pawn shop. Joy calls the investigator and gives him everything she has discovered. The investigator charges the suspect with the burglary and the case is ready for trial. The suspect's defense attorney files to suppress the neighbor's in-court identification of the suspect based on the improper pretrial identification. Discuss in detail whether you believe the in-court identification will be admitted or suppressed and why.

20. The We Forgive All nondenominational church was broken into last week. It appears that entry was gained through the back door by breaking out the window on the door and unlocking the door from the inside. A small safe was taken from the pastor's office. The church does not have surveillance and there were no witnesses. The police dust for prints on the interior knob of the back door where the glass was broken and on the pastor's doorknob where the safe was stolen. A clear print was found on both locations. The police ran the print through their database of prints, and it is a match for Lucifer Cribs, a known thief in the area. Lucifer is interviewed by the detectives and denies having anything to do with a break-in at the We Forgive All Church. When detectives tell him that his prints were found inside the church, he says that he has attended the church in the past and may have touched something coming or going from the church. The detectives notice a cut on Lucifer's right wrist and ask him about it. Lucifer explains that he cut himself doing yard work the previous day. Can the prints obtained be used as identification of Lucifer as the burglaries? Why or why not? What are the strengths and weaknesses of this identification?

References

Illinois v. Gates, 462 U.S. 213 (1983), https://supreme.justia.com/cases/federal/us/462/213/.
Illinois, 462 U.S. 21.
Terry, 392 U.S. 1.
Florida v. J. L., 529 U.S. 266 (2000), https://supreme.justia.com/cases/federal/us/529/266/.
Hiibel v. Sixth Judicial District Court of Nevada, 542 U.S. 177 (2004), https://supreme.justia.com/cases/federal/us/542/177/.
Terry, 392 U.S. 1.
United States v. Brignoni-Ponce, 422 U.S. 873, 881 (1975).
United States, 422 U.S. (quoting Terry, 392 U.S. at 29.
Berkemer v. McCarty, 468 U.S. 420 (1984).
Kirby v. Illinois, 406 U.S. 682 (1972), https://supreme.justia.com/cases/federal/us/406/682/.
United States v. Wade, 388 U.S. 218 (1967), https://supreme.justia.com/cases/federal/us/388/218/.
Wong Sun v. United States, 371 U.S. 471 (1963), https://supreme.justia.com/cases/federal/us/371/471/.
Gilbert v. California, 388 U.S. 263 (1967), https://supreme.justia.com/cases/federal/us/388/263/.
United States v. Ash, 413 U.S. 300 (1973), https://supreme.justia.com/cases/federal/us/413/300/.
United States v. Amrine, 724 F. 2d 84 (1983), https://casetext.com/case/united-states-v-amrine.
United States ex rel. Hall v. Lane, 804 F2d 79, 80 (1986), https://casetext.com/case/united-states-ex-rel-hall-v-lane.
United States, 388 U.S. 218, https://supreme.justia.com/cases/federal/us/388/218/.

Chapter 3

Keeping the End in Mind

Introduction: Building a Case That Will Result in a Conviction

Once a suspect is identified, as discussed in the previous chapter, then it is the officer's responsibility to make sure he builds a case that will result in a conviction. Good investigators can identify suspects and build a case, but great investigators identify suspects, build cases, and can see the case on to conviction. Documentation is the key to building a case that will result in conviction. Unfortunately, there is often a delay in the time from arrest to conviction and in some circumstances, that delay can be years. Even great investigators can forget important details with the passage of years and must rely on their prior documentation. This chapter gives tips and recommendations to law enforcement for documentation of the crime and crime scene, including incident reports, witness statements, photographs, videos, diagrams, and more.

Chapter Objectives

In this chapter students will learn:

- How to obtain information for an intent report
- How to document witness statements
- How to make sketches and diagrams for use in court
- How to take photographs and present them in the courtroom
- How to preserve and present audio and video recordings
- How to strengthen the visual evidence with written documentation
- How to use supplemental reports to preserve information
- The differences in public records and private records

Key Terms

Key terms and professional terminology that are used in this chapter include:

- **Incident/offense report**
- **Initial report**
- **Supplemental report**
- **Public records**
- **Work product**
- **Primary witness**
- **Secondary witness**
- **Investigative photography**
- **Intentional video recordings**
- **Unintentional recordings**
- **Drone videos**
- **Diagrams and crime scene sketches**

Documentation of a crime scene is critical for building a case for prosecution. Report writing, photography, videography, and investigatory diagrams are a part of every case.

Documentation by Report Writing

The most common way to document a crime is report writing. Before the advent of modern technology, report writing was the way crime scenes were documented. Today, most police departments have mandatory written reporting policies for most crimes reported. For example, in most states, domestic violence calls require a mandatory written report. Historically, it was a common practice in domestic violence calls for the responding officer to act as a counselor/mediator at the scene. The officer would cool tempers, suggest a night of separation, and leave the scene without a written report (because the victim did not want to press charges). Now, most state statutes have been written foreseeing domestic violence calls escalating and requiring officers to document the call no matter if an arrest is made. These statutes mandate a report; hence, officers not writing a report and leaving the scene could be exposed to civil liability should something happen later between the two parties. Most state statutes also have mandatory report writing statutes for child abuse calls, elder abuse calls, and others. It is important for an officer to know which crimes require mandatory reports in his or her jurisdiction.

Report writing is an unavoidable constant in law enforcement. Most people go into law enforcement with no real idea of the amount of paperwork involved. Writing and computer skills are essential to the profession. Reports are the permanent written record of the crime scene. They will be examined over and over again by other officers, prosecutors, defense attorneys, judges, juries, and the media. These reports are not just filed away; they are used by everyone in the progression of the criminal case.

Effective written communication can be accomplished many ways, but most good reports have consistent components:

- Organization
- Objectiveness
- Clear and concise language
- Thoroughness
- Professionalism

Below we will look at each one of these components in depth.

Organization

The easiest way to organize a report is to write the report in chronological order. The brain works logically in chronological order, making the report easily read and understood. Also, the report writer is less likely to leave out information if the report is written chronologically. For example, "Chris went to Rowdey's house to watch the game. As they were watching the game, Chris cheered for his team and said negative things about Rowdey's team. This angered Rowdey and Rowdey asked Chris to leave. Chris did not leave and continued to talk negatively about Rowdey's team. Rowdey went to his bedroom, retrieved a shotgun, and shot Chris in the living room."

The report could also be organized by grouping information about a portion of the case together. This could be helpful when the crime involves multiple victims or multiple offenders, or multiple offenses between the same victim and offender. For example, a victim's credit card could have been stolen and used by the same offender on multiple occasions. In this case, the report writer may choose to group the information about each transaction separately. Each transaction may include separate witnesses to the crime, and those witnesses may not have been interviewed in chronological order corresponding to the credit card use.

The writer's organization of the report will allow future readers to move quickly to the next step in the investigation rather than backtrack with questions about the order of events initially reported.

Objectiveness

Police reports should only contain facts. They should contain all facts, including facts that are favorable and unfavorable. This is sometimes hard for law enforcement officers to understand. Why should the law enforcement officer's report contain information that is not favorable? The simple answer is that the government's responsibility is to see that justice is done, not that a certain person is convicted. If there is evidence that is favorable to the suspect, it should be examined by all those involved in the case. For example, if the officer is writing a report about a traffic stop wherein illegal substances are found in the vehicle, it is important to include information about who owns the vehicle. If the suspect does not own the vehicle and the illegal substance is in the trunk, then there is a question of whether the suspect knew the illegal substance was in the vehicle.

The word choice is important. Conclusions and opinions should be avoided. The report should only contain factual statements. You need to ask the following question to identify if it is a factual statement: Can the statement be proven to be true? If the statement can be proven, it is factual. If a statement is an opinion, it cannot be proven to be true. Opinion statements also may contain biased words such as *worse, better, best, worthless.*

Compare the below examples of fact versus opinion:

Fact	Opinion
The victim was crying.	The victim was sad.
The witness said, "I hated him."	The witness hated him.
The ground was wet.	It rained. (Opinion, unless seen.)
She said, "I still love him."	The victim will want to drop charges.
The door had pry marks.	The suspect pried the door open. (Opinion, unless seen.)
Social media apps were visible on the suspect's phone.	The suspect used social media accounts.
The suspect is six feet taller and one hundred pounds heavier than the victim.	The suspect is stronger than the victim.
The driver had an odor of alcohol on his breath.	The driver had been drinking.
The picture depicted a father and adult daughter cuddling in bed.	The picture was inappropriate.
I saw the suspect standing over the victim and holding the knife.	The suspect used the knife to stab the victim.

An officer making a report needs to state the facts and let the reader form the conclusions. The more specific the facts, the easier it will be for the reader to form the same conclusion the officer is trying to convey in the report. For example, in a report alleging a charge of incest between a father and a daughter compares the following two different reports:

Chris Child was interviewed and disclosed that her father, Craig Creepo, bargained for sex. There were text messages on her phone wherein he offered her deals.

Chris Child was interviewed and disclosed that her father, Craig Creepo, provided her marijuana and liquor in return for sexual favors. There were text messages on Chris's phone from Craig saying, "If you will have sex with me tonight I will give you $20."

The first example states the officer's conclusion: the father is bargaining with his daughter for sex acts. This is a conclusion and will not be allowed in testimony. The fact finder, whether it is the judge or the jury, will be the one who draws the conclusion, not the witness.

In the second example, the officer reports specific facts that allow the fact finder to form the same conclusions the officer formed in the first example. This is the better report because it will refresh the officer's memory about the facts when the case comes to trial. The officer will be able to testify about the facts in the courtroom and the fact finder will form the conclusions.

Similarly, the opinions of others should not be noted in the report. When an officer is on a crime scene, inevitably he will get witness statements in the form of opinions. If a witness's opinion gives insight into the crime, it may be important to note the witness's opinion in the report. If this is done, the officer must make certain the report reflects the statement is a witness opinion. Compare the following two reports:

- This officer responded to 123 Sleepy Valley Lane in reference to a woman being hit with a motorcycle. The witness on scene said that the suspect was driving down the road at ninety miles per hour and it is a thirty miles per hour zone. The witness said that the suspect was probably high because he smokes meth every day. The witness said that the whole neighborhood is tired of the suspect driving like a jerk down this road.
- This officer responded to 123 Sleepy Valley Lane in reference to a man driving under the influence of illegal substances. The man was driving a motorcycle at a high rate of speed, and well over the posted thirty miles per hour speed limit.

In the first example, the officer clearly states what the witness sees. The witness is stating an opinion that may be relevant to a later investigation into the cause of the wreck. In the second example, the officer is reporting opinions with no source, therefore becoming the source. If this officer is later questioned about the opinions in his report, he will not have a basis for them.

Clear and Concise Language

Concise writing is not necessarily short writing. Concise writing is direct, impactful, clear writing. A concise report means that every word counts, there are no wasted words, and every word is intentional. Concise writing can be lengthy, but the words are not mere space fillers.

Clear and concise report writing usually means using an active voice rather than a passive voice. In active voice writing, the subject does the action. In passive voice writing, the action happens to the subject.

For example:

Active Voice	The suspect hit the victim.
Passive Voice	The victim was being hit by the suspect.
Active Voice	The neighbor abused the victim.
Passive Voice	The victim was abused by the neighbor.

Concise Reports Avoid Wordiness

Concise	**Wordy**
The man had a tattoo.	The man had a mark on his skin that looked like a tattoo.
The roads were wet.	It looked as if it may have rained earlier.
The car was red.	The car had a reddish tint in the sun.

Another way to clarify a statement in a report is to use quotation marks. This is especially helpful when the quote is of high value to the case. For example, the witness said, "She looked like Carrie from the movie standing there covered in blood."

Words and phrases may also need their own clarification because words and phrases can have multiple meanings. The exact meaning of the word or phrase needs to be clear to the reader and not assumed. For example, in the statement "The two generators were reported stolen by the Smallville Police Department," did the police department report that two generators were stolen or did the police department steal the generators?

The officer needs to also be clear in the report about who said what. Compare the following two reports:

- When officers arrived on scene, there was a crowd of people standing around the body of the young, white male who had been shot. Witnesses said that there was one shot heard from inside the house and then the victim came running out the front door. He collapsed in the front yard after just a few steps. The suspect came out running just after the victim and continued to run down the street toward the park. The report lists John, Bill, and Mike as the witnesses.
- When officers arrived on scene, there was a crowd of people standing around the body of a young, white male who had been shot. John heard one shot from within the house and then saw the victim run out of the house and collapse in the yard. He also saw the suspect run out of the

house and down the road toward the park. Bill heard one shot inside the house and saw the victim run out of the house and collapse in the yard. Bill turned to retrieve his phone to call 911 and did not see the suspect run out of the house. Mike heard one shot from within the house and retrieved his cell phone to call 911. When Mike returned, he saw the victim lying in the yard and did not see the suspect.

The first example gives the reader the impression that all witnesses saw the same thing. This makes the case sound strong, since there will be at least three witnesses who would be able to describe the man running from the crime scene. However, when the officer takes the time to detail what each witness sees, the case is slightly weaker.

Thoroughness

The basic components are Who? What? When? Where? Why? An initial report is generally taken right after a crime has occurred and the facts are fresh on the witness's mind. It is important to get all the basic information at this time. Memories fade over time and it is acceptable for witnesses to refresh their recollection of an event by reading a report. The officer should also note the mannerisms of the witnesses. The emotional state of the witnesses could be important later in the investigation.

The officer should make careful documentation of the state of the crime scene and be thorough in the details he or she observes on the scene. This is the officer's opportunity to list the facts that he or she sees that no one will likely see again, things such as the hood of the car was hot, there was dew on the ground but not on the shirt laying on the ground, and the suspect was sweating profusely despite the cold temperature. The officer will likely visit many more crime scenes before being called to testify on this case, and the crimes scenes may all begin to run together in his or her mind. The officer, like any witness, may review his own report or notes to refresh his memory of the event. For example, if the initial report is a traffic stop wherein illegal drugs are found inside the vehicle, the report should detail exactly where the drugs were located in the vehicle. The trail of the case could be several months if not years from the initial traffic stop. Where the drugs are found could be crucial to whether the defendant had knowledge of the illegal drugs.

Compare the following two examples:

Example 1: On January 1, 2023, Smallville officers made contact with the defendant and other occupants of the Honda Pilot. The officer knew the driver had outstanding warrants for his arrest. After making contact with the occupants of the vehicle and running all names through central dispatch, the defendant was arrested for outstanding warrants. The officer asked the defendant if he had any illegal substances on him and the defendant replied yes. A baggie containing methamphetamine was found in his front pants' pocket. The vehicle was searched and a meth pipe was found along with a large amount of marijuana. Both the driver and the defendant were arrested for possession of a controlled substance and possession of drug paraphernalia. He said, "Y'all got me."

Example 2: On January 1, 2023, Officer Ford made contact with Paul Passenger and the driver of the Honda Pilot. Ford knew that David Driver had outstanding warrants for his arrest. Officer Bentley arrived on the scene and assisted with the traffic stop. Bentley ran both Paul Passenger and David Driver's names through central dispatch and found that Paul Passenger also had a warrant for his arrest. Paul Passenger was arrested. Bentley asked Paul Passenger if he had any illegal substances on him and he replied yes. Ford searched the vehicle and found a meth pipe in the front passenger floorboard. Bentley found a large baggie of marijuana in the center console. Paul Passenger made a spontaneous statement of "Y'all got me."

Notice in the first example that the report is not clear about who said what. It is also not clear where the controlled substances and paraphernalia were found. This will become very important if either David or Paul requests a trial on the issue of possession. The second example isn't necessarily any longer than the first (only three words difference), but the wording is much clearer. It gives the future report reader a lot more information for further investigation or prosecution. It also protects the officer's potential fading memory when he is called to testify a year later.

Professionalism

It goes without saying that we are in the information era and computers are correcting grammar on a regular basis. Most officers use a computer to type reports, and those computers are constantly making suggestions to the inputter of grammatical changes needed. Some computers will autocorrect on their own with the push of the spacebar. Autocorrect errors may be acceptable in text messages to friends but not in police reports. Misinterpretations could have catastrophic results. For example, the police officer's report meant to say, "I was driving when I saw the car on the side of the road," but the report said, "I was drinking when I saw the car on the side of the road." Autocorrect could also misidentify a suspect. For example, the report should have said, "The witness, Annette Miller, said she saw the accident," but the report said, "The witness, Annex Miller, said she saw the accident." If the officer is hasty in his or her report writing, these types of mistakes could be extremely embarrassing to the officer at a later date.

Be aware of word choice. Every profession uses jargon to communicate within the profession. This is certainly acceptable up to certain points and there can be a difference in using jargon verbally versus in written reports. Slang and shortcut verbiage will be interpreted as unprofessional. Some officers have terms to describe certain individuals—for example, "methhead," "crackhead," and "hot pants." These and other similar terms may be common in officer talk but have no place in professional reports.

Also be cautious when using words that have a legal definition. Meanings of words can change when they are in a legal context. Suppose an officer is taking a report of a burglary. There are three burglary suspects who are nineteen years old. Instead of being specific, the officer reports that "the juveniles broke into the residence." The officer has used a common word, *juvenile*. This officer may use the word *juvenile* in casual conversation to refer to a teenager, someone living at home, or someone too young to drink alcohol (depending on the state). However, the word *juvenile* could be interpreted to others reading the report that the suspects should be charged in juvenile court. If another officer reading the report isn't good at math or doesn't notice the date of birth, he or she could mistakenly try to file charges within the juvenile court instead of the adult court.

Types of Reports

There are essentially two types of **initial incident/offense reports** used in law enforcement: the **initial report** and the **supplemental report**. The initial report is usually a brief overview of the crime. It will include the basic components listed above. The supplemental report is any report that supports the initial report. The supplemental report can be done by the initial officer, other officers or supervisors, or investigators. The supplemental report can be an important part of the case organization. Often a case is not solved for days, weeks, or months, and the organization of incoming facts is critical to future readers.

The Differences in Public and Private Records

Public records contain information and/or any other documents that a governmental body is required to maintain. This information is accessible to the public. The Freedom of Information Act was adopted in the United States in 1967 with the purpose of informing citizens about their government. Each state handles public records in its own way. Just because the record is public, it may not be free. Each state can and does enact laws for accessing its public records.

Private records contain information about a particular individual's affairs. These records are not assessable to the public. This would also include confidential records.

The federal courts have left this determination to each state to determine what is consider a public versus private record. In some states the practice is that the incident report is available to the public, but the supplemental information is not. Every officer should have a clear understanding of what will be given over with a request for public records. This is sometimes subject to the discretion of the supervisor making the determination. Each officer should prepare reports as if they will be disclosed to everyone.

Other Information to Gather

Supplemental reports can include any information that could be relevant to the case, such as the following:

Prior Contact with the Victim

This becomes important in cases involving family members, such as domestic violence. It gives others reading the report an opportunity to see the larger picture of what is going on between the victim and the defendant. This could give insight to the prosecutor or others making decisions in the case as to how the parties react to each other.

Prior Contact with the Defendant

The defendant's other bad acts could be admissible in the current case, if the other acts are similar to the crime charged. Modus operandi, or MO, is a method of operation or the manner in which the perpetrator committed the crime. This could be relevant to identification of the suspect.

Existence of Any Court Orders

Prior convictions could enhance charges or weigh into what the defendant's bond should be. If the victim or defendant are involved in court proceedings, there could be orders determining property rights or no contact orders. This could also be relevant to the amount of a bond or sentencing in the case.

How a Suspect Was Established

Often reports say, "John Doe was established as a suspect" and then progress from there. It is helpful to others to know how John Doe was established as a suspect.

Details, Details, Details

Small details can have a large impact on the case. For example, if the clerk remembers that the suspect was drinking a Grapico during the robbery, this should be noted. If an empty can of Grapico is found in the parking lot of the convenience store robbed, litter in a parking lot would not be relevant or collected, but this Grapico can may need to be collected and fingerprinted as evidence to support the charges against the suspect.

This figure depicts an example of a uniform incident report that would be filed by the police upon a crime occurring. The uniform reports could vary state to state but would contain the same basic information.

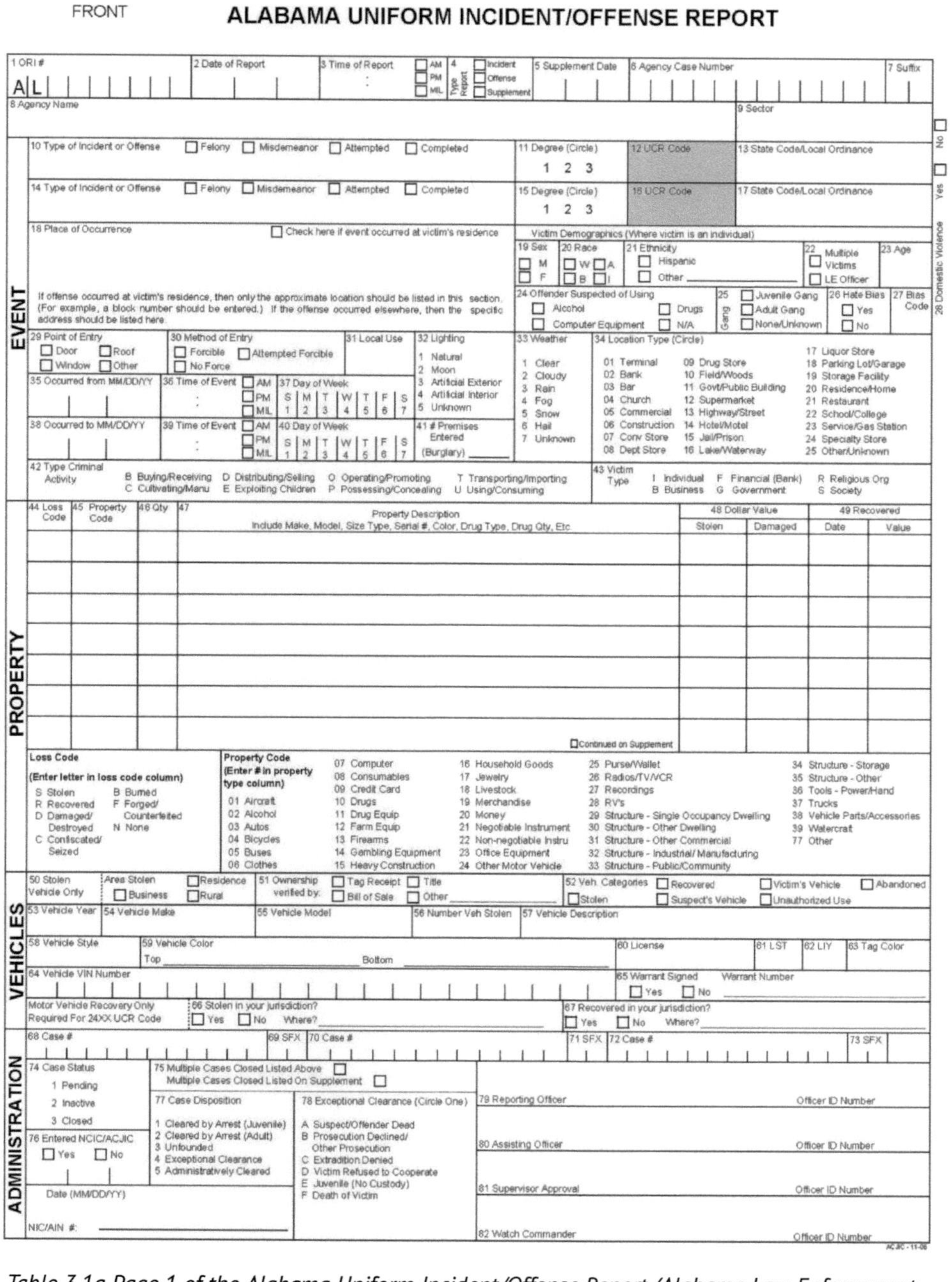

FRONT

ALABAMA UNIFORM INCIDENT/OFFENSE REPORT

1 ORI # A L | 2 Date of Report | 3 Time of Report ☐ AM ☐ PM ☐ MIL | 4 Type Report ☐ Incident ☐ Offense ☐ Supplement | 5 Supplement Date | 6 Agency Case Number | 7 Suffix

8 Agency Name | 9 Sector

EVENT

10 Type of Incident or Offense ☐ Felony ☐ Misdemeanor ☐ Attempted ☐ Completed | 11 Degree (Circle) 1 2 3 | 12 UCR Code | 13 State Code/Local Ordinance

14 Type of Incident or Offense ☐ Felony ☐ Misdemeanor ☐ Attempted ☐ Completed | 15 Degree (Circle) 1 2 3 | 16 UCR Code | 17 State Code/Local Ordinance

18 Place of Occurrence ☐ Check here if event occurred at victim's residence

Victim Demographics (Where victim is an individual): 19 Sex ☐ M ☐ F | 20 Race ☐ W ☐ A ☐ B ☐ I | 21 Ethnicity ☐ Hispanic ☐ Other | 22 ☐ Multiple Victims ☐ LE Officer | 23 Age

If offense occurred at victim's residence, then only the approximate location should be listed in this section. (For example, a block number should be entered.) If the offense occurred elsewhere, then the specific address should be listed here.

24 Offender Suspected of Using ☐ Alcohol ☐ Drugs ☐ Computer Equipment ☐ N/A | 25 Gang ☐ Juvenile Gang ☐ Adult Gang ☐ None/Unknown | 26 Hate Bias ☐ Yes ☐ No | 27 Bias Code

28 Domestic Violence Yes ☐ No ☐

29 Point of Entry ☐ Door ☐ Roof ☐ Window ☐ Other | 30 Method of Entry ☐ Forcible ☐ Attempted Forcible ☐ No Force | 31 Local Use | 32 Lighting 1 Natural 2 Moon 3 Artificial Exterior 4 Artificial Interior 5 Unknown | 33 Weather 1 Clear 2 Cloudy 3 Rain 4 Fog 5 Snow 6 Hail 7 Unknown

35 Occurred from MM/DD/YY | 36 Time of Event ☐ AM ☐ PM ☐ MIL | 37 Day of Week S M T W T F S 1 2 3 4 5 6 7

38 Occurred to MM/DD/YY | 39 Time of Event ☐ AM ☐ PM ☐ MIL | 40 Day of Week S M T W T F S 1 2 3 4 5 6 7 | 41 # Premises Entered (Burglary)

34 Location Type (Circle): 01 Terminal, 02 Bank, 03 Bar, 04 Church, 05 Commercial, 06 Construction, 07 Conv Store, 08 Dept Store, 09 Drug Store, 10 Field/Woods, 11 Govt/Public Building, 12 Supermarket, 13 Highway/Street, 14 Hotel/Motel, 15 Jail/Prison, 16 Lake/Waterway, 17 Liquor Store, 18 Parking Lot/Garage, 19 Storage Facility, 20 Residence/Home, 21 Restaurant, 22 School/College, 23 Service/Gas Station, 24 Specialty Store, 25 Other/Unknown

42 Type Criminal Activity: B Buying/Receiving, C Cultivating/Manu, D Distributing/Selling, E Exploiting Children, O Operating/Promoting, P Possessing/Concealing, T Transporting/Importing, U Using/Consuming

43 Victim Type: I Individual, B Business, F Financial (Bank), G Government, R Religious Org, S Society

PROPERTY

44 Loss Code	45 Property Code	46 Qty	47 Property Description Include Make, Model, Size Type, Serial #, Color, Drug Type, Drug Qty, Etc	48 Dollar Value Stolen	48 Dollar Value Damaged	49 Recovered Date	49 Recovered Value
			☐ Continued on Supplement				

Loss Code (Enter letter in loss code column): S Stolen, R Recovered, D Damaged/Destroyed, C Confiscated/Seized, B Burned, F Forged/Counterfeited, N None

Property Code (Enter # in property type column): 01 Aircraft, 02 Alcohol, 03 Autos, 04 Bicycles, 05 Buses, 06 Clothes, 07 Computer, 08 Consumables, 09 Credit Card, 10 Drugs, 11 Drug Equip, 12 Farm Equip, 13 Firearms, 14 Gambling Equipment, 15 Heavy Construction, 16 Household Goods, 17 Jewelry, 18 Livestock, 19 Merchandise, 20 Money, 21 Negotiable Instrument, 22 Non-negotiable Instru, 23 Office Equipment, 24 Other Motor Vehicle, 25 Purse/Wallet, 26 Radios/TV/VCR, 27 Recordings, 28 RV's, 29 Structure - Single Occupancy Dwelling, 30 Structure - Other Dwelling, 31 Structure - Other Commercial, 32 Structure - Industrial/Manufacturing, 33 Structure - Public/Community, 34 Structure - Storage, 35 Structure - Other, 36 Tools - Power/Hand, 37 Trucks, 38 Vehicle Parts/Accessories, 39 Watercraft, 77 Other

VEHICLES

50 Stolen Vehicle Only | Area Stolen ☐ Business ☐ Residence ☐ Rural | 51 Ownership verified by: ☐ Tag Receipt ☐ Bill of Sale ☐ Title ☐ Other | 52 Veh. Categories ☐ Recovered ☐ Stolen ☐ Suspect's Vehicle ☐ Victim's Vehicle ☐ Unauthorized Use ☐ Abandoned

53 Vehicle Year | 54 Vehicle Make | 55 Vehicle Model | 56 Number Veh Stolen | 57 Vehicle Description

58 Vehicle Style | 59 Vehicle Color Top Bottom | 60 License | 61 LST | 62 LIY | 63 Tag Color

64 Vehicle VIN Number | 65 Warrant Signed ☐ Yes ☐ No Warrant Number

Motor Vehicle Recovery Only Required For 24XX UCR Code | 66 Stolen in your jurisdiction? ☐ Yes ☐ No Where? | 67 Recovered in your jurisdiction? ☐ Yes ☐ No Where?

68 Case # | 69 SFX | 70 Case # | 71 SFX | 72 Case # | 73 SFX

ADMINISTRATION

74 Case Status: 1 Pending, 2 Inactive, 3 Closed

75 Multiple Cases Closed Listed Above ☐ Multiple Cases Closed Listed On Supplement ☐

76 Entered NCIC/ACJIC ☐ Yes ☐ No Date (MM/DD/YY)

77 Case Disposition: 1 Cleared by Arrest (Juvenile), 2 Cleared by Arrest (Adult), 3 Unfounded, 4 Exceptional Clearance, 5 Administratively Cleared

78 Exceptional Clearance (Circle One): A Suspect/Offender Dead, B Prosecution Declined/Other Prosecution, C Extradition Denied, D Victim Refused to Cooperate, E Juvenile (No Custody), F Death of Victim

79 Reporting Officer — Officer ID Number

80 Assisting Officer — Officer ID Number

81 Supervisor Approval — Officer ID Number

82 Watch Commander — Officer ID Number

NIC/AIN #:

ACJIC - 11-08

Table 3.1a Page 1 of the Alabama Uniform Incident/Offense Report (Alabama Law Enforcement Agency, "Alabama Uniform Incident/Offense Report," https://www.una.edu/police/docs/forms/IO%20Report.pdf. Copyright © by Alabama Law Enforcement Agency.)

BACK

THIS SIDE OF FORM IS CONFIDENTIAL UNLESS RELEASED AT THE DISCRETION OF THE CHIEF LAW ENFORCEMENT OFFICER

Incident/Offense Report - Continued

83 Date of Report (MM/DD/YY) | 84 Time of Report ☐ AM ☐ PM ☐ MIL | 85 Agency Case Number | 86 Suffix | 87 ☐ Offender ☐ Suspect ☐ Missing Person | ☐ Check if Multiple

88 Reported By (Last, First, Middle Name) ☐ Victim Or | 89 Suffix | 90 ☐ Resident ☐ Non-Resident | 91 Home Phone | 92 Work Phone | 93 Other Phone

VICTIM INFORMATION

94 Victim # | 95 Victim (Last, First, Middle Name) | 96 Suffix | 97 Address (Street, City, State, Zip) | 98 Home Phone | 99 Work Phone | 100 Other Phone

101 Employer/School | 102 Occupation | 103 Address (Street, City, State, Zip) | 104 Work Phone | 105 Other Phone

106 Sex ☐ M ☐ F | 107 Race ☐ W ☐ A ☐ B ☐ I | 108 Language ☐ English ☐ Spanish ☐ Other ______ | 109 HGT | 110 WGT | 111 Date of Birth | 112 Age | 113 Victim SSN | 114 Complainant SSN

☐ Multiple Victims ☐ LE Officer 115 | 116 Ethnicity ☐ Hispanic ☐ Other ______ | 117 Injury ☐ Yes ☐ No | 118 Offender known to victim? ☐ Yes ☐ No | 119 Victim was? (Explain Relationship.) | 120 Relationship Code

121 Weapons Used ☐ Firearm ☐ Knife ☐ Hands, Fist, Feet, Voice, etc. ☐ Other Dangerous | 122 Description of Weapons/Firearms/Tools Used in Offense ☐ Handgun ☐ Rifle ☐ Shotgun ☐ Unknown Describe ______

123 Place of Occurrence (Enter exact street address here.) | 124 Type Injury: N None, B Broken Bones, I Internal Injury, L Severe Laceration, M Minor Injury, O Other Major Injury, T Loss of Teeth, U Unconscious | 125 Sector

126 Circumstances: Homicide & Assault | 127 Location: Rape | 128 Assault ☐ Simple ☐ Aggravated | 129 Treatment for Assault? ☐ Yes ☐ No | 130 Verify for Rape Exam? ☐ Yes ☐ No | 131 Treatment for Rape? ☐ Yes ☐ No

SUSPECT INFORMATION

132 Off # | 133 Name (Last, First, Middle) | 134 SFX | 135 Alias | 136 Social Security # | 137 Race ☐ W ☐ A ☐ B ☐ I | 138 Sex ☐ M ☐ F | 139 Date of Birth | 140 Age

141 Address (Street, City, State, Zip) | 142 HGT | 143 WGT | 144 Ethnicity ☐ Hispanic ☐ Other ______ | 145 Language ☐ English ☐ Spanish ☐ Other

146 Probable Destination | 147 Eye | 148 Hair | 149 Complexion | 150 Armed ☐ Yes ☐ No ______ Weapon

151 Clothing | 152 ☐ Scars ☐ Marks ☐ Tattoos ☐ Amputations | 153 ☐ Arrested ☐ Wanted ☐ Dual Arrest (Domestic Violence)

154 Off # | 155 Name (Last, First, Middle) | 156 SFX | 157 Alias | 158 Social Security # | 159 Race ☐ W ☐ A ☐ B ☐ I | 160 Sex ☐ M ☐ F | 161 Date of Birth | 162 Age

163 Address (Street, City, State, Zip) | 164 HGT | 165 WGT | 166 Ethnicity ☐ Hispanic ☐ Other ______ | 167 Language ☐ English ☐ Spanish ☐ Other

168 Probable Destination | 169 Eye | 170 Hair | 171 Complexion | 172 Armed ☐ Yes ☐ No ______ Weapon

173 Clothing | 174 ☐ Scars ☐ Marks ☐ Tattoos ☐ Amputations | 175 ☐ Arrested ☐ Wanted ☐ Dual Arrest (Domestic Violence)

WITNESSES

Name (Last, First, Middle)	Sex	Race	Date of Birth	Address	Contact Telephone Numbers	
176	177 ☐ M ☐ F	178 ☐ W ☐ A ☐ B ☐ I	179	180	181 Home	182 Work / 183 Other
184	185 ☐ M ☐ F	186 ☐ W ☐ A ☐ B ☐ I	187	188	189 Home	190 Work / 191 Other
192	193 ☐ M ☐ F	194 ☐ W ☐ A ☐ B ☐ I	195	196	197 Home	198 Work / 199 Other

200 Witness # 1 SSN | 201 Witness # 2 SSN | 202 Witness # 3 SSN

NARRATIVE

203

☐ Continued on Supplement

204 Continued on Supplement ☐ Yes ☐ No | 205 Assisting Agency ORI | 206 Assisting Agency Case Number | 207 SFX | 208 Warrant Signed ☐ Yes ☐ No Warrant # | 209 Add. Cases Closed Narrative ☐ Y ☐ N

I hereby affirm that I have read this report and that all the information given by me is correct to the best of my knowledge. I will assume full responsibility for notifying the agency if any stolen property or missing person herein reported is returned. | 210 ______ Signature | 211 Local Use | 212 State Use

ACJIC - 11-08

Table 3.1b Page 2 of the Alabama Uniform Incident/Offense Report

ALABAMA UNIFORM INCIDENT/OFFENSE REPORT SUPPLEMENT

OFFICER'S WORK PRODUCT MAY NOT BE PUBLIC INFORMATION

1 ORI # A L | 2 Agency Name | 3 Date and Time of Report M D Y | AM PM MIL | 4 Case # | 5 SFX

EVENT

6 Victim's Name (Original Report) | 7 Original Offense Date M D Y | 8 Type Report ☐ Continuation ☐ Follow-Up

9 Original Incident/Offense | 10 UCR Code | 11 State Code/Local Ordinance

12 New Incident/Offense | 13 UCR Code | 14 State Code/Local Ordinance

15 Has an Arrest Been Made? 1 Yes 2 No | 16 Date of Arrest M D Y | 17 Has a Warrant Been Obtained? 1 Yes 2 No Warrant # | 18 Date of Warrant M D Y | 19 Prior Year Premise Weapon

20 ☐ Defendant ☐ Suspect
Name:
Race 1 W 3 A 2 B 4 I | Ethnicity 1 Hispanic 2 Other | Sex 1 M 2 F | DOB M D Y | Age

21 ☐ Defendant ☐ Suspect
Name:
Race 1 W 3 A 2 B 4 I | Ethnicity 1 Hispanic 2 Other | Sex 1 M 2 F | DOB M D Y | Age

DOLLAR VALUE

S R D C

22 Local Use
23 State Use

Each of the following entries has lines marked S R D C B F:

24 Aircraft | 25 Alcohol | 26 Autos | 27 Bicycles | 28 Buses
29 Clothes/Furs | 30 Computer Hardware/Software | 31 Consumables | 32 Credit/Debit Cards | 33 Drugs/Narcotics | 34 Drugs/Narcotics Equipment
35 Farm Equipment | 36 Firearms | 37 Gambling Equipment | 38 Heavy Construction/Industrial Eq | 39 Household Goods | 40 Jewelry/Precious Metals
41 Livestock | 42 Merchandise | 43 Money | 44 Negotiable Instruments | 45 Non-negotiable Instruments | 46 Office Equipment
47 Other Motor Vehicle | 48 Purses/Handbags/Wallets | 49 Radios/TV/VCR | 50 Recordings - Audio/Visual | 51 Recreational Vehicles | 52 Structure - Single Occupancy Dwelling
53 Structure - Other Dwelling | 54 Structure - Other Commercial | 55 Structure - Industrial/Manufacturing | 56 Structure - Public/Community | 57 Structure - Storage | 58 Structure - Other
59 Tools | 60 Trucks | 61 Vehicle Parts/Accessories | 62 Watercraft | 63 Other

Motor Vehicle Recovery Only Required for 24xx UCR Code | 64 Motor Veh. Stolen in Your Jurisdiction? Y N Where? | 65 Recovered in Your Jurisdiction? Y N Where?

MULTIPLE CASES CLOSED | 66 Case # | 67 SFX | 68 Case # | 69 SFX | 70 Case # | 71 SFX | 72 ADDITIONAL CASE'S CLOSED NARRATIVE ☐ Y ☐ N

ADMINISTRATIVE

73 Case Status
1 Pending
2 Inactive
3 Closed
Entered ACIC/NCIC Y N M D Y

74 Case Disposition:
1 Cleared by Arrest (Juvenile)
2 Cleared by Arrest (Adult)
3 Unfounded
4 Exceptional Clearance
5 Administratively Cleared

Exceptional Clearance (Circle One)
A Suspect/Offender Dead
B Prosecution Declined/Other Prosecution
C Extradition Denied
D Victim Refused to Cooperate
E Juvenile (No Custody)
F Death of Victim

75 Reporting Officer ID #
76 Assisting Officer ID #
77 Supervisor Approval ID # | 78 Watch Cmdr ID #

TYPE OR PRINT IN BLACK INK ONLY

AC/IC - 08-07

Table 3.1c Page 2 of the Alabama Uniform Incident/Offense Report

OFFICER'S WORK PRODUCT MAY NOT BE PUBLIC INFORMATION

ADDITIONAL INCIDENT/OFFENSE NARRATIVE CONTINUED

79 Date and Time of Report (M D Y)	1 AM / 2 PM / 3 MIL	80 Case #	81 SFX
82 Type Report: ☐ 1. Continuation ☐ 2. Follow-up			

NARRATIVE

NARRATIVE

NARRATIVE

☐ Continued on Additional Supplement

TYPE OR PRINT IN BLACK INK ONLY

AC.IC - 11-06

Table 3.1d Page 2 of the Alabama Uniform Incident/Offense Report

DOMESTIC VIOLENCE DUAL ARREST ☐

ALABAMA UNIFORM ARREST REPORT

Fingerprinted: 1 Yes / 2 No — R84 Completed: 1 Yes / 2 No

OFFICER'S WORK PRODUCT MAY NOT BE PUBLIC INFORMATION

IDENTIFICATION

1 ORI # A L | 2 Agency Name | 3 Case # | 4 SFX

5 Last, First, Middle Name | 6 Alias AKA

7 Sex: 1 M, 2 F | 8 Race: 1 W, 2 B, 3 A, 4 I | 9 Ethnicity: 1 Hispanic, 2 Other | 10 Hgt | 11 Wgt | 12 Eye | 13 Hair | 14 Skin | 15: 1 Scars, 2 Marks, 3 Tattoos, 4 Amputations

16 Place of Birth (City, County State) | 17 SSN | 18 Date of Birth (M D Y) | 19 Age | 20 Miscellaneous ID #

21 SID # | 22 Fingerprint Class: Key, Major, Primary, SCDV, Sub-Secondary, Final; Henry Class; NCIC Class | 23 DL# | 24 St

25 FBI # | 26 Identification Comments

27: 1 Resident, 2 Non-Resident | 28 Home Address (Street, City, State, Zip) | 29 Residence Phone ( ) | 30 Occupation (Be Specific)

31 Employer (Name of Company/School) | 32 Business Address (Street, City, State, Zip) | 33 Business Phone ( )

ARREST

34 Location of Arrest (Street, City, State, Zip) | 35 Sector # | 36 Arrested for Your Jurisdiction? Yes / No; 1 In State, 2 Out of State Agency

37 Condition of Arrestee: 1 Drunk, 2 Drinking, 3 Sober, 4 Drugs | 38 Resist Arrest? 1 Yes, 2 No | 39 Injuries? 1 None, 2 Officer, 3 Arrestee | 40 Armed? 1 Y, 2 N | 41 Description of Weapon: 1 Handgun, 2 Rifle, 3 Shotgun, 4 Other Firearm, 5 Other Weapon

42 Date of Arrest (M D Y) | 43 Time of Arrest: AM, PM, MIL | 44 Day of Arrest: S 1, M 2, T 3, W 4, T 5, F 6, S 7 | 45 Type of Arrest? 1 On View, 2 Call, 3 Warrant | 46 Arrested Before? 1 Yes, 2 No, 3 Unknown

47 Charge - 1: 1 Fel, 2 Misd | 48 UCR Code | 49 Charge - 2: 1 Fel, 2 Misd | 50 UCR Code

51 State Code/Local Ordinance | 52 Warrant # | 53 Date Issued (M D Y) | 54 State Code/Local Ordinance | 55 Warrant # | 56 Date Issued (M D Y)

57 Charge - 3: 1 Fel, 2 Misd | 58 UCR Code | 59 Charge - 4: 1 Fel, 2 Misd | 60 UCR Code

61 State Code/Local Ordinance | 62 Warrant # | 63 Date Issued (M D Y) | 64 State Code/Local Ordinance | 65 Warrant # | 66 Date Issued (M D Y)

67 Arrest Disposition: 1 Held, 2 Bail, 3 Released, 4 Tol - LE, 5 Other | 68 If Out On Release What Type? | 69 Arrested with (1) Accomplice (Full Name) | 70 Arrested with (2) Accomplice (Full Name)

VEHICLE

71 VYR | 72 VMA | 73 VMO | 74 VST | 75 VCO Top / Bottom | 76 Tag # | 77 LIS | 78 LIY

79 VIN | 80 Impounded? 1 Yes, 2 No | 81 Storage Location/Impound #

82 Other Evidence Seized/Property Seized — ☐ Continued in Narrative

JUVENILE

83 Juvenile Disposition: 1 Handled and Released, 2 Ref. to Juvenile Court, 3 Ref. to Welfare Agency, 4 Ref. to Other Police Agency, 5 Ref. to Adult Court | 84 Released To

85 Parent or Guardian (Last, First, Middle Name) | 86 Address (Street, City, State, Zip) | 87 Phone ( )

88 Parents Employer | 89 Occupation | 90 Address (Street, City, State, Zip) | 91 Phone ( )

RELEASE

92 Date and Time of Release (M D Y): 1 AM, 2 PM, 3 MIL | 93 Releasing Officer Name | 94 Agency/Division | 95 ID #

96 Released To | 97 Agency/Division | 98 Agency Address

99 Personal Property Released to Arrestee: 1 Yes, 2 No, 3 Partial | 100 Property Not Released/Held At: | 101 Property #

102 Remarks (Note Any Injuries at Time of Release)

Local Use

103 Signature of Receiving Officer | 104 Signature of Releasing Officer | State Use

MULTIPLE CASES CLOSED: 105 Case # | 106 SFX | 107 Case # | 108 SFX | 109 Case # | 110 SFX | 111 MULTIPLE CASES CLOSED NARRATIVE ☐ Y ☐ N

112 Arresting Officer (Last, First, M.) | 113 ID # | 114 Arresting Officer (Last, First, M.) | 115 ID # | 116 Supervisor ID # | 117 Watch Cmdr. ID #

TYPE OR PRINT IN BLACK INK ONLY

ACJIC - 11-06

Table 3.1e Page 2 of the Alabama Uniform Incident/Offense Report

OFFICER'S WORK PRODUCT MAY NOT BE PUBLIC INFORMATION

ADDITIONAL ARREST NARRATIVE CONTINUED	118 Date and Time of Arrest M D Y	:	☐ AM ☐ PM ☐ MIL	119 Case #	120 SFX

NARRATIVE	121 Additional Arrest Information
NARRATIVE	
NARRATIVE	☐ Continued on Additional Supplement

TYPE OR PRINT IN BLACK INK ONLY

ACJIC - 11-06

Table 3.1f Page 2 of the Alabama Uniform Incident/Offense Report

A defendant's MO could be identified through small details in reports—for example, if there have been three different robberies of convenience stores and in each case, when the clerk hesitates, the defendant says, "You think I'm playin'? This is no joke."

Once the report is concluded and the suspect is arrested, the officer usually moves on to the next case. Memories fade and important facts could be forgotten unless memorialized in the report. The report writer may need to take a pause after the report is drafted to think about any additional details that can be added.

Report Writing for Self-Preservation

Most officers will agree that one thing in the forefront of his or her mind when generating a report is self-preservation. This is commonly referred to as covering one's backside. Any officer who has been in law enforcement long enough will be able to tell a horror story of a report that came back to bite him or her, either because it did not contain enough information or it contained the wrong information. Embarrassment is often a good teacher and changes behaviors. For example, Officer Smalltown is the first responder to a traffic accident wherein a man driving drunk hit a school bus full of children. The officer reports the facts surrounding the wreck, witness statements, and observations. He fails to note that the defendant had slurred speech and told the officer he only drank two beers. The officer testifies at trial that the defendant admitted to drinking and driving, yet it was not included in the police report. The defense attorney accuses the officer of making up facts to convict the defendant because he requested a trial. This circumstance could have been easily avoided with proper documentation.

Report Writing versus Notes

There is a clear distinction between a police report and an officer's notes. A police report is an official document that is readily available to many others in the criminal justice system. It is often given to the defense attorney, and therefore the defendant, during the discovery process. These reports could end up posted on social media pages or given to the media for larger dissemination. An officer's notes, on the other hand, are given greater protection. An officer's notes are often referred to as **work product** and have specific state statutes that protect their disclosure.

However, just because a state statute may give protection to an officer's work product, it does not mean they will not be disclosed. A police file is always subject to the court's subpoena power and the orders of the court. If a persuasive argument is made and it is convincing, the officer's notes could be disclosed. Given this, officers need to take the same pains with note taking as with report writing.

Another alternative for officer note taking is to take temporary notes. These are notes that are scribbled quickly at the time information is gathered. The purpose of temporary notes is short-term use by only the officer taking the notes. The officer then, within a short time, reduces the notes to a report and shreds the notes. Of course, the defense could make an argument that the officer "destroyed evidence," but that argument is not successful if the timing from incident to notes to report writing is short.

The most important thing about taking notes is to make sure they are clear and correct. Notes are often taken informally on a smaller flip pad or sometimes on the backs of handy scrap paper. This can make the notetaker feel informal. Informality can lead to sloppiness. If the notes are incorrect, the final report will be incorrect. This could be a real problem for the investigation. Consider a large case where multiple investigators are taking notes during witness accounts. Then, when they compare notes later, the notes are inconsistent. Who is right and who is wrong?

Reports in the Courtroom

As a general rule, police reports are not admissible in a criminal case, but an officer should never rely on that general rule. The legal profession is built on the exceptions to the rule and most good attorneys practice within the exceptions.

When an officer receives a subpoena to be a witness in a criminal case, he or she should first review any reports he or she made in connection with that case. After all, a primary reason to have a police report is to refresh memories. It is perfectly permissible to refresh one's memory by reviewing a police report.

The prosecutor will generally not want the police officer to take the reports to the courtroom at the time of the trial. Depending on the contents of the police report, it is generally not discoverable to the defense, and taking it to the courtroom could make it available to the defense.

It is also distracting to the jury if the witness is reading from a report rather than telling what he or she remembers about the case. Juries come to jury duty with high expectations that every witness will remember all the facts of the case like it were yesterday. The witness's credibility also is heightened when the testimony is told rather than read.

However, there could be times when the witness has difficulty remembering details contained in a police report. This happens when the case is complicated with lots of names and dates to remember. In this case, the best practice is to make a note card to take to the witness stand. This could be any type of document that the witness is using to refresh his or her memory at the time of the testimony. This allows the witness to "tell" the story to the jury and have the details correct.

From time to time a police report will be used as impeachment. This could be for several reasons. Maybe the police officer wrote something incorrectly on the report. In this case, it is turned over to the defense and the officer is questioned about the report. An officer's report could also be used to bolster the testimony of certain witnesses. Historically, a police report is hearsay, but there are states that have statutes allowing hearsay when it is an excited utterance or a child abuse victim, for example. A police report could also be used to impeach a witness who is changing his or her story from the original report to the time of trial. This can be seen in domestic violence cases or other familiar cases where time changes the dynamics of a relationship, and witnesses change their stories. The police report could be used to impeach those witnesses in front of the jury.

Documenting Witness Statements

All crimes have witnesses, but sometimes the only witness is the offender. Taking the suspect's statement is a complicated matter and will be discussed in future chapters along with the constitutional implications surrounding taking the suspect's statement.

There are two kinds of witnesses: primary witness and secondary witness. The **primary witness** is someone who saw the crime occur and whose statement can aid in the apprehension and prosecution of the perpetrator. The primary witness can also be known as the eyewitness or the ear witness. The primary witness can be the victim or complaining witness, but not always. If the victim or complaining witness did not see the crime, that person is not a primary witness, but a secondary witness.

A **secondary witness** is a witness who did not see or hear the crime as it was in progress but may have information about the happenings before or after the crime. For example, a secondary witness may not have seen the perpetrator break into the building but did see the perpetrator in possession of the stolen goods at a later date.

Keep in mind that the victim is a witness, and the victim's statement, along with all other witness statements, is evidence in the case. When the victim makes the initial report, part of his or her statement is the basis of the initial incident report. There could be other cases where the victim is not the initial complaining witness, such as when the victim is a child. There are also situations where the victim is the last to know the crime occurred, such as a burglary when the victim is out of town, the victim whose credit card company has noticed the fraud first, or the victim of a theft whose property is discovered missing by a third party. In all these examples, there will be numerous witness statements. It is important to consider the best way to document those statements—in writing, or with an audio or video recording. These different recording mechanisms are explained in depth later in this chapter but suffice it to say, the content should be the same.

The witness statement should include attention to detail and follow the same guidelines as explained earlier relative to report writing. The emotional state of the witness should be noted, but it is difficult to explain without crossing the factual line and giving an opinion. This is a caveat where some degree of opinion is required. However, the opinion of the emotional state of the witness needs to be thoroughly backed up by facts observed about the witness. This is the witness's body language. The officer can report, for example, that the witness was crying, shaking, short of breath, and/or hunched over to express an opinion that the witness was "excited." The term *excited* has special meaning within the law as it applies to witnesses. If a witness is "excited" when recounting an event that has just occurred, there is greater indicia of reliability about that statement, and it may be admissible into evidence if the witness is unavailable. If, for example, a police officer is called to a domestic violence scene and the victim is "excited" when disclosing the facts of what happened, the statement may be used later if the witness becomes unavailable. The witness may become unavailable because she is invoking her marital privilege not to testify against her husband. If her earlier statement is an "excited utterance," the statement could be testified to by the law enforcement officer rather than the victim herself. If the law enforcement officer failed to note the demeanor of the victim in that case, it would be hard to later testify that the victim was excited. The defense would surely argue that the law enforcement officer is merely saying that now that the victim will not cooperate.

Since the witness statements will be reviewed by other officers, investigators, prosecutors, defense attorneys, judges, and maybe even the media, it is important that the same level of objectiveness, clear and concise language, thoroughness, and professionalism are used as when writing a report.

What was the witness wearing? Did the witness have wet clothes? Did the witness appear to be under the influence of a substance? Did the witness appear to have a relationship with another witness on scene or party to the case? Did the witness have anything unusual to note? Keep in mind that a witness could turn into a suspect or codefendant later in the investigation.

Witness Statements in the Courtroom

Like police reports, witness statements are generally not admissible in a criminal case. However, the officer taking the statement should always take the statement with the end in mind, thinking that the statement could be used in a courtroom. Witness statements are hearsay unless the witness giving the statement is the one testifying.

The most common reason that a witness statement is used in the courtroom is for impeachment of a witness. If a witness's testimony is different from a previous statement, the attorney can use the statement and ask questions such as "Didn't you tell Detective Lockemup you didn't know Jeremy?"

Documentation by Photograph

Investigative photography is an important part of documentation of the crime scene. A photograph captures the image as it was at a certain time. It freezes the crime scene to allow others to view it at any future time. Photography becomes particularly important in the presentation of the case to others who did not have the benefit of seeing the crime scene. Investigators can present photographs to judges or magistrates in an application for a search warrant. Investigators can present photographs to prosecutors to help them get an overall understanding of the crime scene. Most importantly, photographs can be presented to finders of the facts in a trial to make the crime seem more realistic.

After a crime scene has been contained for safety, photography is usually the first documentation done by law enforcement. This is because it is important not to touch anything or move anything at the crime scene before photographs can be taken. The photography will preserve the crime scene exactly how it looks, forever. These photographs will be key elements in following up with the investigation and prosecution of the case.

Investigators are usually the ones who record the photographic evidence; however, initial officers, crime scene techs, and attorneys could also take photographs or video at a crime scene. Consistency in who is taking the photographs is the key. If one officer is dedicated to crime scene photography, it makes documentation of the crime scene much easier. The same officer takes the photos, understands the importance of the photos, downloads the photos, and testifies about the photos.

3D Photography

Some departments across the nation are using three-dimensional, or 3D, photography to capture a broader prospective of the crime scene. These devices are designed to use Google Maps along with photography from the scene to give the viewer full information about the area. While these are great tools to use to document a crime scene, they present some concerns. These cameras move in a circle and are self-automated, so others standing around the crime scene could be unaware their photos are being captured. If a department employee uses such cameras, there needs to be a clear protocol of when these cameras will be utilized.

Important Considerations in Photographic Documentation

Most investigators are trained to take photographs from a broad perspective and then a close perspective. This allows the viewer to get an idea of the overall crime scene before noticing smaller items. This is a natural approach because usually an investigator approaches the crime scene taking in the totality of it with his senses and then focuses on the smaller details.

The Use of Markers, Numbers, and Placards in Crime Scene Photography

Image 3.1

It is the practice of some police departments to use markers, numbers, or placards during the photographic documentation portion of the investigation. This can be a way for the investigators to stay organized. However, this can also be distractive to the later viewer of the photograph. Consider this scenario: Investigator Lockemup arrives at a crime scene to find multiple dead bodies inside a single-family residence. Lockemup uses numbered placards while he photographs the scene. In making his initial assessment of the scene, he determines that first the adult male was killed in the living room of the home, then the female was shot in the kitchen of the home, and finally the two children were killed in their bedrooms upstairs. Lockemup places numbered placards around each victim and documents each room in order. Then, as the investigation unfolds in the following weeks, he learns that there was another teenage child in the home who committed the crime and that the children were the first to be shot. The teenager confesses to using two different types of handguns, one of which was a revolver. Lockemup learns that the shell casings found by the body in the living room were from the bullets used to kill the children upstairs; the casings were only downstairs because the suspect reloaded downstairs. Now, when

Lockemup presents these photographs to a jury in a courtroom, his numbering system is confusing and inconsistent with the forensic evidence and other testimony in the case. If he had not used the numbers, the photographs could be presented in any order at a future time to give a clearer reenactment of the crime as it unfolded.

Use Of Photos in the Courtroom

Photos are used routinely in the courtroom. They are a great storytelling tool for the attorneys trying the case. The photo is marked as an exhibit and then shown to the witness, and the witness is asked whether he or she can identify what is in the photograph. If the witness can identify the subject of the photo and testify that the photo fairly and accurately depicts the subject matter therein, then the photo becomes admissible. A common misconception is that the witness must have taken the picture to identify it. That is incorrect. Any witness who has seen the subject matter of the photograph can testify about the photograph.

Everyone has heard the saying "a picture is worth a thousand words." This is true when presenting a criminal case to a judge or jury. The government is telling a story of a set of facts, and those facts become more real when the fact finder can see them. The law enforcement officer needs to be prepared to explain every detail of the photo. Sometimes this gets monotonous because several pictures may display the same subject matter—for example, "This is a picture of the shell casing laying on the floor," "This is a picture of a shell casing laying on the floor seen from the other direction," "This is a close-up picture of the same shell casing."

Image 3.2

Examine these two photos and ask yourself if they are good investigative photos. What do each of the two pictures teach us about the respective crime scenes? The photo of the person in sneakers is a close up of the feet and leg area. There appears to be a plastic bag wrapped around the legs. The legs could also have come through a hole in the bag. It is hard to tell from the photograph. The lighting is bad on this photograph. This picture does not highlight any certain area of the crime scene. It highlights neither the general area nor a specific item, so what is the purpose of this photo?

Image 3.3
Copyright © 2012 Depositphotos/Demian.

In contrast, the second photo of the woman lying on the floor in the office space seems to be better thought through. The photographer must have squatted down low to capture this angle. The intention seems to be to show the white pieces of paper in close proximity to the victim's body. It also shows the victim's entire body in relation to the crime scene. Does this help tell a story about what happened at this crime scene?

The law enforcement officer may be given a pointer or be asked to step down from the witness stand to point at a certain area of a photograph. The photograph also may be projected onto a smart board or something similar to give the witness the ability to mark on the photograph. The mechanisms for presentment to a jury are unlimited, and the law enforcement officer must be ready for anything.

Documentation by Video Recordings

Videography is also an excellent mechanism in preserving a crime scene for use later. Videos provide a real-life reenactment of the crime scene but can be a little more problematic because they usually capture sound. There are typically two types of video evidence in a crime scene: **intentional video recording** and **unintentional video recording**. Usually, the investigator is the one who documents the evidence through videotaping, but responding officers, crime scene techs, and attorneys on scene can also record video of a crime scene.

Intentional Video Recording

A well-done crime scene video can make a jury understand exactly what the scene was like at the time of the crime. For the finders of fact to convict, it is helpful when the prosecutor presenting a case makes it feel real. If an investigator chooses to document a crime scene using video, several things should be considered. First, the scene should be clear of most people. This is more important with video recording than photographic documentation because the viewing picture is broader when using video. A photographer can angle the camera to remove people from the photo or simply ask someone to step out of the way momentarily, but a videographer cannot do so without distraction. Second, other distractions should be minimized before recording. If the purpose is to preserve the crime scene through video, the videographer must see the video as someone else will in the future. Listen for barking dogs, sirens, people talking loudly from distant locations, radio noise, or other such noises that will distract a later viewer. Sometimes the heavy breathing of the videographer can be distractive and should be minimized if possible.

Consider this: Investigator Lockemup arrives at the scene of a multiple homicide. He decides to take a video recording of the scene for presentation at a later time. He begins recording the scene as he walks into the residence. Immediately, a rookie law enforcement officer approaches him and starts giving him a summary of what he thinks happened. There are several law enforcement officers milling about the scene, making offhanded comments about things in the residence, making small talk about nonrelevant things, and even laughing and making jokes. While comedy is a coping mechanism for many first responders, it is inappropriate in a crime scene video that will later be watched in a public courtroom by the victim's loved ones. Now, Lockemup's video is more of a hinderance to the prosecution than a help.

An officer should also consider recording a witness's statement. This is recommended with a reluctant witness. This will be discussed later in this chapter, but it is important to know that the same advantages and disadvantages of recordings apply. A second reason an officer should consider video recording the witness's statement is if the witness is an animated speaker. Sometimes a witness's actions could speak louder than his or her words. For example, a witness may be describing an argument between two people that escalated into an assault. The witness is giving a play-by-play rendition of the escalation, including statements like "Then, bam, he stabbed him" and produces an animated scream. Keep in mind that per the Sixth Amendment to the US Constitution, recorded statements cannot be substituted for live testimony in the courtroom in a criminal case, but they can be used if there is an attempt to impeach that witness.

Arial Photography/Videography /Drones

Another intentional form of photography or videography could be accomplished with the use of a **drone**. The application of drones equipped with optical, zoom, and/or thermal cameras allows law enforcement agents to monitor many different activities. The aerial vantage points can help document accidents and crime scenes and give a better reconstruction of the event. Drones can also be used to respond to emergency situations, like active shooters or protests. This allows law enforcement to see the activity but keep a safe distance.

If a police department uses department resources to purchase drones, there must be written policies in place. There must be a specific plan for the storage and dissemination of the data and images collected by the drones.

Many states have drafted laws regulating citizen and law enforcement use of drones. Be sure to check your state's policy before relying on a drone to document your crime scene. There are US Supreme Court cases regulating airspace usage.

In *Florida v. Riley*, the US Supreme Court looked at whether the open air above a residence was protected under the Fourth Amendment to the US Constitution. In this case, the police flew over a greenhouse located on defendant's property in a helicopter at four hundred feet, looked into the greenhouse, and saw marijuana. The police then obtained a search warrant for the greenhouse and seized the marijuana. The defendant argued that the search was improper because the defendant no doubt intended and expected that his greenhouse would not be open to public inspection. The defendant took precautions to protect against ground-level observation, but the sides and roof of his greenhouse were left partially open and were visible from the air.

This case hinged on how high the helicopter was when the officers saw the marijuana. The court ruled that since the helicopter was within Federal Aviation Administration regulations, the police officers were in place lawfully when they saw the marijuana. The court stated that the defendant could not reasonably have expected the contents of his greenhouse to be immune from examination by an officer seated in an aircraft flying in navigable airspace at an altitude of five hundred feet where such private and commercial flight at that altitude was routine.

This same case would be applicable to drones.

Figure 3.1 This drone picture shows a nice layout of city streets. This could assist a judge or jury in seeing the path of travel testified about.

Satellite Images

Another form of photography could be the use of internet sites that include mapping, such as Google Earth. These sites are readily available to law enforcement and the public. Law enforcement officers can take screenshots of a certain area to give an overall view of the terrain and location. These photos can be used to help a witness explain the facts in directional terms. For example, a witness may say the suspect ran north. The law enforcement officer can clarify with the witness the direction that he or she believes is north by pointing to a satellite photograph of the crime scene.

Overhead satellite images can be very useful when presenting the case to the finder of fact. The judge or jury may not be familiar with the area discussed, and a satellite image can make the testimony clearer. The satellite images can also give the judge or jury a better understanding of distances testified about. For example, if the defendant was seen approaching on foot the home he burglarized, it would be helpful to point out that the defendant's house is two blocks away and there is a clear path between the two homes.

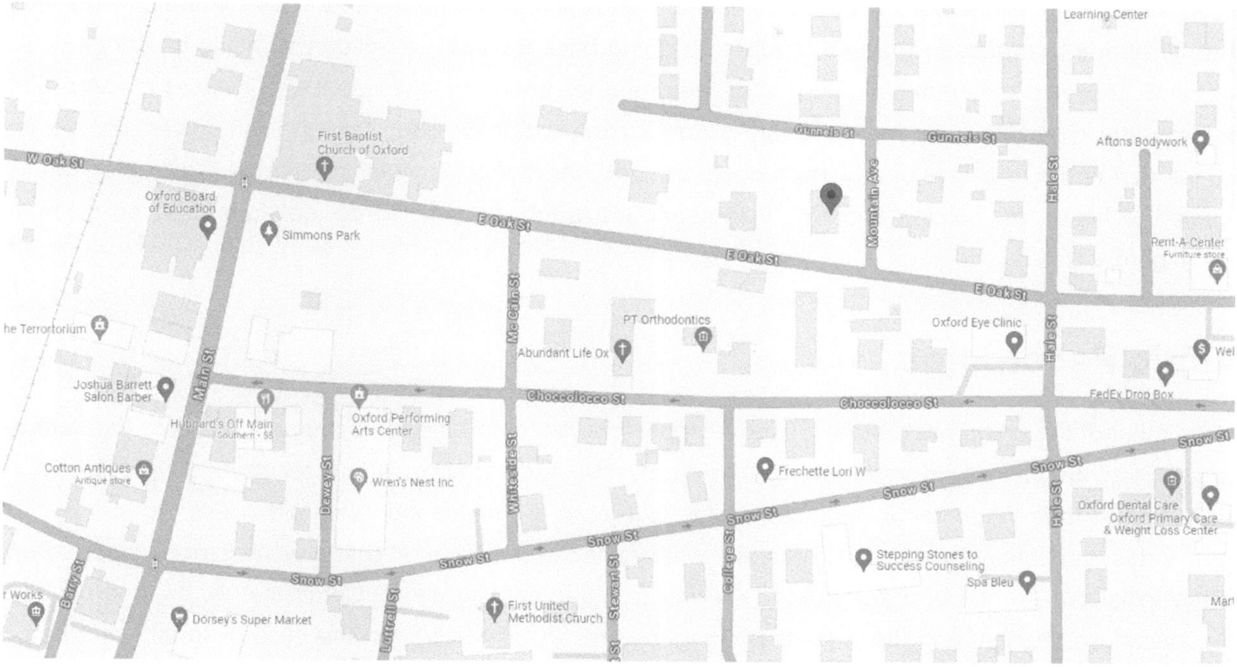

Image 3.4

Unintentional Video Recording

More often than intentional video recording of a crime scene, crime scene videos are made unintentionally. This is with the use of home security systems and police body cameras. Home security video systems are the best tool for solving a crime—what better evidence than the existence of video of the crime itself. Law enforcement officers need to be especially conscious that their actions may be recorded upon their approach to a crime scene and throughout the crime scene investigation if the location has surveillance video. Obtaining a search warrant or consent for preinstalled surveillance will be important in preserving the crime scene for future viewing.

Unintentional recording of a crime scene with body cameras is quite common. This is important documentation and can include many interesting things for fact finders to view later. Many officers wear body cameras as a part of their uniform and are so accustomed to them they often forget they are recording. These cameras can be running constantly or can be turned on and off as needed by the officer. When an officer turns on a body camera and approaches a crime scene, he or she can get distracted with the stress of the crime scene and forget that the camera was initiated. For example, an officer approaches the residence he was called to for a domestic disturbance. The victim describes how she was hit by her boyfriend, who also lives there. She tells the law enforcement officer that she wants him to be removed from the residence but does not want to press charges. The law enforcement officer returns to his car and calls his supervisor. In relaying the situation to his supervisor, the officer explains his disgust of the victim's appearance and that she does not want to press charges. He hangs up the phone and then decides that he needs to urinate in the tree line before going back toward the residence. While he urinates, his girlfriend calls and they make dinner plans. Then he goes back to the residence, convinces the victim to press charges, and starts writing his report. All this is captured on his body cam and can be very distracting for the fact finder who is later making a decision about the domestic violence charge. While everyone is entitled to his or her opinion about how someone looks or what they to do, opinions have no place in investigatory files.

Audio Recordings

While most of the principals discussed above apply to audio recordings, it is important to note that audio-only recordings can be an important tool in an investigator's toolbox. Audio recordings typically occur on a crime scene when the investigator wants to record a conversation with a witness. As mentioned above, this is recommended with a reluctant witness. It can be common that a witness gets wrapped up in the initial occurrence of a crime and is willing to tell everything seen. Unfortunately, as time passes, circumstances change, and the witness no longer wants to be involved in the case or to tell what he or she saw. This occurs for various reasons, such as the witness and defendant have a relationship and the witness feels guilty about "telling on" the defendant. The witness could also become labeled a "snitch" and feel threatened in the community. The witness could also have reached an agreement wherein he or she would not testify in exchange for payment. The reasons a witness could change his or her story are unlimited.

Even the smallest departments have the budget for a recording device. These can be small handheld electronic devices that can remain in the officer's car or duty case. The officer should remember to keep the device charged or additional batteries on hand, to make sure the device is ready to go when needed. Caution should be used when contemplating the use of one's personal cell phone to record statements in the field. Many pitfalls could arise if the officer used his or her own device to record statements.

> Investigator Lockemup suspects the manager of the bank was involved in the robbery of the bank. He already has his personal cell phone in his hand because he was snapping photographs and decides to turn on the audio recorder on his phone. He engages the bank manager in a conversation that later incriminates the manager in the robbery. That audio recording can be seized by the federal officers as evidence in the case, therefore depriving Lockemup of his personal phone.

Also, a recording could be lost or interrupted if an officer is using his or her own cell phone to record. For example, an officer is using his or her personal device to record a statement of a victim. The victim is about five minutes into recounting the events when the officer's supervisor calls to get an update on the case. The officer takes the phone call, and therefore the recording automatically pauses. The officer does not realize that the recording is paused and continues the interview. When the officer's supervisor is reviewing the statements weeks later, the supervisor asks the officer where the rest of the interview is, only to find it doesn't exist.

Advantages and Disadvantages of Photographic and Video Evidence

As with most investigative actions, there are advantages and disadvantages to photographic and video evidence. It is important to weigh these at the onset of the investigation. Along with the advantage of preserving the crime scene for viewing later, discussed above, photos and video can preserve evidence that may disappear quickly. For example, in a home invasion robbery where the suspect shot through the glass back door of the residence, a photograph of the glass door could be important because at any point, the glass could fall to the floor and the height of the hole in the glass would not be preserved. Also, photographs of outdoor scenes can preserve evidence for testing and measurement if imminent rain threatens destruction of that evidence.

Some disadvantages are that photographic and video evidence can distract the fact finder from the facts of the crime. In addition to the disadvantage examples given above, photographs and video can distort distances, sizes, and coloring. There could also be operator error such as lens caps left on, incorrect time stamps, or complete equipment malfunction. In these cases, the investigator is left spending more time explaining the mishap than how the crime was committed.

A common mistake when law enforcement takes photographic or video evidence is that the officer takes this evidence on his or her personal device. Photos and recordings made on personal devices not only can give the appearance of a lack of professionalism, but also can result in the officer giving up his or her personal device to an evidence sticker.

Investigator Lockemup is called out to a bank robbery in the middle of the night. In his dreamy state of mind, he forgets his department-issued camera bag. When he arrives on the scene, he notices footprints in the dirt below the shrubbery lining the bank's sidewalk. He also hears a crack of thunder and senses impending rain. He pulls out his personal cell phone and snaps photographs of the footprints. Since his phone is in his hand, he then decides to snap photos inside the bank as well. At the end of the evening, he speaks with an agent of the secret service, who informs Lockemup that the federal authorities will be taking the case and that his phone will be needed as evidence.

Use of Audio and Video Recordings in the Courtroom

With cameras now readily available, audio and video recordings are a part of most criminal trials. The attorneys will choose the most effective way to present the recording to the fact finder. The law enforcement officer providing the recording to the attorney needs to alert the attorney to any possible issues with the recording that will affect the way the fact finder views and/or hears the recording. For example, the recording may be very difficult to see. Consider a confidential informant who is wearing a hidden wire to record a drug transaction. The confidential informant may be listening to music in the background, wearing clothing that is rubbing the hidden microphone, breathing loud, or some other distracting behavior. The hidden camera could be a fake key fob that the informant is holding in his or her hand. Watching the video feels like being on a roller coaster ride.

The law enforcement officer also needs to alert the attorney if there are any inappropriate behaviors on the video. Sometimes law enforcement officers forget that he or she is wearing a camera and goes to the bathroom or makes a personal phone call to a relationship partner. In such cases, the officer could be embarrassed by what is shown, and perhaps the attorney could not show that portion of the video.

The attorney could also make still shots from the video and present the photos to the witness in the courtroom. This is yet another reason the law enforcement officer needs to have watched the video evidence before going into the courtroom.

The recordings could potentially be difficult to hear. One microphone may be closer to one party, making one voice loud and the other barely audible. The speaker could have a speech disorder or a thick accent making the words hard to decipher. When this happens, the attorney may have the recording transcribed. The law enforcement witness may be asked to listen to the recording while simultaneously reading the transcript to ensure its accuracy.

Documentation by Sketch or Diagram

An effective way to document a crime scene is by making a sketch or **diagram**. This can be done simply with pen and paper or with a complex computer software program. Despite the method used, the basics of production and use are the same.

Below are some tips for creating effective **crime scene sketches** that convey the scene to individuals who were not present.

- Set the parameters of your diagram. Before beginning the sketch, determine how much of the area to illustrate: just the evidence seized, the number placard beside the piece of evidence seized, the area surrounding the piece of evidence, the entire room.
- Gather information. Take measurements of the entire space, note distances between objects, and note larger items to use as reference points. Remember, when you or others look back on this sketch, it could be months or even years later and memories fade. It is important to document as much information as possible and include it in the sketch at the time the sketch is created.
- Add details. Note placement of people, vehicles, animals, and any other object that is readily movable. Also add anything the perpetrator may have left behind or displaced in the area.
- Make a key. Label each piece of evidence with a number or symbol. Then use arrows and text to show additional details or give information about that item.
- Verify the sketch. Consult with witnesses and authorities who are knowledgeable about the area to confirm the information depicted in the diagram.

Sketches

Per the US Department of Justice, the purpose of an investigative sketch is to provide a correct record that shows the scene as it was found that can be examined at a later date. There is no requirement that the drawer have any artistic ability, as after all, the sketch should be for the drawer's own use. The sketch is supplementary to the investigator's field notes. Sketches should record only those items that seem important at the time. It is important to label every object of importance. This enables the viewer to take in the entire area at a glance; for example, a crime scene that includes a house, garage, outbuilding, and neighbor's property line could be sketched to give the later viewer a perspective of the different structures. Sketches are not meant to identify small objects but rather give the bigger picture to the later viewer. It isn't important to record measurements accurately, but the proportions need to be close to accurate. Inaccuracy could be viewed by a later fact finder as a trick to sway the judge or jury.

Keys, symbols, and labels are necessary and valuable to any sketch, but apply caution when deciding what to use. For example, an investigator may think he or she has the crime scene figured out and indicates "first shell casing," "second shell casing," and so on. Then, as the investigation unfolds, the investigators's theory of the order of the shots conflicts with the witness statements. It is best to follow the same rule of thumb used when generating a report—facts, not opinions. Even labeling something as "blood droppings" could be a point for argument later with a defense attorney because the “blood droppings” were not tested and therefore not verified as blood. Seasoned investigators have been down this road and use the term “red brown stain” instead. This allows the fact finder to make the determination that it is blood and eliminates objections from the defense.

Diagrams

A crime scene diagram visually documents the setting of a crime as it appeared when it was discovered. It is similar to a sketch but may look neater and more professional than a sketch. The diagram might be produced using mapping software or crime scene reconstruction software that provides straight lines and perfect 90-degree angles. It typically includes a layout of the environment, location of the victim(s), blood splatter, and possible items of interest like weapons, footprints, dirt, and clothes, along with written details and pictorial evidence. A properly prepared crime scene diagram is very useful for investigative and forensic work in the criminal justice system. A supplemental vehicle diagram may be used in the event the crime took place in or involved a car, truck, van, or other type of vehicle.

The same rules regarding the uses of keys, legends, and labels discussed above apply to diagrams. Getting a diagram to scale may be difficult or impossible, even with expensive software systems. It may be the better practice to label the diagram “not to scale,” even if it may be. There is usually someone who could find a small disparity in measurement, thus tainting the entire diagram if it were reported to be “to scale” but wasn’t.

Use of Sketches or Diagrams in the Courtroom

Sketches and diagrams are great tools to explain the crime scene to a jury. They will be presented to the jury in the same general way as photographs. Chances are the sketch has been reduced to a diagram and that is what will be presented to the fact finder. The attorney may have a trial presenter that acts as a newer version of an overhead projector. This allows the attorney to place the exhibit on a screen and project it to a wall or digital screen. If this is the case, the law enforcement officer will need to be able to explain everything on the diagram and possibly use a pointer. The police officer presenting the diagram is usually the one who produced the diagram, but the presenter could also be another witness present at the scene.

Written Documentation to Accompany the Photographic, Video, or Diagram Evidence

Although a picture can be worth a thousand words, it is still necessary for the investigator to thoroughly document the purpose of the photos and videos taken. Unfortunately, it can be months or years before a case comes to trial and inevitably the law enforcement officer will have worked on many other crime scenes in between. The officer will be expected to answer questions such as what the photo shows and why the officer took it. Most of the photos will be easily explained with a common sense approach, but there are those outlier photos that need documentation. For example, consider photographs from a burglary scene. The photos document the pry marks on the door and items in disarray throughout the house, and then there is a photograph of a gouge in sheetrock. It is a close-up photo, making it impossible to know which room it was take in. The officer is asked on the witness stand why he or she took this picture, what room is it in, and what it tells us about the crime scene. Without written documentation, the officer could fall short in response.

Every investigator must stay abreast of the newest technology available for crime scene reporting and evidence collection. Some new technologies that may be a part of every future crime scene are alternative light photography, high-speed ballistics photography, and Video Spectral Comparator 2000.

Alternative Light Photography

Alternative light photography is a tool used to see damage to the body before it is visible to the naked eye. An Omnichrome camera uses blue light and orange filters to clearly show bruising below the skin's surface. A person must be specially trained to use this important forensic tool to detect injuries below the skin.

High-Speed Ballistics Photography

Forensic scientists can also use high-speed cameras to detect path and directions of bullet paths. A bullet can be fired in the laboratory through wood, metal, or glass, for example, to determine how the hole was created. That knowledge can then be applied to the items collected from the crime scene. This may give the scientists a better understanding of what happened at the crime scene and enable them to testify about bullet trajectories, impact marks, and exit wounds.

Video Spectral Comparator 2000

This specialized machine is used for analysis of papers that may contain words or images useful as evidence in a case where such evidence has been damaged by fire, water, or other means. This machine can mimic lifting fingerprints, but instead can lift words and images from papers to aid law enforcement in solving a case.

Rules to Remember

- An offense report should contain facts not opinions.
- An offense report should answer Who? What? When? Where? and Why?
- An officer should always use clear, concise, and professional language in his or her reports.
- Supplemental reports should include prior contacts with the victim, prior contacts with the suspects, the existence of court orders, how the suspect was established, and any additional details of the offense known to the officer.

- Witness statements can be recorded in writing, on audio recording, or on video recordings.
- Photos at the crime scene should be taken from broad to narrow prospectives.
- An officer should minimize distractions when producing an intentional video recording of a crime scene.
- Officers should be aware that recording devices are everywhere, and their actions will be judged at a later date.
- Officers should be aware that recordings on devices capturing crime scenes need to be preserved before they are recorded over.
- Sketches can be used as a tool for law enforcement to remember a crime scene to later diagram the scene.
- Diagrams are usually not to scale but should be reasonably proportionate.
- Photos, recordings, and diagrams should always be accompanied by written descriptions and reports of what is depicted.
- Officers should be aware of changing technology that can assist with crime scene documentation.

End of Chapter Comprehension and Application

Directions: Use what you have learned in this chapter to help you respond completely and correctly to the question or prompt below.

1. What relevant information should a police report contain?
2. List three purposes for writing reports and why each is important.
3. When should notes be taken? Not taken? What is the purpose of the notes?
4. Do you think police officers should retain or destroy personal notes taken during an investigation?
5. What types of information should be included in supplemental reports?
6. Should a witness statement be taken in writing or recorded? What are the advantages/ disadvantages of each?
7. What are three reasons a witness may change his or her initial statement about a crime occurring?
8. Should more than one officer take notes during an investigation? Why or why not?
9. In what types of cases are photographs likely to be important to the investigation?
10. What is the most effective way to take photographs? Why?
11. What are two types of video recordings, and how can they help document a crime scene?
12. What are some things officers need to be cautious about when videoing a crime scene?
13. In what circumstances would an officer want to audio-record a witness statement?
14. What are some considerations when capturing arial photos or video?

15. What should an officer do to prepare when testifying in a case with recorded documentation?
16. In what types of cases is a diagram or sketch useful? Why?
17. What should an officer do if he finds himself at a crime scene without a recorder and needs to take a recorded witness statement? Explain your answer.
18. Are police reports available to the public? Explain.
19. What should accompany photographic evidence, video recordings, and/or diagrams? Why?
20. What is wrong with each sentence below? Reword these sentences to emphasize clarity. You can add facts to express your reasoning.
    a. "She said she was the one who started the fight."
    b. "I know I locked the door after I walked the dog."
    c. "The chair was out of place, but it was windy that day."
    d. "He was okay before I went to the dentist, but when I got back, he was unconscious."

References

Florida v. Riley, 488 U.S. 445 (1988), https://supreme.justia.com/cases/federal/us/488/445/.

For more on modern forensic science technologies, see https://www.forensicscolleges.com/blog/resources/10-modern-forensic-science-technologies.

Chapter 4

Evidence Collection–The Search Warrant

Introduction: Obtaining Evidence That Will Be Admissible in Court

In this chapter students will explore the Fourth Amendment's reasonableness requirement and study the US Supreme Court cases interpreting the reasonableness requirement. Students will also be introduced to the exclusionary rule and the exceptions to the exclusionary rule.

Chapter Objectives

In this chapter students will learn:

- What the Fourth Amendment to the US Constitution means for evidence collection
- What the US Supreme Court believes is a reasonable search
- What is required to obtain a search warrant
- How to draft a search warrant
- What are some special conditions for search warrants
- How the exclusionary rule is applied and what is its purpose
- What are the exceptions to the exclusionary rule
- What is a reasonable expectation of privacy
- How to obtain evidence with the use of subpoenas and court orders

Key Terms

Key terms and professional terminology that are used in this chapter include:

- **The Fourth Amendment to the US Constitution**

- **Search**
- **Search warrant**
- **Seizure**
- **Reasonableness**
- **Expectation of privacy**
- **Probable cause**
- **Open field doctrine**
- **Staleness**
- **Knock and announce**
- **Anticipatory search warrant**
- **Standing**
- **Exclusionary rule**
- **The fruit of the poisonous tree doctrine**
- **Inevitable discovery**
- **Good faith exception**

The Fourth Amendment to the United States Constitution

When we read the **Fourth Amendment to the US Constitution**, we hear terms that give us guidance on how searches must occur. The Fourth Amendment states that "the right of the people to be secure in their persons, houses, papers, and effects, against unreasonable searches and seizures, shall not be violated, and no Warrants shall issue, but upon probable cause, supported by Oath or affirmation, and particularly describing the place to be searched, and the persons or things to be seized." In examining the Fourth Amendment to the Constitution, we notice:

First, the things that are protected in the Fourth Amendment are persons, houses, papers, and effects.

Second, those things are protected from unreasonable searches.

Third, warrants shall only be issued upon probable cause supported by an oath and particularly describing the place to be searched, and the persons or things to be seized.

What Is a Search?

A **search** can be defined as "to look into or over carefully or thoroughly in an effort to find or discover something."

In *Kyllo v. United States*, federal agents suspected Kyllo of growing large amounts of marijuana inside his home. Agents traveled to the residence with the purpose of utilizing a thermal imaging device to scan the building for a high heat source. The device was aimed at the building and displayed a reading showing a high amount of heat was being admitted from a concentrated area. This was consistent with using lights to grow marijuana in a house. The federal agents put this information in an affidavit and obtained a **search**

warrant to search the residence. The agents found an indoor growing operation with more than one hundred marijuana plants. The issue was whether the use of the thermal imaging device was a search without a warrant. The Court defined a search as something meant to look over or through for the purpose of finding something; to explore; to examine by inspection. The Court also acknowledged that the thermal imaging device wasn't something readily available to the public, which is an important distinction when you consider other devices that can be used such as binoculars. Ultimately, the Court ruled the search warrant invalid as it was based on the use of the thermal imaging device, which was in itself a search.

> Remember that there are many different ways a search can be executed. A search can be done by listening, looking, touching, or smelling. The question is whether any of these things violate a reasonable expectation of privacy.

The Balancing Test for Searches

In assessing the reasonableness of an invasive search, we "balance the invasion of personal rights caused by the search against the need for that particular search," examining the search in context and considering "(1) the scope of the particular intrusion; (2) the manner in which the search was conducted; (3) the justification for initiating the search; and (4) the place in which the search was performed."

What Is a Seizure?

The Fourth Amendment used the term **seizure** broadly to encompass not only seizure in the possessor sense of things, but seizure in the controlling sense over a person.

It is relatively easy to understand when an item has been seized. It is when the item is taken into possession by the government. For example, when a vehicle is impounded by the police because the driver is arrested for driving under the influence, the vehicle is seized by the police. The physical possession of the vehicle is transferred from the suspect to the government.

People can also be seized under the Fourth Amendment's definition of seizure. At common law, it was believed that a person was seized by the government when the government official laid hands on the suspect. This could be ever so slight, even the touch of a finger. The person was believed to be under arrest or seized by that touch. The seizure of a person plainly refers to an arrest. The arrest of a person is quintessentially a seizure.

The courts have moved away from that notion of the need for a physical touching to be a seizure and have found more creative ways that seizures can occur. A seizure requires the use of force with intent to restrain. Accidental force will not qualify. Nor will force intentionally applied for some other purpose satisfy this rule. Only force used to apprehend will be a seizure.

One type of force used to apprehend a suspect is the use of a firearm. The Court in *Torres v. Madrid* was asked to determine whether a seizure occurs when an officer shoots someone who temporarily eludes capture after the shooting. Their answer was yes. The application of physical force to the body of a person with intent to restrain is a seizure, even if the force does not succeed in subduing the person.

The *Torres* Court also stated that the seizure depends on the subjective perceptions of the seized person. Torres claims to have perceived the officers' actions as an attempted carjacking. Torres's subjective thoughts of the circumstances of the encounter do not determine whether a seizure occurred. Instead, the conduct of the officers ordering Torres to stop and then restraining her (by shooting) satisfies the objective test for a seizure.

This builds on a much older case, *United States v. Mendenhall*. The *Mendenhall* Court held that a person has been seized within the meaning of the Fourth Amendment only if, in view of all the circumstances surrounding the incident, a reasonable person would have believed that he was not free to leave. Mendenhall establishes that the test for existence of a "show of authority" is an objective one: not whether the citizen perceived that he was being ordered to restrict his movement, but whether the officer's words and actions would have conveyed that to a reasonable person. This is an objective test rather than a subjective test application.

Once it is determined that a seizure has occurred, the natural question to follow is, How long does the seizure last? The *Torres* Court rules that a seizure that occurs by force, absent submission, is still a seizure. The time frame of the seizure lasts the same time as the time the force is being applied. In this case, the time of the seizure was as long as the bullet striking Torres.

> Remember that a seizure occurs when an object is taken by a governmental agent. A person also can be seized when his or her movement is restricted by a government agent.

The Scope of The Objects Subject to The Search or Seizure

In *Warden v. Hayden*, the US Supreme Court tells us that if a search is **reasonable**, then the police may search and seize the following:

- The instrumentalities of a crime
- The fruits of the crime
- The contraband
- The evidence related to the crime

The Fourth Amendment Protects Persons, Houses, Papers, and Effects

The Fourth Amendment protects more than persons, homes, papers, and effects. It has been expanded over the decades to include many other things such as cars, computers, and internet cloud accounts. The Fourth Amendment question is whether the person has a reasonable **expectation of privacy** in what is searched.

Persons

We can all agree that we have a reasonable expectation of privacy in our bodies. The question becomes, to what degree. Does a person have a reasonable expectation of privacy in the way that he or she looks? We know that photos and images can be used in lineups, and there is no need for a search warrant to produce images of an individual. We must explore where the privacy begins.

Think about the searches that could occur surrounding the body. Photographs of private body parts, fingerprints, bodily sounds (voice or other), measurements of body parts, skin and nail scrapings, DNA swabs, X-rays, head and pubic hair cuttings, head and pubic hair pullings, removal of items from the body. We will explore each of these below.

Private Body Parts

The intimate or private parts of an individual may become the target of a search warrant if probable cause can be established to show an item of evidence of a crime is on or inside a private part. For example, if a man is suspected of solicitation of a child by electronic devices and alleged to have sent photographs of his penis to a child, then there may be a need to photograph his penis to compere to the image sent. Likewise, if there is an allegation of sexual abuse, wherein the child states that there is a unique characteristic to the man's penis, then there may be a need for a search warrant for a photograph.

An investigator also may need to view the skin of a suspect. Perhaps the victim disclosed that she bit her attacker on his inner thigh. The investigator would want a warrant to view and photograph the inner thigh of the suspect.

Since photographs and inspection of one's body parts is an invasive search, there will also be a balancing test applied when determining probable cause of the warrant. The courts will always balance the depth of the invasion of privacy against the government's need of the item sought.

Nonprivate Body Parts

A search warrant can be a useful tool in obtaining photographs of nonprivate body parts. Suppose, for example, that a robbery occurred at a convenience store. The clerk who was robbed at gunpoint described the assailant as having a tattoo of Mickey Mouse on his forearm. When Investigator Lockemup interviews the suspect, the suspect is wearing a long sleeve shirt and refuses to answer any questions. Lockemup would like to know if the suspect has a tattoo of Mickey Mouse on his forearm, but he must have probable cause to request a search warrant.

Bodily Sounds (Voice or Other)

A seizure of a person's physical attributes is not subject to the warrant requirements. The physical characteristics of a person's voice, its tone and manner, are constantly exposed to the public. Like a man's facial characteristics or handwriting, his voice is repeatedly produced for others to hear. No other person can have a reasonable expectation that others will not know the sound of his voice.

Fingerprints

Fingerprints are routinely gathered from crime scenes and compared to a known sample. Most law enforcement agencies have access to a database of known samples of fingerprints for comparison. Those databases contain fingerprints from individuals who have been fingerprinted in the past, perhaps at a prior arrest. However, there could be an occasion wherein the suspect in a crime has no known fingerprint on file, and the law enforcement officer would like a fingerprint from the suspect. The officer can obtain the fingerprint by surveilling the suspect and waiting on the suspect to abandon an item touched (e.g., a soft drink can) or the officer can apply for a search warrant for the suspects fingerprints.

Measurements of Body Parts

The size of a suspect's body part could become relevant to a crime scene investigation. Suppose that a boathouse was broken into and the intruder was barefoot. The intruder walked through wet paint at the boathouse and left a footprint at the crime scene. The police could probably estimate the size of the suspect's footprint by looking at his or her shoe, but the thorough investigator would want an exact match of size. The investigator would need to have **probable cause** to request a warrant for a measurement or imprint of the suspect's foot.

Nail Scrapings

When the searches requested align closer to invasive rather than noninvasive, there must be a balancing test accompanying the probable cause standard. In rape cases or other types of assault cases, a struggle may have occurred between the victim and the offender. If the victim has injuries caused by the suspect's nails, an investigator will want to obtain a scraping from the suspect's nails for comparison. This can be an invasive search and a judge must balance the intrusive nature against the government's need for the invasion. Timing is also a factor, as nail scrapings may not prove helpful after hand washing or bathing.

DNA Swabs

When a suspect leaves DNA at a crime scene, it is only incriminatory if it is matched to a known sample. As with fingerprint databases, law enforcement officers have access to databases containing DNA samples. In many states, when a person is convicted, a DNA swab is taken for identification purposes. Those samples are kept in a database. If a DNA sample is collected at a crime scene and then matched to a DNA sample in a database, the law enforcement officer would have probable cause to obtain a DNA swab from the suspect. This may seem redundant because there already is a match. However, the prudent law enforcement officer will not want to depend on the match to the sample. The database sample may have been taken years prior and it may be too difficult to prove the chain of custody on the swab in the database. This could leave the identification of the DNA swab from the database subject to attack at trial. "How do we know beyond a reasonable doubt that this swab is the defendant's?" "How do we know the swabs weren't mislabeled by a corrections officer twenty years ago?" "How do we know the swab wasn't contaminated by the person who took the swab, because we do not know who took the swab?" "How do we know a qualified technician extracted the DNA from the swab, because we do not know who the technician is?" These will be only a few of the questions raised by a competent defense attorney if there is not a fresh swab taken from the suspect.

X-rays

Similarly to a thermal imaging device, an X-ray machine takes photographs of the inside of the body that cannot be viewed by the naked eye. Therefore, it constitutes a search. This can be another area of the body that an investigator needs to search. For example, suppose Investigator Lockemup is investigating a cold case murder. The suspect was also shot during the altercation. Now years later, Lockemup gets a tip naming the suspect. The tipster produces a recorded phone call wherein the suspect confesses to the tipster and tells the tipster that the bullet from the shooting is still in his hip and bothers him daily. Lockemup wants to get an X-ray of the suspect's hip to confirm there is a bullet there. This should be sufficient probable cause to obtain a search warrant.

Removal of Items from the Body

In the X-ray example above, Investigator Lockemup may also want to request a search warrant for removal of the bullet lodged in the suspect's hip for comparison to the gun the victim used to shoot his attacker. A matching bullet would be a great piece of evidence for Lockemup to use in his case, but it must be balanced against the extreme intrusion of a surgical procedure. In *Carlton v. Pytell*, the suspect was shot during a robbery and the bullet was lodged just under his skin on his back. The law enforcement officer obtained a warrant to remove the bullet, because the suspect refused to have it removed, and it was removed by the ER doctor. The Michigan Supreme Court upheld the removal, while balancing the intrusion to the body. The courts have been consistent in balancing the intrusion of the surgery with the state's need for the evidence. In some cases, such as *Carlton v. Pytell*, that involve a minor procedure, the courts have allowed removal of evidence from the body. However, in other cases, where the defendants showed a risk involved to the health and safety of the patient, the courts have declined to approve a search warrant or removal of an item from within the body.

Head and Pubic Hair Cuttings

An investigator who finds hair at the scene of a crime will surely want a known sample for comparison. Hair cuttings can be subject to a search warrant if the requisite probable cause exists. Certain technological factors may prevent exact matches based on hair cuttings due to the nature of the hair follicle breaking down over time. An expert may be able to give testimony relative to a hair being consistent with another rather than an exact match.

Head and Pubic Hair Pullings

Human hair with the root attached can provide a greater level of identification than hair clippings. The root of the hair can contain mitochondrial DNA, which can identify a suspect. For example, if a victim reports that she ripped hair from her attacker's head, more than likely the root was attached to the hair follicle. This small amount of tissue gives technicians much more to work with for identification purposes. An investigator will surely want to obtain a search warrant for pullings for the suspects' hair if probable exists.

House

At the very core of the Fourth Amendment stands the right of a person to retreat into his or her own home and there be free from unreasonable governmental intrusion. With few exceptions, the question whether a warrantless search of a home is reasonable and hence constitutional must be answered no.

As discussed earlier in this chapter, *Kyllo v. United States* was a case involving federal agents using a thermal imaging device outside Kyllo's home, which revealed unusual heat patterns and an unusual amount of heat radiating from the roof and side walls compared with the rest of the house, leading the agents to believe he was using high-intensity lamps common in cannabis cultivation. The imaging was done without a warrant and therefore was an unreasonable search. The Kyllo Court discussed "vantage point."

The lawfulness of a vantage point is relevant to the definition of a search. Surveillance taken from a vantage point outside of a private area is more likely constitutionally sound. In common terms, if the government agent was lawfully where he or she should have been when he or she saw what he or she saw, then it is constitutional.

Clearly a street, sidewalk, common hallway, or public airspace would all be a lawful vantage point. Private property can be a lawful vantage point. For example, suppose the suspect's house is across the street from a multistory shopping mall. The government could lawfully be on the private property of the mall looking down into the suspect's back yard. The police could also be lawfully inside a neighbor's apartment overlooking the suspect's yard.

The law enforcement officer could also lawfully be inside the curtilage of the suspects' dwelling when the officer sees illegal activity.

> Suppose Investigator Lockemup suspects drug activity at a residence. He can walk to the front door of the residence and knock. There is a caveat that the front door must be accessible and not intentionally shielded from visitors. In other words, if the Girl Scout could walk up and knock on the door, then so can Lockemup. Suppose Lockemup walks up to the door and knocks. When he knocks, he sees through the window what he believes through his training education and experience to be a methamphetamine lab. Can Lockemup draft an application for a search warrant based on his viewing of the methamphetamine lab through the window of the private residence?

Keep in mind that the term "house" in the Fourth Amendment refers not only to a private home, but also to a business establishment, an industry, or a commercial facility.

The Open Field Doctrine

Under the **open field doctrine**, areas outside the curtilage and held out to the public and are subject to the police search without violating the Fourth Amendment. The curtilage of a house or dwelling is the land immediately surrounding it, including any closely associated buildings and structures. The common law distinguished "open fields" from "curtilage." In contrast to the sanctity of the private home, the open field does not provide an expectation of privacy. An "open field" doesn't need to be a "field" or "open."

The test of whether an expectation of privacy is legitimate for Fourth Amendment purposes is not whether the individual chooses to conceal "private" activity; rather, the correct inquiry is whether the government's intrusion infringes upon the personal and societal values protected by the Fourth Amendment.

Limitations on the Expectation of Privacy

While the US Supreme Court has taken great measures to protect the privacy interest of citizens in individual homes, there are limits. One important limitation is in items removed from the home and made available for sanitation collection. In *California v Greenwood*, the police suspected Greenwood of trafficking in narcotics. The law enforcement officer asked the sanitation service to collect Greenwood's trash as usual, but keep it separate from his neighbors and then turn it over to law enforcement. The law enforcement officer found evidence of a controlled substance crime and used it against Greenwood. The issue in the case was whether an individual citizen has a reasonable expectation of privacy in the items left for trash collection. The Court ruled that there is no expectation of privacy in items left for sanitation collection. There are certain limitations to this ruling. One limitation is that the police cannot seize trash that has not been placed in its normal location for pick up.

In *United States v Dunn*, the Court ruled that not all outbuildings are within the curtilage of a home. In this case, the Court considered four factors to consider in making a determination of whether the outbuilding is within the curtilage.

- Proximity of the home to the area claimed to be curtilage
- Whether the area is included in an enclosure that surrounds the home
- The nature of the use of the area
- The protections taken by the homeowner to protect the area from observation

Ariel Flyovers

Similarly to Oliver in *United States v. Oliver*, Ciraolo was growing marijuana in his back yard. The police got an anonymous tip that Ciraolo was growing marijuana in his back yard. They went to the location and could not see in the back yard because of two high fences. The police made the decision to conduct surveillance from overhead. The plane flew over the yard and took pictures. Since the flyover was in publicly navigated airspace and the crops were seen with the naked eye, it was not a violation of privacy in the curtilage. Similarity, in *Florida v. Riley*, the flyover was with a helicopter to peer into a partially covered greenhouse and it was not in violation of the open fields doctrine because it was visible to any other craft flying over.

Papers

When the word *paper* was drafted into the Fourth Amendment, there was no such thing as Instagram. Yes, papers still play an important role in crime scene investigation, but digital papers play a greater role. Individuals tend to document their daily lives on social media accounts and this is a vice relied upon by law enforcement officers routinely. Law enforcement officers draft more social media search warrants than any other group. These warrants still have the same legal requirements as any other warrant, but the terminology is unique. For example, a search warrant could request UGLI information. This is an acronym for user-generated location information.

Most Americans can remember January 6, 2021, when the Capitol Building was stormed by protesters during a meeting certifying the vote count for the Electoral College of the 2020 presidential election. Many rioters recorded and photographed themselves and others on the restricted grounds and inside the Capital Building. Americans watched on platforms such as Facebook Live as this occurred. As part of the investigation, the government requested from Facebook the identification information from accounts of anyone broadcasting from the Capitol area. Once that account holder information was obtained, the government applied for search warrants requiring Facebook to disclose various records and content associated with the accounts that would be evidence of a crime. Defendant Matthew Bledsoe is the owner of one such account. He argued that the government did not obtain a search warrant for the user identification information and therefore the information was due to be suppressed.

The Bledsoe court referenced the *Carpenter v. United States* case. In Carpenter, the government's acquisition from Facebook of noncontent information derived from user-generated content of a highly public event that reveals the user's location—that is, user-generated location information (UGLI)—was a Fourth Amendment search requiring a probable cause warrant. The Court stated, "A 'search' for purposes of the Fourth Amendment occurs when government action infringes a sphere an individual seeks to preserve as private and the expectation of privacy is one society considers reasonable under the circumstances." The *Carpenter* Court acknowledged that this narrow holding left open a range of questions about the application of the Fourth Amendment to cell-site location information (CSLI), other types of data revealing location information, and other business records that might incidentally reveal location information.

The Court noted that the defendant bears the burden of proving that he had a legitimate expectation of privacy. This is a significant ruling because usually the state bears the burden of proof for most issues in criminal court. The Court also noted that the user's privacy settings are a factor in determining whether the user has an expectation of privacy on the account.

> Investigator Lockemup takes possession of Dennis's cell phone and retrieves stored numbers for all the men Dennis said were involved in the murder. Lockemup calls Fred Fed, who worked for the FBI, and asked for an immediate phone trace on each of the numbers. The federal authorities have access to cell phone towers and can determine the location of a phone and give historical data of the phone's location. Within the hour, Lockemup has phone data supporting Dennis's story. He also has the current location of Melvin's and Andy's (Dennis's codefendants) phones. If further evidence is collected based on the information gathered from the cell phone tracking, will it be admissible? If admissible, who could it be admissible against?

With the use of technology at the forefront of daily lives, an investigator will find him or herself drafting search warrants daily for social media accounts, cell phones, and digital storage locations. Search of these areas requires the same Fourth Amendment protections as a home or body.

Effects

The term *effects* can be quite broad. It means the personal effects of a person, which could be any item a person possesses or owns. This is a catch-all category to include anything other than things from the person, houses, or papers. This can include items such as a cellular phone, briefcase, or purses and the like. Law enforcement routinely writes search warrants for these items.

The owner or possessor of a car, like one who owns and possesses a house, almost always has a reasonable expectation of privacy in it. "One of the main rights attaching to property is the right to exclude others," and, in the main, "one who owns or lawfully possesses or controls property will in all likelihood have a legitimate expectation privacy by virtue of the right to exclude." (Blackstone 1765). We can use this same analogy as it relates to a person's cell phone because others can be excluded with password protection.

Another common item that could hold evidence related to a crime is an automobile. An investigator must be careful when contemplating the search of an automobile because it has a unique exception (which will be covered in another chapter) to the search warrant requirement. The question becomes, is a search warrant necessary? To answer this question, an investigator must look at the placement of the automobile at the time of the search. Automobiles travel on public roads and are subjected to regulatory restrictions (licensing and inspection) that homes are not. Therefore, if the automobile is in a public area at the time of the search, then probable cause may be enough for the law enforcement officer to gain access to the vehicle. However, if the vehicle is within the curtilage of a home, the officer must have probable cause and a warrant to search that automobile. For example, in *Collins v. Virginia*, a motorcycle was parked in a section of a partially enclosed driveway when the police searched it. The Court reasoned that the legal ability to view items within the curtilage of one's home is different than entering into the curtilage of one's home for the purpose of a visual inspection. This was an unreasonable search.

Drafting a Search Warrant

Search Warrant Requirements

A valid legal search warrant must contain the following:

- A detailed description of the place to be searched
- A detailed description of the thing to be seized
- Probable cause to believe that the item sought will be in the place searched

A valid legal search warrant must also have the following:

- A sworn application to a neutral and detached judge or magistrate
- Recent information

A Detailed Description of the Place to Be Searched

Every search warrant must contain a detailed description of the place to be searched. The details must be real and specific. The warrant clause of Fourth Amendment categorically prohibits the issuance of any warrant except one particularly describing the place to be searched and the persons or things to be seized. The manifest purpose of this particularity requirement is to prevent general searches. By limiting the authorization to search to the specific areas and things for which there is probable cause to search, the requirement ensures that the search will be carefully tailored to its justifications and will not take on the character of the wide-ranging exploratory searches the Framers intended to prohibit. The scope of a lawful search is defined by the object of the search and the places in which there is probable cause to believe that it may be found. Just as probable cause to believe that a stolen lawn mower may be found in a garage will not support a warrant to search an upstairs bedroom, probable cause to believe that undocumented aliens are being transported in a van will not justify a warrantless search of a suitcase.

In *Maryland v. Garrison*, Baltimore police officers obtained and executed a warrant to search the person of one McWebb and "the premises known as 2036 Park Avenue third floor apartment" for controlled substances and related paraphernalia. The police reasonably believed that there was only one apartment on the described premises, but in fact the third floor was divided into two apartments, one occupied by McWebb and one by the respondent. Before the officers became aware that they were in the respondent's apartment, they discovered the contraband that provided the basis for the respondent's conviction for violating Maryland's Controlled Substances Act. The question became whether the warrant was specific enough in its description of the place to be searched since it did not outline that the third floor contained two separate apartments.

The Fourth Amendment states that "no Warrants shall issue, but upon probable cause, supported by Oath or affirmation, and particularly describing he place to be searched, and the persons or things to be seized." The particularity-of-description requirement is satisfied where "the description is such that the officer with a search warrant can with reasonable effort ascertain and identify the place intended."

Practically, in most incidents, the officer applying for the search warrant has total knowledge of the facts and circumstances surrounding the warrant. The officer may have worked surveillance or personally received the information that is the basis of the application for the warrant. Therefore, the officer making the application for the search warrant knows exactly what is intended to be searched. This is the circumstance that makes it easy to underdescribe the place to be searched. An officer drafting a search warrant must describe the place with specificity as if an officer knowing nothing about the case could execute the warrant with ease. If a warrant is unnecessarily broad, the discovery of facts during the execution of the warrant will not retroactively cure the defect.

In *Maryland v. Garrison*, the Court looked at what the officers knew at the time of the application for the search warrant. "But we must judge the constitutionality of their conduct in light of the information available to them at the time they acted. Those items of evidence that emerge after the warrant is issued have no bearing on whether or not a warrant was validly issued." The *Maryland* Court stated that just as the discovery of contraband cannot validate a warrant invalid when issued, so is it equally clear that the discovery of facts demonstrating that a valid warrant was unnecessarily broad does not retroactively invalidate the warrant. The validity of the warrant must be assessed on the basis of the information that the officers disclosed, or had a duty to discover and to disclose, to the issuing judge or magistrate.

A Detailed Description of the Item to Be Seized

Just as the Fourth Amendment requires the specificity of the place to be searched, the same specificity requirement exists for theaters to be seized. The officers must make great efforts to describe the items that are the subject of the warrant and use as much specificity as possible. In *Marcus v. Search Warrant of Property*, for example, the warrant lacked specificity in the items to be seized, and therefore the warrant was invalid.

In *Marcus v. Search Warrant of Property*, a city police officer appeared in a state trial court and filed a sworn complaint that each of the appellants—a wholesale distributor of magazines, newspapers, and books, and the operators of five retail newsstands—kept "obscene" publications for sale. A judge issued search warrants authorizing police officers to search the appellants' premises and seize all "obscene" material. Different police officers searched the appellants' premises and, after hasty examination, seized all copies of all publications which, in their judgment, were obscene. The US Supreme Court found that the procedures followed in this case lacked the safeguards that due process demands to assure nonobscene material the constitutional protection to which it is entitled. The warrants gave the broadest discretion to the executing officers and left to the individual judgment of each of the many police officers involved the selection of such magazines as in his view constituted "obscene . . . publications." The only officer who had viewed any of the materials was the one officer who purchased obscene materials as the basis for the search warrant application. The court conducted a hearing and found that only one-third of the publications seized were finally condemned, and the remainder of the materials were not contraband. Procedures that sweep so broadly and with so little discrimination are obviously deficient in techniques required by the Due Process Clause of the Fourth Amendment to prevent erosion of the constitutional guarantees.

A law enforcement officer must do the best he or she can to specifically describe the item or place to be searched. Some items may be hard to describe, such as a cell phone that is uncharged and not marked with a brand. Some officers may want to take the phone apart to find a serial number, but this could be interpreted as a search. One way to specifically describe an item is to take a photo of the item and attach it to the search warrant. Remember, a picture is worth a thousand words. It may also be a good idea to place a tag on the item to be searched with a specific identification number and take a photo of the identification number along with the item to include in the search warrant. It's important for the law enforcement officer to draft the search warrant as if a stranger were going to execute the warrant. In most cases, the search warrant is executed by the officer who signed the affidavit; however, the courts will interpret it with no additional knowledge. This is sometimes called the "four corners" of the search warrant, meaning that everything must be contained in the four corners of the search warrant and not supposed or inferred.

The Probable Cause Requirement

The Fourth Amendment gives us the legal standard of proof required for a valid search warrant: probable cause. The probable cause outlined in the search warrant may be based on credible hearsay. Hearsay is information acquired by a third party and not by the person making application for the search warrant. This allows an officer to be the affiant of a search warrant and to use information from another source. For example, an officer may use information he gathered from another officer, witness, or police informant. No matter the course of the hearsay information, its reliability will be judged on the totality of the circumstances. All the allegations in the affidavit, taken together, must permit the magistrate to make a common sense evaluation that there is a fair probability that contraband or evidence of a crime will be found in a particular place.

This is perfectly reasonable because probable cause requires only a probability or substantial chance of criminal activity, not an actual showing of such activity. In making a determination of probable cause, the relevant inquiry is not whether particular conduct is "innocent" or "guilty," but the degree of suspicion that attaches to particular types of noncriminal acts.

In *Illinois v. Gates*, the police received an anonymous tip that a husband and wife were drug dealers. The tipster stated that one spouse would drive to Florida on a particular day and then the other would fly down shortly thereafter to drive back in the car loaded with drugs. The police confirmed this information supplied by the informant and obtained a warrant based on the couple's travel plans. There was nothing in the affidavit to confirm the informant's reliability or prior interaction with the police. Generally, an affidavit should contain a statement validating the informant's reliability or prior credible information. The *Illinois v. Gates* Court ruled that the informant's recitation of detailed facts, though relating to innocent activities, when corroborated by observation by police officers, afforded probable cause to believe that respondents had drugs in their possession, thus confirming the use of the totality of the circumstances test in determining whether legal probable case exists.

Informants certainly could have their own agenda for giving information to the police. Perhaps a relationship between the two went wrong and one is exacting revenge on the other by supplying information to the police that is not true. This is why it is important for the officer to access the credibility of the informer. Generally, a statement that the informant has been credible on several prior occasions is sufficient. Another indication of reliability is when the informant's information tends to cast a bad light on the informer. For example, in *United States v. Harris*, the informer admitted to purchasing illegal whiskey from a bootlegger. The court reasoned that common sense in the important daily affairs of life would induce a prudent and disinterested observer to credit these statements. People do not lightly admit a crime and place critical evidence in the hands of the police in the form of their own admissions. Admissions of crime, like admissions against proprietary interests, carry their own indicia of credibility—sufficient at least to support a finding of probable cause to search. That the informant may be paid or promised a "break" does not eliminate the residual risk and opprobrium of having admitted criminal conduct. Concededly, admissions of crime do not always lend credibility to contemporaneous or later accusations of another. But here the informant's admission that over a long period and currently, he had been buying illicit liquor on certain premises, itself and without more, implicated that property and furnished probable cause to search.

The law enforcement officers' probable cause must be real and specific. It must be specific to the item to be searched for and the place it is to be found. There must be a real connection between the two, and facts to support that the evidence will be there. It is easy to want to throw everything into the search warrant and hope that some evidence is found, but this could invalidate an otherwise good warrant. Compare this example:

- Investigator Lockemup sends a confidential reliable informant to Little Jimmy's house to make a purchase of controlled substances. The informant buys a quantity of controlled substance from Little Jimmy. The entire transaction was captured on a hidden camera that the confidential informant was wearing. Lockemup drafts a search warrant for Little Jimmy's house, any person present at the residence, any vehicle parked at the residence, outbuildings, and curtilage. Upon arrival, there are five other people at Little Jimmy's residence, they all get searched, all their cars get searched, and there is contraband found on all of them. They are all individually arrested. Did the buy of a controlled substance from Little Jimmy provide enough probable cause to search others present? Probably not. There could be exceptions, such as these people being present during the controlled buy, but even so, they would need to have some kind of involvement.

In the example above, what is the probable cause to search the outbuildings on the property? Perhaps it could be argued that the outbuildings are within the curtilage of the residence and therefore can be searched. However, what if this is a two-hundred-acre farm and there are multiple barns and outbuildings? It is a slippery slope to include "all" buildings.

What can be done to remedy this? One way is to keep the search warrant as clean as possible, meaning only list the items and places having clear probable cause. Then, let the facts unfold as the search warrant is executed. For example, if the search warrant in the above example is just for Little Jimmy and his residence, upon arrival, if others are present, Investigator Lockemup has the right to identify people present. If when running identifications, anyone has an outstanding warrant, they will be searched. Lockemup can also ask anyone at the scene for consent to search his or her person or vehicle. Surprisingly, most people consent to searches. Lockemup also may walk by an outbuilding on the property and see or smell something in plain view that gives new probable cause for an additional search warrant for the building. The bottom line is that the search warrant must be very specific and have clear probable cause. If while executing the search warrant, new probable cause if developed, a new search warrant can be drafted. Also, exceptions to the search warrant (which are discussed in following chapters) could apply.

Neutral and Detached Magistrate

A search warrant must be issued by a "neutral and detached" magistrate. A magistrate is a judicial officer who has received some training but is not usually an attorney. A magistrate is not authorized to sign a search warrant if the magistrate has a bias or interest for one party to the search warrant. For example, a prosecutor is not a neutral and detached magistrate. A magistrate cannot be paid for issuing a warrant. A magistrate cannot be related to one of the involved parties. A magistrate cannot participate in the investigation of the case or the execution of the warrant.

Staleness

The probable cause that supports the affidavit for the search warrant must not be **stale**. The information supplying the basis of the search warrant must show that the item sought was recently in the place to be searched. The totality of the circumstances test is still applied, and the courts must analyze the type of item sought under the search warrant. Usually, the probable cause must be close in time to the issuance of the search warrant. For example, if an informant saw narcotics in a residence, usually the affidavit would need to be sworn within a few days of the informant seeing the narcotics. If the item sought is something not readily movable, the affidavit may be able to be a few days longer. There are even incidences where the courts have approved affidavits signed several months after the item was seen in the place to be searched. This is usually in the instances of child pornography. It is well known that individuals who possess, manufacture, and distribute child pornography usually keep their stored images indefinitely.

In *Adams v. State*, Adams argued that there were not sufficient facts to establish probable cause to support the issuance of the warrant because, he says, three months had elapsed between the alleged incident and the issuance of the warrant, and thus the information was too stale to support a finding of probable cause. In this case, the police officer wrote in her affidavit that "when a person 'deletes' a file on a home computer, the data contained in the file does not actually disappear; rather, that data remains on the hard drive until it is overwritten by new data. Therefore, deleted files, or remnants of deleted files, may reside in free space or slack space—that is, in space on the hard drive that is not allocated to an active file or that is unused after a file has been allocated to a set block of storage space—for long periods of time before they are overwritten. In addition, a computer's operating system may also keep a record of a deleted data in a 'sway' or 'recovery' file. Similarly, files that have been viewed via the Internet are automatically downloaded into a temporary Internet directory or 'cache.' The browser typically maintains a fixed amount of hard drive space devoted to these files, and the files are only overwritten as they are replaced with more recently viewed Internet pages. Thus, the ability to retrieve residue of an electronic file from a hard drive depends less on when the file was downloaded or viewed and more on a particular user's operating system, storage capacity, and computer habits." In this case, only three months had elapsed from the date the child pornography was discovered by the internet company to the date that the search warrant was executed. Child pornography images are typically saved and, if erased, are easily recoverable from a computer or electronic device. In fact, most individuals in possession of child pornography "hoard" those images. The information in this case was not stale despite the passage of three months and it furnished sufficient probable cause for the issuance of the search warrant.

An investigator must be careful not to think any warrant for child pornography is not stale, as it certainly can be. All facts must be gathered to defend a "fresh" position. Consider a police department getting notification from a social media internet carrier that images containing depictions of child pornography have been from a specific IP address. The first thing the investigator should do is to check the date of the internet post. If it has been several months, the investigator will need to do some leg work to determine whether the information is stale. If the illegal post was made on May 1, and the police department got notification on July 1, the investigator will need to determine if the same individuals are still living at that indicated residence. This can be done by checking the utility bills and rental agreement (if the residence looks like a rental location), and by taking statements of neighbors. The only problem with taking statements from neighbors is that the suspect could be alerted to the police involvement and destroy the evidence before the search warrant can be obtained.

Execution of Search Warrants

Just as there are rules established for obtaining search warrants, there are rules established for the execution of search warrants.

Timing of Search Warrants

Search warrants must be executed within a reasonable time from the date of issuance. This is different than in the case of arrest warrants, which have no time requirement for service. Usually, the judge or magistrate will enter the number of days the search warrant will be valid on the face of the warrant. If the warrant is not served within that time frame, the officer will need to refresh the probable cause and make another application for the search warrant. For example, Amy makes a report that she was raped by Scott, and a rape kit is collected. Investigator Lockemup may seek a search warrant for a mouth swab from Scott to confirm or exclude his DNA for comparison. If the judge signs the search warrant allowing Lockemup ten days to obtain Scott's DNA, the warrant will not be valid on the eleventh day. Lockemup cannot find Scott within ten days, and the warrant goes stale. In this example, the probable cause will not go stale, because Scott's DNA will always be Scott's DNA. Lockemup will need to prepare a new application for the search warrant (which will include virtually the same facts as the first) and get it resigned.

Investigator Lockemup has a reliable informant who has given him credible information in the past. The informant tells Lockemup that he saw drugs in Jake's house two days ago. Lockemup puts this information in an affidavit and submits this for approval to Judge Jones. Jones signs the search warrant and gives Lockemup ten days to execute the search warrant. The next day, a doctor is killed in Smallville and Lockemup begins working on that case. With the pressures to solve the murder of the doctor, Lockemup forgets about the search warrant for the drugs in Jake's house. On the twelfth day, Lockemup sees the search warrant for Jake's house sitting on his desk and realizes his mistake. What can Lockemup do to search Jake's house? Is his information now too stale to refresh the search warrant?

Who Can Execute a Search Warrant

Only police officers can execute search warrants. Police officers may take along individuals who will assist in the execution of the search warrant. For example, the police may have knowledge that there are children in the home and ask child service workers to accompany them for the execution of the search warrant. Or the police may need the expertise of an individual to assist in the execution of the search warrant—for example, the warrant may be to recover a delicate or fragile object that needs particular handling. In these instances, a non-law enforcement actor may accompany the police. The US Supreme Court in *Wilson v. Layne* stated that it was unreasonable for law enforcement to allow the media to accompany them on a search warrant of a private residence. The media did not serve any particular purpose to assist in the execution of the warrant, thereby infringing on individuals rights protected by the Fourth Amendment.

Knock and Announce

When executing a search warrant, it is necessary for the police to announce their intentions. When executing a search warrant on a residence, the courts have required law enforcement officers to "**knock and announce**." However, the police are excused from this requirement if they can show that knocking and announcing would be dangerous or futile. This is called a "no knock" entry. This can be written in the actual search warrant, wherein sufficient facts are included in the probable cause statement to show that a "no knock" warrant is necessary. For example, Investigator Lockemup is requesting a warrant based on a reliable and credible confidential informant who stated that the residence to be searched housed narcotics. The informant states that all the drug dealers inside the residence carry guns. This information could be enough to allow Lockemup to apply for a "no knock" warrant. A regular warrant could turn into a "no knock" warrant if upon arrival Lockemup sees the homeowner sitting on the front porch run inside and slam the door. Lockemup could reasonably believe that the man is going inside to destroy the drug evidence. This is quite reasonable when it comes to evidence that is readily destroyable. (This would not be the case if the object of the search was a stolen lawn mower.) Lockemup could enter the residence without knocking and announcing and waiting because he would be able to articulate his belief that the homeowner was entering the residence to destroy the evidence and it was necessary for Lockemup to act quickly. The "no knock" entry requires a reasonable suspension of standard of proof, which is the lowest standard of proof in criminal law.

Manner of Execution

The search must conform to the requirements set out in the search warrant. The search cannot be any broader than what was contemplated by the neutral and detached magistrate upon review of the affidavit. If the affidavit alleges that the item subject to the search is a lawn mower, then the police officers executing the search of the residence may not look in the kitchen cabinets for the lawn mower. This is why it is important to draft your search warrant to include a search for the smallest possible object you have probable cause to look for. Perhaps when the lawn mower was stolen, it still had a key in the ignition. This would be a small piece of evidence that could also be the subject of the search. If included in the warrant itself, the law enforcement officers would have the ability to look in the smallest of compartments.

If while executing a search warrant for specific item, an officer runs across another item of known contraband, he or she may seize the new item. For example, if officers are executing a search warrant in a shed for a stolen lawn mower and key, the officers may look in small containers for the lawn mower key. If while looking in a small container, the officer sees cocaine, the officer may seize the cocaine, as it is immediately apparent to be contraband.

When executing a search warrant, officers may detain those persons present at a residence while the officers execute the search warrant. This does not mean that the officers may search these individuals, unless they are named in the search warrant. The individuals can only be searched if the officer has individual probable cause. The officers may pat down these individuals if there is reasonable suspicion that the individual is armed or dangerous. The officer may not simply pat down the individual because he or she is present at a place being searched. The officer also may not search other vehicles present on the property or within the curtilage, if those vehicles belong to other parties not named in the search warrant.

Anticipatory Search Warrants

An **anticipatory search warrant** is a warrant based upon an affidavit showing probable cause that at some future time (but not presently) certain evidence of crime will be located at a specified place. Most anticipatory search warrants subject their execution to some condition precedent other than the mere passage of time—a so-called triggering condition. For instance, execution of a search warrant would not occur unless and until specific contraband had been received by a person(s) and had been physically taken into the residence. If the government were to execute an anticipatory warrant before the triggering condition occurred, there would be no reason to believe the item described in the warrant could be found at the searched location; by definition, the triggering condition that establishes probable cause has not yet been satisfied when the warrant is issued.

Probable cause exists when there is a fair probability that contraband or evidence of a crime will be found in a particular place. Anticipatory search warrants are no different in principle from ordinary search warrants. They require the magistrate to determine that (a) it is now probable that (b) contraband, evidence of a crime, or a fugitive will be on the described premises when (c) the search warrant is executed. It should be noted, however, that where the anticipatory search warrant places a condition (other than the mere passage of time) upon its execution, the first of these determinations goes not merely to what will probably be found if the condition is met. (If that were the extent of the probability determination, an anticipatory search warrant could be issued for every house in the country, authorizing search and seizure if contraband should be delivered, though for any single location there is no likelihood that contraband will be delivered.) Rather, the probability determination for a conditioned anticipatory search warrant looks also to the likelihood that the condition will occur, and thus that a proper object of seizure will be on the described premises.

In *United States v. Grubbs*, the defendant purchased a videotape containing child pornography from a website operated by an undercover postal inspector. Postal inspection officers arranged a controlled delivery of a package containing the videotape to the defendant's residence. A postal inspector submitted an application for a search warrant to a magistrate judge, accompanied by an affidavit describing the proposed operation in detail. The magistrate judge issued the search warrant on the basis of an affidavit explaining that the search warrant would be executed only after the controlled delivery, but that triggering condition was not listed in the warrant. The Court held that anticipatory search warrants were lawful and that the occurrence of the triggering condition plainly established probable cause for the search. In addition, the affidavit established probable cause to believe the triggering condition would be satisfied since although it was possible that the defendant could have refused delivery of the videotape he had ordered, that was unlikely.

Below is a sample application for search warrant:

State of Timbuktu Unified Judicial System	APPLICATION FOR SEARCH WARRANT	Case or Warrant Number

IN THE COURT OF Smallville, Timbuktu

[X] STATE OF TIMBUKTU

V. INVESTIGATION, Defendant

I, the undersigned, hereby make application for the issuance of a Search Warrant as I have probable cause to believe and do believe that the following personal property, to wit: (***Fully describe Property***): A mechanical device intended for the purpose of producing an explosion capable of causing injury to persons or damage to property or containing oxidizing and combustible units or other ingredients in proportions or quantities that ignition, fire, friction, concussion, percussion, or detonator may produce an explosion capable of causing injury to persons or damage to property relevant to the Pending Felony Investigation

is located or concealed in or upon (***Fully Describe Person, Place, Premises, and/or Vehicle to be searched***) and **that said property** (***Check appropriate grounds***): A residence located at 522 Russell Road, Smallville, County, State of Timbuktu. The residence being further described as a red brick home with tan trim. This is to include the residence, its curtilage, and any outbuildings that are located at 522 Russell Road, Smallville, County, State of Timbuktu (photo attached). The directions to 522 Russell Road, Smallville, County, State of Timbuktu, are starting at the intersection of Granttown Road and Cole Road, travel 0.1 miles and turn right onto Russell Road, travel 0.5 miles, and 522 Russell Road, Smallville, County, State of Timbuktu, will be on the right-hand side of the road (photo attached);

and that said property

_____ was, or is expected to be, unlawfully obtained;

_______ was, or is expected to be, used as a means of committing or attempting to commit an offense contrary to the laws of the State of Timbuktu or political subdivision thereof, to wit: in violation of Section of the Code of Timbuktu.

_____is, or is expected to be, in the possession of another with intent to use it as a means of committing a criminal offense, or is in the possession of another to whom it was delivered for the purpose of concealing it or preventing its discovery.

__X__ constitutes, or is expected to constitute, evidence of a criminal offense under the laws or the State of Timbuktu or a political subdivision thereof; to wit: Pending Felony Investigation.

Applicant states that his (her) request is based upon the facts stated in the affidavit(s) attached hereto.

Dated: __________________ Applicant: _________________________________

Figure 4.1 Photo taken by Christina Kilgore

Below is a sample affidavit in support of the application for search warrant:

State of Timbuktu Unified Judicial System	AFFIDAVIT IN SUPPORT OF APPLICATION FOR SEARCH WARRANT	Case or Warrant Number

IN THE COURT OF Talladega County TIMBUKTU

(Circuit, District or Municipal)

[X] STATE OF Timbuktu

V. INVESTIGATION, Defendant

Application for a Search Warrant having been made or to be made to the Court, I, the undersigned, after being duly sworn to tell the truth and in support of said application, hereby depose and say as follows:

My name is Will Lockemup. I am an Investigator with Smallville Police Department. I have been employed in law enforcement since 2002. I graduated from the Northeast Smallville Law Enforcement Academy in 2009. I have been assigned to general investigations since 2015. I have attended numerous classes on the investigation of property crimes and crimes against persons, including homicide investigations and sex crimes investigations. I have been assigned to numerous investigations involving violent crimes. My investigations have kept me in close contact with other investigators investigating various property crimes and crimes against persons.

On May 24, 2022, at approximately 10:00 p.m., law enforcement received information from a concerned citizen that Max Blowhard made comments about re-creating a mass shooting event. Law enforcement determined that Max Blowhard lived in Smallville County, Timbuktu. On May 25, 2022, law enforcement located Max Blowhard at 522 Russell Road, Smallville County, Timbuktu. Max Blowhard stated that he lived at the residence and denied making any comments about re-creating a mass shooting. Max Blowhard stated that he was fascinated by the Columbia High School shooting and identified with one of the shooters. Max Blowhard also stated that he had never had a desire to harm anyone other than himself. Max Blowhard denied consent to search his bedroom at the residence. Max Blowhard agreed to be transported to Smallville ER for a mental health evaluation after stating that he has been committed to Smallville Hospital in the past for mental health treatment.

On May 30, 2022, law enforcement was contacted by Smallville Hospital and informed that Max Blowhard may have a pipe bomb or other explosive device in his bedroom. Law enforcement requested Max Blowhard's medical records from Smallville ER regarding his medical treatment on May 25, 2022. Law enforcement received the medical records on June 1, 2022. A review of the medical records showed a note from Savannah Stern, RN, that Max Blowhard stated that he thought he had a pipe bomb in his bedroom. Max Blowhard continued to state, "You can put staples, BBs, anything sharp in there and when they go off that stuff hits anyone around." Law enforcement contacted Savannah Stern, RN, at Citizens ER on June 1, 2022. Savannah Stern confirmed that she heard Max Blowhard make the statement while in the emergency room and that she entered the statements into his medical records. Savannah Stern also stated that Max Blowhard was talking about his cat and that he was worried about his cat getting into his bedroom immediately prior to making the statements about having a pipe bomb in his bedroom.

Law enforcement secured the residence at 522 Russell Road, Smallville County, Timbuktu, prior to obtaining a search warrant. While securing the residence, Max Blowhard's father stated that Max Blowhard does stay at the residence but does not have a specific room inside the residence and that Max Blowhard stated that he had recently built his first pipe bomb.

Based on the foregoing, as well as my knowledge, training, and experience, I have probable cause to believe and do believe that mechanical devices intended for the purpose of producing an explosion capable of causing injury to persons or damage to property or containing oxidizing and combustible units or other ingredients in proportions or quantities that ignition, fire, friction, concussion, percussion, or detonator may produce an explosion capable of causing injury to persons or damage to property relevant to the pending felony investigation is presently located at 522 Russell Road, Smallville County, Timbuktu (photo attached). Therefore, I respectfully request a search warrant for the residence, curtilage, and any outbuildings that are located at 522 Russell Road, Smallville County, Timbuktu.

____________________________________, Affiant

Sworn to and subscribed before me on this, the

________day of __________________, 20 ______.

____

Judge/Magistrate

Below is a sample search warrant:

State of Timbuktu Unified Judicial System	SEARCH WARRANT	Case or Warrant Number

IN THE COURT OF Smallville **Timbuktu**

(Circuit, District or Municipal)

[X] **STATE OF TIMBUKTU**

V. INVESTIGATION, **Defendant**

TO ANY LAW ENFORCEMENT OFFICER AUTHORIZED TO EXECUTE THIS WARRANT:

Proof having been made before me on this day by Investigator Will Lockemup, that he (she) has probable cause to believe and does believe that (*Description of Property to be Searched For*): A mechanical device intended for the purpose of producing an explosion capable of causing injury to persons or damage to property or containing oxidizing and combustible units or other ingredients in proportions or quantities that ignition, fire, friction, concussion, percussion, or detonator may produce an explosion capable of causing injury to persons or damage to property relevant to the Pending Felony Investigation

is presently located or concealed in or upon (*Description of the Person, Place Premises and/or Vehicle to be searched*): A residence located at 522 Russell Road, Smallville, County, State of Timbuktu. The residence being further described as a red brick home with tan trim, (photo attached). This is to include the residence, its curtilage, and any outbuildings that are located at 522 Russell Road, Smallville, County, State of Timbuktu. The directions to 522 Russell Road, Smallville County, Timbuktu, are starting at the intersection of Granttown Road and Cole Road, travel 0.1 miles and turn right onto Russell Road, travel 0.5 miles and 522 Russell Road, Smallville, County, State of Timbuktu, will be on the right-hand side of the road;

and that said property (*Check Applicable Ground(s)*):

____was, or is expected to be, unlawfully obtained;

____was, or is expected to be, used as the means of committing or attempting to commit a criminal offense contrary to the laws of the State of Timbuktu or political subdivision thereof;

____ is, or is expected to be, in the possession of another with intent to use it as a means of committing a criminal offense, or is in the possession of another to whom it was delivered for the purpose of concealing it or preventing its discovery.

_X__ constitutes, or is expected to constitute, evidence of a criminal offense under the laws of the State of Timbuktu or a political subdivision thereof, to wit: Pending Felony Investigation.

NOW, THEREFORE, by virtue of the authority given to me by Rule 3, Timbuktu Rules of Criminal Procedure, incorporating all of the above mentioned information contained in Will Lockemup'saffidavit, you are hereby commanded to make a search of the above described person or premises □ IN THE DAYTIME □ AT ANYTIME OF THE DAY OR NIGHT and within ______ days (*not to exceed 10 days*) in Smallville County, Timbuktu, for the above-described personal property and to make due return of this

warrant, along with an inventory of any property seized, to the undersigned as required by Rule 3, ARCrP.

ISSUED to ____ at _____________o'clock _____M.

on this the ________ day of _________________________, 20_______.

____, Judge/Magistrate

The style of the search warrant can vary, but the content cannot. This same search warrant can be used for any item: DNA swab, blood draw, vehicle, home, boat, internet cloud account, cell phone, etcetera.

Analysis of the Fourth Amendment

Every analysis of a Fourth Amendment issue begins with four questions. These questions are the foundational requirements for an analysis of whether a search warrant is necessary.

1. Was This a Search or Seizure by the Government?

The Fourth Amendment only applies to actions taken by the government. This can be any level of government—local, state, or federal. The Fourth Amendment does not, however, apply to any action taken by a private citizen or a nongovernment entity. This seems like a fairly black-and-white rule, but it still can become blurred if an individual or private entity is directed by a governmental agent. For example, Investigator Lockemup suspects Dennis Driver of being involved in the murder of Victor Victim and wants to search Dennis's apartment for evidence related to the murder. Lockemup goes to the apartment complex where Dennis lives and speaks with the manager. Lockemup convinces the manager that crucial evidence to the murder investigation could be found in Dennis's apartment. The manager uses his master key and unlocks Dennis's apartment and allows Lockemup to search. If Lockemup finds evidence that is relevant to the murder, it will not be admissible in court because it was found in violation of the Fourth Amendment.

Investigator Lockemup suspects Victor Victim's wife, Trina, as being involved in the murder of Victor Victim. He thinks that she may have some bank records at her office. Lockemup travels to her office and knocks on the door. Lockemup is met by a woman who appears to be hired to clean the office space. He tells the woman that he needs to look around the office for possible evidence related to the murder of Victor Victim. She tells him that she needs to call Trina to get approval. She tries Trina's cell phone, but gets no answer, so she lets Lockemup in to search the office.

Is this a violation of the Fourth Amendment?

Yes, it is. Lockemup needs a warrant to search a private space, such as an office, and he does not have one. He knows that the cleaning lady does not have the authority to allow him consent because she tells him that she has to call Trina for approval. Therefore, the cleaning lady is acting as an agent of the government and the search is not good.

Suppose Lockemup tells the cleaning lady that he is looking for bank statements and asks the her to retrieve the bank statements from inside the office. Lockemup stays outside while the cleaning lady searches for the bank records. She eventually finds them and turns them over to Lockemup.

Is this a violation of the Fourth Amendment?

Yes, it is. In this scenario, Lockemup is using the cleaning lady as an agent of the police. He is asking her to do what he needs a warrant to do. Just because she agrees to help does not make it constitutional.

2. Did the Defendant Have a Reasonable Expectation of Privacy in the Area Searched?

The second question that must be asked in determining whether the search is constitutional is whether the defendant had a reasonable expectation of privacy in the area searched. Public areas are not subject to the Fourth Amendment's protections. The Fourth Amendment protects an individual's privacy. The courts have consistently applied a totality of the circumstances approach to determining whether privacy interests exist.

A defendant's mere presence during a search does not give him or her a privacy interest in the area being searched.

Defendants can give up privacy interests in areas or in items by abandonment or leaving them in plain view to the public.

In *Rakas v. Illinois*, the passengers in an automobile claimed that they had an expectation of privacy in an automobile that they did not own or claim an interest in. The automobile was searched by the police and a rifle and shells were found that was linked to a robbery. The passengers did not claim ownership of the rifle or shells. The question was whether an individual's rights could be violated where the individual had no legitimate expectation of privacy or property interest. Fourth Amendment rights are personal rights that, like some other constitutional rights, may not be vicariously asserted. A person who is aggrieved by an illegal search and seizure only through the introduction of damaging evidence secured by a search of a third person's premises or property has not had any of his Fourth Amendment rights infringed. Since the exclusionary rule is an attempt to effectuate the guarantees of the Fourth Amendment, it is proper to permit only defendants whose Fourth Amendment rights have been violated to benefit from the rule's protections.

Standing

Only a person with a reasonable expectation of privacy may challenge a search. This concept is called "**standing**." The issue of standing involves two inquiries: first, whether the proponent of a particular legal right has alleged injury in fact, and second, whether the proponent is asserting his own legal rights and interests rather than basing his claim for relief upon the rights of third parties. To have standing to challenge a search under the Fourth Amendment, a person must have a reasonable expectation of privacy in the area or thing searched. The same totality of the circumstances test applies as discussed above.

In general, a person does not have a reasonable expectation of privacy in objects held out to the public. Some examples of these items can include smells emitted from an object, the sound of one's voice, a person's handwriting, bank records, and the movement of one's vehicle on a public road.

The next question regarding expectation of privacy is when the setting is more private, such as a guest inside another's home. An overnight guest will have the same expectation of privacy as the homeowner, but a day guest may not. The courts have also analyzed whether there is a difference in an expectation of privacy for a guest in a home for commercial purposes. For example, in *Minnesota v. Carter*, a police officer looked through a window blind in a lessee's apartment based on an informant's tip. The officer observed Carter bagging cocaine in the apartment. Based on that observation, a warrant was issued, and respondents were arrested and charged with conspiracy to commit a controlled substance crime. The court held that an overnight guest in a home could claim the protection of the Fourth Amendment, but one who was merely present with the consent of the householder could not. In addition, property used for commercial purposes was treated differently for Fourth Amendment purposes than residential property.

Investigator Lockemup is working a murder investigation where Victor Victim was murdered in his home in Smallville. Lockemup interviews Dennis Driver and Dennis Driver admits that he drove Melvin and Andy to Victor's home just before Victor was killed. Lockemup searches Dennis's car and finds a piece of paper with Victor's home address written on it and collects it. The paper with the address is also a child support document containing identification information of Melvin. Melvin's attorney objects to the paper being submitted into evidence in the case against Melvin because Lockemup did not get a search warrant or consent to search Dennis's car. Will Melvin be successful in objecting to evidence found in Dennis's car?

3. Was There a Search Warrant?

Always, always, always consider obtaining a search warrant for the item to be searched or seized. If probable cause exists and search warrant requirements can be met, there is no reason to forgo the warrant requirement. In years past, the logistics (getting a computer, supervisor approval, or a judge to sign) of obtaining a warrant encouraged law enforcement to find a way around them. However, since technology is making warrants easier to obtain, there is no excuse not to obtain one.

4. Did an Exception to the Search Warrant Requirement Exist?

While all searches without a warrant are presumed unreasonable, the US Supreme Court has carved out certain exceptions to the search warrant requirement. Each exception has its own set of rules that must be satisfied for the search or seizure to be constitutional. Each of these exceptions will be explored in the following chapter. If there is no search warrant or the search warrant is invalid and there is no exception that applies, the search or seizure is unlawful.

The Exclusionary Rule

The **exclusionary rule** was established to prevent evidence seized in violation of the Fourth Amendment from being introduced in evidence in a trial against a citizen. The exclusionary rule, like Miranda, is not a constitutionally created rule. It is a judicially created remedy designed to safeguard an individual's Fourth Amendment rights and deter police conduct outside of the Fourth Amendment parameters.

In **Mapp v. Ohio**, the US Supreme Court made the exclusionary rule applicable to all states. In this landmark case, Ms. Mapp was involved in an illegal gambling and pornography operation. The police officers went to her residence announcing that they had a search warrant for her residence. Ms. Mapp demanded to view the search warrant and was handed a piece of paper. At that time, Ms. Mapp stuffed the piece of paper down her shirt and a struggle ensued to retrieve the piece of paper. Ms. Mapp's residence was searched, and several items of contraband were found and seized. At the trial against Ms. Mapp, the search warrant was not produced and there was no valid exception to the search warrant requirement. Therefore, all of the evidence against Ms. Mapp was surpassed and disallowed into evidence against her.

The purpose of the exclusionary rule is to deter bad police conduct. If the police act outside of the scope of the Fourth Amendment, then the evidence collected as a result of their bad act will not be allowable in court. This often will mean that a case must be dismissed all together. It is important to understand this purpose because the exceptions will make more sense.

The Fruit of the Poisonous Tree Doctrine

The exclusionary rule applies not only to illegally seized evidence, but also to evidence obtained as a result of the illegal seizure. If a piece of seized evidence is excluded because of a Fourth Amendment violation, then one must examine whether any other evidence seized after the first illegally seized evidence is also due to be suppressed. For example, Investigator Lockemup improperly seizes GPS information to determine locations of cell phones. Then he travels to the location of the cell phones and ultimately discovers narcotics. The narcotics could be considered the "**fruit of the poisonous tree**." The question is whether the evidence has been acquired as a result of the illegal search or obtained "instead by means sufficiently distinguishable to be purged of the primary taint."

Exceptions to the Exclusionary Rule

1. Independent Source: Evidence police are able to obtain from an independent source not connected to the illegal search or seizure. For example, Karen is robbed walking home from work and got a good look at her assailant. With this good description, the police suspect Michael as her assailant. They find Michael and arrest him for old traffic tickets. During the booking process, they photograph Michael and then show the photograph to Karen. She identifies Michael as the robber. The identification will not likely be suppressed under the exclusionary rule, because Karen would have been able to identify Michael at the trial independently of the photograph that was taken.
2. Inevitable Discovery: Evidence that would have been discovered despite bad police conduct will be admissible under the **inevitable discovery** rule. For example, the police pull over Jake for a DUI. Jake fails the field sobriety tests administered roadside and can hardly stand unsupported. Jake is arrested, his car is searched, and cocaine is found. Since the police did not have probable cause to search Jake's car, they would have violated his Fourth Amendment rights during the search. In this situation, an argument could be made for inevitable discovery because the police department's policy dictates that when an individual is arrested for DUI, the car must be impounded. Every car is searched upon impound and the cocaine would have been inevitably discovered.

3. Good faith: The US Supreme Court has held that when police officers act on an objectively reasonable belief that their conduct is not violating the suspect's rights, the evidence can be admitted under a **good faith** exception. It is important to always contemplate the purpose of the exclusionary rule—to deter bad police conduct—to determine whether the good faith exception may apply. If the application of the exclusionary rule would not deter bad police conduct in a certain situation, then the evidence need not be suppressed under the rule. For example, Investigator Lockemup is investigating a case in which many luxury vehicles were stolen. He obtains probable cause to believe that the vehicles are being stored in a warehouse and prepares a search warrant for the warehouse. He gets Mary Magistrate to sign the search warrant and indeed finds the stolen vehicles. Unbeknownst to Lockemup, Mary's husband was the owner of one of the stolen vehicles. The search warrant requires a signature form a neutral and detached magistrate, which Mary is not. Mary had a strong personal interest in the recovery of the stolen vehicles. If the search is not valid, the evidence will be excluded. However, would excluding the evidence deter Lockemup from behaving in the same manner in the future? No. If suppression of the evidence will not deter bad police conduct, then the purpose of the exclusionary rule is not fulfilled. Therefore, the good faith exception would apply.

Rules to Remember

Below is a list of rules to remember from this chapter:

- The Fourth Amendment to the US Constitution protects against unreasonable search and secure.
- The courts apply a totality of the circumstances test in determining whether an individual has reasonable expectation of privacy.
- Searches conducted with a warrant are presumed unreasonable. It is the government's burden to show that the search is not unreasonable.
- Limitations on privacy interest can include items held out for the public to view, such as curtilage of a home or trash set out for pick up.
- A search warrant must contain a specific description of the place to be searched, a specific description of the thing to be found, and probable cause to believe that the thing will be found in the place searched, and be issued by a neutral and detached judge or magistrate.
- If a Fourth Amendment violation occurs, the remedy is to exclude the evidence from admission in court.
- The purpose of the exclusionary rule is to deter bad police conduct.
- Exceptions to the exclusionary rule include independent source, inevitable discovery, and good faith.
- For an individual to object to a search, he or she must have standing to object to the place searched.

End of Chapter Comprehension and Application

Directions: Use what you have learned in this chapter to help you respond completely and correctly to each question or prompt below.

1. Define person, house, paper, and effect as used under the Fourth Amendment.
2. Under what circumstances does the Fourth Amendment apply?
3. Explain reasonable expectation of privacy. When does a person not have a reasonable expectation of privacy? Cite relevant cases in your explanation.
4. Is there a reasonable expectation of privacy in a cloud storage facility? What is the rationale behind the rule?
5. What is the exclusionary rule and what is its purpose?
6. What are three exceptions to the exclusionary rule?
7. If a police officer stood on public property and listened into a private home with a high-tech listening device, would that be a violation of the homeowner's Fourth Amendment rights? Why or why not?
8. What is a seizure and when does to occur? Give an example of a seizure of a person.
9. When can private persons be considered government agents for purposes of the Fourth Amendment? Give a factual example.
10. What are the Fourth Amendment implications for the use of drones by police for surveillance?
11. Explain the open field doctrine.
12. What are the steps in obtaining a search warrant?
13. What is an anticipatory search warrant, and in what circumstances would an officer want to request one from a judge or magistrate?
14. What does it mean to have standing to object to a search? Give an example of when someone would not have standing to object to a search.
15. Under what circumstances are police authorized to conduct no-knock searches?
16. Investigator Lockemup is called in to investigate a shooting. He is told that Jerry was at his home sitting on the porch when a black car with tinted windows drove by and opened fire toward Jerry. Jerry was shot multiple times and is in critical condition at the hospital. Jerry has a camera on his porch pointed in the direction of the street. Lockemup wants to obtain the camera and possible footage of the shooting. What are things he should consider relevant to the Fourth Amendment in obtaining this evidence?
17. Investigator Lockemup is called by child services. Lockemup is told about a ten-year-old boy who has disclosed his mother's boyfriend has been touching him inappropriately. The boy disclosed that it started about six months ago when his mother's boyfriend showed him videos of young boys doing bad things with adult men. The boy isn't sure if his mother's boyfriend ever took a video of him, but he remembers one time when his mother's boyfriend aimed his cell phone with the flashlight on toward the boy. The mother's boyfriend has just been picked up on an old

warrant and is in jail awaiting a hearing on that case. When the mother's boyfriend was booked into the jail on the warrant, he had a cell phone on his person; it is currently in the property room at the jail. Can Lockemup search the cell phone? What are the Fourth Amendment considerations?

18. Investigator Big City calls Investigator Lockemup for assistance on a search warrant needed in Smallville. Big City tells Lockemup that he has been tracking a counterfeiting ring, and the ring has an address in Smallville. Big City wants to obtain a search warrant for the address. Big City has a witness who was in the residence at the address in Smallville three months ago and saw several computers, printers, and blank checks inside the residence. The witness has provided reliable information to Big City in the past. Big City asks Lockemup to assist in obtaining a search warrant from a local judge in Smallville. What should Lockemup do? Explain your answer fully.
19. Investigator Lockemup is called to the scene of a murder. The victim was the wife of the accused. The neighbor tells Lockemup that he heard the couple arguing; he then heard a single gunshot and saw the husband flee the scene by vehicle. The neighbor called 911 and Deputy Dawson arrived on scene just minutes later. Dawson went inside the couple's residence and found a gun hidden inside the refrigerator. Dawson gave the weapon to Lockemup. Using the information above, Lockemup obtained a search warrant for the residence for any firearms, ammunition, and projectiles. Do you see any problems with the search warrant? What, if any?
20. Laura Landlord goes to her tenant's house to collect late rent due. When Laura arrives, she finds no one home. She decides to use her key to look around inside the house. When she enters the residence, she sees what she believes is a methamphetamine lab. She immediately leaves and calls the police. The police arrive to find the front door open (because Laura left in such a hurry) and see a methamphetamine lab in plain view from the porch. The police obtain a search warrant for the residence based on their plain view of the methamphetamine lab. Is the probable cause of the search warrant good? Why or why not?

References

Blackstone, Sir William. *Commentaries on the Laws of England*, Oxford: Clarendon Press, 1765-1769.
Fourth Amendment to the US Constitution, https://constitution.congress.gov/constitution/amendment-4/.
Merriam Webster, s.v. "search (v.)," accessed June 21, 2023, https://www.merriam-webster.com/dictionary/search.
Kyllo v. United States, 533 U.S. 27 (2001), https://supreme.justia.com/cases/federal/us/533/27/.
Sims v. Labowitz, 885 F.3d 254, 261 (4th Cir. 2018), https://casetext.com/case/sims-v-labowitz-4.
Payton v. New York, 445 U.S. 573, 585, 100 S. Ct. 1371, 63 L. Ed. 2d 639 (1980), https://casetext.com/case/payton-v-new-york-riddick-v-new-york
County of Sacramento v. Lewis, 523 U.S. 833 (1998), https://supreme.justia.com/cases/federal/us/523/833/.
Torres v. Madrid, 141 S.Ct. 898, 991 (2021), https://www.lexisnexis.com/community/casebrief/p/casebrief-torres-v-madrid-430755109.
United States v. Mendenhall, 446 U.S. 544 (1980), https://supreme.justia.com/cases/federal/us/446/544/.
United States, 446 U.S. 544.
Warden v. Hayden, 387 U.S. 294 (1967), https://supreme.justia.com/cases/federal/us/387/294/.
United States v. Mara, 410 U.S. 19 (1973), https://supreme.justia.com/cases/federal/us/410/19/.
Carlton v. Pytell, 1993 U.S. App Lexis 3510.
Kyllo, 533 U.S. 27.
United States v. Oliver, 466 U.S. 170 (1984), https://supreme.justia.com/cases/federal/us/466/170/.
California v. Greenwood, 486, U.S. 35 (1988), https://supreme.justia.com/cases/federal/us/486/35/.

United States v. Dunn, 480 U.S. 294 (1987), https://supreme.justia.com/cases/federal/us/480/294/.
California v. Ciraolo, 476 U.S. 207 (1986), https://supreme.justia.com/cases/federal/us/476/207/.
Florida v. Riley, 488 U.S. 445 (1989), https://supreme.justia.com/cases/federal/us/488/445/.
United States v. Bledsoe, 2022 U.S. Dist., https://law.justia.com/cases/federal/appellate-courts/ca3/22-2022/22-2022-2022-08-18.html.
Carpenter v. United States, 138 S. Ct. at 2221, https://www.lexisnexis.com/community/casebrief/p/casebrief-carpenter-v-united-states.
Collins v. Virginia, 138 S. Ct. 1663 (2018), https://casetext.com/case/collins-v-virginia-1.
United States v. Ross 456 US 798, 824 (1982), https://supreme.justia.com/cases/federal/us/456/798/.
Maryland v. Garrison, 480 U.S. 79 (1987), https://supreme.justia.com/cases/federal/us/480/79/.
Steele v. United States, 267 U.S. 498, 503 (1925), https://supreme.justia.com/cases/federal/us/267/498/.
Maryland v. Garrison, 480 U.S. 79 (1987), https://supreme.justia.com/cases/federal/us/480/79/.
Marcus v. Search Warrant of Property, 367 U.S. 717 (1961), https://supreme.justia.com/cases/federal/us/367/717/.
Illinois v. Gates, 462 U.S. 213 (1983), https://supreme.justia.com/cases/federal/us/462/213/. Illinois, 462 U.S. 213.
United States v. Harris, 403 US 573 (1971), https://supreme.justia.com/cases/federal/us/403/573/.
Adams v. State, 316 So3d 260 (2020), https://casetext.com/case/adams-v-state-2148.
Wilson v. Layne, 526 U.S. 603 (1999), https://supreme.justia.com/cases/federal/us/526/603/.
United States v. Grubbs, 547 U.S. 90 (2006), https://supreme.justia.com/cases/federal/us/547/90/. United States, 547 U.S. 90.
Rakas v. Illinois, 439 U.S. 128 (1978), https://supreme.justia.com/cases/federal/us/439/128/.
Minnesota v. Carter, 525 U.S. 83 (1999), https://supreme.justia.com/cases/federal/us/525/83/.
Mapp v. Ohio, 367 U.S. 643 (1961), https://supreme.justia.com/cases/federal/us/367/643/.
Wong Sun v. United States 371 U.S. 471 (1963), https://supreme.justia.com/cases/federal/us/371/471/.

Chapter 5

Evidence Collection—Exceptions to the Search Warrant Requirement

Introduction: Obtaining Evidence That Will Be Admissible in Court without a Warrant

In this chapter students will explore the exceptions to the Fourth Amendment's warrant requirement for arrest, search, and seizure.

Chapter Objectives

In this chapter students will learn:

- The proper procedure for conducting a warrantless arrest
- The proper procedure for conducting a warrantless search
- How a Terry patdown is different from other types of searches
- The eight common exceptions to the search warrant requirement
- How to properly collect evidence using an exception to the search warrant requirement

Key Terms

Key terms and professional terminology that are used in this chapter include:

- **The Fourth Amendment to the US Constitution**
- **Warrantless arrest**
- **Terry patdown (also known as Terry frisk, Terry search, or patdown)**
- **Reasonable suspicion**

- **Warrantless search**
- **Consent search**
- **Voluntariness**
- **Plain view**
- **Plain smell**
- **Vehicle exception to the search warrant requirement**
- **Exigency**
- **Emergency**
- **Hot pursuit**
- **Regulatory searches**
- **Inventory searches**
- **Search incident to arrest**

Warrantless Arrests

In the previous chapter, we learned that the **Fourth Amendment to the US Constitution** mentions the requirements for a warrant. In this chapter we will learn that the Fourth Amendment does not require a warrant in all circumstances. “No warrant shall issue, but upon probable cause, supported by Oath or affirmation and particularly describing the place to be searched and the persons to be seized.” The US Supreme Court has interpreted the circumstances in which a warrant is required for arrest, search, or seizure.

An arrest warrant will rarely be required to make an arrest unless the arrest is to take place within a private home. If there are exigent circumstances, an officer may enter a private home in order to effectuate an arrest. These circumstances are typically when an officer is in hot pursuit of a suspect and the suspect flees into a private residence. It makes sense that the officer would not then be stopped at the threshold, unable to enter in pursuit. Another circumstance where a **warrantless arrest** is proper is when there is a possibility that evidence will be destroyed.

These exceptions do not apply to arrests for minor crimes. However, there is an exception to this exception when a minor crime takes place within the viewing of the officer. In other words, if an officer sees the crime, he or she may make a warrantless arrest no matter the seriousness of the crime.

The same standard applies for both arrests with a warrant and arrests without a warrant: probable cause. There must be probable cause that the crime was committed and that the person arrested was the person who committed it.

Many states impose a statutory requirement for warrantless arrests such as authorization for minor arrests occurring in the officer’s presence. For example, an officer may arrest for a misdemeanor drug possession that he sees, if his state gives him jurisdiction to make warrantless arrests on misdemeanor offenses.

Warrantless Searches

The general rule is that a search warrant is required, unless one of the exceptions is fulfilled. Remember from the previous chapter that the Fourth Amendment states that "the right of the people to be secure in their persons, houses, papers, and effects, against unreasonable searches and seizures, shall not be violated, and no Warrants shall issue, but upon probable cause, supported by Oath or affirmation, and particularly describing the place to be searched, and the persons or things to be seized."

The exceptions to the search warrant requirement have been created by the US Supreme Court and its interpretation of the Fourth Amendment. The exceptions are as follows:

1. Terry patdown
2. Consent
3. Plain view/plain smell
4. Vehicle exception
5. Emergency/exigency
6. Regulatory
7. Inventory
8. Search incident to arrest

Terry Patdown

The **Terry patdown** is one of the most commonly used exceptions to the search warrant requirement of the Fourth Amendment. It is known in law enforcement communities as a "Terry frisk," a "Terry patdown," or simply a "patdown." The Terry patdown is called "Terry" because of the name of the case that created this exception. In *Terry v. Ohio*, an experienced police officer saw Terry and his companion walking back and forth near businesses that were closed for the evening. The officer thought that they were "casing the place." The officer stopped Terry and his companion and patted Terry down. The officer felt a gun on Terry. Terry was convicted of carrying a concealed weapon and appealed the issue of whether the officer had reasonable suspicion to stop and frisk. In this landmark case, the US Supreme Court carved out an exception to the probable cause requirement, they calling it "**reasonable suspicion**." The Terry Court held that an officer could stop and "frisk" or "patdown" if the officer observed conduct that would lead a reasonable person to conclude that criminal activity was afoot. The officer may then identify him or herself as a police officer and ask questions to gather further information to substantiate or dispel his suspicions.

The Terry Court gave parameters for this type of "reasonable suspicion" search. The search must only be of the outer layer of clothing of a person to check for weapons. The Terry Court did not constitute this as a seizure that would carry the usual Fourth Amendment protections. This type of investigatory stop must be brief and no longer than necessary to accomplish its purpose.

There are parameters to the officer's reasonable suspicion search. The identity of the object must be "immediately apparent" to the officer. In **Ex parte Gardner**, Gardner was charged with possession of methamphetamine. The officer who testified at the suppression hearing was not the officer who patted Gardner down. The officer testified: "Once she got out of the car, you could tell that she had some kind of a nervous look on her face as to why we were there. Once she approached us asking why we were there, we asked her to put her hands, I believe it was, on the car and at which time she kind of got nervous and didn't want to put her hands on the car for the pat-down search. And then once we did pat her down, like I said, we felt a bulge in her left pocket that was consistent—once we grabbed hold of it, was crunchy, which is consistent with methamphetamine. It's kind of like salt. You know when you grab hold of it. And that's when we went into the pockets." This witness testified that he did not believe that the bulge was a weapon and that he, based on his training and experience, he would not confuse 0.2 grams of methamphetamine with a weapon. The defense argues that the officer's manipulation of the bag (squeeze) pushed the Terry patdown outside of the bounds of *Terry v. Ohio*. The Court agreed and stated that under the plain-touch doctrine, if a police officer lawfully pats down a suspect's outer clothing and feels an object whose contour or mass makes its identity immediately apparent, there has been no unreasonable invasion of the suspect's privacy. If the object is contraband, the officer can retrieve the object under the plain-feel doctrine. The Alabama Supreme Court interpreted *Minnesota v. Dickerson* as requiring three prerequisites for an officer to seize contraband under the plain-feel doctrine:

1. The officer must have a valid reason for the search—that is, the patdown search must be permissible under *Terry*.
2. The officer must detect the contraband while the Terry search for weapons legitimately and reasonably is in progress.
3. The incriminating nature of the object detected by the officer's touch must be immediately apparent to the officer so that before seizing it, the officer has probable cause to believe the object is contraband.

In practice, the "immediately apparent" requirement is always attacked. This is a reasonable person standard wherein the officer must know from his or her training and experience that the item felt on the patdown is a weapon or contraband. The officer's explanation of how the object was immediately apparent must be reasonable. In the 1990s and early 2000s, when people used cameras with film, a common container used to transport narcotics was in film containers. Officers would patdown suspects and feel a container they knew to be a film container. After opening the film container and finding controlled substances, the suspect would be arrested for possession of the controlled substance. The problem with this patdown and search is that feeling the film container did not make it immediately apparent that the suspect was in possession of controlled substances. The arguments for both sides were "in my training education and experience, people transport drugs in film containers" versus "we all know that film containers usually contain film." The latter always prevailed.

Investigator Lockemup receives a tip from the National Internet Crimes against Children Agency that they have discovered several images depicting children less than ten years old preforming sexual acts with adults from an IP address located in Lockemup's jurisdiction. Lockemup arrives at the residence in question and knocks on the door. A man in his early thirties answers the door and steps outside. Lockemup informs the man of the reason for his visit and asks whether anyone else lives at the residence. The man states that he is the only person who lives at the residence and denies viewing or uploading images of child pornography. The man also denies being in possession of any digital devices that can connect to the internet. After about ten minutes of conversation, the man changes his demeanor and begins stating that he has an addiction to viewing child pornography and has considered suicide multiple times. The man has his hands in his pockets and begins fidgeting with an item in his pocket. Lockemup pats the man down and retrieves a cell phone from the same pocket that the man was fidgeting his hand in. Lockemup seizes the cell phone and secures a search warrant for the device. It is later determined that the device contained hundreds of images of child pornography and the man is charged with possession of child pornography. This patdown and seizure were reasonable under the circumstances. Lockemup can articulate why he believed the man could be hiding a weapon (he was acting nervous, crying, and talking about suicide). This reasonable suspicion allows Lockemup to put his hands on the suspect for a patdown. Then, Lockemup feels something that he knows is immediately apparent as a cell phone in the suspect's pocket. Since Lockemup is investigating an internet crime involving children and the suspect has denied possessing a cell phone, it is reasonable for Lockemup to believe the cell phone is evidence.

2. Consent

One of the more widely used exceptions to the Fourth Amendment's search warrant requirement is **consent**. The Fourth Amendment protects against unreasonable search and seizure, and if a person consents to a search, it is deemed reasonable. There are some caveats to that rule. For the consent to pass constitutional muster, it must be voluntarily given. Note that this is not "knowingly and voluntarily," as we see in Miranda issues. In the context of consent, the state must only show that the consent was voluntarily given. This means that the consent was not obtained while the suspect was intoxicated, under mental duress, or threatened in any way. The consent does not have to be knowing. The US Supreme Court in *Schneckloth v. Bustamonte*, Bustamonte was pulled over on a traffic stop and the police asked if she would consent to a search of the vehicle. Bustamonte told the police that the car was her brother's but consented to the search. The Court found that based on the totality of the circumstances, Bustamonte's consent was voluntary (no duress or coercion). The issue was whether the police should have told her that she had the right to refuse consent. The Court stated that an individual's knowledge of his or her right to refuse consent would be a factor in weighing the totality of the circumstances for voluntariness, but not necessary.

Another consideration in determining whether the consent is valid under the Fourth Amendment is whether the person giving consent had the ability. As we saw in *Schneckloth v. Bustamonte*, the owner of property is not the only person who may give consent to search the property. Anyone with a possessory interest in the property may give legal consent. For example, family members who share common access to a house or apartment may have sufficient joint interest in an area to consent in the absence of others. It is not necessary for law enforcement officers to get permission from every occupant to search the premises.

Consent is fairly straightforward when the person consenting has actual ownership or possession of the area to be searched. It gets a little more complicated when a third party gives the consent. There is a difference in actual and apparent authority to consent. In the aforementioned examples, actual authority was discussed. There are situations where the person giving consent does not have the actual authority to consent but has the apparent authority to consent. If the authority to consent is apparent to the law enforcement officer asking, then the consent will be valid.

When the courts look at apparent authority, they question whether the officer's belief was reasonable based on the totality of the circumstances. In *Illinois v. Rodriguez*, the police arrived at a domestic assault call. Ms. Fischer showed visible signs of being beaten and referred to the apartment as "our apartment." She told the officers that the man who beat her (Rodriguez) was inside the apartment asleep on the sofa and that she had a key and could let them in. When police made entry into the apartment, there were drugs and paraphernalia in plain view. Mr. Rodriguez was arrested for the drug crimes. Mr. Rodriguez contested the search saying that Ms. Fischer had moved out weeks earlier and had no authority to consent to the search of his apartment. The court reasoned that it was reasonable for the officer to believe that Ms. Fischer could consent to the search of the apartment and therefore the apparent authority was sufficient. This makes sense when we go back to the purpose of the exclusionary rule: to deter bad police conduct. If the police activity is reasonable and is not bad conduct, it does not serve the purpose of the rule: to exclude evidence.

Third-party consent must be examined carefully. If there is not actual or apparent authority, the consent will be invalid. For example, the court in *Stoner v. California* held that the motel clerk could not give consent to the police to search a hotel room that was legally rented. When a person rents a hotel room, he or she has a reasonable expectation of privacy in the hotel room. That is a right protected by the Fourth Amendment; therefore, a warrant must be obtained unless a valid exception exists. The hotel clerk may not enter the room at any time; therefore, the hotel clerk may not give consent. The circumstances change when the checkout time has passed. Then, the guest loses his or her reasonable expectation of privacy in the room. The law enforcement officer needs to read the hotel policies closely if the officer intends to use this type of consent. Some hotels could give late checkout times or charge fees for continued stays if the checkout time is not honored. In that circumstance, the guest still has the right to the room.

Consent can be given in writing or verbally or can be implied. Many states have enacted implied consent laws that require motorists to submit to breath or blood tests if requested by law enforcement.

These are considered a condition to the ability to drive on the public roadways. Many states have enacted penalties for failing to submit to the required tests ranging from losing one's license for a period of time to actual criminal charges for refusal to comply. This means that an unconscious driver is presumed to have consented and cannot withdraw consent because of his or her condition. For example, an impaired driver has an accident, is unconscious, and is taken to the hospital. The driver's blood may be drawn under the implied consent laws since he or she is not able to withdraw consent. This type of consent is a close neighbor to the exigent circumstances exception to the search warrant requirement. The idea is that the alcohol in the breath and blood breaks down quickly, and if time is taken to obtain search warrants, evidence may be lost.

It is important to note that minors can give consent to search their property. If sixteen-year-old Sara is pulled over on a traffic stop and the law enforcement officer asks her for consent to search, she can give it because she is in possession and control of the vehicle. It is not necessary for the law enforcement officer to track down her parents (or the lawful owner of the vehicle) to gain consent. However, it is important to note that minors may not be able to give consent to an adult's residence. For example, Investigator Lockemup wants to search Joe's house because he believes Joe is manufacturing controlled substances in the residence. Lockemup waits down the street for Joe to leave, then approaches the house. Joe's twelve-year-old daughter answers the door and gives Lockemup consent to search the residence. When Joe returns, Lockemup arrests him for the illegal controlled substances and paraphernalia inside. If Joe complains that there was no actual or apparent authority of the twelve-year-old to consent, he will prevail.

Now consider the reverse. The parent can consent to a search of a minor's possessions. For example, Investigator Lockemup is investigating reports of kids at the high school producing, saving, and disseminating nude pictures of each other. Lockemup approaches one of the parents of a child reported to have sent several images and asks for consent to search the minor's phone. The parents give consent. This will be accepted as actual consent.

Investigator Lockemup is investigating the theft of a piece of heavy equipment. The city employees routinely leave the keys in the heavy equipment because it is stored in a locked and fenced yard. The city discovered the bulldozer gone on a Monday morning and reviewed surveillance footage from the lot. The surveillance footage showed a man approaching on foot, cutting the lock on the gate, and entering the heavy equipment storage yard. It showed him getting in the bulldozer and driving it away. Lockemup recognized this man as Burt Hustler, who was known for acquiring stolen property, posting the property on social media, and selling it quickly to an unsuspecting victim. Lockemup traveled to Burt's residence and immediately notices tracks consistent with a bulldozer going through the yard and disappearing in a wooded area behind the residence. Lockemup makes contact with Burt, who was working on a car in the front yard. Lockemup asks Burt if he has any knowledge of a stolen bulldozer. Burt denies any knowledge of a stolen bulldozer. Lockemup asks Burt for consent to search the property for a bulldozer and Burt gives consent. Lockemup walks about one hundred yards into the wooded area and finds the stolen bulldozer. Burt is arrested for theft of property. The bulldozer's discovery will be entered into evidence against Burt because the consent was given freely and voluntarily.

3. Plain View/Plain Smell

The **plain view** doctrine generally states that a police officer does not commit a Fourth Amendment violation if he or she sees an object in plain view of the officer. The officer must lawfully be in the place he or she viewed the object for the plain view doctrine to apply. Plain view was discussed briefly under the open fields doctrine in the search warrant chapter and has the same meaning. It is important to note that if the officer's location is in plain view of an illegal object, and the officer is lawfully in the location, what the officer sees will be considered in plain view.

The plain view exception also applies to the other bodily senses, such as plain hear or **plain smell**. Those terms are not as readily used in the field, but the concept is the same as plain view. If an officer is in a lawful location and hears something that gives the officer probable cause to seize or search, the officer may act on that sense of hearing. Likewise, if the officer is in a lawful location when he or she smells something that gives him or her probable cause to search or seize an item, the officer may rely on his or her sense of smell for that determination.

The important to note that the plain view rule is designed to permit warrantless seizures, as opposed to searches. The US Supreme Court in *Coolidge v. New Hampshire* carved out the plain view doctrine to allow seizure of an item without a warrant if (a) the police were lawfully in the area from where the item was seen, (b) the item was immediately apparent as evidence of criminal activity, and (c) the discovery of the evidence was inadvertent. The Coolidge Court stated that plain view alone is never enough to justify the warrantless seizure of evidence. Plain view must be coupled with another exception, such as **exigency** or emergency.

Plain view situations are when an officer isn't looking for evidence, yet he or she sees what is immediately apparent as such, or when an officer is in the midst of searching for evidence and sees more evidence during the search. Below we explore each of those two scenarios.

1. When the officer isn't looking for evidence, yet sees, hears, or smells what is immediately apparent as such.

For example, in *Colorado v. Bannister*, an officer observed a vehicle speeding but did not make a traffic stop. A short time later, the officer heard on the police radio that a vehicle matching the description of the vehicle he saw speeding had been involved in a theft. A few minutes later, the officer spotted the same vehicle he had observed speeding that was thought to be involved in the theft. The officer initiated a traffic stop on the vehicle and approached it to issue a traffic citation to the driver. From standing outside of the vehicle, the officer observed chrome lug nuts in an open glove compartment and lug wrenches in the back seat, all of which were in plain view and illuminated by outside light. Recognizing that both occupants of the vehicle matched the police description of those suspected of stealing motor vehicle parts, the officer arrested them and seized the lug nuts and wrenches. Performing the analysis stated in Coolidge, the officer was lawfully where he should have been when he saw the evidence (lawful traffic stop). The item was immediately apparent as evidence of the stolen lug nuts and wrenches that had been described over the police radio and the discovery of the evidence was inadvertent.

2. When the officer is in the process of executing a search warrant or searching under a valid exception to the search warrant requirement and sees, hears, or smells what is immediately apparent as other evidence.

The plain view doctrine may be used when a lawful search is underway for evidence and the police come across other evidence not originally contemplated. This could happen, for example, if the police were executing a valid search warrant for a residence. Consider a search warrant containing probable cause to enter the residence to search for stolen property. If during the search of that residence, the police officers see illegal substances in plain view, the officers may then seize the controlled substances as evidence even though they were not stated with particularity in the original warrant. The rationale is that seizing this new piece of evidence does not intrude on the Fourth Amendment rights of the property owner because the property is already being searched.

One police tactic in drafting search warrants is to list the smallest possible item as evidence of the intended search. This will give the police officers executing the search warrant the ability to look in small areas inside the residence and possibly discover other evidentiary items in plain view. For example, consider a search warrant for a building purported to house riding lawn mowers that were stolen from a local store. If the keys were also stolen with the lawn mower, the officer could list the key as an item being searched for. This would allow the officers to open small drawers and look in small areas within the building. Then, if the officers see other items of illegal evidence, the officers will lawfully be looking where authorized. On the other hand, if the search warrant only listed the stolen lawn mowers, the officer would have no lawful purpose to look in drawers and cabinets for a riding lawn mower.

This exception also applies to searches under consent, vehicle exception, hot pursuit, regularity searches, and others. If the police officer undertaking a search pursuant to one of these exceptions and sees other evidence in plain view, he or she may seize that evidence under the plain view exception. Consider the scenario wherein an officer approaches a parked vehicle. The officer suspects the driver to be up to no good and asks the driver if he has any weapons or narcotics in the vehicle. The driver denies any wrongdoing and gives the officer consent to search the vehicle. During the search of the vehicle, the officer finds several counterfeit one-hundred-dollar bills. The officer may seize the counterfeit money as evidence, although the original consent was contemplated for drugs or weapons.

Mechanical Devices May Be Used to Facilitate the Plain View

The courts have allowed the use of vision-enhancing cameras to photograph areas under the plain view doctrine, but the technology must be readily available to the public. This means that police may station themselves in an area that is accessible to the public and use the camera to view areas that may not be visible to the naked eye. This can include the air, in instances of flyovers. The same rules apply to flyovers as discussed in a previous chapter discussing the open fields doctrine.

Courts have consistently upheld the use of cameras or binoculars by officers perched in trees or neighboring apartments, but the officer must make sure the device is not too high tech. The courts have not allowed the use of high-tech gear that is not readily available to the public. In *Kyllo v. United States*, the police suspected Kyllo was growing marijuana in his home. The police did not have enough probable cause to obtain a search warrant, so they decided to use a high-tech thermal imaging device to detect heat signatures from inside the home. This device is not readily available to the public. The device showed a heat signature coming from the attic area above the garage of the residence consistent with the amount of heat emitted from grow lamps commonly used to grow marijuana indoors. Based on tips from informants, utility bills, and the thermal imaging, a federal magistrate judge issued a warrant authorizing a search of the home, and agents found an indoor growing operation involving more than one hundred plants. Use of a thermal imaging device aimed at a private home from a public street to detect relative amounts of heat within the home constitutes a search within the meaning of the Fourth Amendment, and use of such imaging, without a warrant, is unlawful. Obtaining by sense-enhancing technology any information regarding the interior of the home that could not otherwise have been obtained without physical intrusion into a constitutionally protected area constitutes a search for purposes of the Fourth Amendment.

Any violation of plain view, plain smell, or plain hear is exclusion under the exclusionary rule of the Fourth Amendment.

Use of Police Dogs

Police dogs are routinely used by larger departments in the plain smell context. Because a dog has a keen sense of smell, a dog can be trained to detect controlled substances, explosives, ammunition, chemicals, bodies, and so much more. A dog's sense of smell is ideal when law enforcement needs to search larger areas or areas which would otherwise be difficult to search. A police dog can be considered an agent of the police and therefore have the same limitations as a law enforcement officer under the Fourth Amendment. In *United States v. Place*, the US Supreme Court ruled that a K-9 sniff of luggage stored in a public place did not constitute a search under the Fourth Amendment. The Court reasoned that the sniff did not open the luggage, yet the smell emitted from the luggage was in the public area.

The most common use for a specially trained police dog is during a search for controlled substances. This is commonly done during a detention involving a vehicle. A vehicle may be detained upon a traffic stop. During the issuance of the ticket, a drug dog may be walked around the car (in the public space) to sniff for controlled substances within the vehicle. The caveat here is that the sniff cannot further delay the traffic stop. Courts have routinely upheld stops that involved police dog's being called to the stop when the stop has lasted up to an hour.

The rules and regulations concerning the certification for the dog and handling agent are ever changing, and an officer who intends to depend on the plain sniff from a police dog should be proficient in those regulations and make sure the dog is properly trained.

Sandy and Scott have been living together for a few years and are known throughout the neighborhood for their loud domestic disturbances. The local law enforcement officers all know the address because they have been called numerous times by the neighbors. On this occasion, the neighbors called reporting Sandy and Scott in an argument that had escalated to shots fired and screaming. Law enforcement officers arrive at Scott and Sandy's residence to find both Scott and Sandy in the yard. Sandy is holding a gun and Scott is bleeding from the arm. Upon approach from the officers, Scott begins saying that he accidentally shot himself in the arm when he was cleaning his gun. Sandy had a bruise on her left eye and looked like she had been crying. Scott was holding his arm and needed medical attention. The law enforcement officers called the paramedics and took more detailed statements from Sandy, Scott, and the neighbors. While standing outside of the residence, a law enforcement officer looks inside the window. He sees what he recognizes as methamphetamine and paraphernalia used to manufacture methamphetamine on a coffee table in the living room. He enters the residence and seizes the methamphetamine and lab components. Scott and Sandy are both arrested for manufacturing a controlled substance. At a pretrial hearing, Scott's attorney moves to suppress the methamphetamine and lab components as fruits of an illegal search. The methamphetamine and lab components are suppressed, and the charges dropped against both Scott and Sandy. What should the law enforcement officer have done differently?

4. Vehicle Exception

The US Supreme Court has carved out another exception; it is commonly referred to as the **vehicle exception**. It is an exception to the search warrant requirement for vehicles that are mobile. This can include cars, boats, airplanes, motorcycles, buses, wagons, and anything that is readily movable. Controlled substances are the most common piece of evidence found during a vehicle search because criminals usually keep the substances close. There are also many good hiding places on a vehicle. Some vehicles also may have hidden compartments that are specially designed to conceal narcotics.

The precedent for a **warrantless search** of a vehicle without a warrant was established in *Carroll v. United States*. The Carroll decision required that if a vehicle was searched without a warrant, two requirements must be met: (1) probable cause to believe the vehicle contains fruits or instrumentalities of a crime, evidence of a crime, or contraband, and (2) the vehicle would be gone before a search warrant could be obtained. This probable cause to search the vehicle may develop as a result of observations after stopping the vehicle. In fact, this is usually how probable cause to search occurs.

The vehicle exception carves out a lower expectation of privacy that allows a warrantless search because of the mobility of a vehicle. This is because the driver of such a vehicle has allowed himself and his vehicle to venture out into the public and away from more private areas such as a home, building, or curtilage. This also applies to mobile recreational vehicles such as a motor home.

> Investigator Lockemup is driving home from his shift and sees a vehicle weaving in and out of traffic at a high rate of speed. Although he is ready to get home, he decides this vehicle is a danger to other motorists. He initiates a traffic stop using the lights on his undercover vehicle. When Lockemup approaches the vehicle, the driver rolls down the window and Lockemup immediately smells the odor of marijuana emitting from the vehicle. Possession of marijuana is illegal in Lockemup's jurisdiction, and this gives him probable cause to believe the vehicle contains evidence of a crime. Lockemup asks the driver to step out of the vehicle and searches the car. This is a permissible search under the automobile exception.

Technological Aids and the Vehicle Exception

Earlier in this chapter we discussed the use of high-tech sensory enhancing equipment for the search of a residence or privately protected area. Let's now examine the use of a high-tech surveillance device placed upon or inside of a vehicle. In *United States v. Knotts*, law enforcement officers suspected Knots and others to be involved in the manufacture and sale of controlled substances. One of the items needed to manufacture the controlled substance was chloroform. Knott's codefendant purchased a container of chloroform, in which the police had previously placed a beeper. This device allowed law enforcement to track the path of the vehicle and ultimately discover the cabin in which the manufacture of controlled substances was happening. The police obtained a search warrant for the cabin based on information supplied by the beeper and ultimately discovered a controlled-substance operation at the cabin. The issue before the court was whether the beeper that was placed within the vehicle was an intrusion on the defendant's Fourth Amendment rights to privacy. The US Supreme Court reasoned that the police could have simply followed the vehicle on the public roadway to the cabin and therefore the beeper did not infringe upon only privacy rights of the defendant. The Court did not find that placing the beeper within the vehicle was a search or a seizure.

Searching Containers or Persons within a Vehicle

As discussed above, if law enforcement has probable cause to search a vehicle, then they may open any container within the vehicle that may reasonably contain the item serving the basis of the probable cause. Below we will discuss if the requirements change when there are other passengers within the vehicle at the time the probable cause is developed and how to approach search of those people or their belongings.

Passengers in the Vehicle

The first question that should be asked when assessing whether the passenger can object to a search is whether there was a Fourth Amendment violation. For there to be a Fourth Amendment violation, there must be a search or seizure. The question becomes whether the passenger is seized when the driver is commanded to pull over by law enforcement. That question is answered in *Brendlin v. California*. When a police officer makes a traffic stop, the driver of the car is seized within the meaning of the Fourth Amendment. The same is true of a passenger. A passenger is seized as well and so may challenge the constitutionality of the stop.

The next question one must ask is whether the passenger has a legitimate expectation of privacy in the vehicle. If the passenger does not have a possessor interest in the area of the vehicle searched, then the passenger cannot complain about the search. As in any case, the issue of standing involves two questions: first, whether the suspect has an injury, and second, whether the suspect is asserting his own legal rights and interests rather than basing his claim for relief upon the rights of third parties. In *Rakas v. Illinois*, the defendant was a passenger in an automobile suspected in a robbery. The police searched the vehicle and found a gun under the seat and ammunition in the glove box. The defendant complained about their admission into evidence. The court found that the passenger in the vehicle did not have any standing to object to evidence found in an area of the car to which the defendant had no possessory interest. Therefore, the evidence was used against him at trial.

Passengers' Possessions within the Vehicle

When law enforcement officers have probable cause to believe the vehicle contains contraband, the officers may search the vehicle and any containers within the vehicle that could reasonably contain the items believed to be contraband. But what if the items within the vehicle belong to other passengers within the vehicle? The courts have not put any duty on law enforcement to determine ownership of the containers found within the vehicle that probable cause was established to search. That would be a near impossible standard, given that the individuals in the car could lie or invoke their rights to silence, rendering ownership too difficult to determine. Nevertheless, ownership or possession must ultimately be determined in order to make charges against an individual. Consider the examples below:

An officer stops a vehicle for a traffic infraction and that vehicle contains four persons. There is a strong smell of marijuana emitting from the vehicle, giving the officer probable cause to search the vehicle for marijuana. This gives the officer the probable cause to look within small containers and compartments in the vehicle. Certainly, the driver and passengers would be able to contest the traffic stop (seizure) and search because their movement was restricted by the stop. Then suppose the police officer finds marijuana in a woman's purse in the back seat floorboard. The search of the purse would be upheld because the smell of marijuana gives the officer the right to search small containers. The fact that the purse is in the back seat floorboard is irrelevant. The fact that the driver is a man is irrelevant. The search and seizure of the marijuana would be within the bounds of the Fourth Amendment. The next practical question that needs to be asked is who could be charged with the marijuana found within the purse. The driver would have a reasonable nexus to the purse because it is within the vehicle that he controls. Also, assume, for this example, that the purse contains a wallet and identification of one of the passengers. This would also give a nexus to the purse to allow arrest of the passenger who can be tied to the purse. It would be unlikely any other passenger could be charged with possession of the marijuana based on these facts.

Using the above example, consider another passenger verbally claims ownership of the purse. Perhaps a chivalrous male shouts, "Whatever is in the purse is mine, not hers." Then he, too, may be linked to the marijuana.

Law enforcement officers may also search containers within a vehicle as long as the container could contain the item or evidence that is the basis for the probable cause. Law enforcement officers may also develop probable cause for the contents of a particular container that is placed within a vehicle, but not have probable cause to believe the vehicle contains other evidence of a crime. In *California v. Acevedo*, the law enforcement officers knew that a FedEx package containing marijuana was picked up from the FedEx hub. The person picking up the package drove to a residence and went inside with the package. Just moments later, the suspect left the residence with a bag that appeared to be the same size as the FedEx package and placed that bag in the trunk of the vehicle. The police stopped the vehicle on the roadway, opened the trunk of the vehicle, and removed the bag from the trunk. The bag contained a large amount of marijuana. The US Supreme Court upheld the search of the container that was taken from the vehicle because the law enforcement officers had probable cause to believe the container contained evidence of a crime. The Court did not permit a search of the rest of the vehicle based on the probable cause only existing to search the container.

It is important to note that for the automobile exception to apply, the vehicle must be mobile. This exception would not apply to a vehicle that is unmovable. A law enforcement officer must be able to articulate that the vehicle is movable. For example, a parked car may be readily movable by starting an engine and driving away. Compare another example: An officer suspects the vehicle contains stolen property. Upon approach, the officer sees in plain view through the windows several laptop computers in the floorboard. The officer also notes that the vehicle parked in the yard does not have wheels and is propped up on blocks. The officer also notes that the grass is growing up tall around the vehicle. The officer would not be able to establish both prongs of the automobile exception to search this car without a warrant.

5. Exigency/Emergency

Evidence may be seized or searched in emergency circumstances. The issue with this exception is what is an **emergency** to one, may not be to another. Therefore, it is important to know the types of cases that have been outlined by the US Supreme Court as constituting an emergency.

Hot Pursuit

Hot pursuit is a classic example of an emergency situation. Police can almost always seize a piece of evidence or search a location based on the pursuit of a suspect. When the police have probable cause to make an arrest and pursue the suspect into a private residence, the police may reasonably seize evidence therein. This is limited to the circumstances of the chase and only allowable when the police are preventing a suspect from escaping. The courts have refused to allow this rule to apply to petty offenses.

An example of a seizure based on hot pursuit follows. A law enforcement officer sees a robbery in progress. The suspect sees that the law enforcement officer has arrived and flees the crime scene. The officer gives chase. The suspect runs into a private residence to escape. The police officer follows the suspect into the private residence. The suspect is found hiding in the back closet of the residence. Also inside the bedroom in which the suspect is hiding is an obvious methamphetamine lab. The officer seizes the lab components and controlled substances and charges the homeowner with manufacturing a controlled substance. The seizure will be proper and the evidence will be admitted because the police officer was in hot pursuit of a fleeing felon at the time he entered the residence. He did not search the home, but reasonably saw the methamphetamine lab in the area of the house where the fleeing felon hid.

Dangerous Emergencies

The courts have ruled that a warrant is not required to search for explosive devices. The reasoning continues that there is not enough time to get a warrant because of the dangerousness of explosives. For example, if the police reasonably believed that an apartment contained an explosive device, law enforcement could enter the apartment to neutralize the explosive device. If while inside the apartment the police see several counterfeiting devices and large quantities of blank checks, the police could seize the counterfeiting evidence.

Other Emergencies

If the police reasonably believe that a child is injured and inside a private residence, the police can enter the residence to check on the welfare of the child. If while conducting a welfare check, the police also see illegal drugs, the police can seize the illegal drugs.

If the police see blood oozing from inside a building, the police may enter the building to check on the welfare of the persons inside. If while inside, the police see illegal substances, the police may seize the illegal substances.

If the police smell the readily identifiable smell of a decaying body, they may not enter the building without a warrant. This is not an emergency. The emergency is long since over and there is time for the police to obtain a warrant.

Evanescent Evidence

The police may seize evidence that is in the process of being destroyed or will be destroyed in the amount of time necessary to obtain a search warrant. For example, the police suspect Joe of trafficking in cocaine. The police go to Joe's residence and knock on the door in hopes of interviewing Joe. When the police knock and announce "Police," they hear sounds of people running and commotion coming from inside the residence. The police hear someone say, "Flush it." The police enter the house and seize the drug evidence before it all is flushed. The warrantless seizure of the drug evidence will be upheld as an emergency exception.

No Crime Scene Emergency Exception

There is no crime scene exception to the search warrant requirement. When police arrive at a murder scene and find a dead body, the excitement is running high. Officers may forget that the same Fourth Amendment rules apply. Once the scene is secure, the police need to back away and obtain a search warrant prior to searching for evidence.

> Investigator Lockemup is called to a murder scene. When he arrives, he speaks with other law enforcement officers who have secured the scene. They tell him that the neighbor called 911 after hearing screams coming from inside the residence. When the first law enforcement officer arrived, he noticed the front door was wide open. He could plainly see from the threshold of the front door that a female was lying motionless on the floor. The officer entered the residence to conduct a welfare check on the female and found that she had no pulse. Upon further inspection, he could see marks around her neck consistent with a cord. What should Lockemup do?
>
> The best practice is for Lockemup to secure a search warrant for the residence to include a search for the murder weapon. Adding a small item as the basis of the search warrant will allow Lockemup to look in small compartments and containers inside the residence. Lockemup may find evidence that there is a male also living in the home and that person could be the suspect. If the suspect had a reasonable expectation of privacy in the home, any evidence Lockemup found without a warrant could be suppressed.

6. Regulatory Searches

Regulatory searches are typically searches done by government officers for a health and safety purpose. These particular searches usually do not require probable cause or a warrant.

Inspection Searches

These types of searches are carved out for the purpose of health and safety of the community at large. These searches can take place in private dwellings, vehicles, or private businesses. For example, most businesses must apply and be granted a business license to operate in a county or city. This means that the business may be required to do or maintain certain things for the health and safety of the business's customers. The agency governing food permits, alcohol permits, and the like can perform random inspections of restaurants and bars to ensure that the business is providing a safe environment for its customers. There is no requirement that there not be a dual purpose for the inspection.

> Investigator Lockemup gets an anonymous tip that Granny's bar is selling narcotics in addition to Granny's special chicken wings. Lockemup does not have probable cause to get a search warrant based on this anonymous tip, but he does know that the state alcohol board licenses Granny's bar for the sale of alcoholic beverages. He calls his friend, Agent Hennassee, who works for the state alcohol board, and asks for the board to do a regulatory inspection at Granny's bar. When Agent Hennassee searches Granny's bar, he finds many kinds and large quantities of controlled substances. The bar is shut down and the operator arrested for trafficking in narcotics. The search will be upheld as a regulatory search.

Border Checkpoints

A border search is sometimes called an immigration search and usually takes place at an international travel crossing point. This could be on a road, or at a train depot, boat dock, or airport. Persons crossing through these areas are subject to having their possessions and person searched without probable cause.

Routine Traffic Stops

Police may lawfully stop a vehicle for a traffic violation. However, law enforcement officers may also stop a vehicle where there is no traffic violation in two manners: random and fixed checkpoint.

Random police stops occur when the police randomly stop a car. The randomness may be accomplished in many ways, but the burden is upon the law enforcement officer to show the randomness is consistent, meaning, for example, that the police may stop every tenth car that passes through an area and inquire whether the driver is licensed and the car is registered. These encounters and questions could lead to the discovery of criminal activity that leads to arrest. Other exceptions would need to apply such as plain view or smell. The police could not select cars in a manner that would tend to profile a particular group.

Fixed checkpoint stops occur when the police physically set up a checkpoint and stop cars for a valid public safety reason. A fixed checkpoint could be set up to check for drivers licensing, vehicle registration, intoxication levels of drivers, or whether a car harbored certain evidence of a crime. For example, police may have received an Amber alert about a missing child in a particular area. The police could decide to set up a fixed checkpoint to check vehicles for the missing child or any witnesses that may have information about the missing child.

Parolees and Probationers

Individuals who are on probation or parole do not have the same level of Fourth Amendment rights as unconnected individuals and can be subject to search without a warrant. The rationale is that a person who is on parole or probation is still "incarcerated" but just to a lesser degree than actually being housed inside the walls of a jail or prison. The guards have the ability to search prisoners confined in a jail or prison; therefore, law enforcement have the ability to search parolees or probationers.

> Investigator Lockemup receives information that Chris was involved in a series of convenience store robberies. Six convenience stores were broken into in one evening and all the cartons of cigarettes were stolen from each store. Lockemup has information from a confidential informant that Chris is talking on the street about having cigarettes for sale and trying to make money selling them. Lockemup does not have probable cause to believe the cigarettes are inside Chris's residence but knows that Chris is on probation for theft of property that occurred last year. Lockemup calls Chris's probation officer and asks the officer to go search Chris's apartment. The probation officer searches Chris's apartment and finds eight hundred cartons of cigarettes. The warrantless search of Chris's apartment by his probation officer will be upheld as a regulatory search.

School Searches

Warrantless searches by school officials are permissible for any student belongings on the school property. The school merely needs to have a reasonable suspicion of the student to conduct the search. The school is also permitted to conduct drug tests (searches) as long as the tests are conducted in a reasonable manner.

New Jersey v. T. L.O.

Read here for a summary of a case regarding an example of a school search. The school search's lawfulness turns on the question of reasonableness, as does most Fourth Amendment questions.

Read at: https://www.law.cornell.edu/supremecourt/text/469/325

Image 5.1

In another example of a case regarding a school search, *Safford Unified Sch. Dist. #1 v. Redding*, the school's policies strictly prohibited the nonmedical use, possession, or sale of any drug on school grounds. A student gave a statement to school officials that another student was possession of and selling pills on school property. This suspicion was enough to justify a search of the student's backpack and outer clothing. The principal further made the student pull down her underwear as part of the body search for pills. There was no indication from the student's original statement that the suspect student kept the pills in her underwear. Thus, the Supreme Court held that the strip search of the student was unreasonable and a violation of the Fourth Amendment.

Government Offices

Government officers may also search the personal belongings and areas of government employees as long as the search is somewhat work related. The courts apply the same reasonableness standard.

7. Inventory Searches

Inventory searches are another exception to the search warrant requirement. There is no requirement for probable cause. There is only a requirement that the property being inventoried is properly seized and the inventory is done within the standard operating procedure.

In *Colorado v. Bertine*, the police arrested Bertine for drunk driving and impounded his vehicle. After impounding the vehicle, the police inventoried the contents of the vehicle according to departmental policy. While doing this inventory, the officers opened a closed backpack and some sealed containers and found that the latter contained narcotics. They charged Bertine with possession of those narcotics. The issue was whether the police exceeded their authority and violated the Fourth Amendment rights of Bertine by opening closed containers found in the vehicle they impounded. The US Supreme Court found that the police did not and that the inventory search was proper. The reasoning was that there was no showing that the police, who were following standardized procedures, acted in bad faith or for the sole purpose of investigation. The police were potentially responsible for the property taken into their custody. By securing the property, the police protected the property from unauthorized interference. Reasonable police regulations relating to inventory procedures administered in good faith satisfied the Fourth Amendment.

The Supreme Court, in later case law, set out criteria for determining whether an inventory search is proper.

- The search must be of lawfully seized and detained property.
- The search must be to ensure the property seized is not harmful.
- The search must be to properly secure valuable items.
- The search must be to protect against false claims of loss or damage.
- As a practical matter, the police need to inventory all property seized, for many reasons.

There could be a need to identify the owner of property that was abandoned. This could occur if the police were in a high-speed chase with a robbery suspect and the suspect wrecked the vehicle and fled on foot. The police would need to secure the vehicle with an impound and inventory the contents. They would also try to locate the identity of the owner of the vehicle. Perhaps the owner was not the fleeing suspect. The car could be stolen or borrowed and due to be returned to its rightful owner.

There could be items in the property seized that are dangerous to the public, such as bombs, chemicals, weapons, razor blades, and/or needles that could harm people in the area in which the vehicle is being stored or to which it is being taken.

To protect the police from claims of theft or damage. The owner of the property could make claims against the individual officer or the department. If there is an accurate record of the items seized, the police officer or department had greater protection.

> Investigator Lockemup arrests Margaret for fraudulent use of a credit card. When he takes her into custody, she has a large purse. Lockemup searches the purse consistent with the departmental policy for listing all contents of property seized during an arrest. Lockemup finds three other stolen credit cards in Margaret's purse along with three other false identifications. Lockemup charges Margaret with three additional counts of possession of stolen credit cards. The search and seizure of the additional credit cards will be upheld because it complies with the Supreme Courts's requirements.

8. Search Incident to Arrest

All individuals who are arrested are searched. This is for the protection of the officers and to inventory items in the possession of the charged. This search is usually twofold. First, there is a cursory search done by the arresting officer. This is usually a patdown and search of the clothing of the arrestee. This is usually done before the suspect is transported to the holding facility or jail. The second search usually takes place at the jail. It is a more invasive search in which the arrestee is usually asked to strip and squat. The genital area is a common hiding place for drugs and has to be examined by officers before the arrestee is placed in a secure facility. The rationale for this exception is that the defendant may have a concealed weapon or a concealed means to escape, or may destroy evidence of a crime.

The US Supreme Court's decision in *Chimel v. California* established that the area around the arrestee that may be **searched incident to the arrest**. One basis of this exception to the search warrant requirement is that the arrest be lawful and custodial. This exception would not apply to the issuance of a speeding ticket, which may be a lawful arrest but is not custodial, meaning the driver is usually free to drive away from the traffic stop with the issuance of a summons and court date information available either electronically or on the written citation. Another requirement of this exception is that the arrest occurs before the search. The search cannot occur before the arrest. For example, if the law enforcement officer knows that he is going to arrest Johnny for a crime, he cannot search Johnny and then place him under arrest for the crime.

Timing Requirement

Just as a search incident to arrest must occur after the arrest, the search must also be soon after the arrest. For example, Johnny is arrested for an outstanding warrant and his vehicle towed. The police cannot go search the vehicle the next day, incident to arrest.

Scope of the Search

The Supreme Court initially states that incident to arrest, the officer may search the arrestee and any nearby area that the arrestee possessed. Then in later decisions, the US Supreme Court modified this area to the "wingspan" of the accused. This area was later expanded to include the area in which the arrestee could lunge for a weapon after arrest. This is in keeping with the rational of the rule to protect the officer making the arrest. The US Supreme Court has also ruled that the arrestee can extend this area through his or her actions. In *Washington v. Chrisman*, an officer arrested a student for underage drinking. The officer asked the student for his identification and followed the student to his room to get it. In plain view the officer saw marijuana and drug paraphernalia. The Court upheld the seizure of the drugs and paraphernalia because it was shortly after the probable cause for the arrest and the student extended the area in his control by entering the room.

Protective Sweep

The US Supreme Court has recognized that items may not be the only thing that puts an officer in danger upon arrest. There also may be additional people present who could put the arresting officer at risk. *Buie v. Maryland* expanded the search area to allow officers to do a protective sweep of the area adjoining the area of arrest. The protective sweep must be limited to the visual inspection of the area and limited to areas in which a person could hide. The police may look in the adjoining room, under the bed, and in the closet, but may not open a kitchen drawer, as a person would not be inside the kitchen drawer.

There are limitations on the protective sweep's application. In *Vale v. Louisiana*, the law enforcement officers had been watching the defendant's home and suspected him of dealing in narcotics. They had a warrant for his arrest that they intended on serving. While they were watching his home, they saw him come out and make what they believed to be a drug deal. The police officers arrested the defendant and then entered his home to search incident to arrest. The defense argued that this was outside of the scope of the protective search and incident to arrest. The Court agreed. The general rule is that if a suspect is arrested outside of the home, the police cannot enter the home to search under the theory of protective sweep or search incident to arrest. However, if the defendant is arrested inside the home, then the police may search the area immediately surrounding the suspect for evidence or weapons, and they may also search the entire residence for dangerous persons.

In practice, a law enforcement officer who has a warrant for a suspect's arrest may prefer to serve the warrant on the suspect at his or her residence. This allows for a greater search of the surroundings. This also needs to be balanced with the level of danger involved in executing a search warrant at a residence.

Some suspects who have knowledge of how the system works will immediately walk outside when they see police arrive at their home. Some never learn, and hole up in their homes until the police announce and enter the home with a lawful arrest warrant; then the police can do a search of the immediate area and a protective sweep of the residence.

> Investigator Lockemup has an arrest warrant for Amelia for distribution of drugs. Lockemup knows that Amelia is home in the early morning hours and plans to take a team to Amelia's home to make the arrest at 6:00 a.m. Lockemup also knows that Amelia is armed and dangerous. She has made comments on social media platforms that she is not going to prison again and that she will defend her property, even against police invasion. At 6:00 a.m., Lockemup and his team approach Amelia's home and forcibly breach the door. They enter quickly, securing the residence and all individuals inside. There is a brief standoff while Amelia decides to lower her weapon. Amelia is taken into custody. While Lockemup is doing a protective sweep of the residence, he sees cocaine in plain view in a back bedroom and therefore also arrests Amelia for that controlled substance. The cocaine will be admissible against Amelia as it was in plain view and the protective sweep was authorized.

Search of a Vehicle Incident to Arrest

The passenger compartment of a vehicle may be searched by law enforcement pursuant to a lawful custodial arrest, if the areas searched are accessible to the car occupants who could retrieve a weapon or destroy evidence. The vehicle can also be searched if it is "reasonable to believe the vehicle contains evidence of the offense of the arrest." Note that this reasonable belief standard is similar to the reasonable suspicion standard the Court carved out for patdown searches in *Terry v. Ohio*. This reasonable suspicion standard is lesser than the required probable cause standard for vehicle searches under the vehicle exception to the search warrant requirement.

Rules to Remember

Below is a list of rules to remember from this chapter.

- The Fourth Amendment to the US Constitution protects against unreasonable search and secure.
- The courts apply a totality of the circumstances test in determining whether an individual has reasonable expectation of privacy.
- Searches conducted with a warrant are presumed unreasonable. It is the government's burden to

show that the search is not unreasonable.

- A prior lawful intrusion is required for plain view to apply. This intrusion can be based on a valid warrant or exception to the warrant requirement.
- Items not contemplated by the initial search may be seized during the search as long as there is probable caused based on plain view.
- Police may not use special sense-enhancing equipment to search a private area.
- Law enforcement officers may only use sense-enhancing devices readily available to the public, such as cameras or binoculars.
- Police dogs can be used consistently with the plain smell doctrine but will be treated with the same constitutional limitations as law enforcement officers.
- A vehicle that is mobile has a lesser degree of Fourth Amendment protection than a residence or building.
- A vehicle and containers found therein may be searched with probable cause that evidence can be found within the vehicle.
- Passengers in a vehicle may contest the seizure and search of the vehicle but only relative to the areas in which they have a possessory interest.
- Probable cause may exist to search a container found within a vehicle without probable cause to search the entire vehicle.
- Police may use technological aids to track the movement of vehicles.
- Evidence found while in hot pursuit of a fleeing felon can be admissible without a warrant under the emergency exception to the search warrant requirement.
- There is no crime scene exception to the search warrant requirement.
- There is no probable cause requirement for regulatory searches.
- Traffic stops can be random or at a fixed checkpoint and do not require probable cause.
- Probationers and parolees can be searched at any time without a warrant.
- Inventory searches must be done of lawfully seized property and for a noninvestigative purpose.
- Law enforcement officers may search the areas immediately surrounding the suspect for weapons or evidence.
- Law enforcement officers may do a protective sweep of a residence if the suspect is arrested inside the residence and the areas searched are large enough to conceal a person.

End of Chapter Comprehension and Application

Directions: Use what you have learned in this chapter to help you respond completely and correctly to each question or prompt below.

1. Define warrantless arrest and give a lawful example.
2. What is the standard of proof required for a Terry patdown? Why is this important?

3. What factors must be present for a Terry search to be lawful?
4. Explain the differences in actual versus apparent authority.
5. What limits has the Supreme Court put on the plain view doctrine? Explain fully.
6. What two requirements must be present to avoid the necessity for a search warrant for a vehicle?
7. What factors must be present for the emergency exception to apply? Give a factual example.
8. Do parolees have the same rights afforded to individuals who haven't been convicted of a crime? Why or why not? Do you agree or disagree with this rule? Give your reasons for your position.
9. What criteria has been set by the US Supreme Court for determining whether an inventory search is proper? What do you think about the criteria? What other criteria could be added to this rule to ensure suspects' rights?
10. What areas may be searched incident to arrest?
11. John Snorty was pulled over by Investigator Lockemup because of an expired vehicle registration tag. When Lockemup approached the vehicle, he asked John for his driver's license and registration. John had neither. Lockemup sees ammunition on the floorboard of the vehicle and asks John if he has any weapons in the vehicle. John says that he does not. Lockemup asks John to step out of the vehicle and then pats him down for weapons. He finds a pistol in John's jacket pocket. After calling in John's name to central dispatch, Lockemup determined that John is a convicted felon. Lockemup arrests John for felon in possession of a pistol and ammunition. Will the pistol and ammunition be admitted into evidence in John's trial for felon in possession of a firearm and ammunition? Why or why not?
12. Investigator Lockemup gets a call to a domestic disturbance between Kim and Kevin Rowdee. Upon arrival, Lockemup gets information from other officers on scene that Kim and Kevin have been in a domestic disturbance and Kim's son called the police. Kim has red marks on her neck and a busted lip. She states that she and Kevin were arguing because he accused her of having an affair. She stated that Kevin has a hot temper and gets paranoid when he does methamphetamine. She said he had smoked some meth earlier in the day and then there was a hang-up call to her cell phone. He flew into a rage about some other man and then began hitting and choking her. Kim's son confirmed this story. Kevin is arrested for domestic violence and taken to the police department for booking. Lockemup asks Kim for permission search the house for methamphetamine. Kim gives voluntary consent to search the residence for drugs. After a thorough search, Lockemup finds a large quantity of methamphetamine in Kevin's tool shed, bedroom, and living room. At trial, Kevin's attorney files a motion to suppress the evidence found, stating that Kim does not have the authority to consent to the search of Kevin's residence. She and her son were merely overnight guests and had no actual rights to the home. Will the evidence be admissible against Kevin? Why or why not?
13. The police department received a call to 13 West Oak Street from a neighbor complaining that young children are home alone. The police department routes the call to social services to assist them on the call due to children being involved. When Investigator Lockemup arrives on scene,

he finds a six-year-old and an eight-year-old home alone. The children look dirty and not cared for. The social worker asks Lockemup to walk with her inside the home to gather some belongings for the children, as they are being placed in foster care. While walking to the children's room, Lockemup sees a variety of pipes used to smoke controlled substances, and he sees the remnants of a methamphetamine lab, and possible methamphetamine residue in a dish on the coffee table. What should Lockemup do? Explain in detail.

14. Dispatch gets a call regarding a suspicious vehicle parked on the side of the road. The caller states that the driver looks asleep. Investigator Lockemup drives to the location and approaches the parked vehicle. He looks in the window and sees a male who appears to be asleep behind the wheel. In the passenger seat of the vehicle is a bag of fast food, some empty beer cans, and a pipe used for smoking a controlled substance. Lockemup bangs on the window until the male wakes up. Lockemup tells the man to step out of the vehicle. Lockemup searches the car. He finds a pill bottle with the label torn off in the center console. The pill bottle contains twenty tablets that appear to be controlled substances. Lockemup asks the driver about the pills. The driver says he has no idea what they are and that they are not his pills. Lockemup arrests the driver for possession of controlled substances and drug paraphernalia for the pipe. Was the collection of the evidence done properly? Why or why not?
15. An alarm call comes in from the Stop and Shop on East North Street. Investigator Lockemup drives to the location just in time to see a red Monte Carlo pulling away from the store at a high rate of speed. Lockemup calls in for back up and purses the Monte Carlo. The two vehicles reach speeds of over seventy miles an hour on a dark country road. Lockemup is familiar with the road and knows there is a hairpin turn just ahead. The Monte Carlo does not slow down, then loses control and wrecks. Both the driver and the passenger flee on foot and Lockemup gives chase. The fleeing suspects in the robbery run in opposite directions. Lockemup pursues the one who appears to be losing speed. The suspect runs through yards and hops a fence, entering the backyard of a residence. Lockemup also hops the fence into the backyard of the residence. He sees the suspect hiding in some bushes, orders him out, and detains him. As Lockemup is reading the suspect his rights and cuffing him, Lockemup realizes that the bushes are all marijuana plants. There are many marijuana plants growing in the private backyard of this residence. The homeowners are arrested for trafficking in marijuana because of the large quantity of marijuana found. The homeowners' attorney files a motion to suppress the evidence arguing that Lockemup should have had a search warrant for the search and seizure of the marijuana. Was the seizure of the marijuana plants proper? Why or why not?
16. Smallville has had a recent increase in traffic accidents involving individuals driving under the influence. One reason is that there is a new club on the south side of town that is offering great prices on alcohol, a popular DJ, and late hours. The police decide that the best way to crack down on people driving under the influence is to set up a traffic safety checkpoint down the street from the new club. The police set up at 10:00 p.m., completely blocking the road and

stopping every car driving down the road. Patty Partier is leaving the club and headed to another club across town. She drives through the checkpoint and the officer asks for her driver's license and insurance. She explains to the officer that she does not have her license because she lost it. The officer runs Patty's name and Social Security number through the database and finds out that Patty has lost her license because it has been revoked for driving under the influence. The officer also sees that there is an outstanding warrant for Patty's arrest for failing to show up for her district court case of driving under the influence. The officer arrests Patty for the outstanding warrant and calls the city wrecker to tow her car. Pursuant to the city's policy, the officer inventories the contents of the vehicle prior to it being towed. The officer finds cocaine in the glovebox and a straw fashioned to snort cocaine through. The officer then adds the charges of possession of controlled substances and possession of drug paraphernalia to Patty's arrest report. Patty contests the search and seizure of the cocaine. Will she prevail? Why or why not? Explain the search and seizure independently.

17. Investigator Lockemup gets information that the new bar in town has a back room with gambling machines and tables. Games of chance are illegal in Smallville. Lockemup knows that the new bar has just obtained a liquor license and that the license is regulated by the State of Timbuktu. The Bureau of Alcohol, Tobacco, Firearms, and Explosives (ATF) regulates licensing for establishments serving food and alcohol. Lockemup calls a friend who works for ATF, Brian, and asks if ATF can conduct a search of the new bar and see if there are any gambling machines on premises. Brian agrees to visit the new bar and plans his visit for the following evening. When Brian arrives, he announces his presence to the new bar manager and asks for a tour. The new bar manager acts extremely nervous and says he has to call the owner first. Brian ignores this request and starts to walk around the new bar on his own. He sees a back room and enters through a beaded curtain. Inside the room there are approximately twenty illegal gambling machines. Every machine is being played and making sounds and lighting up. Brian calls Lockemup, who arrives with several other officers. They shut down new bar and seize all the illegal gambling machines. The owner of the new bar shows up demanding to know what is going on wherein he is arrested for possession of illegal gambling machines. Was the search and seizure of the gambling machines proper? Why or why not?
18. Investigator Lockemup is headed to a local coffee shop to revive after his last call when a Nissan Maxima sped by his unmarked car at an extremely high rate of speed. Lockemup really wants to get his coffee but decides that something needed to be done about this dangerous driver. Lockemup initiates his lights. The speeding car immediately reduced speed and pulled over. Upon approach to the driver's side of the vehicle, Lockemup notices that there are two passengers inside. The driver's side window is rolled about half-way down. Lockemup immediately smells a strong order of marijuana. He asks the driver where he is headed. The driver's answer does not make sense based on his location and home address. Lockemup asks the driver and occupant to step out of the vehicle. Lockemup begins searching the vehicle.

Immediately visible are some pieces of marijuana on the floor of the vehicle on the passenger side. Lockemup thinks the plastic compartment under the steering wheel looks misplaced, so he tugs on it slightly and the entire piece of plastic falls off. Inside the hidden compartment is approximately $51,000 in United States currency. Lockemup seizes the currency and marijuana pieces. Smallville has a state statute that allows for condemnation of money that is directly related to drug sales. Lockemup arrests the driver for possession of the marijuana. Lockemup calls a wrecker service to tow the vehicle consistent with the departmental policy after arrest of the vehicle's driver. Prior to the vehicle being towed, Lockemup seizes a black backpack from the trunk of the vehicle. Inside the backpack is a box of ziplock baggies, digital scales, and a ledger of names and amounts of marijuana. Which pieces of evidence were obtained properly and which were not? Discuss any exceptions that apply to each piece of evidence.

19. Investigator Lockemup is called out to a murder scene. The location is a private residence. Upon arrival, Lockemup is briefed about what is known about the murder. The suspect came home and was upset about something. The two children, who are less than six-years-old, were told by the suspect to go to their room and play. The one child said that he heard Mama and Daddy arguing and then heard a gunshot. The suspect is the person who called 911, reporting an accidental shooting and requesting an ambulance. The female was dead on the kitchen floor when paramedics and police arrive. She had a gunshot to her right temple that exited through the top of her head. The suspect told the initial officer that he was taking the gun out of his pocket and placing it on top of the refrigerator. The suspect says this is his regular storage place where the kids can't reach it. He said that he was lifting the gun up and it just went off, striking his wife in the head. The officers ran the suspect's name through the database and determined that he has a prior conviction of violence and cannot be in possession of a firearm. They arrested him for felon in possession of a firearm and have taken him to the station. Lockemup walks through the entire residence to see if there are any other adults there. He sees a dresser drawer not completely closed and decides to open the drawer to see what is inside. He sees a holster that would fit the size of gun that was fired. He also sees a box of ammunition. He collects this evidence to dispel the suspect's statement that he regularly stores the firearm on the top of the refrigerator. He also collects the shell casing from the floor in the kitchen and swabs the blood on the kitchen floor. He looks in the kitchen closet and finds a sawed-off shotgun propped in the corner. He seizes that as well and adds a count to the suspect's arrest report for possession of a sawed-off shot gun. Discuss the seizure of each piece of evidence and whether any Fourth Amendment violations occurred.

20. Bo Fluke is pulled over for driving at excessive speeds on a country road on the outskirts of Smallville. His brother Luke is in the passenger seat. The officer who pulls Bo over approaches the vehicle and asks Bo why he was driving so fast. Bo just smiles and says he didn't think they were going that fast. The officer runs Bo's name through the database and finds out that Bo has an arrest warrant outstanding for bear wrestling, which was a felony in Smallville. The officer

asked Bo to step out of the vehicle and starts patting Bo down for weapons. The driver's door is still open and the officer can see in plain view that there is a small bottle of liquor in the driver's side door pocket. It is against the law to transport liquor in the city of Smallville. The police officer seizes the bottle of liquor but does not add an additional charge. Then the officer looks over at Luke and notices a small bottle of liquor between his legs as he sits in the passenger seat. The officer gets Luke out of the vehicle and seizes the bottle of liquor that Luke possesses. The officer charges Luke with possession of alcohol in a dry county. Explain which items of evidence were properly seized and the rule that allows the seizure. If any evidence was improperly seized, explain why.

References

Fourth Amendment, US Constitution, https://constitution.congress.gov/constitution/amendment-4/
Terry v. Ohio, 392 U.S. 1 (1968), https://supreme.justia.com/cases/federal/us/392/1/
Ex parte Gardner, 329 So. 3d 64 (2020), https://casetext.com/case/ex-parte-gardner-2021
Minnesota v. Dickerson, 508 U.S. 366 (1993), https://supreme.justia.com/cases/federal/us/508/366/
Schneckloth v. Bustamonte, 412 U.S. 218 (1973), https://supreme.justia.com/cases/federal/us/412/218/
Illinois v. Rodriguez, 497 U.S. 177 (1990), https://supreme.justia.com/cases/federal/us/497/177/
Stoner v. California, 376 U.S. 483 (1964), https://supreme.justia.com/cases/federal/us/376/483/
Coolidge v. New Hampshire, 403 U.S. 443, S.Ct. 2022 (1971), https://supreme.justia.com/cases/federal/us/403/443/
Colorado v. Bannister, 449 U.S. 1 (1980), https://supreme.justia.com/cases/federal/us/449/1/
Kyllo v. United States, 121 S.Ct. 2038 (2001), https://supreme.justia.com/cases/federal/us/533/27/
United States v. Place, 462 US 696 (1983), https://supreme.justia.com/cases/federal/us/462/696/
Carroll v. United States, 267 U.S. 132 (1925), https://supreme.justia.com/cases/federal/us/267/132/
United States v. Knotts, 460 U.S. 276 (1983), https://supreme.justia.com/cases/federal/us/460/276/
Brendlin v. California, 551 U.S. 249 (2007), https://supreme.justia.com/cases/federal/us/551/249/
Rakas v. Illinois, 439 U.S. 128 (1978), https://supreme.justia.com/cases/federal/us/439/128/
California v. Acevedo, 500 U.S. 565 (1991), https://supreme.justia.com/cases/federal/us/500/565/
New Jersey v. T. L. O., 469 U.S. 325 (1985), https://supreme.justia.com/cases/federal/us/469/325/
Safford Unified Sch. Dist. #1 v. Redding, 557 U.S. 364 (2009), https://supreme.justia.com/cases/federal/us/557/364/
Colorado v. Bertine, 479 U.S. 367 (1987), https://supreme.justia.com/cases/federal/us/479/367/
Chimel v. California, 395 U.S. 752 (1969), https://supreme.justia.com/cases/federal/us/395/752/
Washington v. Chrisman, 455 U.S. 1 (1982), https://supreme.justia.com/cases/federal/us/455/1/
Buie v. Maryland, 494 US 325 (1990), https://supreme.justia.com/cases/federal/us/494/325/
Vale v. Louisiana, 399 U.S. 30 (1970), https://supreme.justia.com/cases/federal/us/399/30/
Arizona v. Gant, 556 U.S. 332 (2009), https://supreme.justia.com/cases/federal/us/556/332/
Terry, 392 U.S. 1.

Chapter 6

Self-Incrimination and Confessions

Introduction: Statements of the Accused

It is the responsibility of every law enforcement officer to build a complete file for every case investigated. An investigation isn't complete unless there is an attempt to speak with the accused. The accused have certain rights that other witnesses do not. One of those is the right to remain silent. Suspects also have the right to tell his or her side of the story. It is an important part of the process.

This chapter will discuss the constitutional implications of taking a suspect's statement.

Chapter Objectives and/or Outcomes

In this chapter students will learn:

- What a Miranda warning is and when to give it
- Restrictions placed on obtaining and using a confession
- What to consider when questioning a juvenile
- What to do when taking multiple statements from one suspect

Key Terms

Key terms and professional terminology that are used in this chapter include:

- **Due process**
- **Sixth Amendment**
- **Passive listening**
- **Miranda warning**
- **Custody**

- **Interrogation**
- **Express waiver**
- **Implicit waiver**
- **Public safety**
- **Impeachment**

The Due Process Analysis

Statements of an accused can only be offered into evidence if they were given freely and voluntarily. The ultimate test for constitutionally permissible interrogation remains the test of voluntariness. Is the confession the product of an essentially free and unconstrained choice by its maker? If it is, if he has willed to confess, it may be used against him. If it is not, if his will has been overborne and his capacity for self-determination critically impaired, the use of his confession offends **due process**. The line of distinction is that at which governing self-direction is lost and compulsion, of whatever nature or however infused, propels or helps to propel the confession.

Statements not given freely and voluntarily violate the Fifth and Fourteenth Amendments. The true test of admissibility is that a confession is made freely, voluntarily, and without compulsion or inducement of any sort.

Statements given in violation of due process will not be admitted into evidence and cannot be used for any purpose.

The court must determine, by a preponderance of the evidence, that the statement was freely and voluntarily made. The court will consider:

1. **The defendant's personal characteristics** (age, experience with the criminal justice system, education or lack thereof).

The courts have consistently looked at the individual person in making determinations of whether he or she can voluntarily waive his or her Miranda warnings. The courts look at whether the accused has a college education, a high school education, some lower grade level of education, or a mental disability. There is no one level of education or low intelligence that will render a statement involuntary alone, but rather this is a part of the totality of the circumstances approach.

The courts have also considered and discussed the accused's prior contacts with the criminal justice system. Perhaps the accused was a police officer for ten years. The courts could consider this in an analysis of whether the accused acted voluntarily in giving a statement.

The courts have also looked at whether the suspect was under the influence of any intoxicating drugs that would render him unable to give a voluntary statement.

2. **The circumstance surrounding the detention** (where and how long was the suspect detained).

Let's consider two different circumstances. First, the accused was picked up from the crime scene, driven to the police department, lead to an interrogation room, and made to wait eight hours before being questioned. Second, the accused drove himself to the police department, was led to the investigator's office by a secretary, and interviewed by an investigator immediately. The accused would have a better argument for an involuntary statement in the first circumstance.

3. **The police tactics used during the encounter** (deception, promises, threats).

There are a wide variety of examples that can fit into this category. What if the investigator interviewing the suspect tells him that there is a witness to the crime when there really isn't? The suspect confesses because he thinks he is caught. The courts have found that such police tactics are permissible. The Fifth Amendment privilege is not concerned with moral and psychological pressures to confess emanating from sources other than official coercion. Other examples include telling the suspect that his DNA was found at the crime scene or that his codefendant has confessed and implicated his involvement. It isn't as easy as it sounds to illicit a confession. Many suspects are street smart and more cunning than the law enforcement officer doing the questioning. A rookie mistake for a new law enforcement officer would be to try a bluff that the suspect knows is untrue. This would ensure that the suspect gets the upper hand in the interrogation and knows that the police were grasping at straws. For example, consider a law enforcement officer telling a suspect that a drive-by shooting was captured on video at the intersection of Street A and Street B. The law enforcement officer based this on his best guess of where the shooting occurred based on witness accounts of hearing gunshots. The suspect knows exactly where the drive-by occurred because he did it and it was two blocks over. At the point the law enforcement officer tries the bluff, the suspect knows he can stick with his "I wasn't there" story.

Contrast this scenario with an accused confessing after being told that he will get leniency if he confesses. The suspect is brought into be questioned about a drive-by shooting. In that shooting, only buildings were hit and there were no persons injured. The law enforcement officer hopes to secure a charge of shooting into an unoccupied building because there is no greater offense that could be charged. The law enforcement officer is playing with the fact that the suspect may or may not know whether he actually hit a person during the shooting. The law enforcement officer tells the suspect, "All you did was shoot into the air; you did not intend to injure anyone." "If you just admit to me that you shot the gun into the air, I can ensure that is all you are charged with, and you will get probation." This confession is almost always held to be involuntary and thus suppressed.

These three areas of analysis of the suspects' due process rights have been known as the totality of the circumstances approach. It is the approach the courts use to determine whether a suspect's due process rights were violated.

Consider now the doctor murder case file and the example below. Do any of the personal characteristics of the accused cause issues with due process?

Personal Characteristics of the Accused

Bobby's attorney files a motion to suppress his statement, alleging that the statement was given involuntarily. Bobby's attorney asks the court to consider Bobby's education, and experience with the criminal justice system. Bobby is young but has had prior involvement with the criminal justice system as a juvenile offender. He has been interviewed by police officers and attorneys since age fourteen. He dropped out of school at age sixteen and does not have a formal education. He does, however, have a street sense of how things work. He appears to be cunning and calculated in his speech. When the police put pressure on him to talk about the Smallville murder, he doesn't seem to be affected. At first, he tells them "I don't know nothing about nothing." They continue to tell him that a man is dead in Smallville, and he will be prosecuted as an accessory if he doesn't tell them the truth. After three hours of interrogation, Bobby tells them that he was the middleman in a murder for hire. He tells them that he was approached by a business partner of Victor Victim. The business partner wanted Victor Victim dead and asked Bobby to find someone to get the job done. Bobby put the word out in Sodom City and found two guys willing to do the job.

Based on these facts, will the statement made by Bobby be suppressed as involuntary? Why or why not?

Often there aren't any personal characteristics of the accused that bring forth due process analysis. Consider the totality of the circumstances in the next example. Think about the circumstances of the police detention and the police tactics used.

Circumstances of the Police Detention

Sam Snitch, who has a tenth-grade education, was arrested on suspicion of theft shortly before 11:45 p.m. on the evening of July 3. He was taken to the police station. He is a diabetic, a condition for which he was taking medication twice a day. Petitioner had last taken food and medication, before his arrest, at 4:00 p.m. He did not have medication with him at the time of the arrest. At the police station, the petitioner was interrogated from 11:45 p.m. until 1:15 a.m. He was not advised of his constitutional rights. Petitioner repeatedly denied guilt. No incriminating statements were made at this time. Sam was booked and fingerprinted and, sometime after 2:00 a.m., he was taken to a cell in the city jail. A plank fastened to the wall served as his bed. Petitioner claims he did not sleep. At 5:00 a.m., petitioner was led from the cell to a "bullpen." At 9:30 a.m. he was placed in a lineup. At 9:45 a.m., his interrogation recommenced. It was conducted by several officers at a time, in a small room. Petitioner testified that in the course of the morning, he was not offered food and that he continued to be without medication. For an hour or two he refused to answer any questions. When he did speak, it was to deny, once again, his guilt. Sometime after 11:00 a. m., petitioner was asked to write out a confession. He refused, stating that "it was against my constitutional rights" and that he was "entitled to have a lawyer." These statements were ignored. No further reference was made to an attorney by Sam Snitch or by the police officers. At about noon, Sam began a series of oral admissions culminating in a full oral confession at about 12:30 p.m. At 2:00 p.m. he was offered food. The confession was reduced to writing around 3:00 p.m. Just before the confession was reduced to writing, petitioner was advised of his constitutional rights. It was at this time he offered to give the police information about a doctor who had been murdered in Smallville. He asked if giving them information on a murder would help him get a lighter sentence on the robbery case. He was told that it might.

Would the circumstances surrounding the detention be a factor in the voluntariness of the confession? If so, do any facts stand out as important? Which ones?

The Sixth Amendment Analysis

The **Sixth Amendment** attaches to an accused when he passes a critical stage in the criminal justice process. Usually, this is the first time the suspect's case is before a court. It can also attach during an in-person lineup procedure.

The Sixth Amendment right to counsel is offense specific. Only statements related to the crime charged will be inadmissible. Statements relative to investigations that have not been charged will be admissible because the Sixth Amendment has not attached. In other words, if a defendant's Sixth

Amendment right to counsel has attached regarding one charge, he may be questioned without counsel about the unrelated charge.

Another important consideration in any analysis of the admissibility of a suspect's statement is to ask whether it was given to a law enforcement officer. It is important to remember that a person working at the direction of the police will also qualify as law enforcement for a Sixth Amendment analysis.

In *Maine v. Moulton*, the defendant made incriminating statements in a meeting with his accomplice, who had agreed to cooperate with the police. During that meeting, the accomplice, who wore a wire transmitter to record the conversation, discussed with the defendant the charges pending against him, repeatedly asked the defendant to remind him of the details of the crime, and encouraged the defendant to describe his plan for killing witnesses. The Court concluded that these investigatory techniques denied the defendant his right to counsel on the pending charges. Significantly, the Court emphasized that because of the relationship between the defendant and the informant, the informant's engaging the defendant "in active conversation about their upcoming trial was certain to elicit" incriminating statements from the defendant. Thus, the informant's participation in this conversation was the functional equivalent of interrogation."

When a suspect is questioned by someone working for the police or by an officer posing as a citizen, the right to counsel is violated if after adversarial proceedings have begun, the police question the defendant outside the presence of counsel or without a valid waiver of the right to counsel.

After Dennis Driver's arraignment for theft of Victor Victim's car, the police decide to send an undercover officer into the jail posing as a recently arrested suspect to talk to Dennis Driver. The undercover officer poses as someone arrested for assault on a police officer and tells Dennis that he hates the police. "They are always trying to control us, and I'm tired of it," said the undercover. The undercover stays in jail three days and over that time, he befriends Dennis Driver. He asks Dennis Driver why he is in jail. Dennis Driver tells the undercover that he was giving some guys a ride to a house to handle a guy they were having trouble with and they killed the guy. Dennis Driver said he only dropped them off and was not involved in the murder.

Is Dennis Driver's statement that he drove the guys to Victor Victim's house knowing the reason was to handle the guy admissible against Dennis Driver if the police upgrade his theft of property charge to murder? Is this statement admissible against him in the theft of property case for which he is in jail?

Compare Active Questioning to Passive Listening

Passive listening is different from active questioning. It is not a violation of constitutional rights to listen passively. The defendant must demonstrate that the police and their informant took some action, beyond merely listening, that was designed deliberately to elicit incriminating remarks. Such statements are considered spontaneous statements of the accused. Spontaneous statements are almost always admissible.

Since the Sixth Amendment safeguards do not apply to passive listening, it is important to note that passive listening can be done with a device. Often individuals who have been arrested for a crime and their Sixth Amendment rights have attached remain incarcerated until their trial. These individuals may have in-person visitors or telephone calls with friends and family members during this time. Detention facilities usually record conversations that occur between family members and friends with the accused. If the accused makes incriminating statements to these family members or friends, they are admissible as spontaneous statements.

The most prevalent place passive listening occurs is on social media. The majority of Americans have a digital footprint, which included some type of social media account. Criminals are no different. These individuals are accustomed to posting their daily lives on social media for everyone to see. You may think that people are not that ignorant as to post something relating to a crime, but you would be surprised. Criminals have peer groups whom they want to impress and can be impulsive. These people are also not selective about setting the social media accounts to a private setting. Even if the social media page can only be accessed by so called "friends," they are not selective about who they allow in as "friends."

Police departments routinely create and rotate fake social media accounts. They make friend requests regularly to the usual suspects of criminal activity. This allows them to "passively listen" to many different people. Criminals will post themselves flashing guns and money or driving a stolen car. This is great evidence against them in court. It is also great for preparation for suspect interviews.

> An undercover officer is placed in the jail cell intentionally with Dennis Driver. Dennis Driver initiates the conversation with the undercover and discloses that he knew they were driving to Victor Victim's house with the intention of murder and theft of his vehicle. The undercover does not ask any questions about the crimes but merely listens to Dennis Driver's recount of events.
>
> Are the statements Dennis Driver made admissible in the theft of property case? Are the statements Dennis Driver made admissible in a potential accessory to murder charge?

Some things that are important to remember about a Sixth Amendment analysis is that it is offense specific, and it does not matter whether the suspect thought he or she was speaking with a law enforcement officer. This is easy to remember when you consider the purpose of the rule. It is to deter police from questioning a suspect, without his /or her counsel present after adversarial proceedings have initiated. It is not about the feelings of the accused.

The Fifth Amendment Analysis

The Miranda Court formulated a warning that must be given to suspects before they can be subjected to custodial interrogation. The substance of the warning must be given to suspects even today. A suspect in custody must be advised as follows: He must be warned prior to any questioning that he has the right to remain silent; that anything he says can be used against him in a court of law; that he has the right to the presence of an attorney; and that if he cannot afford an attorney, one will be appointed for him prior to any questioning if he so desires.

Miranda warnings are necessary:

1. When a suspect is in custody
2. When a suspect is being questioned (or the functional equivalent)
3. By law enforcement

Let's explore each of these below.

1. What Is Custody?

A person is in **custody** if his freedom of movement has been restricted by the police. The test depends on the objective circumstances of the interrogation and not on the subjective views of the person being questioned. A person will be found to be in custody if a reasonable person under the circumstances would have not felt free to leave.

Relevant factors to consider in an analysis of custody are:

- Location and ability of suspect to leave
- Number of officers, uniform, firearms, and showings of authority
- Language and tone used
- Promises, inducements, or threats

Location and Ability of Suspect to Leave

Many interviews are conducted in the field, so there is no time for planning. If this occurs, it is important for the officer to record the interview as close to verbatim as possible. If the officer is wearing a body camera or has a recording device, this is simple. If the officer doesn't, it is important to use quotes when possible when recording by hand what the suspect said at the scene of the crime.

If time permits, it is always better to set the stage for an interview with a suspect. The officer should review reports and interview as many witnesses as possible to gain a full understanding of the crime before interviewing the suspect. The suspect should be interviewed separately and in private.

Whether the interview is at the scene or at a remote location, the officer should consider whether a reasonable person would feel free to leave given the circumstances. Merely removing hand restraints may not free the suspect from "custody" in the eyes of a court reviewing the case down the road.

Consider the location and the ability of the suspect to leave in the example below.

Investigator Lockemup drives to Sodom City to find Dennis Driver for a theft of property charge. Lockemup locates Dennis hanging out at a service station. Lockemup is in an unmarked undercover police car and is wearing a shirt and tie. He has a badge clipped to his belt along with his service weapon; he is approximately fifty years old, six feet tall, and 230 pounds. Another investigator is also with him, Investigator Patience. Patience is slightly shorter and heavier than Lockemup. He also wears a shirt and tie, a badge clipped to his belt, and service weapon visible. They both exit the vehicle and walk toward Dennis Driver. They walk with authority and use a straightforward tone when telling Dennis Driver that he needs to come with them to give a statement. They drive Dennis Driver back to Smallville. It takes about an hour and Dennis Driver asks a few times where they are going and why. He is told that he needs to be thinking about his future and whether he plans to be honest with them when they get to the police department for an interview. In Smallville, they enter the police department and walk to an interview room at the back of the building. Dennis Driver is not restrained in any way. After Dennis Driver takes a seat, the investigators leave the room. They return ten minutes later and offer Dennis Driver a drink. They begin asking him questions about Victor Victim's murder.

Is Miranda required before the interview?

Number of Officers, Uniform, Firearms, and Showings of Authority

Remember that our standard of whether a person is in custody is measured by the reasonable person standard, not what the actual suspect felt at the time. This may not seem fair, but it is the Court's solution to an even application of the law. The easiest way to think about this portion of the analysis is on a sliding-scale spectrum. At one end of the spectrum, you have a suspect who is interviewed by one plain-clothes officer who doesn't have a weapon visible. On the other end of the spectrum, you have a suspect who is surrounded by the biggest, baddest uniformed officers who are stacked with duty belts full of weapons. A person who is speaking one on one with the plain-clothes officer would reasonably feel free to leave at any time and conclude the interview. On the other hand, the person who was surrounded by large, weapons-yielding officers may feel like he or she is in custody.

Language and Tone Used

Often officers will attempt to develop a rapport with a suspect before formal questioning. This is arguably the most critical factor in any interview. The rapport is an understanding between the suspect and officer that will set the undertone for the interview. This can be created by the use of language and tone of speech between the two. Suspects with longer criminal histories will often try to set this rapport with the officer before the officer has a chance to do the same. An analysis of the language and tone can be done on a sliding spectrum also. On one side of that spectrum, you have an officer who is making casual conservation, making jokes, and speaking in a friendly tone to the suspect. On the other side of the spectrum, you have an officer who is demanding, bullying, and using profanity with the suspect. Keeping in mind that it is still a totality of the circumstances analysis, consider the example below.

> Terry has a long criminal history and has been to prison on multiple occasions. He is a suspect in a drive-by shooting where a rival gang member has been shot. He has been secured in an interview room and an officer is attempting to interview him. When the officer enters the room and introduces himself, Terry does not acknowledge the officer. The officer tells Terry that he would like to hear his side of what happened. Terry uses profanity toward the officer and indicates he doesn't have anything to say. The officer replies in kind, using profanity and street slang in the conversation with Terry. The officer says things like "you know how this works" and "we don't have to do this the hard way," as well as several profane words.

Promises, Inducements, or Threats

A promise is a declaration that something will occur. An inducement is leading or moving by persuasion or influence as to some action. A threat is a declaration of an intention to inflict punishment or injury conditionally on some action or statement. A law enforcement officer cannot promise a suspect any benefit in return for a statement or action. A law enforcement officer cannot threaten the suspect or induce him or her to make a statement. If any of these things occur, the statement will be suppressed and not allowed in court.

2. What is Interrogation?

A suspect's statement is only subject to Miranda if it is given in response to questioning by the police or the functional equivalent. Direct questioning is self-explanatory and is exactly what is commonly known an **interrogation**. There is very little interpretation by the courts as to what direct questioning is. Most of the case law surrounds the area of the functional equivalent to questioning. This is an area that has been addressed by the US Supreme Court many times. The functional equivalent of questioning could not be questioning at all; rather, it could be speaking to another officer in the suspect's presence to purposely elicit a response by the suspect. When the suspect makes a spontaneous statement in response, it must be examined. Spontaneous statements not made in response to any questioning by police are not subject to Miranda protections. However, if the spontaneous statement was made because the police intentionally made remarks or did other actions that would reasonably elicit a response, it is the functional equivalent of questioning.

One of the most cited cases regarding the police not questioning a suspect yet the suspect's statement being suppressed because it is the functional equivalent of questioning is the Christian burial speech case. This case is *Brewer v. Williams*. Williams was arrested for the abduction of a missing girl. His attorney advised him that police officers would be transporting him to another city, that the officers would not interrogate him, and that he should not talk to the officers until consulting with the attorney. After William's arraignment, another attorney similarly advised Williams. The officers gave Williams Miranda warnings. During the trip, Williams expressed no willingness to be interrogated. In the car, one officer discussed how expected snow might make recovery of the body and a Christian burial impossible, and that Williams was the only one who knew where the body was. Williams eventually led the officers to the body. The Court held that Williams was entitled to a new trial because he was deprived of the Sixth Amendment right to assistance of counsel, as judicial proceedings had been initiated against him before the start of the car ride, and the officer deliberately set out to elicit information from him when he was entitled to the assistance of counsel. Williams did not waive his right to counsel because he consistently relied upon the advice of counsel in dealing with the authorities.

3. Law Enforcement

Miranda relates to custodial interrogation by law enforcement. It was born of a police-dominated atmosphere. If the person is not a law enforcement officer or acting at the direction of law enforcement, Miranda is not triggered. If a school principal questions a student about a crime that occurred on campus, there is no requirement that the student be Mirandized before the statement is admissible. This is easily understood when you look back to the purpose of the rule: to deter improper police conduct. The purpose is not to deter citizens from demanding answers to questions.

The analysis would be the same of a homeowner who catches a thief on his property. The homeowner holds the thief at gunpoint and asks, "Why do you keep stealing from me?" This is clearly custody because a thief would not feel free to leave if he were being held at gunpoint. This would also be an interrogation because a direct question designed to elicit a response is being asked. However, there is no requirement for Miranda warnings because it is not law enforcement doing the detention or questioning.

Consider this change in facts. The homeowner has had his property broken into several times in the past and has made several police reports. However, the police were never able to determine who was doing the break-ins. The police officer tells the homeowner, "If you ever catch the person breaking in and can get them to confess to the prior break-ins, we can charge him. But if I have to do a formal interview, I will need to Mirandize him and he probably won't confess." In this case, an argument could be made that the homeowner is acting at the direction of the police when he takes the thief into custody and interrogates him. If this is true, then the statement would be inadmissible. This is also in keeping with the purpose of the rule, deterring bad police conduct.

Miranda's Origin

Miranda v. Arizona was a 1963 case in which Ernesto Miranda was charged with kidnapping and rape. Upon his arrest, he was questioned by police officers. After several hours, he confessed. His confession was reduced to writing on a form that indicated that Miranda understood that his confession would be used against him in court. The form also stated that the confession was given voluntarily and not coerced. There was never mention of Miranda's right to have an attorney. Miranda was described as severely mentally ill and English was not his first language. He was eighteen years old at the time of the statement.

The confession was used against Miranda at trial and he was convicted. His attorneys appealed, stating that he should have been told of his right to have an attorney present, and because he was not, his confession should be suppressed. The US Supreme Court agreed and suppressed the statement.

Ernesto Miranda was retried, without the use of the confession and still convicted. He was sentenced to twenty to thirty years. After his release from prison, Miranda ended up in the state of Texas. There he got in a fight, was stabbed, and died from resulting injuries. The man who stabbed him exercised his Miranda rights, refused to give a statement, and was released.

Miranda rights are not constitutional rights. They dance around the Fifth Amendment right to silence and the Sixth Amendment right to counsel, but Miranda is not constitutional in and of itself. Despite this, in practice, many law enforcement officers, attorneys, and judges talk about the constitutional violation of someone's Miranda rights.

Waiving Miranda

Even absent the accused invocation of the right to remain silent, the accused's statement during a custodial interrogation is inadmissible at trial unless the prosecution can establish that the accused in fact knowingly and voluntarily waived Miranda rights when making the statement. The waiver inquiry has two distinct dimensions: (a) the waiver must be voluntary in the sense that it was the product of a free and deliberate choice rather than intimidation, coercion, or deception, and (b) it was made with a full awareness of both the nature of the right being abandoned and the consequences of the decision to abandon it. Some language in Miranda could be read to indicate that waivers are difficult to establish absent an explicit written waiver or a formal, express oral statement. Miranda said a valid waiver will not be presumed simply from the silence of the accused after warnings are given or simply from the fact that a confession was in fact eventually obtained. In addition, the Miranda Court stated that a heavy burden rests on the government to demonstrate that the defendant knowingly and intelligently waived his privilege against self-incrimination and his right to retained or appointed counsel.

The suspect may make either an express waiver of Miranda or an implicit waiver of Miranda.

Express Waiver

An **express waiver** of Miranda is exactly what the name implies. It is when the suspect is directly asked if he or she wishes to waive his or her Miranda rights and an acknowledgment is made. This acknowledgment can be verbal, nonverbal (a head shake), or in writing. An express waiver is always the least complicated means by which to show the constitutional rights were waived.

> Investigator Lockemup sits down with Bobby to take a statement. Lockemup Mirandized Bobby by reading the Miranda rights from a form and then allowing Bobby to review the same form. Lockemup discussed with Bobby his ability to read and write. After going over the form, Bobby tells Lockemup that he will talk and wants to tell his side of the story but is not signing any forms. Lockemup notes on the form that "suspect wishes to verbally waive his Miranda rights."
>
> Is the statement that Bobby made an express waiver?

Implicit Waiver

The prosecution does not need to show that a waiver of Miranda rights was express. An **implicit waiver** of the right to remain silent is sufficient to admit a suspect's statement into evidence. A waiver of Miranda rights may be implied through the defendant's silence, coupled with an understanding of his rights and a course of conduct indicating waiver.

If the state establishes that a Miranda warning was given and the accused made an uncoerced statement, this showing, standing alone, is insufficient to demonstrate a valid waiver of Miranda rights. The prosecution must make the additional showing that the accused understood these rights. Where the prosecution shows that a Miranda warning was given and that it was understood by the accused, an accused's uncoerced statement establishes an implied waiver of the right to remain silent.

> Investigator Lockemup sits across the table from Bobby in the interview room. Lockemup starts making small talk with Bobby and then recites from memory the Miranda warnings. Lockemup tells Bobby, "I've looked at your arrest history and I'm sure you have been told these rights many times before." Bobby chuckles and nods his head. Lockemup says, "You probably can recite these better than I can." Bobby says, "Yeah." Then the two engage in more small talk. They eventually get to the topic of the murder for hire and Bobby tells the entire story.
>
> Is this an implicit waiver of the Miranda warnings? Why or why not?

Invoking Miranda

In the context of invoking Miranda rights to counsel, a suspect must do so unambiguously. If an accused makes a statement concerning the right to counsel that is ambiguous or equivocal or makes no statement, the police are not required to end the interrogation or ask questions to clarify whether the accused wants to invoke his or her Miranda right.

Even absent the accused's invocation of the right to remain silent, the accused's statement during a custodial interrogation is inadmissible at trial unless the prosecution can establish that the accused in fact knowingly and voluntarily waived Miranda rights when making the statement. The waiver inquiry has two distinct dimensions: (a) the waiver must be voluntary in the sense that it was the product of a free and deliberate choice rather than intimidation, coercion, or deception, and (b) it was made with a full awareness of both the nature of the right being abandoned and the consequences of the decision to abandon it. Some language in Miranda could be read to indicate that waivers are difficult to establish absent an explicit written waiver or a formal, express oral statement. A valid waiver will not be presumed simply from the silence of the accused after warnings are given or simply from the fact that a confession was in fact eventually obtained. In addition, the Miranda Court said that a heavy burden rests on the government to demonstrate that the defendant knowingly and intelligently waived his privilege against self-incrimination and his right to retained or appointed counsel.

Once the suspect has invoked Miranda, the interrogation must immediately stop. For example, when Investigator Lockemup is talking to Trina, she seems distant and not forthcoming with information. Lockemup presses her, and she gets frustrated with his accusing nature. Trina tells him that he needs to talk with her attorney if he wants any further information. Lockemup leaves but returns the following day. He finds Trina sitting outside on her porch. She has a bottle of wine and it is half gone. She is crying and he asks her what is wrong. She tells Lockemup that maybe she did lead Manny Maintenance on and give him the wrong impression of their relationship. She tells Lockemup that she often complained to Manny about her relationship with her husband. She did not feel that her husband treated her fairly, and he was verbally abusive. When she told Manny this, he said, "I can take care of him for you." She responded, "That would be nice." She is now worried that Manny could have taken that statement as her asking him to kill her husband. Lockemup is secretly recording this conversation. If Trina is later arrested for solicitation of murder for hire, her statement would not be admissible because just the day before, she invoked her right to speak with an attorney. Although Lockemup did not read her the Miranda rights, she can still invoke them. He cannot reinitiate a conversation with her after she has invoked those rights. There are exceptions when much time has passed, but one day is certainly not enough time.

The request for an attorney must be clear and unambiguous. If an accused makes a statement concerning the right to counsel that is ambiguous or equivocal or makes no statement, the police are not required to end the interrogation or ask questions to clarify whether the accused wants to invoke his or her rights. For example, Investigator Lockemup wants to take a statement from Manny Maintenance. He sits down with Manny and reads the Miranda rights to Manny. Manny's reply, "Maybe I should talk to a lawyer," is not unambiguous.

The suspect has to be the one invoking Miranda. Oftentimes, the police will try to make contact with a suspect and interact with family members in the process. A suspect's friends and family cannot invoke Miranda; only a suspect can invoke Miranda. For example, when Investigator Lockemup was talking with Trina, he asked to speak with her son. Trina made it clear that she did not want her son involved in the case or to give a statement to the police. This was ambiguous at best and probably could not be argued to invoke the right to an attorney, especially without the rights having been read to her. However, even if Lockemup had read her the Miranda rights, she cannot invoke them for her son. Only the person giving (or not giving) the statement can invoke the rights.

One issue that is worthy of note when discussing Miranda is the verbiage of the parties. If a law enforcement officer reads the Miranda rights to a suspect, there are several ways the waiver could be asked. The law enforcement officer could ask, having these rights in mind, "Do you wish to talk with me?" If the suspect says no, it is over. Contrast a suspect saying, "I don't need no lawyer, but I don't want to talk right now." This would not be an invocation of the rights. This would leave it open for the investigator to come back the next day and initiate a conversation without a Miranda violation.

Subsequent Statements and Rewarnings

Timing of Miranda

The length of time that elapses between the commission of a crime and a police interview that takes place when a person voluntarily comes to the police station has no relevance in determining whether a Miranda warning is required. There is no prejudice to a suspect for a lengthy investigation. The fact that a person who voluntarily engages in an interview with police is unaware of the consequences of his participation does not transform the voluntary interview into a custodial one so as to require Miranda warnings.

Midstream Miranda

Midstream Miranda can occur for a number of reasons. It is important to examine the intent of the officer and the police department practice behind the occurrence.

Midstream Miranda can be an oversight. Often, suspects are taken into custody in the heat of the moment, just after a crime has occurred. The emotions and heart rate could be elevated after a chase and capture, and an unexperienced officer could simply forget about Miranda. For example, a police officer performs a random traffic stop. The officer approaches the vehicle and asks for identification. The suspect pretends to be retrieving identification and instead runs from the traffic stop. A chase ensues, and the suspect is apprehended by the officer some hundred yards away. The officer is out of breath and frustrated that the traffic stop did not go as usual. The officer asks the defendant, "Why did you run?" The suspect replies, "Because I have dope in my pocket." The officer sits the defendant in the back the patrol car, calls in the arrest to dispatch, and wipes sweat from his brow. He opens the back door of the patrol car and reads the suspect his Miranda warnings. The suspect agrees to talk to the officer. The officer asks the suspect again why he ran. The suspect gives the same reply. This statement is offered into evidence against the suspect at his trial.

There are two admissions in this example, and it is important to examine them separately. The first admission is when the defendant is in custody, interrogated, and not apprised of his Miranda rights. The second admission is when the defendant is in custody, interrogated, and given his Miranda rights. Brief interrogation at the onset of an investigation could be acceptable without Miranda, as happened in this example. The suspect could have run for many reasons, and the officer needs to know why the suspect ran. The second admission was done properly and would only be suppressed if it were tainted by the first statement. The law enforcement officer's right to request information while discharging his law enforcement duties will hinge on the manner and intensity of the interference, the gravity of the crime involved, and the circumstances attending the encounter. In this example, the officer only knows that the defendant has committed a traffic infraction and the question "Why did you run?" could be accepted by the court as a traffic encounter.

Subsequent Miranda

Let us compare and contrast a scenario when a statement is given without Miranda, and then the suspect is Mirandized and gives a statement. This is sometimes known as the "cat out of the bag" analysis. The courts generally frown on this practice because the idea is that if the suspect is questioned without Miranda and then gives a statement against his own interest, then he or she is more likely to give the same statement again after Miranda. In that case, it is hard to know if the suspect gave the statement because he or she understood and voluntarily waived Miranda or because he or she figured "the cat was out of the bag" so he or she may as well give the statement.

A police officer performs a random traffic stop. The officer approaches the vehicle and asks for identification. The suspect pretends to be retrieving identification and instead runs from the traffic stop. A chase ensues, and the suspect is apprehended by the officer some hundred yards away. The officer is out of breath and frustrated that the traffic stop did not go as usual. The officer asks the defendant, "Why did you run?" The suspect replies, "Because I have dope in my pocket." The dope is retrieved from the suspect's pocket and the officer books the suspect in for possession of a controlled substance. The next day, the case is assigned to an investigator. The investigator travels to the city jail and attempts to take a statement from the suspect. The investigator reads the defendant his Miranda rights and interrogates him about the cocaine found in his pocket. The suspect makes a full confession. The prosecution intends to offer the confession given to the investigator.

Again, it is important to analyze both statements. The first statement has the same analysis as above. The second statement to the investigator was while in custody and subject to interrogation, and the suspect was given his Miranda rights. That statement would be admissible unless it was tainted by the first statement to the officer on the scene.

Let's look at another example to further understand the point of subsequent Miranda warnings.

A police officer performs a random traffic stop. The officer approaches the vehicle and asks for identification. The suspect pretends to be retrieving identification and instead runs from the traffic stop. A chase ensues, and the suspect is apprehended by the officer some hundred yards away. The officer is out of breath and frustrated that the traffic stop did not go as usual. He cuffs the suspect and walks him back to the patrol car. On the walk, he asks the defendant, "Why did you run?" The suspect replies, "Because I have dope in my pocket." The dope is retrieved from the suspect's pocket and the officer books the suspect in for possession of a controlled substance. The next day, the case is assigned to an investigator. The investigator travels to the city jail and attempts to take a statement from the suspect. The investigator asks the suspect about the encounter the evening before and tells him that he has reviewed the body camera footage and knows that he confessed to the possession of dope. The investigator asks the suspect a series of questions about the dope and then tells him that he needs to now take a "formal statement." The investigator reads the defendant his Miranda rights and interrogates the suspect about the cocaine found in his pocket. The investigator records the interview and reduces it to writing for the suspect to sign. The suspect makes a full confession. The prosecution intends to offer the recorded statement in the trial of the suspect.

The same analysis applies to the first statement given to the officer at the scene of the traffic stop. We must examine the second statement closely. In the second statement, the investigator clearly knows that he is going to the jail to take a statement from the suspect. He knows that the suspect is in custody and that he will be questioning him while in custody. The investigator interrogates the suspect first without informing him of his Miranda rights. This is a clear violation of the suspect's rights. The fact that the investigator later informs the suspect of his rights does not save the tainted confession.

This reveals a police strategy adopted to undermine Miranda. This police practice was a common way to circumvent the Miranda Court's ruling and was termed the "cat out of the bag" theory. The police believed that if they could get a confession without warning the suspect of his or her Miranda rights. Then, they could reinterview the suspect and properly Mirandize him or her and have a clean admissible confession. The courts refused to agree.

In *Oregon v. Elstad*, the Oregon court identified a subtle form of lingering compulsion, the psychological impact of the suspect's conviction that he has let the cat out of the bag and, in so doing, has sealed his own fate. After an accused has once let the cat out of the bag by confessing, no matter what the inducement, he is never thereafter free of the psychological and practical disadvantages of having confessed. He can never get the cat back in the bag. The secret is out for good. In such a sense, a later confession may always be looked upon as fruit of the first. "But this Court has never gone so far as to hold that making a confession under circumstances which preclude its use, perpetually disables the confessor from making a usable one after those conditions have been removed."

A series of relevant facts bear on whether Miranda warnings delivered midstream could be effective enough to accomplish their objective: the completeness and detail of the questions and answers in the first round of interrogation, the overlapping content of the two statements, the timing and setting of the first and the second, the continuity of police personnel, and the degree to which the interrogator's questions treated the second round as continuous with the first.

Rewarnings

A suspect can be Mirandized multiple times. The number of Miranda warnings that a suspect receives has no constitutional merit for or against the admissibility of a statement. The questions arise in assessing why the suspect was re-Mirandized.

It is important to examine what the circumstances were surrounding the re-Mirandization of a suspect. Analysis could include whether the Miranda warnings came from the same officer or different officers; whether the Miranda warnings came from the same officers within one agency or different agencies; whether the defendant waived his or her rights in the first instance or invoked his or her rights to an attorney in the first instance; whether the interrogations involved the same crime, related crimes, or unrelated crimes; and what the time frame was between the first and subsequent Miranda warnings.

For example, Defendant was arrested in connection with the investigation of robberies. After being advised of his rights, Defendant stated that he did not want to talk about the robberies. Defendant was thereafter questioned at another police station about a homicide and confessed to the murder. The Court found that the subsequent confession was proper. The stated "the right to remain silent" encompassed within the Miranda rights was not a right to permanently remain silent but was a right that had to be scrupulously honored by the police. The Court concluded that when the questioning was for different crimes, by a different police officer, in a different station, after an extended period without questioning, the request to remain silent had been scrupulously honored.

Exceptions

Most rules have exceptions and Miranda is no different. The US Supreme Court has given us exceptions to the rule requiring suspects to be Mirandized when in custody and questioned. Those exceptions are for public safety, for use when impeaching witnesses, and for simple traffic encounters.

Public Safety

When the police officers ask questions reasonably prompted by concern for **public safety**, the suspect's response need not be suppressed in court, even though the suspect was in police custody when the statements were made and the facts come within the purview of Miranda. The public safety exception should not be judged by the subjective thoughts of the officer present but rather by an objective standard—whether a reasonable officer under the circumstances would think there was a public danger.

For example, in *New York v. Quarles*, a police officer pursued Quarles into a supermarket after a woman identified him as the man who raped her. The officer frisked the respondent and discovered that he was wearing an empty shoulder holster. After handcuffing Quarles, the officer asked him where the gun was. Quarles said, "The gun is over there." After the officer retrieved the loaded gun, he placed Quarles under arrest and read him his Miranda rights. The Supreme Court held that there was a "public safety" exception to the requirement that Miranda warnings be given before a suspect's answers could be admitted into evidence, and that the availability of that exception did not depend upon the motivation of the individual officers involved.

This reasonableness exception to the Miranda requirements could not apply if Miranda were constitutional. Since Miranda is a US Supreme Court decision, the Court can use reasonableness in its application.

Impeachment

If a statement is given in violation of the requirements set out in *Miranda v. Arizona*, the statement may be admissible for **impeachment** of the defendant at trial. The statement, however, must be voluntarily given. This means that even if the police officers neglected to Mirandize the defendant, if he takes the witness stand in his defense, the prosecution will be able to use his prior statement against him, if he deviates from it. The exception to this is if the defendant's statement was taken involuntarily. For example, if promises, threats, or inducements were made to the defendant to get him or her to give a statement, the statement cannot be used for any purpose.

Traffic Encounters

Under the Fourth Amendment, a police officer who lacks probable cause but whose "observations lead him reasonably to suspect" that a particular person has committed, is committing, or is about to commit a crime, may detain that person briefly in order to "investigate the circumstances that provoke suspicion." The stop and inquiry must be "reasonably related in scope to the justification for their initiation." Typically, this means that the officer may ask the detainee a moderate number of questions to determine his identity and to try to obtain information confirming or dispelling the officer's suspicions. But the detainee is not obliged to respond. And, unless the detainee's answers provide the officer with probable cause to arrest him, he must then be released. The comparatively nonthreatening character of detentions of this sort explains the absence of any suggestion that Terry stops are subject to the dictates of Miranda. The similarly noncoercive aspect of ordinary traffic stops prompts the conclusion that persons temporarily detained pursuant to such stops are not "in custody" for the purposes of Miranda.

Either a rule that Miranda applies to all traffic stops or a rule that a suspect need not be advised of his rights until he is formally placed under arrest would provide a clearer, more easily administered line. However, each of these two alternatives has drawbacks that make them unacceptable. The first would substantially impede the enforcement of the nation's traffic laws by compelling the police either to take the time to warn all detained motorists of their constitutional rights or to forgo use of self-incriminating statements made by those motorists—while doing little to protect citizens' Fifth Amendment rights. The second would enable the police to circumvent the constraints on custodial interrogations established by Miranda.

In *Pennsylvania v. Bruder*, when a Pennsylvania local police officer observed a motorist driving erratically and ignoring a red light, the officer stopped the motorist's vehicle. After smelling alcohol and observing the motorist's stumbling movements, the officer administered field sobriety tests, including asking the motorist to recite the alphabet, and inquired about alcohol. The motorist failed the sobriety tests, whereupon the officer arrested the motorist, placed the motorist in a police car, and gave the motorist Miranda warnings. Later, at a Pennsylvania trial in which the motorist's statements and conduct prior to arrest were admitted into evidence, the motorist was convicted of driving under the influence of alcohol. On appeal, the issue was on the ground that certain of the motorist's statements prior to arrest had been elicited through custodial interrogation and should have been suppressed for lack of Miranda warnings The US Supreme Court followed its prior ruling in *Berkemer v. McCarty* that ordinary traffic stops do not involve custody for purposes of the requirement to give Miranda warnings before beginning custodial interrogation. A single police officer asking the motorist a modest number of questions and requesting the motorist to perform a simple balancing test at a location visible to passing motorists is not custodial as required by Miranda.

For example, a police officer pulls over Dennis Driver, who is on the way home after dropping off Melvin and Andy at Victor Victim's house, for an expired registration tag. The officer asks Dennis Drive for his driver's license and proof of insurance. Dennis Driver cannot produce proof of insurance and the officer calls in Dennis Driver's name to check for outstanding warrants. While waiting for the dispatcher to advise about the warrants, he asks Dennis Driver where he was coming from. Dennis admits that he was in Smallville but says he was there visiting a friend. Later in his trial for aiding and abetting the theft of the vehicle, the state wants to use this statement admitting he was in Smallville. The statement will likely be admitted.

Minors and Miranda

By its very nature, custodial police interrogation entails "inherently compelling pressures." Recognizing that the inherently coercive nature of custodial interrogation blurs the line between voluntary and involuntary statements, the Supreme Court in Miranda adopted a set of prophylactic measures designed to safeguard the constitutional guarantee against self-incrimination. Prior to questioning, a suspect must be warned that he has a right to remain silent, that any statement he does make may be used as evidence against him, and that he has a right to the presence of an attorney, either retained or appointed. The four warnings Miranda requires are invariable, but the Supreme Court has not dictated the words in which the essential information must be conveyed. And, if a suspect makes a statement during custodial interrogation, the burden is on the government to show, as a "prerequisite" to the statement's admissibility as evidence in the government's case in chief, that the defendant "voluntarily, knowingly and intelligently" waived his rights.

No matter how sophisticated, a juvenile suspect of police interrogation cannot be compared to an adult subject.

In *J. D. B. v. North Carolina*, a uniformed police officer removed the thirteen-year-old seventh-grade student from his classroom and escorted him to a closed-door conference room, where he was questioned by police for at least half an hour regarding home break-ins. Prior to the commencement of questioning, the student was not given Miranda warnings. The student confessed. In denying the student's motion to suppress, the state courts found that he was not in custody when he confessed, declining to extend the test for custody to include consideration of the age of an individual subjected to questioning by police. The Supreme Court determined that remand was warranted because a child's age properly informed the Miranda custody analysis since, inter alia, (1) a reasonable child subjected to police questioning will sometimes feel pressured to submit when a reasonable adult would feel free to go, and courts can account for that reality without doing any damage to the objective nature of the custody analysis, and (2) a child's age differed from other personal characteristics that, even when known to police, have no objectively discernible relationship to a reasonable person's understanding of his freedom of action.

The Court reversed the judgment of the North Carolina Supreme Court and remanded for a determination whether the student was in custody under the proper analysis (5–4 decision, 1 dissent).

So long as the child's age was known to the officer at the time of police questioning, or would have been objectively apparent to a reasonable officer, its inclusion in the custody analysis is consistent with the objective nature of that test. This is not to say that a child's age will be a determinative, or even a significant, factor in every case. It is, however, a reality that courts cannot simply ignore.

Juvenile Miranda

A distinction needs to be made between a minor and a juvenile. The US Supreme Court has addressed Miranda as it relates to minors in *J. D. B. v. North Carolina*. States are free to set the age of minors within their states. This age usually varies between eighteen or nineteen years old. The word juvenile denotes a category of person according to state statute. States have varying legislative codes as relate to juvenile offenders. In some states, the juvenile code requires that if the suspect is a minor and will be charged as a juvenile, then the "juvenile Miranda warnings" must be waived by the suspect for the statement to be admissible. This often includes the same four rights that are stated in *Miranda v. Arizona* and adds one additional right, the right to have a parent or guardian present during questioning.

Statements to Parole and Probation Officers

The general obligation to appear before a probation officer and answer questions truthfully does not in itself convert a defendant's otherwise voluntary statements into compelled ones.

As in a Fourth Amendment analysis, we see that a suspect on parole or probation is separately considered in a constitutional analysis. When a person is on probation, he or she is subject to being called in at any time for questioning or drug testing. This is mandatory; otherwise, the probationer could lose freedoms. Some argue that this is akin to custody and any statement made by the probationer needs to be subject to Miranda. However, the courts have refused to make this finding.

> Manny Maintenance is called in by his probation officer to answer questions about the murder of Victor Victim. He confirms that he is having a relationship with Victor's wife but denies any involvement in the murder. He also denies knowing Melvin, Andy, or Dennis. The state wants to admit this statement because his admission of an affair will set up the motive for the murder.
>
> Will this statement be admissible?

Practical Application

Ideally, investigators trained in conducting interviews should do most of the questioning, but on-scene statements are important too.

The Balancing Act:

- Erring on the side of getting the statement
- Erring on the side of giving Miranda

It is always important to get the suspect's side of the story. Knowing the defense helps investigators direct the investigation. For example, if the defense is self-defense, the investigators will question the witnesses closer about what the parties were doing just before the crime. In contrast, if the defense is that the suspect wasn't there and did not commit the crime, then the questions may center around identification

Often, the most truthful statement is the one that is made before there is time to concoct a lie. If the immediate statement is a lie, it is one made in haste and will fall apart. Patrol officers and first responders are in the best position to record these initial statements. These statements can be recorded on body cameras or noted with pen and pad. They are usually in response to a question posed by a law enforcement officer or third party on the crime scene. However, suspects can make spontaneous statements just after the crime has been committed, as in the following example.

Officers responded to a shots fired call. When they arrived, they find a female standing outside of a residence with three small children in the yard. She is hysterical and tells the responding officer that her friend is shot and inside the house. The officer asks her, "Who shot your friend?" The female responds, "I don't know." After everyone is interviewed, including the children, it is determined that the two females were in a relationship, and after an argument, the female standing outside shot the deceased female inside. This now makes the initial statement critical to the investigation because it is a lie.

Recording Interviews and Having Multiple Witnesses in Interviews

If a statement of an accused is offered into evidence, it must be proven, the same as every other piece of evidence presented. This proof is usually in the form of sworn testimony from the person hearing the statement. In the years before technological advances, this was the only way that a statement was offered. However, with the use of modern technology, these statements are often recorded.

There are several advantages to recording a statement. First, a recorded statement speaks for itself. There is no room for interpretation by the hearer of what was said by the speaker. This can be important when details of the crime are at issue. For example, a suspect is being interviewed for a statutory rape case wherein the age difference of the parties makes it illegal to have sexual intercourse. The police officer testifies at the trial that the defendant denied having sexual intercourse with the victim. The defendant's DNA was found inside the vagina of the victim. This would appear that he lied to the investigator. However, the defendant testifies that when the investigator asked him if he slept with the victim, he denied doing so because he left the bedroom after they had sex. The defendant testifies that the investigator never asked if he had sexual intercourse with the victim. If this statement were recorded, there would be no dispute.

Another advantage to a recorded statement is that you hear the voice inflections of the parties. Often, after a suspect gives a confession to the police, he later regrets giving that statement and wants to take it back. The suspect may say that he was coerced or intimidated into giving the statement. If the statement isn't recorded, the jury can weigh the testimony of the police officer against the testimony of the defendant about what went on during the interview. Historically, this was always weighed in favor of the police officer. However, in some communities there is a growing distrust of police, and the police officer's testimony may not be believed without a recording.

This leads to the third reason that not only is a recording is preferred, it is expected. Recording devices are readily available and economical for departments to issue to their officers. Many investigators may also purchase their preferred devices with their personal funds to be more helpful to their individual cases. Also, with so many television shows and movies portraying police recordings being taken, juries expect to hear the statements rather than only hear a rendition from the officer who took the statement.

There are also disadvantages to recorded statements. First, if a statement is recorded, it must be preserved. This becomes an issue when there are technical difficulties with devices. In the early years of recorded statements, there were issues of operator error. This would include devices with short battery lengths. An officer would have intentions of recording a suspect statement and place his handheld recorder on the table during the interview. Then, two hours later when the interview was concluded, the officer would realize that his batteries had given out after the first ten minutes. Similarly, an officer may know that the batteries were low on his own recording device and thus borrow his partner's device. The partner's device was more sophisticated and required a press-and-hold for three seconds to activate the recording feature. Not knowing this, the officer just pressed the record button, thus none of the conversation was recorded. Although recorded statements are not required, the fact that the officer attempted and failed makes the officer look inept. It is the practice of some officers to use two different recording devices when taking statements from suspects in major cases. This minimizes the chances of mishaps.

Preservation of Evidence

Preservation of the evidence is usually not given a second thought, but it should be. The police officer follows the standard protocol for downloading the statement to a station house server and deletes the recording from his individual recorder. As you are probably imagining, this could not go as planned. The download could malfunction and the officer not notice that the file is not stored on the server. Then, several months later when the case goes to trial, it is not there. This could also happen through no fault of the officer. Consider that the officer did everything right in the download and even listened to the statement on the server to make sure it transferred before deleting it from his personal recorder. Then, several weeks later the server crashes and there is no cloud backup system.

Destruction of evidence is a terrible thing to be accused of as a law enforcement officer. Destruction of evidence can occur purposely or inadvertently. The difference is substantial. Purposeful extraction of evidence can result in a dismissal of charges against the accused. Of course, a malfunction in technology usually cannot be attributed to a purposeful act. In this case, the destruction of evidence would be inadvertent and not call for an automatic dismissal of charges. The officer is left to explain himself on the stand, which will usually make him look incompetent.

Another reason not to record suspect statements is that consistency may be a problem. Law enforcement officers often justify their interaction with suspects with consistency. An officer can always listen to a suspect statement and reduce it to writing later. However, if an officer records only sometimes, it is harder to explain to juries. An officer maybe called out in the middle of the night to respond to a call and forgets his recording device. Therefore, in that instance, he reduces the suspect statement to writing. However, the officer's consistent practice is to record suspect statements. When called to testify, the officer would be questioned by the defense and made to look like there was an ulterior motive for not recording the statement.

One more reason not to record statements is that the conversation could stray far away from the relevant topic. Law enforcement officers have different tactics for speaking with suspects. Sometimes the officer will try to befriend the suspect by making small talk before getting to the point at hand. This could relax the suspect and get him or her talking. The small talk could be related to prior criminal acts of the suspect or other criminal acts that surrounded the topic of the interrogation. For example, if the officer and the suspect have a prior relationship, the officer could say things like, "I know you know how to get rid of stolen property because you did it last year with that Dodge Charger I arrested you on." These types of statements concerning the prior criminal acts of the accused would be inadmissible in the current case. If later in that same conversation the suspect confessed to stealing a BMW and changing VIN numbers, only the potion of the statement relevant to the BMW could be played for the jury. This puts the prosecutor in the position of figuring out how to redact a video or audio statement. It could also cause the jury to question what was going on during the portions of the statement that were inadmissible. This kind of distraction is never good for the prosecution.

When confronted with the question of whether to record or not record, officers could choose a hybrid approach. This approach allows for a preinterview statement that is not recorded followed by a formal statement that is recorded. The Miranda rules still apply. The officer needs to Mirandize the suspect, if he is in custody, before any questioning occurs. There is no requirement that the Miranda be recorded or in writing. Then, the officer can proceed with the small talk, the talk about prior criminal history of the suspect, or any other subject matter relevant or irrelevant to the subject of the interrogation. Then, the officer can move into the interrogation on the relevant crime. If the suspect continues to deny and the officer feels that the statement would not move the prosecution forward, the officer ends the interrogation. However, if the officer elicits any incriminating responses from the suspect, the officer could elect to start a recording. The recording usually starts with the officer saying, "I am Officer Lockemup present with Ted Thief and today's date is July 4, 2024. You and I have been speaking informally about the theft of the victim's car, is that right?" This allows the suspect to answer on the recording. "Prior to beginning our conversation, I informed you of your Miranda rights and you agreed to waive those rights, correct? Now tell me about how you stole the victim's car." This makes for a much cleaner version of the statement and avoids unnecessary redaction of portions later. Of course, the downside to this is that the officer must defend what was said off recording.

Officers who pursue this hybrid interrogation technique often work in partnership. One officer will take the lead in the interrogation while the other officer simply observes. The observing officer could be in the room or viewing from a two-way glass or closed-circuit channel. If the defendant later makes allegations of misconduct by the interrogating officer, there is a witness.

It is also preferred to have two officers involved in taking a statement from the suspect in case one officer is unavailable at the time of trial. Unfortunately, a career in law enforcement has the potential to be life threatening; it would be unfortunate to lose the admissibility of a confession because the officer who took the statement was deceased. To a lesser degree, officers can be unavailable for other reasons. Perhaps the officer who took the statement is also in the Army Reserve and is called away to duty and unavailable at the time of trial. Perhaps the officer who took the statement has moved to a remote location and it wouldn't be cost effective for the government to pay for his travel back to testify.

Rules to Remember

Below is a list of rules to remember from this chapter:

Voluntariness Rules

- When doing an analysis of a suspect's statement, you must first ask whether the statement was taken by a law enforcement officer or agent thereof.
    - If the statement was taken by a non-law enforcement agent, it will be admissible.
- Next, you must ask whether the statement was given voluntarily.
    - A statement can be rendered involuntary for many reasons.
    - Most appeal cases involve issues of accused intimidation by law enforcement officers toward the suspect during questioning.
    - Mental health and voluntary intoxication could also render a statement involuntary.
- If the statement is involuntary, it cannot be used for any reason.
- If the statement is voluntary, it is not automatically admissible. This is when the Miranda analysis begins.

Miranda Analysis

- If the suspect is not in custody, then no Miranda is required. Remember, the term custody isn't just the physical arrest or restraint.
- If the suspect is in custody, then the next question is whether there was an interrogation. Interrogation can be the standard questioning, but it can also be the "functional equivalent" of questioning.
- If there is custody and interrogation, then Miranda warnings are required.
- If Miranda warnings are given to the suspect, the suspect must make a voluntary waiver of those rights. Here, the same questions surrounding voluntariness of the statement apply as above—that is, intimidation, mental health, intoxication.

In Addition

- Suspect statements may be verbal or in writing. Departmental policies will vary on when to take either and how to preserve statements that are memorialized.
- The Supreme Court has left it up to each state to determine how juvenile Miranda warnings are administered. Some states require an extra right be waived by a juvenile suspect. This is the right to have a parent or guardian present during questioning.

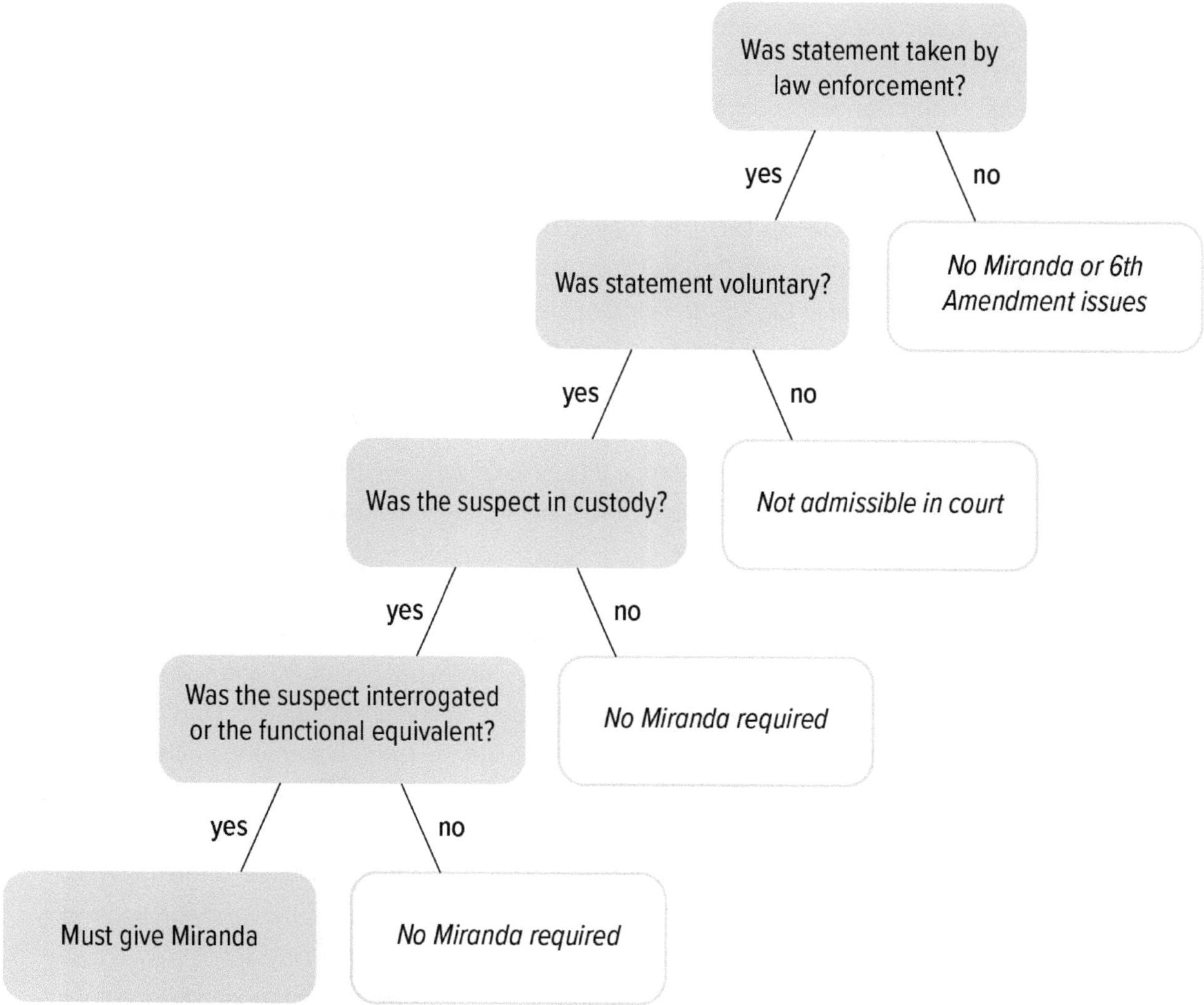

Figure 6.1 Miranda chart

End of Chapter Comprehension and Application

Directions: Use what you have learned in this chapter to help you respond completely and correctly to each question or prompt below.

1. What can make a statement voluntarily given?
2. Can a nonvoluntary statement be used for any purpose?
3. Is Miranda case specific? Explain.
4. Can a statement be taken from a defendant after indictment? Why or why not?
5. What are three advantages of recording a suspect's statement?
6. What are the differences in the Fifth Amendment and Sixth Amendment right to counsel?

7. Discuss the public safety exception to the Miranda requirement.
8. How many times can a suspect be Mirandized?
9. Under what circumstances would a suspect need to be re-Mirandized?
10. How can a suspect invoke his Miranda rights?
11. Investigator Lockemup is looking for Dennis Driver to interview him about the murder of Victor Victim. Lockemup finds Dennis Driver hanging out at a service station in Sodom City. Lockemup exits his vehicle and approaches Dennis Driver. Lockemup asks Dennis Driver to follow him down to the police department in Big City to talk. Dennis Driver agrees to talk and drives himself to the police department, which is one mile away from the service station. Dennis Driver parks his vehicle and enters the police department. He meets Lockemup in the lobby and they walk to an interview room down the hall. Is Miranda required before the interview? Why or why not?
12. How would your opinion of custody change if Dennis Driver were patted down and his cell phone taken by Investigator Lockemup before entering the interview room? Is Miranda required before the interview? Why or why not?
13. How would your opinion of custody change if Dennis Driver was left sitting in the interrogation room an hour before questioning? Is Miranda required before the interview? Why or why not?
14. When Dennis Driver is arrested for theft of property, officers pat him down and find a pill bottle in his right pants pocket. The officers open the pill bottle and find crack cocaine. Dennis Driver says, "That's not my pill bottle, I'm just holding it for a friend." Is this statement admissible without Miranda? Why or why not?
15. When Dennis Driver is arrested for theft of property, officers say in his presence: "We're going to get a search warrant for his phone and I bet we will find texts between him and the guys who killed Victor Victim." Dennis responds, "Sure you are going to find texts between me and them. We are friends." Is that statement admissible without Miranda? Why or why not?
16. Investigator Lockemup wants to take a statement from Manny Maintenance. He sits down with Manny and reads the Miranda rights to Manny. Manny replies, "Maybe I should talk to a lawyer." Lockemup continues to ask him questions and Manny makes statements. Will those statements be admissible? Why or why not?
17. The defendant gave a statement that was voluntary, but he was in custody and not Mirandized at the time of the statement. The defendant takes the witness stand in his trial for possession of cocaine and tells the jury that he did not know that the cocaine was in console of the vehicle he was driving because it was not his vehicle. Can the prosecutor impeach his trial testimony with a statement the police obtained voluntarily that he knew the cocaine was in the vehicle? Why or why not?
18. Using the same facts as above, but if the statement that the defendant gave the police about knowledge of the cocaine was not voluntary, how could it be used in the case against Manny Maintenance?
19. Based on Melvin's statement and the other evidence in the case, Investigator Lockemup obtains

a murder warrant for Andy. Lockemup goes to the jail to speak with Andy. Immediately, Lockemup realized that Andy appears to be a person with an intellectual disability. Lockemup reads Andy his Miranda rights and Andy asks for an attorney. Lockemup tells Andy that he can exercise his right to an attorney, but asks, "Are you sure that's the way you want to go with this?" Andy asks, "What do you mean?" Lockemup says, "Everyone else has given me their side to the story and I just want to give you the chance to do the same." Andy makes an incriminating statement. Would this statement be admissible? Why or why not?

20. While Sam Snitch was giving a statement to Investigator Lockemup about the murder investigation, he also gives a statement about his own robbery. He says, "Man, I only took a few dollars, this is so stupid." The prosecution in Sam Snitch's robbery case wants to use that admission against Sam Snitch. Will it be admissible? Why or why not?

References

Culombe v. Connecticut, 367 U.S. 568 (1961), https://supreme.justia.com/cases/federal/us/367/568/
Berghuis v. Thompkins, 560 U.S. 370 (2010), https://supreme.justia.com/cases/federal/us/560/370/
Illinois v. Perkins, 496 U.S. 292 (1990), https://supreme.justia.com/cases/federal/us/496/292/
Maine v. Moulton, 474 U.S. 159 (1985), https://supreme.justia.com/cases/federal/us/474/159
Kuhlmann v. Wilson, 477 U.S. 436 (1986), https://supreme.justia.com/cases/federal/us/477/436/
Messiah v. United States, 377 U.S. 201 (1964), https://supreme.justia.com/cases/federal/us/377/201/
Kuhlman v. Wilson, 477 U.S. 436 (1986), https://supreme.justia.com/cases/federal/us/477/436/
Miranda v. Arizona, 384 U.S. 436 (1966), https://supreme.justia.com/cases/federal/us/384/436/
Brewer v. Williams, 430 U.S. 387 (1977), https://supreme.justia.com/cases/federal/us/430/387/
Miranda v. Arizona, 384 U.S. 436 (1966), https://supreme.justia.com/cases/federal/us/384/436/
Davis v. United States, 512 U.S. 452 (1994), https://supreme.justia.com/cases/federal/us/512/452/
Moran v. Burbine, 475 U.S. 412 (1986), https://supreme.justia.com/cases/federal/us/475/412/
California v. Beheler, 463 U.S. 1121 (1983), https://supreme.justia.com/cases/federal/us/463/1121/
Oregon v. Elstad, 470 U.S. 298 (1985), https://supreme.justia.com/cases/federal/us/470/298/
Missouri v. Seibert, 542 U.S. 600 (2004), https://supreme.justia.com/cases/federal/us/542/600/
Michigan v. Mosley, 423 U.S. 96.(1975), https://supreme.justia.com/cases/federal/us/423/96/
New York v. Quarles, 467 U.S. 649 (1984), https://supreme.justia.com/cases/federal/us/467/649/
Berkemer v. McCarty, 468 U.S. 420 (1984), https://supreme.justia.com/cases/federal/us/468/420/
Pennsylvania v. Bruder, 488 U.S. 9 (1988), https://supreme.justia.com/cases/federal/us/488/9/
J. D. B. v. North Carolina, 564 U.S. 261 (2011), https://supreme.justia.com/cases/federal/us/564/261/
Minnesota v. Murphy, 465 U.S. 420 (1983), https://supreme.justia.com/cases/federal/us/465/420/

Chapter 7

Pretrial Hearings

Introduction: Preparing for Pretrial Hearings

In this chapter students will learn the different types of pretrial hearings, and what an officer needs to do to prepare for pretrial hearings, such as initial appearances, preliminary hearings, and other motion hearings.

Chapter Objectives

In this chapter students will learn:

- What an officer should do when receiving a subpoena for a pretrial setting
- What is relevant in a bond hearing
- How an initial appearance differs from a preliminary hearing
- The standards of proof required for preliminary hearings
- The differences in presentment of evidence at pretrial hearings
- The different types of motion hearings that could require officer testimony
- What rights a defendant has at each type of hearing
- The types of pretrial pleas
- The considerations for plea negotiations
- What is the purpose of a grand jury proceeding, in states that have grand jury proceedings
- What pieces of evidence are discoverable to the defendant from the government
- What pieces of evidence are discoverable to the government from the defendant
- What types of evidence can be suppressed at a suppression hearing
- What issues are rated in competency hearings

Key Terms

Key terms and professional terminology that are used in this chapter include:

- **Pretrial hearing**
- **Initial appearance**
- **Bond hearing**
- **Preliminary hearing**
- **Grand jury**
- **Subpoena ad testificandum**
- **Subpoena duces tecum**
- **Arraignment**
- **Allocution**
- **Nolo contendere**
- **Plea negotiations**
- **Suppression hearing**
- **Competency hearing**
- **Other hearings: bad acts, stand your ground**

Initial Appearance/Probable Cause Hearing

Once a suspect has been arrested, he or she is usually booked into the system, which involves documenting the arrest. This is the same whether the arrest is with a warrant or without a warrant. Depending on the jurisdictional rules, the suspect will next be afforded an initial appearance. Each jurisdiction is free to set the rules surrounding this process. Some jurisdictions require that the hearing take place in less than twelve hours after arrest, some require less than twenty-four hours and some up to seventy-two hours after arrest.

In US Supreme Court case *Gerstein v. Pugh*, individuals were arrested in Florida with a prosecutor's information (which is similar to a warrant but without a judge's review). Florida law allowed individuals to be arrested without judge's review and held for a substantial period of time without judicial review. The US Supreme Court ruled that a timely judicial determination of probable cause was a prerequisite to detention. However, the Court did not agree that the Fourth Amendment required the determination of probable cause to be in the form of an adversary hearing.

The initial appearance has many purposes:

- **Notifications of charges**
- More often than not, the suspect knows what he or she is being charged with at the time of arrest. However, there could be times where the suspect is unable to appreciate the situation based on intoxication, mental illness, or physical health at the time of arrest.

- **Notification of the right to remain silent**
- The initial appearance is usually the accused's first opportunity to interact with a neutral and detached judge or magistrate. The judge or magistrate will gather important identifying information from the accused, such as the correct spelling of the accused's name and the accused's address. This information will be kept in the court's file for future mailouts and correspondence regarding court dates and times. The judge or magistrate will inform the accused that he or she has the right to remain silent and does not have to communicate with any law enforcement or otherwise. Sometimes, the accused will take this opportunity to tell his or her side of the facts to attempt to persuade the judge or magistrate. If this happens, the officer attending the initial appearance should supplement his or her report with the accused's statement. This could become very relevant to the investigation and prosecution of the case.
- **Notification of the right to counsel**
- The accused will be notified that he or she has the right to counsel and that one will be provided to him or her for further progression of the case. Each jurisdiction may conduct this process differently. Some jurisdictions will have counsel present and available at the initial appearance, while other jurisdictions will have a list of attorneys and send the attorneys an electronic communication telling the attorney the name of the client, charge, and court date.
- **Identification of counsel**
- The **initial appearance** is usually the first time the suspect meets his or her counsel. There is not much that counsel can add at this stage except to remind the suspect of his right to remain silent.

Pretrial Release

Most arrestees have the right to pretrial release. The right to pretrial release is grounded in the Eighth Amendment. The Eighth Amendment to the US Constitution states that "excessive bail shall not be required." The granting of bail is certainly a privilege, and it does not have to be granted. However, there are many reasons that every jurisdiction grants bail as a matter of right in most cases. First, the local jails cannot sustain housing for everyone arrested until the outcome of the case. This would place an unreasonable burden on the government to fund housing for individuals awaiting trial. Second, there is a presumption of innocence that attaches to each accused. This presumption stays with the accused until conviction by judge, jury, or plea of guilt. It is unreasonable to take the liberty of an individual charged with a minor offense and presumed innocent for the long period between arrest and conclusion of the case.

The procedures used for the issuance or setting of pretrial release have been left to each jurisdiction to implement. States are permitted to legislate their own pretrial release requirements. Usually, pretrial release is accomplished in three ways:

1. Own Recognizance

An arrestee may be released on his or her own recognizance, or "OR bond." This is basically a promise by the arrestee to show up at a future certain date and to comply with the law. This is the usual course for speeding tickets. Some jurisdictions allow for arrest upon traffic violations. Traffic violations are usually minor offenses that do not involve injury to the public and are commonly committed by noncriminally minded citizens. Most people do not expect to be jailed for a speeding ticket. Most jurisdictions have moved to a digital issuance of tickets, but in years past, traffic citations were in paper form. The law enforcement officer would hand write the ticket and then have the person sign the bottom of the ticket. This was commonly known as signing his or her own bond. This was a recognizance bond, a simple promise to show up to the traffic ticket court date or to pay the amount before the court date.

A traffic ticket is the classic example of a minor offense that would offer the offender a recognizance bond, but these types of pretrial releases can occur in serious offenses as well. For example, if an arrestee is eight months pregnant and the jail does not want to incur the medical expenses associated with the delivery of the baby, the law enforcement officer may ask the judge to allow the arrestee to be released on her own recognizance. Similarly, if an arrestee has a serious medical condition that will incur additional expenses for the government, the law enforcement officer may ask for an "OR" bond. This also could occur if the arrestee is suffering from a severe mental health disability. In this case, the law enforcement officer may ask for an OR bond so that the arrestee can be placed in an appropriate institution instead of a local jail to await resolution of the case.

Practically, the request for a release on one's own recognizance could occur anytime after arrest. This could be immediately, as in the traffic ticket example. This could also occur anytime before the resolution of the case. Perhaps, in the example of the pregnant arrestee above, she is given a standard bond amount at initial arrest. Then after a few days or weeks, it becomes evident that no one will make her bond for her. At that time, the law enforcement officer or the arrestee's attorney can go back to the judge or magistrate and request an OR bond. Often, on felony offenses, the law enforcement officer will wait to see if the arrestee can make the bond before making any special requests on the arrestee's behalf. Remember that every decision that the law enforcement officer or government official makes could be publicly scrutinized. Often, it is not acceptable to the public to offer pretrial release on one's own recognizance on a serious offense because there is a possibility of reoffense.

2. Bail or Bond Amount

The purpose of bail or bond is to assure the presence of the arrestee at future court appearances. An arrestee may be required to pay or promise to pay a certain amount of money to be released pending the resolution of the case. This process is commonly known as making bail or bonding out. The question becomes what amount should be set. Remember that the Eighth Amendment does not require that an arrestee be released pretrial, but it does contemplate that it can occur by bail, as long as it is not excessive. The US Supreme Court has not ruled that the Eighth Amendment applies to the states. Therefore, the issue of pretrial release is jurisdiction specific. Each state can create its own bail schedule and even attach fees to those schedules for collection upon conviction. The bail schedules usually track the seriousness of the offense. Misdemeanor offenses carrying a low amount and higher-class felony offenses carrying a higher amount. Bail schedules are often the subject of attack and criticism because an amount that may seem high to one person may seem low to another person.

Below is the State of Alabama's recommended range bond schedule.

Felonies:	
Capital felony	$50,000 — No Bail Allowed
Murder	$15,000–$1,500,000
Class A felony	$10,000–$60,000
Class B felony	$5,000–$30,000
Class C felony	$2,500– $15,000
Drug manufacturing/trafficking	$5,000–$1,500,000
Class D felony	$1,000–$10,000
Misdemeanors:	
Class A misdemeanor	$300–$6,000
Class B misdemeanor	$300–$3,000
Class C misdemeanor	$300–$1000
Violation	$300–$500
Traffic-related Offenses:	
DUI	$1,000–$7,500
Reckless driving	$300–$1,000
Speeding	$300–$500
Other traffic offenses	$300–$500

Some states have a much more complex bond schedule that lists each individual crime and gives a recommendation for each. States can also give judges and magistrates the ability to deviate from the bail schedule depending on the facts and circumstances of a particular case. This can also attract criticism from the public at large. Consider the following examples.

- Jeremy is arrested in Smallville for distribution of a controlled substance. He is a known drug dealer in Smallville and has the reputation of being able to supply anyone with any drug of choice because if his connections to Mexico. He rents a nice condominium in Smallville, drives an expensive car, and appears to be wealthy. The state's bail schedule calls for an amount not exceeding $30,000 for distribution of controlled substances. The law enforcement officer who arrested Jeremy knows that Jeremy has no connections in Smallville and he is a flight risk. Therefore, the officer asks the judge to set bail in the amount of $100,000, which is substantially outside of the legislated bail schedule. The judge sets bail for Jeremy at $100,000, which Jeremy immediately posts, and he is released.

- Maria is arrested in Smallville for distribution of a controlled substance. She is a known drug dealer in Smallville and has the reputation of being able to supply anyone with any drug of his or her choice. She is known to have contacts with Mexico and has no family in Smallville. Maria rents a tiny apartment above a garage in the bad part of town. She drives a used, older-model vehicle and has three children. The state's bail schedule calls for an amount not exceeding $30,000 for distribution of controlled substances. The law enforcement officer believes that Maria is a flight risk and requests that the judge go outside of the bail schedule and set Maria's bond at $100,000. The judge sets bail for Maria at $100,000, which Maria cannot post, and Maria remains in jail.

How do the above two examples make you feel? Was the judge justified in going outside the bail schedule in both cases? Do you believe the judge could receive any public criticism for his actions in either or both cases? Would it make a difference to you if Jeremy and Maria had been charged with violent crimes?

States give judges the ability to set bail based on a number of factors. For example, in Alabama, the state legislature has codified Rule 7 of the Alabama Rules of Criminal Procedure to read as follows:

Rule 7.2. Right to release on one's personal recognizance or on bond

Read at: https://casetext.com/rule/alabama-court-rules/alabama-rules-of-criminal-procedure/rule-7-release/rule-72-right-to-release-on-ones-personal-recognizance-or-on-bond.

These are factors that require the subjective judgment of the judge or magistrate. The judge or magistrate is also not required to specifically state his or her reasons for the deviation in bail amounts. Often, the courts orders simply read "based on Rule 7.2, the Court finds that the bond amount is set at $100,000." In this instance, no one really knows what factors persuaded the judge's ruling.

Practically Making Bail/Bond

Each state is tasked with making its own procedures of how an accused suspect can make bail or bond. Usually, the judge or magistrate indicates that the bail can either be cash or professional surety or property. A cash bond means that the accused individual must post the amount of bail in cash. For example, if the bond is $10,000, then the accused must post $10,000 with the sheriff in order to be released. At the conclusion of the case, the $10,000 cash will be returned to the person posting that amount, as long as the accused appeared for the court date.

If professional surety is indicated by the judge or magistrate, then the accused can use a professional surety company, also known as a bail bonding company. These companies are essentially betting against the odds that the accused will show up for the court appearance. Each surety will look at things like the accused's flight risk and past history before deciding to post bond for that individual. The sureties usually charge a percentage of the bond amount. For example, if the bond amount is $10,000, the bonding company may require that the accused give the surety $1,000 in cash, and in turn the surety will post $10,000 with the sheriff. If the accused does not show up for the court date, the surety will lose the $9,000. If the accused does show up for the court date, the accused does not get refunded the $1000. That is the cost of the loan from the surety.

If the judge or magistrate allows a property bond, the accused (or family or friend) can sign over the deed to real property to the sheriff to secure the amount of the bond. If the accused fails to show for the court date, the sheriff's office could place a lien on the property and force collection by sale of the property or otherwise.

1. Conditional Requirements of Pretrial Release

Just as the judge or magistrate may use his or her discretion to set an amount of bail or bond, the judge or magistrate may use his or her discretion to set certain conditions of pretrial release. Most states do not have a suggested list of conditions, but merely have a broadly stated rule that will allow the judges to "set conditions as required by justice" or similar language. Some jurisdictions have a standing judge's order requiring certain conditions be set on certain types of offenses. For example, a jurisdiction may have a standing order that mandates no contact as a condition of release in domestic violence cases. A no-contact order as a condition of pretrial release is a restraining order. These could be added as conditions on any case. Also, conditions restraining a person from a certain area could be ordered in pretrial release. For example, an arrestee who was charged with theft from a department store may be restrained from visiting the department store as a condition of pretrial release. The law enforcement officer would simply need to make this request at the time of the bond request. The pretrial release condition need be rationally related to the crime charged. For example, if an arrestee were charged with selling narcotics, the judge could require the arrestee to post a sign in his or her yard stating, "There are no drugs for sale here." Ultimately, the condition can be as creative as the judge or magistrate wishes, until challenged.

Enforcement of conditions of pretrial release is only possible if the court is notified of the violation of the condition. For example, if a pretrial release of no contact is entered in a domestic violence case and the arrestee and victim continue having contact without reporting that contact, it will never be enforced. However, if the victim reports the contact by the arrestee, the remedy for enforcement is revocation of bond.

Consider the below examples:

- Robbie is arrested for domestic violence. It is a misdemeanor offense involving physical injury to the victim, Trina. The maximum bail schedule amount is $6,000. The judge knows Robbie and knows that he has been arrested multiple times for domestic violence with the same victim. Trina usually makes Robbie's bond and then gets back together with Robbie. The judge thinks that if he can keep Robbie locked up for a while, Trina will move on and not get back together with Robbie. The judge sets Robbie's bond at $50,000 and places a condition of no contact with Trina on the bond. Robbie cannot post that large of a bond and has been sitting in jail five weeks awaiting trial.
- Chris is arrested for domestic violence. It is a misdemeanor offense involving physical injury to the victim, Jon. The maximum bail schedule for the misdemeanor domestic violence charge is $6,000. The judge knows that Chris and Jon have had prior incidents of domestic violence, where they have both been charged and both been victims in the past. The judge is tired of dealing with them and sets a bond in the amount of $6,000 and a condition of no contact with Jon. Jon is at the initial appearance and requests that the judge not put a condition of no contact on the bond. Jon states that he has forgiven Chris and wants to see Chris. The judge instructs the law enforcement officer obtaining the warrant to drive by Chris and Jon's residence every day to check on the no-contact condition of the bond. The law enforcement officer drives by the residence on the day after Chris's release and sees Jon and Chris sitting on the front porch together. The law enforcement officer informs the judge and the judge revokes Chris's bond.

Food for Thought

What do you think about the above examples? Do you think the $50,000 bond that the judge set for Robbie is reasonable? Do you think that he should have set a similar bond in Chris's case? Do you think the judge should have set a condition of bond when the victim did not want the condition in place? Do you think Chris's bond should have been revoked even though no one was complaining about the contact between Jon and Chris?

Another common condition of pretrial release is that the arrestee submit to a random drug test. With the use of illegal substances at an all-time high across the country, this condition is often violated and the bond surrendered because of a positive test.

The arresting officer or investigator can have input on the conditions of release, including the amount or bail and/or the conditions of release added to the bond. The arresting officer may have important information that will effect the amount of bail or need for conditions of release. The prosecuting attorney may call the law enforcement officer as a witness to give testimony concerning pretrial release. As you see in the Alabama Rule of Criminal Procedure above, many factors can be considered by the judge or magistrate. The law enforcement officer may be sworn in as a witness and asked about the facts of the case, the criminal history of the accused, or the flight risk involved in any given case. The officer making an appearance at an initial appearance or **bond hearing** need be prepared to answer these types of questions.

Changing Conditions of Pretrial Release

There are many moving parts in a criminal case, and often there are changes from the onset of a case to the end of the same case. There are many reasons a pretrial condition may need to be amended or changed prior to the resolution of the case. As discussed in earlier examples, the mental or physical health of the arrestee could be a basis to change the condition of release from a bail amount to an OR bond. Other examples of common reasons for changes are listed below.

An arrestee cannot post the set amount of bond and requests that he be allowed to serve his pretrial commitment in a drug rehab facility prior to resolution of the case. Some jurisdictions will allow arrestees awaiting trial to receive in-house drug treatment if requested. The arrestee is informed that leaving the rehab facility will be considered an escape, similarly as it would be for leaving the jail. This helps curb the temptation of walking away from the drug treatment facility. But this is a slippery slope because it also gives the prosecution the possibility of compounding charges if the temptation takes over.

A law enforcement officer or prosecutor may also request a change in pretrial release. This could happen if the case against the arrestee suddenly changes—for example, if the only eyewitness dies. The government could ask that the defendant be released on his own recognizance pending presentation of the case for dismissal (no bill) by the grand jury.

A law enforcement officer may also ask for new conditions to be added to a pretrial release after the arrest has been released. For example, the defendant is charged with simple assault of his cousin. The defendant makes bond and immediately contacts the cousin, asking cousin to drop the charges. The cousin is in fear and does not want any more contact with the defendant. The state could request that an additional condition be added to the bond that was not originally included.

The defendant could ask for a change on condition as well. For example, the defendant is arrested for burglary of a business and makes bond. While awaiting trial, the defendant is offered a job by a family member out of state. The defendant can request that the judge allow him to travel out of state to start the new job and promises attendance at every court proceeding.

One of the most common reasons that a condition of pretrial release changes is that the accused commits another crime while out on bond. Not violating the laws of any jurisdiction is a condition on all bonds. Unfortunately, individuals who have committed an offense and are awaiting trial often commit the same or similar offenses prior to the resolution of the first case. When this happens, the state usually files a motion to revoke the defendant's bond and requests the defendant's bond be revoked. The defendant can submit and agree or request a hearing on the issue. If a hearing is requested, often the law enforcement officer with knowledge about the new charge is called to testify. Other witnesses also may be called, such as the victim of the new charge or an eyewitness to the crime. The standard of proof is relatively low at this hearing and is only that the judge is reasonably satisfied that the defendant committed the new crime. Considering the ultimate standard of proof in a criminal case is proof beyond a reasonable doubt, this is a low burden at a revocation hearing.

The change in type and condition of pretrial release can be done by either party at any time between arrest and final resolution. Most of the time, these changes occur before a finding of guilt or no guilt but can be after such finding. In fact, many states have separate bail schedules that apply after conviction. Some jurisdictions have a practice of not allowing bail or bond after conviction, or of significantly increasing the amount of bail after conviction. It goes without saying that a defendant found not guilty is released from all pretrial conditions. This change in circumstance after conviction becomes significant when there is a long delay between conviction and sentencing. In some jurisdictions, a defendant could have a trial and be convicted, and then the sentencing could occur two to three months later.

Problems with the Bond/Bail System

As noted above, there can be controversy surrounding the pretrial release of accused defendants. The courts usually take into account the accused's financial status in making bail decisions. This is an important factor for the judge to consider so as to avoid irrational decisions. Bail can be denied simply because the accused is unable to pay it. The disparity in socioeconomic status has been a point of criticism for advocate groups over the decades.

Preliminary Hearing

The **preliminary hearing** is a formal process in which the accused and the government are subjected to judicial accountability. Both parties, the government and the accused, are present, and the government has the burden of proof to show that the accused committed the crimes charged. The preliminary hearing is distinguished from the initial hearing/probable cause hearing in that the preliminary hearing is more akin to a trial. It is an adversarial hearing. It is also distinguished by the facts that the initial appearance hearing is a justification for the arrest. The preliminary hearing is held to determine whether the case should proceed with trial. The burden of proof at a preliminary hearing is the same burden as required for an arrest or warrant: probable cause. The state has the duty to call witnesses to prove the case to a judge. This is a public proceeding conducted in a public courtroom. The government usually calls a minimum number of witnesses for the purpose of providing probable cause to the hearing judge. The law enforcement officer is usually chosen over a victim or other witness because the rules of evidence are relaxed at a preliminary hearing. A testifying witness can testify about hearsay, so it is not necessary to subject the victim or other witness to cross-examination so early in the case.

The preliminary hearing is a time that the defense learns what the government's case is and the strength of the evidence against the accused. The defense can use the preliminary hearing to gather information to be used to later attack the case. It is important to note that the rules of discovery are different in civil and criminal cases. In civil cases, both sides turn over copies of the files to the other side, and each knows the substance of the plaintiff's and defendant's case. In criminal law, it is not required that each side turn over a copy of the file. Only certain items from either side's files are turned over in discovery. Each state may enact rules calling for greater discovery, but most do not. For example, the government may have statements from six witness to a shooting. Five of those statements say the accused was the only shooter. One of those statements says that there was another shooter present. The government would be required to give the defense the one statement that indicates someone else could have committed the crime. This is known as exculpatory evidence. The government is required to give the defense any exculpatory evidence in the case, but not any inculpatory evidence (tending to show the accused did commit the crime). Likewise, the defense is not required to give the government any statements. Each state can require other items be transferred in discovery, such as expert reports or any physical evidence intended to be presented at the trial of the case. This would include photographs, videos, and other tangible things.

The defense can also attack the government's evidence at the preliminary hearing itself. If the government's case is weak and the judge does not find probable cause, the case could be dismissed against the accused at this stage in the proceeding. This rarely happens since the burden of proof is only probable cause. This standard is the same that was used to arrest the accused to bring him or her before the preliminary hearing. However, things could change between arrest and the preliminary hearing, such as witnesses changing their stories or becoming unavailable.

Because the burden of proof is so low at the preliminary hearing stage, often the accused will waive the right to a preliminary hearing. At first glance this may seem odd. Why would an accused waive this procedural right? Consider the prominent member of the community who was charged with a theft. The preliminary hearing may bring forth a large amount of media attention. The accused may waive the preliminary hearing to avoid the embarrassment of media attention.

Since preliminary hearings have compulsory process (subpoena power), witnesses may be called by either side. As noted above, there is a strategy to which witnesses the government will call and whether the defense will call any witnesses at all. The law enforcement officer investigating the case should assume that he or she will be called as a witness at a preliminary hearing and not be surprised to receive a subpoena for a preliminary hearing. The officer should contact the prosecutor and discuss the need for that officer's testimony. There are several reasons for the officer to make contact with the prosecutor:

- The officer may have been subpoenaed in error. The initial file may have been turned in through a standard process wherein clerical staff from the court clerk's or prosecutor's office subpoenas the officer who turned in the file. This may not be the officer who actually has knowledge of the facts of the case.
- The officer may be unavailable during the date of the preliminary hearing. Officers have many commitments for training or testifying. There may be a conflict wherein the officer has received two subpoenas for the same dates in two different courts and would be unavailable for one. In that case, the prosecutor could request a continuance or a special setting.
- There may be another officer who could serve as a better witness. The officer who is in charge may not be the officer the prosecutor wishes to call at the preliminary. The prosecutor may wish to call a witness with less knowledge of the facts so as to not disclose all the facts of the case at the preliminary hearing.
- There may be a confidential informant or a witness who needs to remain confidential. If the officer has an informant who is working undercover, the officer needs to inform the prosecutor. The prosecutor can request that person remain confidential until a later time.

Once a determination has been made about who is going to testify for the government, the officer needs to know the following information:

- **What is expected from his or her testimony.** The officer should briefly speak with the prosecutor and determine how much evidence the prosecutor intends to present at the hearing. The officer also needs to know what evidence the prosecutor does not want revealed during the preliminary hearing.
- **What has changed since the initial arrest.** The officer testifying should review his or her file and make contact with crucial witnesses before the preliminary hearing, making sure nothing has

changed. For example, if the defendant and victim are related, the defendant could have convinced the victim not to pursue charges.

- **The status of any codefendant cases.** Defense attorneys are always interested in codefendant cases. Codefendants are always a good way to cast doubt of guilt from the accused to another. Also, defense attorneys often look for plea agreements early in the case. Offering up testimony on a codefendant is one way to secure a plea agreement from the prosecutor.
- **Criminal history of the accused.** The preliminary hearing can morph into another request for a bond or change in bond condition by the defense. The defense attorney may make an oral motion for a lower bond amount, and the prosecutor will need to be able to question the law enforcement officer about the accused's criminal history.

Investigator Lockemup gets a report of a theft of property. Margaret Mercy reports that her jewelry has been stolen from her jewelry box in her bedroom. She suspects her nephew Nick because he has stolen from her in the past. She tells Lockemup that Nick was at her house the day before asking if he could borrow some money. She told him that he could not because she was tired of loaning money. She tells Lockemup that Nick has a drug problem and needs some help. She also tells Lockemup that she is tired of Nick stealing, and that even though she has not pressed charges in the past, she wants to this time. She also tells Lockemup that Nick's girlfriend, Sara, is a bad influence and the reason he is addicted to drugs. Lockemup obtains Nick's contact information from Margaret and travels to Nick's address to interview him. Nick is with Sara and Lockemup interviews them both at their residence. Nick tells Lockemup that he took the jewelry because he needed money to pay his bills. He pawned the jewelry at Joe's Treasure Chest and intends to get it back as soon as he gets paid for a job he did. Lockemup arrests Nick for theft of property. Lockemup receives a subpoena for the preliminary hearing on Nick's theft of property case. He phones Margaret to notify her that the hearing is upcoming and to ask if she has received the appraisals he requested concerning the jewelry. Margaret begins to cry and tells Lockemup that Nick has been fired from his construction job because of this arrest, and her brother, Nick's father, is upset with her for pressing charges. Margaret tells Lockemup that she no longer wishes to prosecute the case against Nick and wants everything dropped. Lockemup tells Margaret that he will relate her wishes to the prosecutor.

Testifying at the Preliminary Hearing

The rules of evidence at a preliminary hearing are markedly different than those in a criminal trial. Hearsay evidence (what the witness heard and is not repeating in court as a witness) is admissible in a preliminary hearing but not in a trial. Cross-examination of a witness may not be permitted. The US Supreme Court has stated that there is no constitutional right to cross-examination at a preliminary hearing. The court conducting the preliminary hearing has the discretion to allow cross-examination and to what extent. The officer should be ready for cross-examination and know the weaknesses of the case that may be attacked.

If an officer is called as a witness, the officer should not take his or her file or any personal information to the witness stand. If the officer takes notes or a file to the witness stand, it is fair game for the defense to mark and review. See the below example:

> Investigator Lockemup is called to testify at a preliminary hearing. He has been busy and not had time to review his case file prior to the court date. He enters the courtroom and introduces himself to the new prosecutor seated at the table. He looks to the defense table and sees a defense attorney he doesn't know representing the defendant. Lockemup decides he needs to take his case file to the witness stand with him to testify. The judge in this jurisdiction routinely allows the defense to cross-examine witnesses at a preliminary. On cross-examination of Lockemup, the defense attorney asks what time of day the crime occurred. Lockemup responds, "Nighttime." The defense attorney asks for the specific time, to which Lockemup resounds, "I don't recall." The defense attorney asks if Lockemup has any information with him on the witness stand that would assist in answering the question. Lockemup responds that he does and indicates his file. At that time, the defense attorney asks the court reporter to mark the entire file as exhibit one and it is marked. Lockemup has made a terrible mistake in taking his file to the stand, as it is now in the custody of the court and part of the public record.

Demeanor and Attire

An investigator called to testify should present in a professional manner. Each jurisdiction will have a police culture or policy in place for appropriate dress. It is important that the officer always looks professional and is prepared for testimony. The preliminary hearing may be the victim's first opportunity to see the court process, and it is important to impress upon the victim and other spectators that the process is taken seriously. Law enforcement officers need be aware that the spectators and victims present will be watching everything, because to them, this is an important case. Officers should refrain from laughing or making unnecessary small talk with others in the courtroom. Even though the law enforcement officer may be fully prepared for the hearing, unnecessary small talk will give the appearance to spectators that the hearing is unimportant.

Bypassing the Preliminary Hearing

There could be times where the preliminary hearing is bypassed. Some jurisdictions use grand juries to indict all serious offenses. A **grand jury** proceeding is another stop in the criminal process. It is another check and safeguard on the rights of the accused. In jurisdictions that use grand juries, the prosecutor could choose to present the case directly to the grand jury instead of the preliminary hearing. The prosecution could also choose to present the case to a grand jury while the case was awaiting the preliminary hearing. Some jurisdictions have backlogged dockets for preliminary hearings, and it can be more efficient for the prosecutor to present the case to a grand jury before the date of the preliminary hearing. This leaves the defense without the opportunity to gain the discovery available during a preliminary hearing. But because the rights of the accused are not infringed because the preliminary hearing is bypassed, there is no avenue for complaint.

Chris Coke was arrested for selling cocaine. The state's evidence is that a reliable confidential informant who had bought from Chris in the past purchased fifty dollars of cocaine from Chris. On this occasion, the confidential informant was given fifty dollars of police funds, wired with a hidden video recorder, and followed to Chris's residence. Investigator Lockemup saw the confidential informant go inside the residence and then come back out in a matter of minutes. Lockemup met the confidential informant a few miles down the road and recovered the cocaine and video recorder from the confidential informant. Lockemup viewed the recording and saw Chris sell cocaine to the confidential informant. Lockemup is using this confidential informant to purchase drugs from several people around Smallville and does not want his name disclosed until the operation is complete. What should Lockemup do to keep his informant's identity confidential?

Grand Jury Proceedings

A grand jury is a body of people selected to hear evidence in a criminal case to determine if there is enough legal evidence for the charge to proceed against the person charged or the suspect. Grand jury proceedings are grounded in the Fifth Amendment to the US Constitution: "No person shall be held to answer for a capital or otherwise infamous crime, unless on a presentment or indictment of a grand jury." The grand jury was intended to be a check on the powers of the US government by having citizen involvement early in the case against the accused. Citizen involvement does not carry over to the states via the Fourteenth Amendment. In other words, that portion of the Fifth Amendment has not been incorporated by the individual states. Each individual state is free to determine whether they will use a grand jury and for what type of case. Some states choose to use grand juries to indict all felony offenses. Other states choose to use grand juries only to indict cases involving capital murder or offenses involving a punishment of death or life without the possibility of parole. Some states choose not to use a grand jury at all in the criminal justice process.

In states that use grand juries, the members of the grand jury are selected in the same manner in which individuals are selected to serve on juries. That selection process must not intentionally exclude a particular group based on race or sex.

In states with grand jury proceedings, cases can be brought to a grand jury in three ways: (a) after the defendant has been formally charged by warrant, (b) as an investigation file, or (c) initiated by the grand jury.

If a criminal defendant is charged by warrant and afforded an initial appearance or preliminary hearing, his or her case will be presented to a grand jury. This will usually be done through the use of witnesses. Perhaps the police officer obtaining the warrant will testify about the probable case he had for obtaining a warrant against the defendant. The victim and other witnesses may also be called, but this is not necessary. The rules of evidence are relaxed in grand jury proceedings and hearsay is generally admissible. The defendant is not present, eliminating any confrontation clause issue. The witnesses will be examined by the prosecutor and/or any member of the grand jury who wishes to ask questions of the witness. In this instance, the defendant knows he has been charged but may not know when the grand jury proceeding occurs because it is a secret preceding.

A case may be presented to a grand jury as an investigative file. This means that there have not been formal charges, and the suspect may or may not know he is under investigation. The case will be presented to the grand jury in the same manner as if there have already been formal charges. The grand jury may not know whether the case is being presented to them as a new investigation or one that has already been charged. This should be of no concern to the grand jury because their duty is the same no matter the procedural history of the case.

A grand jury may open a new investigation into new charges on a criminal defendant. This usually occurs when they are already hearing the facts of a case being presented and those facts lead to other potential investigations. These investigations may be on the same individual or a different individual or different charges on the same individual. For example, Investigator Lockemup is presenting a charge of theft of property to a grand jury on Richard Smith. Smith has already been charged by warrant. During Lockemup's testimony, he discloses that Smith has also stolen three other vehicles in addition to the one he has already been arrested for stealing. The grand jury may inquire of Lockemup his level of proof on the additional three cases and begin an investigation on those additional charges on the same defendant. Also consider another example: Investigator Lockemup is presenting a case of theft of property wherein Richard Smith has been charged by warrant. During his testimony in front of the grand jury, it is learned that his girlfriend, Karen Brown, was with him and drove him to the location to get the stolen vehicle. The grand jury may open a new investigation on Karen Brown for a new charge of theft of property as an accomplice.

The prosecutor has the discretion to bring cases to a grand jury by use of a warrant or as an uncharged investigation. There may be pros of each.

- The pros of bringing a case by warrant:
  - The defendant is immediately arrested.
  - The victim is satisfied.
- The pros of bringing a case directly to the grand jury without a warrant:
  - The defendant is arrested.
  - The victim testifies in a closed preceding rather than at a preliminary hearing after warrant.
  - The facts of the prosecution's case aren't disclosed early in the case's progression through the system.

Investigator Lockemup takes a report of sexual abuse that alleges Nina's stepfather, Robert, has been molesting her for a number of years. Lockemup sets up a third-party phone call with Nina and Robert wherein Nina confronts Robert with what he has been doing. Lockemup is listening in on the call. Nina tells Robert that she wants him to promise to stop because she doesn't like it. Robert apologizes to Nina and agrees to stop. The call is ended and Lockemup has the recording. Should Lockemup obtain a warrant or present the case to a grand jury (assuming Lockemup is in a state that utilizes grand juries)?

If Investigator Lockemup obtains a warrant for Robert, Nina may be subpoenaed for the preliminary hearing by the defense attorney. At the preliminary hearing, the defense attorney aggressively cross-examines Nina, and she gets very confused about all the dates and incidences wherein she was molested by her stepfather. She has a horrible experience and leaves the stand in tears. When the case progresses to a trial docket, the prosecutor reaches out to Nina. Nina says that she cannot testify again because of the emotional trauma she suffered. The prosecutor is forced to dismiss the case because moving forward will be detrimental to Nina's mental health. The prosecutor also knows that Nina will be impeached, given all the inconsistencies she explained while confused at the preliminary hearing.

If Investigator Lockemup decides to skip the warrant process and present the case directly to the next available grand jury, Nina will be subpoenaed by the government to testify at the grand jury proceeding. Since it is a closed preceding, the defense attorney is not present and Nina is gently questioned by the prosecutor. The grand jury returns an indictment and Robert is arrested. The case is set for trial. Nina is prepared and confident to testify because she feels good about how her testimony went at the grand jury proceeding. The case proceeds and the jury convicts Robert of sexual abuse.

These are extreme examples of why a prosecutor may elect to present a case directly to a grand jury (in states where that is available), but they make the point that early case decisions can have an impact on the case at a later time.

The court is responsible for empaneling the grand jury, but the prosecutor is responsible for most grand jury procedures. The prosecutor's office usually lines up the cases and witnesses to be presented to the grand jury and is present to question witnesses. The witnesses are sworn. The testimony received in a grand jury proceeding is secret and not open to the public, judge, or defense. Grand jurors are instructed that they can never disclose or discuss the cases heard as a grand juror. Prosecutors may disclose the content of witness testimony at a grand jury proceeding only in very limiting circumstances. One of these circumstances is when the testimony is exculpatory to the defendant.

Grand juries have investigative duties and can issue subpoenas to produce testimony (a **subpoena ad testificandum**) or a subpoena for documents (**subpoena duces tecum**). A grand jury has the power to hold a witness in contempt for failing to appear. The grand jury can invoke civil or criminal contempt sanctions to include incarceration for failing to appear. The grand jury cannot, however, compel a person to testify. The witness may invoke a Fifth Amendment right not to testify.

If the grand jury hears a case and determines there is probable cause evidence to believe the defendant committed the crime charged, the grand jury shall return an indictment. An indictment is a written instrument that is a charging instrument, similar to an arrest warrant that will command the defendant to be brought before the courts of justice to address the charges. This is also called a "true bill." If the grand jury does not find sufficient probable cause to bring an indictment against the defendant for a crime, it is called a "no bill." If a defendant's case is no billed by a grand jury, that is the end of the process for that case. It does not continue forward, and if the defendant was incarcerated, he is released. If a case is no billed, jeopardy has not attached and the defendant can be charged or investigated again for the same charge.

A grand jury may also continue a case forward for investigation to themselves or to another grand jury. Grand juries are usually impaneled for a short period of time, perhaps one to three months. During this time, they may not meet daily but rather at the request of the prosecutor when there are cases to be heard. At the end of one grand jury's service, another grand jury can be empaneled and hear the same case. Of course, they will not have the knowledge of any of the prior testimony, so the testimony would need to begin again.

Grand jury indictments can be challenged on a constitutional basis if the defendant can show (a) lack of evidence, (b) prosecutorial misconduct, (c) that the jurors were selected in an unfair, biased manner, and (d) the evidence presented at trial is substantially different than the evidence presented to the grand jury. This is a high burden for the defendant to prove, given there is no transcript record of the grand jury proceedings and the participants are sworn to silence regarding the proceeding.

Arraignment

An **arraignment** is a proceeding that notifies a person of the formal charges against him or her. In states that have grand juries, arraignment occurs after formal indictment by a grand jury. This is a public proceeding where the accused has the right to enter a formal plea to the charge. If the case was presented directly to a grand jury and did not begin with a warrant, then this will be the opportunity for the accused to receive court appointed counsel. The Sixth Amendment to the US Constitution requires that defendants have representation at arraignment procedures. Counsel can enter the accused's formal plea. These pleas could be guilty, not guilty, not guilty by mental disease or defect, or nolo contendere.

Guilty Plea

A defendant has the opportunity to enter a guilty plea at an arraignment proceeding. In some jurisdictions, the defendant can enter a guilty plea at the preliminary hearing stage. If the defendant enters a guilty plea at the arraignment, there must be an allocution. An **allocution** is a statement of the facts that are the basis of the charge. The allocution can be done by either the prosecutor or the defense. But no matter the party that states the facts against the defendant, the defendant will have to agree to the facts during the plea proceeding. The facts must include all the elements required to prove the charge against the defendant. It can be as simple as reading the warrant or indictment that the defendant is charged with or closer to an opening statement including all facts and witnesses. Once a defendant enters a plea of guilty to the charge, there aren't further **pretrial hearings**. The defendant can reserve the right to appeal certain issues, but those will be handled at the appellant level, not the trial level. These issues could include claims that the court does not have jurisdiction over the defendant or that the crime charged is unconstitutional. Once the plea is entered, the court will move to sentencing.

Not Guilty Plea

A defendant can enter a not guilty plea at arraignment. There is no other explanation necessary. It is the government's burden to prove the case against the defendant. If the defendant enters a plea of not guilty, then the case will proceed with other pretrial hearings and trial.

Not Guilty by Mental Disease or Defect

If the defendant pleads not guilty by reason of mental disease or defect, then the defendant is representing that he did commit the crime, but he is due to be released from the crime because he didn't appreciate the wrongfulness of his actions at the time of the crime. If a defendant pleads not guilty by mental disease or defect, the court may also inquire about the defendant's competency to stand trial. If the defendant is indigent, the court will usually order an evaluation by a mental health professional to determine the defendant's competency at the time of the crime and the defendant's competency to stand trial. If the defendant is not indigent, he or she can hire his or her own mental health professional to conduct an evaluation. The government may also hire a mental health professional to evaluate the defendant.

Nolo Contendere

A **nolo contendere** plea is sometimes called a best interest plea. This is a plea that occurs in the same manner as the guilty plea described above, but the defendant does not admit guilt. The defendant is listening to the facts that the government intends to prove and is agreeing that if the government proves those facts, he would be guilty. This is a small semantic distinction, but it is big legal difference. The defendant is telling the court that it is in his best interest to plead guilty based on the government's evidence, not because he is guilty. There are two notable issues surrounding nolo contendere pleas: First, crime victims often want to hear the defendant admit to the crime and the nolo contendere plea does not satisfy this wish. Second, the nolo contendere plea cannot be used as a prior conviction against the defendant for future sentencing enhancements. It is for these reasons that many states do not allow a nolo contendere guilty plea.

The arraignment is not usually a hearing in which witnesses are called. It would be unusual to have law enforcement testify at an arraignment unless there was an accompanying motion, such as a bond motion.

Plea Bargaining

Plea bargaining is a necessary part of the progression of a criminal case. If everyone charged with a crime requested a trial, the criminal justice system would not be able to accommodate those requests with current staff and funding.

Constitutional Issues Surrounding Guilty Pleas

The US Supreme Court in *Brady v. United States* held that they would not hold unconstitutional the state extending a benefit to the defendant and the defendant extending a benefit to the state. The rights a criminal defendant has during **plea negotiations** are not the same rights that a defendant enjoys at or after trial. However, there are several rights that the defendant has during plea negotiations:

The defendant has the right to counsel. The US Supreme Court in *Kirby v. Illinois* gives defendants the right to counsel after charges have been filed.

The right to effective counsel rises from the Sixth Amendment. This means that at a minimum the defendant's attorney must investigate the case so that he or she can effectively advise the defendant of the possible charges and sentence ranges that would be available during a plea negotiation.

Defendants do not have the right to be present at plea negations between defense counsel and the prosecution. Counsel for the defendant must share with his or her client any and all plea offers from the government. Some prosecution offices make all offers in writing, and it is copied to the defense attorney. Other prosecutor offices only convey offers orally. Competent counsel must also ensure that the defendant fully understands the consequences of a plea. This is often memorialized in an explanation of rights form that the defense attorney goes over with the defendant prior to the plea proceeding.

At a plea hearing, the court will go through a plea colloquy. This is a procedure in which the court explains the defendant's rights to plea or to have a trial. The court will notify the defendant of the range of punishment he will be facing upon a plea of guilt and any enhanced punishments that apply to the charge. The defendant will be asked by the court whether he or she still wishes to move forward with the plea. The court will also ask the defendant if he or she has been satisfied with their attorney in the case. If the defendant answers in the affirmative to all these questions, the judge will continue and accept the plea.

The Right to Exculpatory Evidence Does Not Extend to Plea Negotiations

A criminal defendant does not have the right to discovery before a plea hearing. The prosecution may provide some discovery to the defense attorney in order to move plea negotiations forward, but it is not required. There is no right to exculpatory evidence or impeachment information from the prosecution regarding witnesses against the defendant at the time of the plea. It is thought that if the defendant is guilty and wants to plead guilty, he or she knows what he or she did.

The defendant's plea must be knowing and voluntary. This can be evidenced by the explanation of rights colloquy and statement of counsel. The defense counsel and the judge both fully inform the defendant of the consequences of the plea and accept that the defendant is acting knowingly when he or she enters the guilty plea. The defendant must also plea voluntarily. This means that he or she cannot be under the influence of any intoxicating substance at the time of the plea, that the defendant cannot be suffering from any mental disease or defect at the time of the plea, or that the defendant cannot be subjected to any threat or duress to induce him or her to plea.

The Remedy: Setting the Case for Trial

Although there are several defendants who regret pleading guilty, a mere change of mind is never sufficient to set aside a guilty plea. Guilty pleas can be set aside if the court finds the plea was not done knowingly and voluntarily. However, the remedy for setting aside a guilty plea is setting the case for trial. This means that the defendant may still be convicted of the crime and potentially receive a greater sentence.

It is common knowledge that a defendant who accepts a plea bargain will surely receive a lesser sentence than a defendant who does not. In some jurisdictions this is called a "trial tax" or a "plea discount." In these cases, the punishment is determined by the attorneys involved in the same rather than a judge or jury. There are several factors that account for this sentencing scheme:

- Type of charge
- Strength of the case
- Criminal history of the defendant
- Requests of the victim

Type of Charge

The type of charge may give the attorneys for each side a starting point for plea negotiations. Many jurisdictions have mandatory sentencing schemes for certain felony offenses. These punishment ranges are set by statute or rule and may set an upper or lower limit in which the sentence must fall. One common way to deviate from the mandatory statutory minimums is to reduce the charge. Reducing charges is a common occurrence, and is expected in some jurisdictions in return for a plea of guilt.

The parties may also reduce the charge to a lesser included offense. The court taking the plea of the defendant must have subject matter jurisdiction to accept the guilty plea. This is shown by the charging instrument in the case: the warrant, the information, or the indictment. The wording in the charging instrument will allege the charge and set out the elements for that charge. If the government and the defendant work out a plea to a reduced charge, the reduced charge must be a technical lesser included offense of the original charge for the court to have jurisdiction to accept the guilty plea. The easiest way to determine whether a charge is a lesser included charge of the original offense is to see if the same elements are in both. The lesser included charge cannot add elements to the charge. For example, burglary in the first degree has the following elements: (a) entering a property unlawfully (b) with the intent to commit a crime (c) while armed with a deadly weapon. Robbery in the second degree has the following elements: (a) two or more persons (b) entering a property unlawfully (c) with intent to commit a crime. If the government and the defendant agreed to reduce the charge to robbery in the second degree, the court would not have jurisdiction to receive that plea because the lesser offense of robbery in the second degree adds an element of another person present.

Unspoken Considerations

There are always considerations made by both parties during the plea bargaining process that are unspoken. When considering whether to reduce a charge, the state must consider how to discuss the reduction with the victim or the victim's family. Sometimes, the name of the charge is very important to victims. For example, if the charge is murder, often the victim's family does not want the charge reduced to manslaughter as a matter of principle. Another consideration is always what the general public will think of the reduction in charge. A prosecutor's position is an elected position and therefore the prosecutor is accountable to the public as a whole. A prosecutor usually does not want to appear soft on crime without an explanation, and reducing a charge can have that appearance.

The Strength of the Case

The strength of the case must be accessed by both sides prior to resolving a case by plea. The government will bear the burden of proof beyond a reasonable doubt, which is a high standard to meet. The government will need strong evidence to convince a jury to convict the defendant. Jurors, as they should, demand that the case be proven and must be comfortable with their verdict, should they convict. The defense shall also review the strengths and weaknesses of their case in determining whether a plea bargain should be reached. The defense attorney will review discovery provided and discuss any defense strategies with the defendant. The attorney can only recommend to the defendant that he or she should plea bargain the case. Ultimately, it is the defendant's choice.

Unspoken Considerations

A prosecutor has the duty to turn over exculpatory evidence in every case. More on this will be discussed in the section on discovery. Suffice it to say now that exculpatory evidence is anything that tends to make the accused look not guilty. As the case progresses through the criminal justice system, witnesses could change their stories, move away, or even die. These are all considerations that the government will take into consideration but may not disclose to the defense during plea negotiations. The defense attorney will also be meeting with the defendant and accessing whether the defense is plausible under the circumstances and could lead to a finding of not guilty.

The Criminal History of the Defendant

The criminal history of the defendant will affect the sentence range. Many states have statutes that call for minimum sentences based on the number of prior felony convictions the state can prove. Some jurisdictions have sentencing worksheets that calculate the number of priors, including misdemeanors, youthful offender convictions, and types of crimes convicted. Keep in mind that the number of prior convictions that a defendant has may differ from the number of convictions that the government can actually prove. For example, if the conviction is thirty years old, whether the government can obtain a certified copy of that conviction may depend on the recordkeeping standards of the jurisdiction. It can be especially taxing for the government to communicate with out-of-state jurisdictions that may require certain certification processes to obtain a certified copy of the conviction. It becomes easier for the government to agree not to prove the prior conviction as the difficulty in obtaining it increases.

Unspoken Considerations

In some cases, the defendant may have a number of prior convictions that enhance his or her mandatory minimum sentence to a high number of years. A prosecutor may elect to not prove a certain number of prior convictions in order to entice the defendant to plead guilty. This could be due to the strength of the case or any other reason.

The Benefits of Plea Bargaining

The plea bargaining process is beneficial to the government because the government has a high standard of proof in criminal cases, and a conviction by plea alleviates the government of this burden of proof. Once the defendant pleads guilty, there is no need to prove any element of the case because the defendant has admitted to commission. If the defendant enters a guilty plea, it also means that the witnesses can be excused, saving the state any expenses related to witness travel or expert fees.

The plea bargain is beneficial to the victims in the case because it can give them control over the case. The victim or victim's family can be involved in the plea bargain negotiation, and once a term of punishment is reached, the victim can have certainty about the sentence. Often victims like the idea of being involved in the bargaining process rather than having a passive role in sentencing. If the case is tried, the jury or judge will solely determine the sentence, if there is a conviction. It also gives the victims a sense of closure because the defendant has admitted the wrong. This closure can come as soon as the plea is entered and the defendant is sentenced. While on the other hand, the trial process can be lengthy and the case could drag out months or years longer awaiting trial.

The plea bargaining process is beneficial to the government because the conviction isn't subject to all the appeals that otherwise would be available to the defendant after conviction. This gives closure to the case and lessens the possibility of the case being overturned on issues surrounding the trial.

The plea bargaining process is beneficial to the court and court officers. The criminal justice system is one of limited resources, and trials can be very taxing on all parties involved. The judges have tremendous caseloads. Setting aside days or weeks for a criminal trial means that everything else must wait. The court clerk's office is also relieved of pretrial motions and other filings that attorneys make when a case is progressing to trial. When a defendant enters a guilty plea, there is no need for many procedural pretrial motions. The sheriff's office is also relieved of the duty of service of subpoenas when a defendant pleads guilty. Serving subpoenas can take many man hours that can be devoted to other tasks when a case is not scheduled for trial and no subpoenas are filed.

The Criticisms of the Plea Bargaining Process

Plea bargaining can get to be so routine that it is expected in every case. When that happens, the government could get into the habit of overcharging offenses in order to reduce the charge to satisfy a plea bargain later in the case. The original charge is something that will remain with the accused on his record despite a reduction and a plea to a lesser charge. This could create unnecessary stigma and prejudice the defendant. For example, a fourteen-year-old victim reports that she had sexual intercourse with a nineteen-year-old boy. She reports that she didn't want to, but he forced himself on her. Instead of investigating what the victim meant by "forced himself," the law enforcement officer charges him with rape in the first degree. The law enforcement officer knows that the government's procedure in his jurisdiction is to offer plea bargains in most every case to a lesser charge. Ultimately, the defendant pleads guilty to a charge of rape in the second degree, which is a charge that requires no force yet is an offense due to the age difference between the victim and the accused, How was the defendant prejudiced by the original charge? It is forever on his criminal history, and when he is applying for employment or schools, it will show a charge of rape in the first degree with a plea to rape in the second degree. This could unduly prejudice the defendant because assumptions will be made about the facts of the case.

Another criticism of the plea bargaining process is that it breeds inefficiency. Officials in the criminal justice system can easily be burned out by the sheer volume of cases. It is much easier to dispose of a case via plea than by having a trial. Trials can be lengthy and stressful and require many hours in preparation. Prosecutors can get complacent in their duties and succumb to the easier route. This could mean that the prosecutor undercuts a case by offering a very low sentence to entice the accused to plea.

Many people believe that the plea bargaining process can undermine the criminal justice process. Plea agreements can be seen as being weak on crime, and it can be said that the defendant got away with his crime. The most serious public criticism of the plea process is that it encourages innocent people to plead guilty.

Plea Bargains Are Still Subject to the Court's Ratification

The plea bargain is usually worked out between the parties to the case: the defendant and the government. The government has the authority to enter into any agreement, even an agreement that the victim is not satisfied with. The prosecutor's role is to be consistent with other similar cases and do what is best for the community as a whole. The opposite is true for the defense. The defendant is the sole decision-maker as to whether a plea will be accepted. The defense attorney can only recommend that the defendant accept or reject a plea agreement but cannot speak for his client. Often, attorneys will get creative in working out a plea agreement that both sides are satisfied with. No matter the plea agreement reached, it is only valid if the judge will accept the terms. Some judges feel that it is not the court's responsibility to interfere and will accept just about any agreement that the parties reach; other judges will make suggestions to the attorneys about the terms of the agreement and not accept the plea bargain unless the parties agree to the judge's notifications.

Discovery

Discovery is the exchange of information between the parties concerning which evidence each will present. The discovery process is outlined in the Federal Rules of Criminal Procedure and is not equal between the parties because of the constitutional rights of the defendant. The Federal Rules of Criminal Procedure specifically list the responsibilities of the government and defense separately. Rule 16 of the Federal Rules of Criminal Procedure states that the Government must disclose the following:

1. Defendant's oral statement. Upon a defendant's request, the government must disclose to the defendant the substance of any relevant oral statement made by the defendant, before or after arrest, in response to interrogation by a person the defendant knew was a government agent if the government intends to use the statement at trial.
2. Defendant's written or recorded Statement. Upon a defendant's request, the government must disclose to the defendant, and make available for inspection, copying, or photographing, all the following:
    - any relevant written or recorded statement by the defendant if:
        - the statement is within the government's possession, custody, or control; and
        - the attorney for the government knows—or through due diligence could know—that the statement exists;
    - the portion of any written record containing the substance of any relevant oral statement made before or after arrest if the defendant made the statement in response to interrogation by a person the defendant knew was a government agent; and
    - the defendant's recorded testimony before a grand jury relating to the charged offense.
3. Defendant's prior record. Upon a defendant's request, the government must furnish the defendant with a copy of the defendant's prior criminal record that is within the government's

possession, custody, or control if the attorney for the government knows—or through due diligence could know—that the record exists.

Some points to note about these rules are that they are prefaced by "upon a defendant's request." Most of the time this is through a written motion for discovery filed with the court. The other important note is that the government must turn over a defendant's statement that is "within the government's possession, custody, or control" and the government "through due diligence could know that the statement exists." This rule puts the burden on the government to seek out any statement of the defendant that may not already be in the possession of the prosecutor. For example, if the defendant made statements to paramedics at the scene of the crime, this may not be in the police file, and therefore not in the prosecutor's file. However, the prosecutor should make inquiry as to whether the defendant made statements to anyone on the scene and provide those statements to the defense. This prevents a prosecutor from using plausible deniability about the defendant's statement: "It wasn't in my file, so I didn't provide it in discovery." The cornerstone of whether the government "could know" is reasonableness. For example, a defendant would not be successful in showing that a prosecutor should have known about a sealed juvenile conviction in another state.

The Federal Rules of Criminal Procedure also have rules dictating the discovery of documents and objects.

1. Documents and objects. Upon a defendant's request, the government must permit the defendant to inspect and to copy or photograph books, papers, documents, data, photographs, tangible objects, buildings, or places, or copies or portions of any of these items, if the item is within the government's possession, custody, or control; and
    - the item is material to preparing the defense;
    - the government intends to use the item in its case-in-chief at trial; or
    - the item was obtained from or belongs to the defendant.
2. Reports of examinations and tests. Upon a defendant's request, the government must permit a defendant to inspect and to copy or photograph the results or reports of any physical or mental examination and of any scientific test or experiment if
    - the item is within the government's possession, custody, or control;
    - the attorney for the government knows—or through due diligence could know—that the item exists; and
    - the item is material to preparing the defense or the government intends to use the item in its case-in-chief at trial.

It is important to note that all these rules also are prefaced with "upon the defendant's request." The rule also includes the language "within the government's possession, custody, or control." This can be interpreted broadly, but the cornerstone is reasonableness. For example, if the 911 emergency call is recorded and time stamped, it may still be in the control of the emergency management agency, not the prosecutor's office. However, this could be reasonably within the prosecutors' control, depending on the jurisdiction's organizational structure.

The government also has the duty to disclose expert witnesses under the Federal Rules of Criminal Procedure.

- Duty to disclose. At the defendant's request, the government must disclose to the defendant, in writing, any testimony that the government intends to use at trial under from an expert witness to include
  - a complete statement of all opinions that the government will elicit from the witness in its case-in-chief, or during its rebuttal to counter testimony that the defendant has timely disclosed;
  - the bases and reasons for them; and
  - the witness's qualifications, including (a) a list of all publications authored in the previous ten years, and (b) a list of all other cases in which, during the previous four years, the witness has testified as an expert at trial or by deposition.

It should be noted that this rule also contains the language "at the defendant's request." Here again, the defendant will usually file a motion requesting notice of state's experts. This request will trigger the government's response.

The government must always discover to the defense any exculpatory evidence. Exculpatory evidence is evidence that is favorable to the defense. Failure to disclose this evidence is a violation of due process. In *Brady v. Maryland*, Brady was convicted on a charge of murder in the first degree (committed in the course of a robbery) and sentenced to death. Later, Brady learned of an extrajudicial confession of his accomplice, tried separately, admitting the actual homicide. This confession had been suppressed by the prosecution despite the defendant's request for it. The US Supreme Court held that the statement should have been disclosed to the defense and failure to do so was a due process violation. The Brady Court went on to state that the suppression by the prosecution of evidence favorable to an accused upon request violates due process where the evidence is material either to guilt or to punishment, irrespective of the good faith or bad faith of the prosecution. Later cases have dictated that the Brady rule applies despite the defendant's request for exculpatory material. Exculpatory material always needs to be turned over to the defense by the prosecutor. Even evidence that is not admissible should be turned over because it could lead to admissible evidence that the defense could use.

Although the above rules make it sound as if a lot of information is discoverable to the defense, but there are several pieces of evidence that are not discoverable.

1. Inculpatory evidence is not discoverable. This is evidence that is used to show the defendant committed the crime. For example, in a robbery case, where the victim and the witness both say the defendant committed the robbery, neither statement is discoverable to the defense because both statements inculpate the defendant.

2. Also, discovery of inspection of reports, memoranda, or other internal government documents made by an attorney for the government or other government agent in connection with investigating or prosecuting the case is not required. This is known as the work product rule. Prosecutors and law enforcement officers do not have to turn over their work product in discovery. For example, witness statements that are inculpatory are not given to the defense in discovery.

Although the rules for providing discovery must be made available for the other side to view, copy, or inspect, most government offices make copies of the discoverable materials for the defense. Electronic files can be copied or transferred via a secure cloud storage site allowing secure access. Some government offices have set fees associated with certain types of copies, while others just absorb the costs. Attorneys who are retained simply pass this cost on to the client. Attorneys who are appointed for indigent defendants can bill the state for expenses. There could also be special circumstances where the state should not allow the defendant to copy the discovery. An example of this would be in a possession of child pornography case.

Each state has their own version of Federal Rule of Criminal Procedure Rule 16 and will be slightly different. The constant is that exculpatory evidence must be discovered to the defense.

There are also rules that govern what the defense must discover to the government. It is not as exhaustive as the government's list because the constitutional rights apply to the defense and not the government. However, there are rules created in fairness to give the government an opportunity to prepare for certain defenses. Rule 16 of the Federal Rules of Criminal Procedure require the defendant, upon request of the government, to disclose the following:

1. Items: Books, papers, documents, data, photographs, tangible objects, buildings, or places, or copies or portions of any of these items if
    - the item is within the defendant's possession, custody, or control; and
    - the defendant intends to use the item in the defendant's case-in-chief at trial.
2. Examinations or tests: The results or reports of any physical or mental examination and of any scientific test or experiment if
    - the item is within the defendant's possession, custody, or control; and
    - the defendant intends to use the item in the defendant's case-in-chief at trial, or intends to call the witness who prepared the report and the report relates to the witness's testimony.
3. Expert witnesses: At the government's request, the defendant must disclose to the government, in writing, testimony of an expert witness that the defense intends to call at trial.

It is important to note, just as in the duties of the government to disclose to the defense, requests for the information is necessary. The Federal Rules of Criminal Procedure also allow the local courts to determine the time frame that is reasonable for the disclosure. The Federal Rules of Criminal Procedure provide for a continuing duty to disclose for both sides. This means that if additional evidence is discovered by a party after the initial discovery, or even after the trial has begun, it should immediately be turned over to the opposing party.

The Federal Rules of Criminal Procedure also provide for sanctions for failure to comply. If a party fails to comply with this rule, the court may

1. order that party to permit the discovery or inspection, specify its time, place, and manner, and prescribe other just terms and conditions;
2. grant a continuance;
3. prohibit that party from introducing the undisclosed evidence; or
4. enter any other order that is just under the circumstances. Each state has enacted a similar rule.

Prosecutors also have a duty to preserve evidence. For example, if the state tests blood samples for a DNA match, the government cannot then throw the sample away once the test is complete. The government has a duty to preserve that evidence in the event the defense requests an independent test.

Suppression Hearings

A common pretrial hearing is a **suppression hearing**. This is a motion filed by the defense to suppress certain pieces of evidence that the prosecution intends to offer in the case. Although the defense files the motion, it is the state's burden to show that the evidence is admissible against the accused and therefore lead the hearing. If the suppression motion moves to suppress a piece of physical evidence, the prosecutor will need a witness to testify about the circumstances under which the evidence was collected. If a search warrant was executed, the prosecutor will need the officer who was the affiant on the search warrant. If the officer receives a subpoena, he or she should immediately contact the prosecutor and determine what type of hearing is requested and what the prosecutor intends to gain from the officer's testimony. This hearing is possibly the first opportunity that the prosecutor has had to review the evidence in the case. This hearing is also the defense's "practice run" with the state's witnesses outside the presence of a jury. The judge will be the finder of the legal determination of whether the piece of evidence was obtained in a constitutionally sound manner. However, the witness should remember that even though there is no jury, there will be a court reporter recording every word of the testimony. The witness should be just as prepared as he or she would be at a trial.

Suppression hearings are not only for challenging physical evidence but for challenging statements of defendants as well. If this is the case, the law enforcement officer who took the statement of the defendant will be called to testify. The voluntariness of the statement will be the issue, along with whether the statement was subject to Miranda. A witness subpoenaed to testify at a suppression hearing regarding the statement of the defendant should also review the circumstances with the prosecutor handling the case.

Competency Hearing

If the accused pleads not guilty by mental disease or defect at arraignment or any other pretrial setting, there will be a need for a **competency hearing**. The first hearing is to determine whether the defendant is competent to stand trial. This is a preliminary matter, because if the defendant is found incompetent to stand trial, all other issues related to the trial procedure are moot.

Burden of Proof

During the hearing to determine competency to stand trial, the government will bear the burden of proving that the defendant is competent to stand trial, this can be done a number of ways. One avenue of proof is to put forward evidence that the defendant suffers from a severe mental disease or defect. The defense could call lay witnesses who are in close contact with the defendant, such as family members or friends. The defense attorney could also call expert witnesses, such as mental health professionals who have treated the defendant in the past. Some states allow the judge to make the decision as to whether the defendant is competent to stand trial. Other states require jury trials on the issue of competency.

The defense could also allege that something happened to the defendant after the commission of the crime but before the defendant's trial and that testimony regarding the defendant's behavior at the time of the crime is irrelevant to his mental state at the time of trial. For example, the defendant could have been in a car accident while out on bond and suffered a traumatic brain injury. This circumstance could render the defendant unable to understand the criminal proceedings of his case and therefore incompetent to stand trial.

The second issue of competency surrounds the defendant's competency at the time of the crime. In order for the defendant to be held responsible for the crime itself, the question will be whether he understood the consequences of his actions at the time of the crime. Sometimes the circumstances surrounding the crime can show the competency of the defendant. The prosecutor can also call witnesses who interacted with the defendant around the time of the crime. Testimony about the contents of conversations with the accused are allowed into evidence because the defendant is present and available to rebut the testimony, if he so wishes.

The defendant entered his place of employment along with other coworkers to start the day. While everyone was at their desks, the defendant went to his supervisor and shot him in the back of the head. The defendant immediately called 911 and requested "extraction," telling the operator that he had killed the target. The defendant's coworkers all gave statements that he was odd and kept to himself. They all were eyewitnesses to the execution-style murder he committed. At the defendant's arraignment, he pleads not guilty by mental disease or defect. Later, at the defendant's hearing on his competency to stand trial and competency to appreciate the wrongfulness of his actions, the state calls witnesses. One witness is the first responder to the crime scene who took the defendant into custody. The witness testified that the defendant was armed with two weapons: a .40-caliber handgun and a .22-caliber handgun. This distinction could be relevant to show that the defendant knew what he was doing at the time of the crime because he used the larger-caliber weapon to accomplish the murder.

Issues can also arise as to the defendant's competency to waive certain rights, such as Miranda rights, before giving a statement. A defendant may argue that he understands the trial process (his competency to stand trial) and he was not incompetent at the time of the crime, yet his Miranda rights were not knowingly and voluntarily waived due to incompetency. The defendant could hire expert witnesses to examine the issues surrounding the Miranda warnings to give testimony that the defendant did not understand the rights and therefore could not waive them. If the defendant is found incompetent to waive the Miranda rights, then the statement would be suppressed, unless it was not custodial or an interrogation.

Other Pretrial Hearings

Other Bad Acts

The general rule is that the trial of the case must be on the merits and facts of the case at the time of the crime. However, some jurisdictions allow other bad acts to be admissible to show things such as intent or identification in limited circumstances. A law enforcement officer may be called to testify that an accused has another bad act that is relevant to the charge before the court. For example, if the defendant is on trial for distribution of a controlled substance and the defendant has been convicted three other times of distribution of the same controlled substance, the prior acts could be admissible to show the defendant's common scheme or plan for selling controlled substances. Of course, the sales need be very similar in facts to show this nexus.

Stand Your Ground

When the defense is self-defense, the defense may be that the defendant had the right to stand his or her ground. There are many states that have enacted certain statutes to allow for pretrial hearings to determine the sufficiency of a stand-your-ground defense. This could be an in-depth pretrial hearing because it would be necessary for the government to prove most aspects of the case for a determination to be made of whether the defendant acted in self-defense.

Rules to Remember

Below is a list of rules to remember from this chapter.

- There are many different types of pretrial release options: own recognizance, cash bond, property bond.
- The judge has great latitude for setting conditions of bail or bond.
- The conditions of pretrial release may be changed anytime at the request of either party or on the judge's own motion.
- The preliminary hearing is a formal hearing wherein the government has the burden of proving the case through witness testimony by a probable cause standard.
- In states with grand jury proceedings, cases can be brought to a grand jury in three ways: (a) after the defendant has been formally charged by warrant, (b) as an investigation file, or (c) initiated by the grand jury.
- Grand juries have investigative duties and can issue subpoenas to produce testimony (a subpoena ad testificandum) or a subpoena for documents (subpoena duces tecum).
- An arraignment is when the defendant enters a formal plea for the charges against him.
- The type of charge, the strength of the case, the criminal history of the defendant, and the requests of the victim are just some of the factors that can affect the government's decision in the plea bargaining process.
- The outcome of a suppression hearing can affect the ability of the government to move forward with the case. If key evidence is suppressed, the criminal case may be dismissed as a matter of law.
- The accused is entitled to a hearing on the issue of competency if there is a plea of not guilty by reason of mental disease or defect.
- Plea agreements that are reached by the parties are still subject to ratification or approval by the judge.
- The government must give notice of intentions to show other bad act evidence. This pretrial notice may necessitate a pretrial hearing on the other bad act evidence.
- The government must discover to the defense any exculpatory evidence, regardless of if the defense requests discovery.

- States that have enacted stand-your-ground self-defense legislation require the court to have a pretrial hearing on the issue of self-defense.

End of Chapter Comprehension and Application

Directions: Use what you have learned in this chapter to help you respond completely and correctly to each question or prompt below.

1. Summarize the different options for pretrial release.
2. What is the purpose of an initial appearance and what are the accused's rights at an initial appearance?
3. Amy was arrested for shoplifting designer clothing. Because the value of the merchandise stolen was greater than five thousand dollars, she was charged with theft of property in the first degree. She has a long history of property offenses and has been given a high bond because of her past history. Amy is eight months pregnant, but the jail does not want to incur her hospitalization expenses for labor and delivery. What can the jail request in order to avoid Amy's medical costs?
4. Jacob Arstop was arrested for trafficking in marijuana. He was caught in possession of ten pounds of marijuana and admitted to selling marijuana to support himself. He also admitted to using marijuana and having dependency on marijuana. Jacob cannot make bond but has asked to be released to a drug rehab program while he awaits trial. Explain what the judge's options will be for Jacob's request.
5. When is the appropriate time to ask for a change in pretrial release conditions?
6. What is the purpose of the preliminary hearing?
7. What should an officer do when he or she receives a subpoena to testify in a preliminary hearing?
8. Explain the different pleas that can be entered at arraignment.
9. Summarize the effects of a plea bargain on all parties.
10. What are the elements of a valid guilty plea?
11. What factors are taken into consideration in the plea bargaining process? Explain each in detail.
12. What are some unspoken considerations in the plea bargaining process? Explain in detail.
13. The defendant files a postconviction motion alleging that his counsel, at the time of plea, did not fully explain the consequences of the plea. What proof would be sufficient for the court to set aside the defendant's guilty plea?
14. What types of pieces of evidence are discoverable to the defendant? When are they discoverable? What triggers discovery?
15. Does the defendant have the right to exculpatory evidence at the time of plea? What is the rationale for this rule?
16. What types of evidence can be challenged at a suppression hearing?

17. Who has the burden of proof at a suppression hearing and why?
18. What two issues of competency must be proven to the court to allow the prosecution to proceed with trial against the defendant? Why?
19. Is it possible for a defendant's competency to change during the course of a criminal proceeding? If so, give an example.
20. Explain other possible pretrial hearings and what can occur at those hearings.

References

United States Supreme Court in Gerstein v. Pugh, 420 U.S. 103 (1975), https://supreme.justia.com/cases/federal/us/420/103/

Bail Schedule, Supreme Court of Alabama, January 14, 2022, https://judicial.alabama.gov/docs/rules/Rule7_2(b)AlaRCrimPOrder.pdf

Schilb v. Kuebel, 404 U.S. 357 (1971), https://supreme.justia.com/cases/federal/us/404/357/

Goldsby v. United States, 160 U.S. 70 (1895), https://supreme.justia.com/cases/federal/us/160/70/

Brady v. United States, 397 U.S. 742 (1970), https://supreme.justia.com/cases/federal/us/397/742/

Kirby v. Illinois, 406 U.S. 682 (1972), https://supreme.justia.com/cases/federal/us/406/682/

Brady v. Maryland, 373 US 83 (1963), https://supreme.justia.com/cases/federal/us/373/83/

Chapter 8

The Adversarial Proceeding

Introduction: Preparing for Trial and the Procedures Involved

This chapter will discuss the procedures involved in a criminal trial.

Chapter Objectives

In this chapter students will learn:

- The standards of proof required for conviction
- How evidence is presented at trial
- The purposes of voir dire
- The purposes of opening and closing statements
- The purposes of direct examination and cross-examination
- Tips for witnesses
- The basis surrounding the right to a speedy trial
- What is meant by a "fair and impartial jury"
- What could be considered "ineffective" by defense counsel

Key Terms

Key terms and professional terminology that are used in this chapter include:

- **Jury trial**
- **Bench trial**
- **Voir dire**
- **Direct examination**

- **Cross-examination**
- **Self-authenticating evidence**
- **Rebuttal witness**
- **Closing arguments**
- **Courtroom technology**
- **Juvenile proceedings**

What Is Meant by "Adversarial Proceeding"?

An adversarial proceeding is a system of law wherein the goal is to find the truth. During this truth-seeking process, opposing parties present their respective sides to a judge or jury whose job it is to determine the truth and pass judgment accordingly. Most defendants' cases will be resolved by guilty plea, but those who wish to have a trial will be granted one. This adversarial proceeding affords the defendant certain rights that may be asserted by him.

The Burdens of Proof

There are multiple burdens of proof utilized in criminal courts. The definitions of each are not crystal clear, yet clear enough to make a distinction.

Proof beyond a Reasonable Doubt

The ultimate burden of proof for a criminal trial is proof beyond a reasonable doubt. This basic right is guaranteed by the due process clause of the Fourteenth Amendment and case law. This standard of proof applies to all criminal cases, no matter the seriousness of the crime. A harassment case must be proven beyond a reasonable doubt the same as a murder case must be proven beyond a reasonable doubt. There have been many definitions given for what rises to the level of proof beyond a reasonable doubt. Some courts define it as a doubt for which one can attach a reason, not a mere speculative doubt. The courts have made it clear that proof beyond a reasonable doubt is more than a probable doubt but less than an absolute certainty.

Often discussed with proof beyond a reasonable doubt is the presumption of innocence. Under the Due Process Clause of the Fourteenth Amendment, a defendant is presumed innocent until proven guilty beyond a reasonable doubt.

Preponderance of the Evidence

This is a standard used in many civil proceedings but also applicable in criminal proceedings. While proof beyond a reasonable doubt is the standard for ultimate conviction of the defendant, there are other instances that need be weighed by the judge during a trial—for example, admissibility of certain pieces of evidence. If a defendant challenges a search and the evidence collected, the judge must determine that the state met the required burden by a preponderance of the evidence.

Proof to Reasonable Satisfaction of the Judge

This is an even lower standard than the preponderance of the evidence standard. This standard is merely that the judge is reasonably satisfied that the proof exists. This standard is used in probation revocation hearings and other like hearings.

The Defendant Has No Burden of Proof (Almost)

A criminal defendant does not have the burden of proving his innocence and has the right to assert no defense at all. A criminal defendant can just argue that the government has failed to prove its case beyond a reasonable doubt. It would be a mistrial for the prosecution or a prosecution witness to comment on any duty of the defendant to prove his or her innocence. There are a few exceptions to this general no-burden rule. One example would be where the defendant asserts an extreme emotional disturbance defense. The defendant would be required to prove this affirmative defense as long as it was not an element of the crime charged.

Preparing for the Adversarial Proceeding

An adversarial proceeding is not an undertaking to go into unprepared. Preparing for an adversarial proceeding can take days, weeks, or months depending on the complexity of the case. An investigator must refamiliarize him or herself with every aspect of the case. This will include reviewing the evidence and reports and speaking with witnesses. Often, there are many months, if not years, in between the commission of the offense and the trial on the matter. Many cases have happened since then and it is easy to forget important details of the investigation.

Reviewing the Evidence

Once an investigator learns that a case will be called to trial, the first thing he or she should do is review the physical evidence. This is the tangible evidence that was collected during the investigation. This could be items such as shell casings or blood swabs. Often these items are sent to a laboratory for forensic testing and then returned to the investigative agency. In large departments, there may be one officer in charge of logging the evidence in and out of the property room. However, that officer is not familiar with the facts of each individual case. If, for example, a piece of evidence was not picked up from the laboratory doing the testing, it will be missing from the evidence room. It is the investigator's responsibility to ensure that all pieces of evidence are still available to be presented at trial.

Investigator Lockemup investigated a murder wherein the victim was shot and killed. The projectile was collected from the victim's body at autopsy and Lockemup collected many shell casings from the crime scene. The state laboratory conducting autopsy examinations has a practice of mailing forensic evidence to the state laboratory conducting ballistics testing. This is done through the US Postal Service. When this case is called for trial, Lockemup collects the evidence and delivers it to the prosecutor's office for pretrial review. The prosecutor and the defense attorney are reviewing the evidence when they notice that the cardboard envelope containing the bullet removed from the victim's body is empty. Upon further examination, a small hole is found in the cardboard envelope. It is concluded that the envelope may have been fed through some type of machine at the postal service that pressed the bullet out of the packaging. There is no other explanation presented. This could be a very disruptive moment if discovered midtrial and is much better to be discovered pretrial.

It is also necessary for the investigator and the prosecutor to discuss the evidence in preparation for trial. The prosecutor may not fully understand why a particular piece of evidence is relevant to the case or put more or less weight on a particular piece of evidence than necessary. The prosecutor is the advocate for the criminal case and must present the case in the most persuasive manner possible. Most pieces of evidence are sealed in containers pending trial. This is necessary to preserve the integrity of the evidence collected. The general practice is for the evidence to be sealed upon collection and initialed by the person sealing the container. Then each person who opens the container initials or signs the container and dates the opening. Usually this occurs when the evidence is tested by the laboratory testing the evidence. It can also occur if the evidence needs to be repackaged for some purpose. This could cause the piece of evidence to have several different markings on it by the time it is presented at trial. This could also be done with a list attached to the piece of evidence documenting each time it was opened and by whom. This is known as the chain of custody. It can also be opened for viewing in preparation for trial. This could occur at discovery proceedings if the defense attorney requests to view all the evidence. The prosecutor handling the case should also open and view each piece of evidence. This could involve wearing masks and gloves so as not to contaminate the evidence if further analysis is required. Some agencies have a practice of photographing or videoing the evidence as it is being sealed. This could be an optional way to view the evidence in preparation for trial.

Investigator Lockemup has investigated a domestic violence case wherein the victim was threatened by the defendant. The victim alleges that the defendant held a knife to her throat and threatened to kill her. She also alleges he strangled her until she passed out. The physical evidence consists of the knife that was collected from the scene and sealed in an opaque container. The prosecutor does not open the container pretrial or when it is exhibited in the container during trial. During closing argument, the prosecutor is passionately delivering a closing argument about the deadly weapon that was held to the victim's throat and how she was in fear for her life. The prosecutor dramatically opens the container in front of the jury only to find a butter knife. This embarrassing moment could have been prevented by simple communication between the prosecutor and investigator or a visual inspection of the evidence.

It is also important to review all reports prior to trial. Depending on the complexity of the case, there could be many types of reports. Every case will have police reports. Incident reports initiate most criminal investigations and contain basic information, such as dates, locations, names, and contact information. Investigators often supplement the initial incident report with documentation of the progression of the case. This gives greater detail about the facts, witnesses, and circumstances. There could also be export reports from various agencies in the case file. For example, if blood swabs were collected from the crime scene, they would have been analyzed for DNA. The DNA report would be part of the file. If there were an autopsy of a body, that report would be part of the file. If a child victim was counseled, that expert report may be part of the file. There are many different reports that the investigator is taxed with imputed knowledge. The investigator needs to read all these reports and be prepared to answer minimal questions about them.

> Investigator Lockemup worked a murder scene wherein the victim was stabbed multiple times. There was a lot of blood evidence at the scene and Lockemup collected swabs of the blood. The body of the victim was sent for an autopsy examination, and DNA swabs were collected from the victim's body at autopsy. Lockemup delivered the swabs he collected from the scene to the laboratory for DNA analysis. The laboratory conducting the autopsy sent the swabs collected from the victim's body to the same laboratory for analysis. The scientist analyzed the two samples submitted and prepared a report. The report states that the swabs collected from the crime scene contain the victim's DNA and a foreign DNA that was typed as male. The scientist's report states that further analysis could be conducted if another DNA sample were submitted. The report is sent back to the Smallville police department. The secretary gets the report and files it in Lockemup's murder file. Then a year later, the case is called for trial. The day of trial, the prosecutor asks Lockemup why he never submitted a swab taken from the defendant for comparison. At this point, Lockemup realizes he forgot to submit the swab and now is left without a potential DNA match at the crime scene. The prosecutor could ask for a continuance, but the judge may or may not grant it.

There should also be a review of the photographs in each case. The investigator may only have digital copies of the photographs, and perhaps the prosecutor prefers to present tangible copies that can be easily viewed by the jury. Perhaps the digital copies have already been turned over to the defense in discovery without review. Digital evidence should always be viewed before being copied. For example, if the law enforcement officer stores all his digital evidence in one folder, he could click the wrong photos to copy and end up turning over a completely separate case to the prosecutor. The prosecutor could in turn copy the photos without review to the defense. This could cause the defendant to be in possession of private and personal information in another case. This could also allow the defense to argue against the government's use of photos at trial because the correct photos were never turned over before trial. Video footage should also be reviewed so as not to make mistakes while copying. In all circumstances, a simple review of the evidence before copying can alleviate these kinds of mistakes.

An investigator should also contact witnesses prior to the case going to trial. As stated earlier, months or years could elapse between the crime occurring and the case going to trial. This gap in time also means that the witnesses' circumstances could change. The address and phone number originally listed might no longer be valid and thus the witness will need to be found. Witnesses could also change their statement for a variety of reasons. If the witness and the defendant had a prior relationship (family, friend, or dating relationship), the witness could not wish to testify against the defendant at trial. The witness could outright lie and say he or she doesn't remember what happened or falsify a version of the facts that would be favorable to the defendant. Witnesses could be intimidated or paid to change their statements or forget what they saw.

An investigator should remember that the case is always ongoing until there is an acquittal or conviction. This means that a witness could also have more information than was originally disclosed. Witnesses generally answer questions posed by the law enforcement officer asking. The law enforcement officer may not have the full facts at the time of the witness statement, and the officer may later develop more facts and therefore some questions go unasked. As a case is approaching trial, the investigator may find it necessary to ask follow-up questions with certain witnesses. The investigator and prosecutor should communicate before this is done because it could be an issue with discovery. The bottom line is that a simple review of witness circumstances can change the dynamics of the case.

The Steps in the Adversarial Proceeding

There are many steps in a trial, whether it is a bench trial or a **jury trial**. A **bench trial**—a trial where the judge is the finder of fact and law—removes the need for jury selection, therefore simplifying the process slightly. A trial by jury, where the jury is the finder of fact and the judge is the finder of the law, adds the additional step of jury selection. This is also known by the French word **voir dire**, which means to speak the truth.

The Voir Dire Process

The voir dire process is generally known to people as jury selection. This can happen in a number of ways, but it will involve questions being posed to jurors and the jurors answering those questions. Some jurisdictions send out jury notices or summons electronically and hope that the requisite number of people will show up for the trial; other jurisdictions hand-deliver subpoenas to prospective jurors.

In *Taylor v. Louisiana*, the US Supreme Court required that jury selection procedures be based on "the concept of the jury being a fair cross section of the community." This ruling allowed challenges to jury selection pools if the defendant could show a systematic exclusion of a sex or race or other protected class of persons. In the Taylor case, the state of Louisiana required women to file and declare their desire to be subject to jury service, thus systematically reducing the number of women eligible and serving on juries in the state of Louisiana. This ruling does not mean that a defendant is guaranteed that his or her sex or race will be a member of the jury, but it does mean that a particular group is not being systematically excluded from service.

Jurors must meet a minimum qualification for service. If a juror does not meet that minimum qualification, the juror will be excused. These qualifications include things such as being able to read, speak, and understand the English language; being over a minimum age required for that jurisdiction; having no prior felony convictions; being a citizen of the United States, and being a resident of the jurisdiction for a minimum amount of time. Each state can set certain minimum requirements along with other no-bias qualifications. Some jurisdictions request jurors to complete an online form prior to the date of the jury service. This allows the Court to excuse jurors who are disqualified prior to the trial date. Other jurisdictions require potential jurors to show in person and state the reasons he or she is disqualified. Once the jurors are qualified for service, many jurisdictions allow questioning by the attorneys about specific opinions or qualifications.

Once those answers are gathered, then the striking process begins.

The judge can and usually does begin the voir dire process with questions to potential jurors. The judge's questions are usually limited to foundational questions, but a judge could ask about any specific issue.

Jury selection is just the opposite—it is done by elimination. Both the defense and the prosecution have an unlimited number of strikes for cause and a limited number of peremptory strikes. Strikes for cause can be used by any party when that party feels that the potential juror is disqualified from service. This could be due to relationships between the potential juror and the defendant or victim in the case. This could be because the juror answered that he or she could not return a verdict and make judgment against a fellow man. This could be because the potential juror answered that he or she knows something about the facts of the case and has already formed an opinion of the defendant's guilt or innocence. The party who believes the juror would be disqualified will make a strike for cause, and the opposing party would agree or make an argument against disqualification. The judge could eliminate the potential juror based on previous answers to questions posed and attorney argument or pose further questions directly to that juror before making a ruling.

Once all disqualified potential jurors are eliminated, the court will notify the parties of the total number of jurors who are in the jury pool for selection purposes. Then the judge and/or parties will agree if there is to be an alternative juror selected. An alternative juror is usually the last juror struck and thus released from duty but for the decision to retain an alternate juror. Trials can be complicated and costly endeavors. If the trial is progressing and a juror because of sickness or otherwise could not attend the rest of the trial, the judge would be forced to declare a mistrial and start again at a later date. However, if there were an alternate juror, then that person could replace the unavailable juror. The alternative juror usually does not know that he or she is the alternative juror until the close of the case. To let the juror know earlier may cause that person to not pay attention or otherwise not take the trial seriously, knowing that he or she wouldn't be involved in the deliberations. Therefore, if a juror becomes unavailable during the trial, the alternate will never know he or she was the alternate. Similarly, sometimes the judges will require the alternate juror stay even after deliberations begin. Deliberations can be lengthy as well, and a juror could become unavailable during deliberations. If that were to happen, the alternate juror would be placed in the jury room and the jurors would be ordered to resume deliberations. All these scenarios prevent a retrial and save taxpayers money.

Once the jury pool numbers are totaled, each party will be told how many peremptory challenges they have based on the total number of potential jurors left in the pool. For example, if there are fifty-one people remaining in the pool and thirteen are needed for the jury, including one alternate, then fifty-one minus thirteen is thirty-eight and each side will have nineteen strikes. The defense's last strike will be the alternate juror. Each party will call out a strike until the potential jurors remaining in the pool are the jurors "selected."

The psychology of the selection process is the peremptory selection process. Each side is armed with the answers each potential juror has given during the questioning. These questions are usually in-depth and personal, questions such as have they or a family member ever been a victim of a crime or have they or a family member ever been accused of a crime. The potential jurors are also asked their professions and opinions on various laws or scenarios. Their responses could trigger the attorney to think he or she would be a bad juror for their side of the case. For example, if a juror responds that he would have a hard time convicting the accused based on the testimony of one credible eyewitness, the prosecutor would strike that juror where the law clearly allows for a conviction with only one eyewitness. The constitutional challenges become relevant if an attorney says he struck a witness for one reason but did not strike another witness of a different race who answered similarly. This when the opposing attorney could make a "Batson challenge."

A Batson challenge is an equal protection challenge alleging the use of peremptory strikes to exclude certain jurors solely on the account of their race or gender. The party alleging the challenge must show a pattern of such striking and that nonminority or male jurors who answered similarly were not stuck. If the party raising the Batson challenge is successful with the challenge, the remedy is to restrict the jury. Upon restrict, the party losing the Batson challenge (the party who illegally struck minorities or women) cannot strike any of the same jurors originally struck. It is important to note that the defendant need not be of a particular minority or female to make a Batson challenge.

The purpose of void dire is to find out as much about the group as possible. It is also the attorneys' first opportunity to present their case. The attorney can bring up weaknesses in the case and ask questions of the potential jurors about those weaknesses. For example, if the case involves a defendant who was driving his own vehicle with narcotics in the center console, an attorney may want to ask potential jurors if they agree that individuals have knowledge of the contents of their own vehicle.

Vior dire is the also the first opportunity for the attorney to get the jury to like them and want to listen to their case. After all, this is the first impression the jury will have of each side. Some attorneys believe that dress is important, style is important, likability is important to the outcome of the case. Consider, for example, the attorney who, hurrying to the courthouse, cut off jurors in traffic, steals a parking place, and rushes past other jurors standing in line to get in the building. Will that attorney be likable when he or she is presenting the case? Probably not, because first impressions matter. Consider also that the case is being tried in a small rural town. One attorney is dressed in a moderate suit and uses simple language. The other attorney is dressed in expensive clothing and uses an advanced vocabulary. Which attorney is the jury most likely going to identify with? The same goes for all witnesses involved.

Attorneys should always share the potential jury list with the law enforcement officers associated with the case. The law enforcement officers may know individuals on the list who would be good or bad for the case and can notify the attorney. Some jurisdictions share the jury list with local law enforcement agencies, probation offices, or others to gain as much background as possible about each juror. It is also possible to run the names through databases to find out about relationships or contacts with the criminal justice system.

Once the jury is selected from the group of potential jurors, they are sworn and empaneled in the case. Jurors lose certain rights while they are on duty. The biggest right the jurors lose is the right to free speech. They will be instructed by the judge that they cannot disclose or discuss the case with anyone, including family and friends. They will be restricted from watching any television accounts of the trial or reading any print material about the trial. The rationale is that if the juror discusses the case with a family member or friend, that family member or friend will inevitably give his or her opinion to the juror. This could taint the juror's verdict. The same holds true if the juror reads a reporter's views of the case.

Opening Statements

The opening statement is always done in a jury trial but not always in a bench trial. The opening statement is the parties' opportunity to state their side directly to the jury. The opening statement is a statement of what each side intends to present at trial. Some jurisdictions will allow attorneys to discuss the law in an opening statement, but it is not common. Opinions are not allowed in opening statements. The prosecution goes first because the government has the burden of proof. The defense can present an opening statement, or choose not to or defer it to the opening of the defense's case. If the defense gives an opening statement, the prosecution can then give a rebuttal opening statement. The government goes last because the burden is on the prosecution.

Presentation of Evidence

Most evidence in a criminal trial is presented through a witness. The prosecution goes first because the government has the burden of proof. When the prosecution calls the witness to the stand and the witness is sworn, the prosecution asks the witness questions. This is known as **direct examination**. The prosecution isn't allowed to ask the witness leading questions. A leading question is a question designed to lead the witness to an answer—for example, "You saw the defendant at the crime scene, didn't you?"

Direct Examination

The law enforcement witness should remember that he or she is on trial too. The jury will be accessing the witness's credibility, knowledge, professionalism, adherence to standard operating procedures, and the witness's protection of the defendant's rights. The law enforcement officer should not take any papers or files to the witness stand. The officer should have reviewed the material and confidently remember certain facts of the case. If the case is complex and witness names and dates voluminous, it may be a good idea to make a short list of notes with just names and dates and such to aid in the officer's memory. The officer should refer to his or her memory of the events rather than notes. Usually, the first question asked is for the law enforcement witness to state his or her training education and experience in the field. The officer should be prepared for this question and be able to state his or her qualifications easily. This is the jury's first impression, and if the witness has trouble with this first question, it is hard to recover.

The law enforcement officer also needs to be prepared to step down from the witness stand and diagram, demonstrate, or otherwise interact with evidence. If the witness collected pieces of evidence from the scene, the prosecutor will pass the evidence to the witness and ask the witness to identify it. The jury will be looking for verbal responses; however, nonverbal responses are also important. Do not underestimate the power of elements such as dress, posture, mannerisms, and eye contact. The witness needs to be aware of any habits that may be annoying to an onlooker, such as chewing gum, touching one's face, or repeated clearing of the throat.

Jurors will hold expert witnesses to high expectations. Expert witnesses can range from the mechanic who has a special knowledge of the workings of an automobile involved in a crime to a doctor who performed brain surgery on the victim of a crime. Formal education or degrees are not necessary to be an expert witness; one simply possess a greater understanding of a subject matter than the average person. An expert witness may be called upon to examine pieces of evidence or give an opinion based on a fact pattern. Usually, law enforcement officers are called as fact witnesses, but they can also be called as expert witnesses. Some jurisdictions allow law enforcement officers to give an opinion on whether a substance is marijuana based on the officer's years of experience interacting with marijuana. An officer may also be called on to give an opinion on the way a firearm ejects bullets based on that officer's training and experience with the weapon. To be prepared, the officer should always inquire with the prosecutor whether the prosecutor intends to use the officer as an expert witness during the trial. The defense may also try to use the law enforcement officer as a witness to bolster the defense. The officer should be cautious about giving expert testimony unless discussions of such have occurred pretrial. The officer needs to be sure that he or she is qualified to give testimony on the subject matter inquired about.

> Officer Newby is called to the witness stand in a murder trial because he was the first officer to arrive on the scene. The prosecution intends to establish who was present on the scene and the placement of the victim's body at the scene. The prosecution does not intend to use Newby as an expert witness. Newby is cavalier in his responses and tends to volunteer more information than is asked for. The prosecution concludes direct examination and turns the witness over to the defense for cross-examination. The defense attorney takes this opportunity to further his alibi defense and tries to establish a time of death with Newby. Newby is not an expert in time of death but has watched many police drama television shows. Newby begins discussing rigidity of the body and rigor. The prosecution objects to Newby's foundational knowledge in the subject matter. At this point, the government is questioning the qualifications of their own witness and trying to silence him. This is not a good look in front of the jury.

Most jurisdictions have rules in place to prevent witnesses from being in the courtroom during other witness testimony on the same case. This rule can be invoked by the judge or either party. This rule makes it harder for a witness to hear another's testimony and thereby change his or her testimony based on what was previously heard. It also gives the witness an unfair advantage to prepare for certain questions and to discuss his or her responses with others.

Cross-examination

Cross-examination of a witness is the asking of questions to the witness called by the opposing side. The purpose of cross-examination is to discredit the witness by challenging or extending the testimony already given. Some defense attorneys look forward to cross-examination as an opportunity to argue with the witness. The witness should never allow this to happen. The witness should remember that he or she is always in control of the testimony. If the defense attorney presents as overly friendly or hostile, the witness should maintain an even demeanor. The witness should not display irritation or disgust with the questions asked. The witness has an obligation to give the jury the facts of the case or an expert opinion in a clear unemotional manner. If the defense attorney attempts to ask rapid-fire questions to confuse the witness, the witness needs to remember the he or she can always slow the pace of the responses. If the defense attorney asks complex or multiple questions, the witness can either answer one question at a time or ask that the attorney repeat the question. Asking an attorney to repeat the question often disrupts the flow of the attorney's thought process and slows the pace of the examination.

If during the cross-examination the witness answers a question and then the defense attorney remains silent, the witness should not volunteer any extra information. Silence in a conversation is uncomfortable for some people. This is what the defense attorney is banking on. The attorney wants the witness to volunteer something that the attorney can seize on because he is running out of questions. It is best that the witness let the silence loom until the judge tells the attorney to move on.

A defense attorney will sometimes ask the same questions over and over in hopes the witness will give a different response he or she can seize on in closing argument. For example, the attorney may ask the law enforcement officer if the car was red. The witness replies, "Yes." Then the attorney asks the witness, "Wasn't it in fact maroon?" And the witness answers, "Yes." Then later in cross-examination the attorney argues that the witness changes his or her answers and cannot be believed. This is an easy trap for law enforcement officers to fall into because the officer is trying to be helpful and agreeable. The proper response is if the witness thinks the car is red, the car is red every time. This will reduce the questioning and communicate to the defense attorney that this tactic will not work with this witness.

The defense attorney may also ask questions with an accusatory tone. The questions may be outside of the realm of facts of the case, questions such as "You've been speaking with the prosecutor about your testimony in this case, haven't you?" This type of question is posed in a manner to imply that the testimony has been invented or embellished. The witness should understand that there is no problem or prohibition in discussing the witness's testimony with anyone pretrial. It is a natural part of preparing for trial. A response of "yes" is sufficient. There is no need for the witness to explain why or offer additional explanation. If this line of questioning continues, the witness can simply answer, "I have discussed this case with many people in my official capacity, but no one has told me what to say or suggested anything of such." This line of questioning is something that can be addressed on redirect examination, if the prosecution thinks necessary.

Defense attorneys will often ask leading questions because they are permissible on cross-examination. These are questions that tend to lead a witness to an answer or a question that includes facts not yet in evidence. For example, if to the question "the car was red, wasn't it," the answer is yes, there is no problem with the witness conceding to the point and answering in the affirmative. However, the witness must listen carefully because the attorney could add multiple adjectives hoping the witness will agree to all of them. For example, if the question is "the car was red, two door, and small, correct?" it is permissible for the witness to subdivide a response, if needed: "The car was red and two door. I would consider it an average-size vehicle."

Sometimes an attorney will try to intimidate the witness by telling the witness that he or she must answer the questions with yes or no answers. This is simply not true. The witness may answer the question in the manner the witness chooses as long as the answer is responsive to the question. For example, if the attorney asks, "The car was red, two door, and small, yes or no," the witness can respond, "The car was red and two door. I would consider it an average-size vehicle." However, the witness cannot go outside of the scope of the question to answer and add facts not asked. For example, if the attorney asks, "The car was red, two door, and small, yes or no," the witness cannot answer "it was red, two door, and weaving all over the road because the driver was intoxicated."

The witness needs to be careful about guessing. As humans, we use estimation in everyday life and it is perfectly acceptable. What time did she arrive? How long did it take for you to get there? How far is it between the door and the road? Are all questions that can easily be answered with an estimation. However, when the answer is coming from the witness stand, the answer should not be estimated, unless the witness makes it clear that the answer is an estimation. For example, "The murder occurred at 2:00 a.m., right?" If the call came into dispatch at 2:03 a.m., the law enforcement officer may jump to the conclusion that the murder had occurred just before and answer yes to this question. The witness is using facts that he or she knows to deduce things that the witness does not know. This is a duty of the jury. They are the ultimate finders of the facts and they are allowed to make certain assumptions from the evidence presented. The witness needs to respond only to the facts that he or she knows—for example, "The call came in at 2:03 a.m. I do not know the actual time of the murder."

The most important thing for the law enforcement witness to remember is to not be emotional on the witness stand. The defense attorney could try to engage the emotional side of the witness by personal attacks or belittling comments. When this happens, it is very hard to stay calm, but for the sake of the case, the witness must. Also, the witness should not regard the defense attorney as an enemy. This could inadvertently cause the witness to come across hostile, sarcastic, or condescending back toward the defense attorney. The jury will certainly pick up on any hostility exhibited by the witness and could hold it against the case.

The witness should refrain from asking questions back to the defense attorney. This often happens when the witness feels pushed into a corner or intimidated. This showing of weakness could be perceived as weakness with the case itself. Defense attorneys will often pose ridiculous questions to elicit such a response from the witness. For example, "If you were the victim in this case, would you want the law enforcement officer to talk to every single witness or just the ones who were easy to locate?" This question is argumentative and can be objectionable. The witness's first response back to the defense attorney may be to say, "Have you ever tried to take statements from witnesses who do not want to be involved or hate the police?" However, the best response would be "I cannot speak for how the victim felt about the investigation because I was not the victim here." Remember that a witness cannot testify as to what someone else felt, opined, thought, saw, or heard.

Objections

Attorneys will inevitably make objections during a witness's testimony. This is the right and privilege of each side during a trial. The judge can also make objections during trial to preserve the record for appeal, but this is rare. The witness should not concern himself or herself with the objections. These are between the judge and the attorneys. An objection does not mean that the witness did anything wrong. In fact, the question is just the opposite. It is an allegation that the attorney has asked an improper question. There are tactical decisions to whether attorneys will use objections during a trial. Sometimes the opposing counsel's questions are objectionable, but the attorney chooses not to object. This could happen to a law enforcement officer. If the prosecutor feels that the answer cannot hurt the case, the prosecutor will not object. Sometimes too many objections may make the jury think one side is trying to hide something from the jury. Inevitably, the jury wants to know everything in the case. Unfortunately, sometimes the attorney does not make objections because he or she is timid and/or does not know what objection to make. If this is the case, the witness must do his or her best to answer the question in a nondamaging way to the case. Sometimes the attorney can make an objection to give the witness a clue about how to answer the question—for example, "Your Honor, I object. This is outside the scope of this witness's training and experience."

The witness needs to be prepared for an objection midsentence. This could be done to intimidate the witness or because the witness is truly improperly answering the question. For example, the witness may be adding facts not asked about. If the question is "what time did the defendant give his statement?" the opposing counsel will object if the answer is "it was about 3:00 p.m. right after he got finished smoking meth." If there is an objection during the witness's testimony, the witness must immediately stop talking. It is not permissible to finish a thought or even a sentence. As a practical matter, the court reporter cannot take down two people speaking at the same time. Moreover, if there is an objection, it means that one side believes illegal testimony will follow, and this is a determination for the judge.

The direct examination and cross-examination can go back and forth indefinitely or as long as the judge will allow. This is called redirect examination and recross-examination. Different jurisdictions have different rules about the content that can be sought in the questioning. Some jurisdictions only allow what is called "scope of direct" cross-examination, which means that the party cross-examining the witness can only ask questions related to the direct examination. Other jurisdictions have "wide open" cross-examination. This means that the attorney may ask questions about any topic relevant and material to the trial regardless of whether the attorney calling the witness discussed that subject matter.

Witnesses should wait until they are excused from the witness stand and courtroom to exit. Some jurisdictions will allow attorneys to reserve the right to recall witnesses, and it can be a tactic in the questioning process. For example, if the defense is unfamiliar with all the facts of the case, it may be difficult to cross-examine the first witness called by the government. The defense may want to reserve the right to recall that witness at a later date and call that same person in the defense's case. The downside of this tactic is that the defense loses the right to lead that witness and must use the direct examination procedure.

Witness Tips

Being a witness in a criminal case can be overwhelming. For people with a fear of public speaking, the thought of testifying cause anxiety or physical illness. Witnesses come in all sizes, shapes, and backgrounds and will be expected to fit into the same category after being sworn in by the judge. All eyes will be on the witness and all those eyes are judging the witness. The jury is told that one of their duties is to judge the credibility of witnesses. The attorneys are sizing the witness for cross-examination. The witness needs to be aware that, if given the opportunity, these judgments will be made prior to the witness taking the witness stand.

Contact between witnesses and parties is often unavoidable, especially if the courthouse is small or not crowded. The jurors may see the witnesses as they exit their cars, as they walk through the halls, or even if they use the same facilities. Witnesses need to be aware that they will be remembered in the short time period between the interaction and the time they take the witness stand. Below is a list of things that a witness should consider prior to taking the witness stand.

- Talking in public. Witnesses need to be careful about talking in the hallway or other public place where jurors could be present. This is especially important for law enforcement officers to remember. For example, if there are several law enforcement officers testifying on a murder case, they could gather in the hallway or other public place. They will pass the time by telling stories or making conversation. Some of that conversation could turn to laughter. Then just as they are all laughing about a story, a juror rounds the corner and gets a first impression that the law enforcement officers are not taking the murder case seriously.
- Talking to other witnesses. It is a natural tendency for witnesses to want to discuss with each other what they know about the case, opinions, and desired outcomes. Witnesses should be

aware that those are all fair game questions for the opposing side to ask. For example, "Have you talked to Wade Witness about what he saw?" If the witness's answer is yes, then the attorney will surely argue that the witness was influenced by what Wade said rather than what the witness actually saw.

- Social media. Social media is the way the world communicates, and witnesses are no different. People are in the habit of posting mundane daily activities for the world to see, and jury service is not excluded. A witness needs to be very careful about posting anything about the case on social media. The witness needs to also be aware that anything posted could be printed and viewed in the courtroom by an attorney to the case.

> Wendy Witness sees a car wreck and posts, "Oh my gosh, I just witnessed a wreck. I don't know if I want to get involved though." In the same post, Wendy talks about going out to a bar with friends that same night. A few days later she posts, "An investigator showed up to talk about the wreck. I'm not sure I told him everything." A week before the trial, she posts, "I'm testifying about a wreck that happened two years ago. I can't remember what I did two weeks ago." The defense attorney gets the government's witness list and checks everyone's social media accounts. He prints out all of Wendy's posts and is ready to confront her with them when she takes the witness stand. This will distract the jury and reduce the effectiveness of her testimony.

Evidence Not Requiring a Witness

During a trial, there may be evidence presented that does not require a witness. This could be what is called "**self-authenticating**" **evidence**. This is a document that can be admitted into evidence without supporting testimony as to its authenticity. Most jurisdictions have statutes that allow certain documents to be admitted into evidence without the necessity of live testimony. These items could be things such as prior court documents that are certified by the clerk of court, medical records that are certified and delivered directly to the clerk of court, or forensic lab reports that are certified by the examiner. States enact these exceptions to prevent the need of common witnesses who are needed in the field.

Rebuttal Witnesses

Both the government and the defense will have the opportunity to call witnesses in the trial. The government goes first in calling witnesses because it has the burden of proof. Then the defense may choose to call witnesses but is not required to do so. **Rebuttal witnesses** are witnesses called by the prosecution after the defense has rested its case. Often it is not necessary to call a rebuttal witness; it will depend on what is presented by the defense. If the government calls a rebuttal witness, the testimony will take place in the same manner as earlier described. The government will take the witness on direct examination, and if the defense has any questions for the witness, it is called cross-examination. Usually, the defense is not allowed to call rebuttal witnesses to the state's rebuttal witnesses, but most jurisdictions leave that in the discretion of the judge and have statutes that allow re-rebuttal in the interest of justice.

Likewise, once the government and defense have closed their case, they cannot call any other witnesses, However, most jurisdictions have statutes that allow either side to reopen its case if justice requires it. For example, the government may have put forward several days of testimony in a murder case, the defense called witnesses, and both sides rested. Then the government realizes that it forgot to prove venue (jurisdiction). This is done in all cases with a simple question of any witness: "Did this happen in [fill in the blank for city and state]?" The judge could allow the government to reopen its case for the purpose of proving venue to avoid a retrial.

> The government is trying a rape case wherein the testimony from the victim is that her stepfather raped her right after school and before her mother got home from work over a period of several months. In the defense's case, the defendant testifies that he could not have raped his stepdaughter after school because he worked every day until 6:00 p.m. and the victim's mother would be home from work by then. To strengthen his testimony, the defendant produced a document that was propertied to be a work record. The government objected to this piece of evidence because the defense had not turned it over in discovery. The defense argued that the work document was just procured the day before trial and was necessary to the defense. The judge allowed the document to be admitted into evidence over the government's objection. At the next break, the prosecutor contacted the defendant's employer and asked that the work record be verified. The employer stated that the work record was a forgery. The government then could call the propertied employer as a rebuttal witness to testify that the document was a forgery and the defendant was not working during those times.

Closing Argument

The **closing argument** is the favorite part of most trials for everyone involved in the case. The attorneys are setting up their closing arguments throughout the case with certain evidence presented. This is a time when the attorney uses his or her persuasive skills to make inferences from the evidence and argue his or her respective side. The attorneys must only argue facts that were presented in evidence. The attorneys can also argue the law and how the law applies to the facts. It is improper for an attorney to argue points that have not been admitted into evidence. It is also improper for the attorney to comment about his or her personal opinion of the facts of the case. Likewise, it is improper for the attorney to ask the jury to place themselves in the position of the victim or defendant in the case. For example, "What would you have done in that situation?" is an improper statement to be made to the jury during the closing argument. The prosecutor has additional restrictions during the closing argument. The prosecutor cannot comment on certain rights of the defendant and doing so could result in a mistrial. For example, if the prosecutor said, "It would have been nice if the defendant told us what happened, but he declined to testify," this statement would improperly comment on the defendant's Fifth Amendment right to silence and could cause a mistrial.

Judge's Instructions

While a judge's instructions usually come at the close of the case, when to instruct is the judge's prerogative. He or she can instruct at the beginning of the trial, midway, or at the end. The judge may instruct on the basic elements at the beginning of the trial and wait until the close of the case to instruct on specific elements proven during the trial. These instructions could include self-defense instructions, mental health instructions, instructions about witnesses with felony convictions, flight, expert witnesses, impeachment of witnesses with prior statements, and a number of other issues. The judge must make sure that the instructions are detailed and complete. Failure of the judge to define certain terms for the jury or instruct on certain issues could result in the case being overturned on appeal.

How the Steps in the Adversarial Proceeding Differ in Bench Trials

The steps of the adversarial proceeding will differ slightly when there is a bench trial. A bench trial is a trial in which the judge is the finder of the facts and the law. There is no jury deciding the facts. Obviously, there is no voir dire process if there is a bench trial. There is also no reason to take up issues outside of the jury's presence. In a jury trial, there may be issues that require argument outside the jury's presence. This slows the process down because the jury has to be excused from the courtroom and arguments are often repeated. For example, if the state wishes to impeach a witness with a prior conviction, this cannot be discussed in front of the jury. The jury will not be able to set aside the fact that the witness has a prior conviction, if instructed. Conversely, the law expects judges to be able to not consider certain evidence if the judge finds it inadmissible.

Bench trials can be held as confidential proceedings. Juvenile and youthful offender status requires that proceedings be closed to the public. These are usually bench trials. The judge controls the number of persons in the courtroom to minimize the possibility of disclosure of the facts to the general public.

Bench trials do not always require opening statements or closing arguments. These are at the judge's discretion. The judge may feel that he or she can hear the facts from the witness stand and does not need a preview in opening statements from the attorneys. Likewise, the judge may feel that he or she can apply the law to the facts presented in evidence and draw conclusions necessary. There can also be less posturing by the attorneys with each witness. Some of the actions of attorneys in the courtroom is just for show, and the judges have seen it numerous times and it has lost its effect.

The Use of Technology in an Adversarial Proceeding

We are a world dependent on **technology**, and this is carried over into adversarial proceedings. Crime dramas are watched by most Americans for entertainment and those Americans are serving on juries. Therefore, the jurors almost expect that some type of technology be used in adversarial proceedings because that is what they see on television. In fact, most of the technology seen in crime drama programming is available in real life. The problem is that many attorneys are not schooled in the use of such technology, which prevents them from using such in an adversarial proceeding. The attorney is driven to present the evidence by the evidence itself. If the evidence is collected using sophisticated technology, the attorney must understand that process to present it to a jury. The problem there is that most police departments do not have the funding to purchase the most sophisticated technological devices and therefore don't use them.

Ultimately, the decision is on the attorney presenting the evidence. Each stage of the trial can involve a different use of technology. An attorney can choose to use technology only in certain stages or all stages, bearing in mind what will be more effective in presenting the case to the jury.

Voir Dire

An attorney can choose to speak the questions or have a visual presentation of the questions to the potential jurors. In this case, the potential jurors are both hearing and seeing the questions asked. This may allow a question to linger in the potential juror's mind longer or register a different way with the potential juror. This could elicit more responses from potential jurors.

Opening

An attorney could also speak the opening statement or choose to have a visual presentation to accompany the opening statement. A visual representation could be helpful with a complicated fact pattern with multiple names, dates, or places. The attorney would be able to visually display the names or relationships of parties. The attorney could also give a timeline of events that the potential jurors could see rather than just guess. The attorney needs be careful about including any actual evidence in the visual presentation as doing so could be grounds for a mistrial. Most jurisdictions will not allow an attorney to show evidence to a jury until it has been admitted.

Direct Examination

Direct examination is a place where parties can get creative with the use of technology during testimony. If a witness is testifying on direct examination, the attorney and witness will have the ability to meet and discuss the testimony prior to trial. In this case, the witness can discuss with the attorney any available technology or evidence that was collected using technology. Photographs have been in use for over a century now but are a common way that technology is used with a witness while testifying. The usual way of presenting a photograph in a trial is marking it as an exhibit and handing it to the witness while the witness is testifying. The attorney would ask the witness if he or she recognized the subject matter in the photograph and if it is an accurate presentation of what was seen by the witness at the time the photograph was taken. If so, the evidence can be admitted into evidence and published to the jury. It is at this point that the attorney needs to have a plan for presentation of that photo to the jury. One way is for the attorney or bailiff to hold the photograph up and show the jury. Another way is for the attorney to pass the photograph around the jury box. Another way is for the attorney to use a trial presenter (a version of an overhead projector) to display the photograph on a large screen. If the attorney chooses this method, the equipment needs to be set up and ready at the time the witness takes the witness stand. The attorney also needs to be educated on how to use the equipment or have an assistant in the courtroom to assist in the presentation. Most trial presenters will allow the user to adjust lighting and glare, or to zoom in on the photograph.

Visual presentations can also be helpful if the witness is showing call logs, bank statements, credit card statements, or any other documents that jurors have never seen before. It helps the juror stay interested in the subject matter of the case and understand what the witness is saying. Having the witness read lists of charges on a credit card cannot be as effective as the juror actually hearing about and seeing the statements.

Technology is also useful in showing how an expert witness arrived at a certain conclusion in a case. For example, if a witness is testifying about the reliability of GPS coordinates to place a person's cell phone in a certain area, projection of a map marked with coordinates may assist the jury in seeing the area that the cell phone traveled. Using technology in all these ways can assist the trier of the fact in understanding the facts. Jurors like to hear and see what happened. They like to feel involved in the fact-finding process. It is often helpful for an attorney using any of these methods of presenting evidence to allow the witness to use the technology as well. This can be accomplished by giving the witness a simple laser pointer and asking the witness to point at a photograph as the witness explains what was present when the photograph was taken.

Cross-examination

Technology can be used in cross-examination in the same manner as on direct examination. For an attorney, it can be a little more challenging because there has been no prior opportunity to discuss with the witness the use of technology. Witnesses are naturally uncomfortable on cross-examination, and this can heighten any anxiety that a witness may be feeling.

Closing Arguments

Technology can be very useful in closing arguments. The closing argument is the time the attorney highlights certain pieces of evidence and tries to convince the jury that his or her position is correct.

Once a piece of evidence has been admitted into evidence, the attorney can highlight certain pieces of that evidence. For example, if the government is trying a drug distribution case wherein the defendant is accused of selling controlled substances, there could be a video of the transaction. It is common practice that controlled buys of controlled substances are captured on audio or video recordings by the confidential informant or undercover agent making the transaction. The transactions in videos can move fast and be hard to hear. It is quite possible that a video can be presented to a jury wherein it is difficult to see where the actual drug transaction occurs because of additional factors. The parties could be using slang language, the lighting can be bad, and the background music can be loud, as well as a number of other factors that could distort what is actually occurring on the recording. This is when technology can be used to cut out relevant portions of the recordings and play just that portion multiple times for the jurors. This will allow them to focus on the relevant parts and disregard the irrelevant parts.

Judge's Instructions

The judge's instructions can contain complicated terms and concepts of law that may be better both seen and heard. The judge could use courtroom technology to present his instructions to the jury to make sure they comprehend each charge. This could be done by use of a projector and screen at the same time the judge is verbally instructing the jury.

No matter the technology an attorney chooses to use, a trial run is always needed. No matter how many times an attorney has used the same equipment and software, different evidence can present in different ways. For example, photos printed on glossy paper can have a reflective quality when using an overhead light. A simple trial run-through with the actual photos being used in the case will allow the attorney to see whether the print quality of the photo matters. Also, sounds can be drowned out in a large courtroom. If a witness intends to play a recorded statement, it is a good idea to test the volume possibilities in the courtroom. Once the statement begins playing is not the time to try finding speakers and extension cords.

Problems with Using Courtroom Technology

While the use of courtroom technology can bolster the jury's understanding of the law and evidence, there are also pitfalls to its use. This occurs when the parties are not equally technologically savvy. For example, if the attorney attempts to display portions of video clips in a closing argument PowerPoint presentation and the judge is unaware of what a PowerPoint presentation is, the judge is likely to disallow the presentation. Judges can also lack the patience needed for the attorneys to set up the technology or to restart devices when there is a glitch. It is best the attorney advise the judge pretrial of the intention to use courtroom technology, minimizing any conflict that could arise between the attorney and the judge.

Technology can also become distracting at an adversarial proceeding. Some devices have a sleep mode or may make certain sounds when not in use. If the attorney is unprepared or simply forgets to adjust the device's settings, many things could go wrong. For example, if an attorney is using an investigator's laptop to project pictures, and then at the close of the presentation the laptop displays the home screen, the picture on the home screen must be appropriate for everyone's viewing. Also, some computers are set for notifications upon receipt of text messages and email. If certain email and text messages appeared on the large screen in the middle of an adversarial proceeding, it could affect the case.

Technology can also be a problem when the use is one sided. Both the prosecution and the defense can decide how best to present evidence in a trial. Should the prosecutor decide to use technology to project pictures, the defense attorney could ask the prosecutor for help in displaying pictures during his or her case. This puts the prosecutor in a precarious position of looking unhelpful to opposing counsel or acting as opposing counsel's assistant. Neither is a good look in front of a jury.

There is also the possibility that technology malfunctions or goes down. An attorney could have a beautifully crafted PowerPoint closing argument and just before time to deliver it to the jury, the computer goes to sleep and will not wake up. Then the decision would be for the judge to delay the proceeding to allow the attorney to figure out what went wrong or tell the attorney to proceed. The latter is more likely. This is why an attorney or witness planning to use courtroom technology should always prepare for a backup presentation.

Juvenile Proceedings

Juvenile proceedings are not technically adversarial proceedings, but to many they can feel as such. Juvenile proceedings are complex proceedings handled by the government but designed to rehabilitate rather than punish the juvenile. The government is thought to act as a substitute parent instead of an adversary. The thought is that if the juvenile criminal behavior is caught and addressed early, then the juvenile will have the opportunity to change behaviors before turning the age of majority. It is also thought that some juvenile crimes occur due to a lack of education or a lack of understanding of the consequences of one's actions that comes with maturity.

Because juveniles may have acted using juvenile judgment, the juvenile proceeding is often closed to the general public to protect the juvenile's future reputation. In jurisdictions that permit closed proceedings for juvenile offenders, it is also improper for any party to the case to discuss the juvenile offense outside of the court process. This protects the juvenile's name from appearing in public databases or in the media.

A juvenile's rights are slightly different than a defendant charged in adult court. The juvenile proceeding does not have a right to jury trial or public trial, but many other constitutional rights still apply. A juvenile has the right to counsel, confrontation of witness, proof beyond a reasonable doubt, a Fifth Amendment right to remain silent at trial, and a double jeopardy protection.

A juvenile can also be initially charged as a juvenile and then transferred to adult court to be tried as an adult. Sometimes the juvenile system does not rehabilitate the juvenile as intended and the juvenile continues to commit other crimes. When this happens, the government has the right to move for the juvenile's case to be transferred to be tried as an adult. This is a substantive right of the juvenile and necessitates a hearing on the issue. Certain states have passed statutes that have been upheld providing for an automatic transfer of juvenile offenders to be charged as an adult without a hearing. These statutes usually have a high minimum-age requirement for the transfer along with requiring a serious offense. For example, a seventeen-year-old juvenile who commits the crime of murder may be automatically charged as an adult in a state that provides a such a statue.

When a juvenile is transferred to be tried as an adult, the state statute can proscribe the appropriate punishment for the juvenile. Some state statutes allow juveniles to be punished equally as adults when their cases are transferred to adult court, while other states proscribe mandatory maximum punishments for the transferred juveniles. The states could also dictate whether the juvenile's conviction will be a matter of public record or sealed.

Juvenile convictions are not considered convictions at all but rather adjudications. This protects the juvenile from the charge later being used to enhance punishments should the juvenile commit future crimes. A juvenile adjudication cannot be used against the juvenile in the future, and if the record is sealed, the juvenile will not be forced to disclose that it ever existed.

Rules to Remember

Below is a list of rules to remember from this chapter.

- There are many different burdens of proof utilized in the criminal justice system: proof beyond a reasonable doubt, a preponderance of the evidence, proof to a reasonable satisfaction.
- A criminal defendant never has to prove his or her innocence. It is the burden of the government to prove that the defendant committed the crime charged.
- All parties must spend time preparing for an adversarial proceeding (trial) by reviewing the facts and evidence in the case.
- Defendants are constitutionally guaranteed to have a jury selected from a fair cross section of the community.
- Attorneys must use their peremptory strikes without purposeful discrimination based on sex or race.
- Opening statements should only be the facts of the case and not contain any opinions of the attorneys.
- Evidence is usually presented through direct examination of a witness but can be presented without the use of a witness if the evidence is self-authenticating.
- When objections are made by either attorney, the witness must stop talking and wait for the judge's ruling.
- Witnesses need to be cognizant of their behaviors pretrial and during the trial when in an area that can be viewed by jurors. Jurors can make first impressions based on those behaviors that could negatively impact the case.
- Attorneys can argue the facts and law and draw inferences from each. Attorneys may not ask

jurors to place themselves in the shoes of either party or give personal opinions.

- A jury trial differs from a bench trial in that in a jury trial, the judge determines the applicable law and the jury decides which facts occurred from the evidence presented. In a bench trial, the judge determines both the law and the facts.
- In a trial, technology can be utilized by either party or the judge to convey the evidence in a clear and concise manner or to argue points for respective sides.
- The purpose of a juvenile proceeding is to rehabilitate the juvenile and will not result in a criminal conviction.
- Juveniles can be transferred and tried in adult court depending on the age of the offender and crime committed as proscribed by statute.

End of Chapter Comprehension and Application

Directions: Use what you have learned in this chapter to help you respond completely and correctly to each question or prompt below.

1. Explain the different burdens of proof in the criminal justice system and give an example of a proceeding that utilizes each different burden of proof.
2. When an investigator receives a subpoena, what steps should he or she take to prepare for testimony?
3. What is constitutionally required for a fair jury selection process?
4. What is a Batson challenge? What must be shown? What is the remedy?
5. What is the difference between a challenge for cause and a peremptory challenge?
6. What is the purpose of opening statements and what could make an opening statement improper?
7. What are some things a witness can do to be effective on direct examination?
8. What are some things a witness needs to be prepared for on cross-examination?
9. What things should a witness be careful about outside of the courtroom pretrial or during trial?
10. Can evidence be admitted into evidence without a witness? If so, what types?
11. What is the purpose of rebuttal witnesses?
12. Who is the finder of fact and who is the finder of the law in a jury trial?
13. How does a bench trial differ from a jury trial?
14. In what ways can technology be used during the different stages of a criminal trial?
15. What are some problems that can arise when using technology during a criminal trial?
16. What is the purpose of the juvenile justice system? How does it differ from an adversarial proceeding?
17. What rights are afforded a juvenile charged in juvenile court?
18. Under what circumstances can a juvenile be prosecuted in adult court?

19. Write a state statute outlining the circumstances when a juvenile may be transferred to adult court.
20. What do you think are the three most important stages of an adversarial proceeding and why?

References

Taylor v. Louisiana, 419 U.S. 522 (1974), https://supreme.justia.com/cases/federal/us/419/522/
Batson v. Kentucky, 486 U.S. 79 (1989), https://casetext.com/case/batson-v-kentucky

Chapter 9

Individual Rights at an Adversarial Proceeding

Introduction: Defendant and Victim's Rights during the Trial

This chapter will discuss the constitutional rights that a defendant is afforded during the adversarial process and how the competing rights of the victim are balanced.

Chapter Objectives

In this chapter students will learn:

- The constitutional rights defendants have at a trial and how they apply at the different stages of the trial
- How the rights of the government and victims balance with the defendant's rights

Key Terms

Key terms and professional terminology that are used in this chapter include:

- **The right to a speedy trial**
- **Impartial judge and jury**
- **Sequestration of the jury**
- **The right to a public trial**
- **Confrontation of witnesses**
- **Change of venue**
- **Effective assistance of counsel**

- **Double jeopardy**
- **Entrapment**
- **Victim's rights**

The Rights Afforded to Parties during an Adversarial Proceeding

If a criminal defendant does not plead guilty, then the case will either be dismissed by the government or there will be a trial. The defendant is afforded certain constitutional rights at a trial that he or she waives if there is a plea. These are the right to a speedy trial, the right to an impartial jury, the right to an impartial judge, the right to counsel, the right to an effective defense, the right to confront witnesses, the right to a public trial, and others. The government is also afforded certain rights to protect victims and witnesses.

The Right to a Speedy Trial

The Sixth Amendment to the US Constitution states that the accused shall enjoy the **right to a speedy trial**. This right is intended to prevent the criminally accused from an undue delay in the time between arrest and commencement of the trial. Otherwise, the time the accused spends awaiting trial could be longer than the actual punishment imposed for the charge. The US Supreme Court in *United States v. Ewell* identified three purposes for having a speedy trial: (a) It prevents excessive incarceration, (b) it minimizes anxiety experienced by the accused as a result of the publicized accusation, and (c) it prevents damage to the defendant's case resulting from too much delay.

The right to a speedy trial applies after a criminal defendant has been charged with the crime. There is no right to a speedy trial that attaches when the defendant is merely a suspect. It is said that a criminal defendant benefits from a lengthy investigation and cannot complain that charges have not yet been brought against him or her. In fact, the investigation may never result in charges against the defendant. Many jurisdictions have statutes regulating the statute of limitations. A statute of limitations prevents the government from charging an individual with a crime after a certain time has passed. For example, a statute of limitation on a misdemeanor offense may be one year. A statute of limitation on a felony may be five years. A statute of limitations on a serious felony offense may be unlimited. Charges for crimes such as rape, robbery, or murder may be brought anytime after the offense date with no limits.

Knowledge of the charges by the criminally accused is irrelevant to whether the right to a speedy trial applies. In *Doggett v. United States*, the defendant was charged with conspiracy to import and distribute cocaine. When government agents went to defendant's home to arrest him, they learned he was in Colombia. In September 1981, agents learned that defendant was in Panama. In September 1982, he passed unnoticed through customs and settled down in Virginia. In September 1988, the government ran a credit check and found within minutes where the defendant lived. They arrested him. Doggett claims he did not know he had been charged with a crime until then. The US Supreme Court held in Doggett that the speedy trial clause of the Sixth Amendment was implicated and reasoned that Doggett had a diminished ability to defend the case against him due to the amount of time that had passed. This decision probably has very little influence on most cases because most defendants know when they are charged.

Many states have enacted legislation proscribing time frames in which the prosecution must occur. The Federal Speedy Trial Act regulates federal prosecution. However, many have left it up the discretion of the trial courts. Trial courts have direction from the US Supreme Court in *Baker v. Wingo*. Baker and a codefendant had been charged with murder. Baker had been arrested and held incarcerated with his trial initially set for September 1958. He made bond on his charges in June of 1959, after spending ten months in jail awaiting trial. The government insisted that it was necessary to try the codefendant's case first and moved to continue Baker's case multiple times. The petitioner made no objection to the first eleven continuances granted by the state trial court, but when the state moved to continue his case for the twelfth time, in February 1962, he filed a motion to dismiss the indictment, which motion was denied. Following the granting of two further continuances, to which the petitioner did not object, his trial was set for March 1963, the first term of court following the other suspect's final conviction. But on the day of trial, the state again moved for a continuance, citing as its reason the illness of the ex-sheriff who was the chief investigating officer in the case. The petitioner objected unsuccessfully to this continuance. One additional continuance was granted for the same reason. Thereafter, the trial was set for October 1963; the petitioner moved to dismiss the indictment on the ground that his right to a speedy trial had been denied; the motion was denied; the trial commenced, with the other suspect as the chief prosecution witness; and the petitioner was convicted and given a life sentence. The Baker Court ruled that a balancing test necessarily compels courts to approach speedy trial cases on an ad hoc basis. The Court established four factors to be balanced in making decisions regarding motions for speedy trials. Those factors are (a) the length of the delay, (b) the reason for the delay, (c) the defendant's assertion of his right, and (d) prejudice suffered by the defendant as a result of the delay.

A prosecutor can dismiss a case to avoid issues of lengthy delays. The prosecution is still restrained by the statute of limitations, so this tactic is often reserved for serious offenses or offenses with longer statutes of limitations. If a case is dismissed or nolle prosequi by the government before jeopardy attaches, there is no constitutional issue with recharging the defendant for the same crime. Jeopardy attaches in several ways: a witness being sworn to testify, a defendant entering a guilty plea, and others. It is important to know that jeopardy does not attach when the defendant is simply charged. If jeopardy has not attached, the government is free to recharge the defendant as long as the requisite statute of limitations is not violated. The *Baker* Court also discussed the government dismissing and recharging a case. The *Baker* Court suggested that the reason for the delay could be important in the trial court's decision on a speedy trial motion. A deliberate attempt to delay the trial to hamper the defense could be weighted heavily against the government. A more neutral reason or a reason that is beyond the government's control would be constitutional. For example, instances such as a delay in testing by a state forensic laboratory, the court's backlog, or the unavailability of a necessary witness would be sufficient reasons for the government to delay prosecution of a case.

If the reason for the delay of the trial is the fault of the accused, he or she shall not be successful on a speedy trial motion. The defendant cannot move for continuances and, if granted, complain that his case was continued. Also, the defendant must assert his need for a speedy trial. He cannot remain silent while his case is continued and then complain after he is convicted that there was an unduly delay.

The Right to an Impartial Jury

Most countries in the world do not have trials by jury; only countries whose laws are derived from the English common law system have trials by jury. This involvement of citizens in the criminal justice system is thought to protect the rights of the criminally accused. Not only do individuals accused of a crime have a right to a trial, they have the right to a jury trial. And not only do they have the right to a jury trial, they have the right to a fair and **impartial jury**. The right to an impartial jury is imparted to criminal defendants by the Sixth Amendment. However, it does not apply in all cases. Of course, if the defendant pleads guilty, he or she is waiving the right to an impartial jury. This Sixth Amendment right is also limited by the type of crime that the defendant is charged with. The US Supreme Court has interpreted the meaning of the Sixth Amendment to only apply to more serious crimes. In *Duncan v. Louisiana*, the Supreme Court carved out a petty crime exception. The *Duncan* Court did not expressly define a petty crime, but later cases concluded that any crime that has a potential punishment of less than six months is a petty offense for the purpose of the Sixth Amendment right to a jury trial.

Misdemeanor and petty offenses can be tried before juries in some states, though the process is longer. Many states have statutes directing that misdemeanor offenses are tried by a judge only. Then, if there is a conviction, the case is appealed to a higher court and subject to a jury trial. This is known as a trial de novo, which means a "trial anew." There is no review of the record of the original trial and the parties assert the evidence as if it were never previously tried. This system allows a larger number of misdemeanor offenses to move forward without the involvement of jury panels. In *Ludwig v. Massachusetts*, the defendant challenged such a system as an impermissible obstacle to exercise the right to a jury trial. The US Supreme Court rejected the challenge, stating that a defendant who insists on a jury trial on a misdemeanor offense can timely admit to a finding of fact in the first trial, which will trigger an appeal and trial de novo on appeal. This process is not any slower than a serious felony going through the criminal justice system and obtaining a jury trial. Therefore, there is no prejudice to the defendant and no constitutional violation of his or her right to a jury trial. In fact, this could mean that defendants are able to try cases in front of juries that were never contemplated by the country's founders to be tried in front of a jury. For example, if Jon has a speeding ticket and knows that a judge will convict him upon testimony from a law enforcement officer that he was driving over the legal limit, Jon can admit to the speeding ticket in the lower court and appeal the conviction to a higher court. Since the trial in the higher court is a trial de novo, the admission is never mentioned and the trial proceeds as if there were no prior trial. The jurors are selected in Jon's speeding trial and law enforcement testifies that Jon was speeding. Depending on the defense that Jon puts forward, the jury may only have testimony from one law enforcement officer that Jon was speeding. During deliberations, the jurors could discuss that they did not like the personality of the law enforcement officer and he seemed like a jerk. They could also feel sorry for Jon. They could feel that the speed limit is unrealistically low on that street, solely for the purpose of catching people like Jon. They could also be upset that their tax dollars were spent on a jury trial for a speeding ticket and feel that they should be hearing something more serious. The jury could find Jon not guilty, and the parties would never know what was discussed during jury deliberations. This is called jury nullification. Jury nullification occurs when the evidence seems clear and uncontested against the defendant, yet the jury does not find the defendant guilty.

There is also no right to a jury trial in noncriminal proceedings. One example of a noncriminal proceeding is a juvenile proceeding. Juvenile proceedings are noncriminal and do not result in punishment. Instead. the focus of juvenile proceedings is to rehabilitate the young offenders rather than punish them. Certainly, spending six months in a juvenile facility probably feels like punishment to a juvenile; the courts, however, have refused to call it punishment.

The US Supreme Court in *Ramos v. Louisiana* held that the Sixth Amendment right to a jury trial, as incorporated against the states by way of the Fourteenth Amendment, required an unanimous verdict to convict a defendant of a serious offense. Louisiana had a statute that allowed a conviction at jury trial with a nonunanimous vote of 10–2. The defendant raised this issue, and the US Supreme Court held that the Sixth Amendment expressly states “unanimous verdict” and the Court cannot interpret this to mean something different.

Waiving the Right to a Jury Trial

Just like other constitutional rights, defendants can waive the right to a jury trial. This is a good decision for defendants in certain cases. A case that is highly sensationalized in the community and will attract much media attention may be better tried without a jury. A case that is sensitive or emotional, such as a child sex case, may be better tried by a judge rather than a jury. The defendant isn’t the only one who has the right to a jury trial. The government also has the right to try a victim’s case in front of a jury. If a defendant requests that a jury be waived, all parties must agree, including the judge. There could be certain situations where the judge wants the jury to return the verdict rather than him or herself. Essentially, this right needs to be waived by the defendant, prosecutor, and the judge.

Pretrial Publicity

The right to a fair and impartial jury can be hampered by pretrial publicity. With the information superhighway open, news travels fast. Most people have smart devices that track the news and are constantly updated about what is happening around them. Potential jurors may already know about the case they are going to hear before they arrive at the courthouse. Most sources of news media tend to pick a side and report facts slanted toward that side. It is no different with reports on crime. Potential jurors may already believe that the defendant is guilty because they have read the story so many times. Media attention to a particular case breeds public opinion on the case. Jurors may have already talked about the case with friends, family, and neighbors. Each of these people may have given an opinion of what they thought about it and what they would do if chosen as a juror on that case. All this pretrial talk leads to an unfair jury.

> The trial of Miles Brookwood is scheduled to begin in two weeks. Miles was fifteen years old when he decided to kill his mother and two twin brothers. He stabbed them in their sleep when his stepfather was away on a business trip. After he stabbed them, he used some of their blood to draw video game characters on the walls and then went to sleep. The next morning, he went to school as usual and stayed all day. After school, he went back home and packed his belongings to leave town. He took the family car and began driving. He was later apprehended in a neighboring state. When the authorities discovered what had happened, the entire community was talking about the case. There were social media posts about the crime. Some were in support of a distraught teenager and others were in support of the family he murdered. Even the stepfather had a difficult time picking a side to support. The defense attorney files a motion to change venue, alleging that teenager cannot get a fair trial in the community because of the overwhelming amount of public opinion. The fourteen-year-old is being tried as an adult because his case was transferred to adult court, after a hearing. There have been many opinionated posts regarding whether a fourteen-year-old should be tried as an adult and subjected to the same punishment. During voir dire, the judge and attorneys ask whether the potential jurors can be fair and unbiased and set aside anything they have heard or read involving this case. They all say that they can, and twelve members are selected. Do you think this is a fair jury? If not, what could be a remedy?

Pretrial publicity can also affect how attorneys present a case. Decisions may be made by each side based on what will look good to the general public rather than to the jury selected. Prosecutors could use the media to further a political career, while defense attorneys could use the media to get more clients. The judge could use the media to further his or her career by appearing a certain way to the voters. All these things distract from the facts and law in the case being presented to the jury.

Minimizing the Effect of Media on Juries

The courts have four ways that they can minimize the effect of pretrial publicity on criminal trial: (a) voir dire, (b) change of venue, (c) sequestration of the jury, and (d) gag orders.

Voir Dire

As discussed earlier, the voir dire process is the questioning of jurors by both parties and perhaps the judge to determine prejudices and biases that could affect their ability to sit as a fair and impartial juror. These questions almost always include "have you heard" questions. These types of questions are asked to determine if prospective jurors have heard any information about the case. This could be a discussion with family, friends, or neighbors, or by reading or watching media accounts of the crime. Since there are often many months or years between the time of the crime and the time of the trial, it is important to inquire about media reports both at the time of the crime and at the time of trial. If the voir dire process occurs in a group setting rather than individual voir dire, the parties must be careful how to ask "have you heard" questions. If an attorney asks the group, "Have you heard any facts about this case?" and a potential juror responds in the affirmative, the natural next question is "What did you hear?" If this is answered in a group setting, then everyone on the jury panel has heard the same thing. An easy solution would be the ask the group the "have you heard" question and then not elicit what they heard in the group setting but rather request individual voir dire on only the individuals who answered in the affirmative. This avoids tainting the entire panel.

Change of Venue

If the voir dire exposes a large number of potential jurors who may be biased from community talk or the media, a change of venue can eliminate the taint. A change of venue means that the trial will be moved to another jurisdiction that may not have had the media coverage or taint that the original jurisdiction had. However, this can be difficult if the crime was widely covered in multiple jurisdictions.

Sequestration of the Jury

If the case is particularly sensationalized by the media, it will certainly get more attention as the trial progresses. This could mean that the voir dire process and the change of venue is not sufficient to protect the defendant's rights. In this case, the jury would need to be **sequestered** to remain untainted by media attention. This is an extreme remedy and is rarely used because it involves isolating the jurors during the duration of the trial. Most people would be highly opposed to being separated from their friends or family for any number of days and kept overnight is a less-than-optimal environment. The courts also would incur the expense of housing, transporting, and feeding the jury for the duration of the trial, which could add up quickly. More commonly, the judge will instruct the jurors not to discuss the case with anyone, not to read any media accounts of the trial, not to watch the news, and not to look at any social media sites.

Gag Orders

There are two basic types of gag orders: media gag orders and individual gag orders. The purpose of a gag order is to reduce the media coverage of a case and reduce the impact of that media on the jury's verdict.

In *Nebraska Press Association v. Stewart*, the trial judge prohibited the media from reporting information that the defendant had confessed in out-of-court pretrial statements. The Supreme Court ruled that restrictions on the media would only be allowable in extreme circumstances and only after considering certain factors. Those factors are (a) the nature and extent of the pretrial coverage, (b) whether other measures could mitigate the effects of the pretrial media coverage, and (c) if a restraining order could accomplish the same result.

Stopping the press from reporting about a trial can be very difficult, especially in light of today's social media presence. It can be near impossible to determine who is responsible for certain posts or reports. Also, the person responsible for the posts may be outside the jurisdiction of the trial court. Therefore, the easier avenue for a trial judge is to restrict the parties from discussing the case with the media. There could be an issue involving the parties' right to free speech, but likely the parties will not contest the judge's ruling. As practical matter, the attorneys may wish to stay in the good graces of the judge they are currently practicing in front of. This could affect rulings, time allotments, or future cases, depending on the personality of the trial judge. Most attorneys will not risk secondary and indirect punishments for violating a gag order.

There are also rules of professional conduct that prohibit attorneys from discussing certain aspects of the case with the media, pretrial. These rules can prohibit the attorneys from discussing the criminal histories of witnesses, whether the defendant confessed to the crime, the conclusions of certain tests performed in the case, and others. The rules of professional conduct can also prevent an attorney from purposefully disclosing information to the media to affect the case. If an attorney violates the rules of professional conduct, the Bar could suspend or even revoke the attorney's license, which carries much greater weight than any threat of a trial judge.

The Right to a public Trial

The US Constitution provides many rights to the criminally accused. The Sixth Amendment provides that "in all criminal prosecutions, the accused shall enjoy the **right to . . . a public trial**." One way to protect the rights of an accused defendant is to have the criminal trial in the public. The US Supreme Court in In re Oliver stated that "the knowledge that every criminal trial is subject to contemporaneous review in the forum of public opinion is an effective restraint on possible abuse of power . . . without publicity, all other checks are insufficient: in comparison of publicity, all other checks are of small account." The Court went on to state, "the presence of interested spectators may keep the defendant's triers keenly alive to a sense of their responsibility and to the importance of their functions." This right to public trial also extends to other pretrial hearings, with the exception of a grand jury proceeding, which is always held in private. Preliminary/

probable cause hearings, suppression hearings, other act hearings, venue transfer hearings, and others are open to the public.

This right is not absolute. Either side may request that the trial be closed to the public in the interest of justice. Since this is the defendant's right, the defendant may request to close the trial without much overall explanation. However, if the state requests that the trial be closed to the public, there is a burden that must be met. That burden was set out in the case of *Waller v. Georgia*. Defendants who were indicted for violating the Georgia Racketeer Influenced and Corrupt Organizations Act and other state gambling statutes moved prior to trial to suppress certain wiretap evidence. The state moved to close the hearing, stating that some of the information revealed on the wiretap would involve other defendants both indicted and not indicted. The US Supreme Court held that the right to a public trial under the Sixth and Fourteenth Amendments applies to a hearing on a motion to suppress evidence. They also held that the closure of the entire suppression hearing was unjustified. The state's proffer was not specific as to whose privacy interests might be infringed if the hearing were open to the public, how they would be infringed, what portions of the wiretap tapes might infringe them, and what portion of the evidence consisted of the tapes. The trial court should consider alternatives to immediate closure of the entire hearing, by directing the state to provide more detail about its need for closure and closing only those parts of the hearing that jeopardized the interests advanced.

To prevail on a motion to close a criminal court hearing or trial, the government must show (a) that there is an overriding interest, (b) that the closure is no broader than absolutely necessary, (c) that reasonable alternatives have been considered, and (d) that adequate findings to support closure are entered by the trial court.

Peter Pervert is on trial for numerous sexual acts on six different children in his home. He was the stepfather of three of the children and the biological father of the youngest three. The youngest child was four years old. Her name was Zoe. Zoe is the last of the children to take the witness stand in the trial and has not seen her father since his arrest months ago. She is qualified as a witness and the prosecutor begins asking questions. She answers the foundational questions without any problem, such as her name, age, and school. When the prosecutor moves into questions about her father, Zoe does not answer. She looks at the floor and fiddles with her hands. The prosecutor asks if she is okay and she shakes her head "no." The prosecutor asks if she will answer the questions about her father now and Zoe shakes her head "no." The prosecutor asks if she is scared of her father and Zoe nods her head "yes." The prosecutor asks if Zoe would answer the questions about her father if she were allowed to go to another room in the courthouse with her father not present. Zoe nods her head "yes." The prosecutor makes a motion to the court to allow Zoe to leave the courtroom and testify via closed-circuit television from an empty courtroom. The judge allows Zoe and the prosecutor to leave the room and testify via a FaceTime setup. The defense attorney, defendant, judge, and jury remain in the original courtroom and view Zoe's testimony on a large screen in the courtroom. The defense attorney is able to cross-examine Zoe, and ultimately the jury convicts the defendant on all counts. Has the court violated the defendant's rights by allowing Zoe to be removed from the courtroom?

The Right to Joinder of Defendants

The federal rules of criminal procedure and many state rules of criminal procedure allow joinder of defendants. This joinder can occur in the original charging instrument or at any later date. This most likely happens when the case involves codefendants. The general reason for allowing joinder of parties for the purposes of trial is judicial economy. This is separate and apart from joinder of charges on a single defendant. Joinder of codefendant who participated in the same crime has the potential to be highly prejudicial to each defendant. For example, if Jack and Jill commit a robbery and are caught, and Jill implicates Jack and gives a full confession, allowing the confession and the portion of the statement implicating Jack could prejudice Jack if Jill refused to take the witness stand. In this example, Jack's attorney will not be able to cross-examine Jill, but only the law enforcement officer who took Jill's statement. This could raise confrontation clause issues for Jack and substantial prejudice.

Judges are cautious to join codefendants in the same trial because at the onset of the case, the judge may not have full information about the facts, and the facts can always play out differently as a trial progresses. Because of this, judges should separate codefendants trials when there is a serious risk that a joint trial would compromise a specific trial right of one of the defendants or prevent the jury from making a reliable judgment about guilt or innocence.[1]

Baby Olivia, three months old, was brought into the emergency room as nonresponsive by her mother and mother's boyfriend. Both the mother and boyfriend gave an account to the nurses that the baby had been sleeping in her bed, which is a mattress on the floor, and crying through the night. They had checked on her multiple times and she seemed fine, just fussy. The last time they checked on her was approximately 3:00 a.m. When they awoke to check on baby Olivia at 10:00 a.m., she was on the floor beside the mattress and nonresponsive. They took her immediately to the emergency room. The doctors worked on Baby Olivia but ultimately she died that same day at the hospital. Her body was examined, and she was found to have bleeding on the brain, swelling of the brain, a cracked skull, petechiae on the eyes, and eight old and healing fractures to multiple areas of her body. The expert physician determined that Baby Olivia died from blunt force injury to her head and that in his opinion this could not have been caused by a low-height fall to the floor. Both the mother and mother's boyfriend were interviewed and never changed their original story. They both said that they were with Baby Oliva the entire twenty-four-hour period prior to bringing her into the emergency room and that no one else was in the home. The expert physician believes that this injury would have occurred within a twelve-hour window before Baby Olivia presented to the emergency room. He cannot give an opinion of a time frame for the eight other healing fractures but does believe that they were intentionally caused due to their placement on Baby Olivia's body. Both the mother and the mother's boyfriend were arrested for the murder of Baby Olivia. The government files a motion for the cases to be consolidated and the defendants joined for a single trial. Why would the government want to try both of these cases together? Is it a violation of the mother's and mother's boyfriend's rights to join these cases for trial?

The Right to Confront Witnesses

The defendant's right to **confront witnesses** is grounded in the Sixth Amendment to the US Constitution. This is the defendant's opportunity to challenge the witness against him or her. This is usually accomplished by the defendant physically being present in the courtroom in which the witness is testifying. This face-to-face encounter clearly complies with the Sixth Amendment confrontation guarantee.

1. *Zafiro v. United States*, 506 US 534 (1993).

The controversy lies around instances where a witness has been allowed to testify in a manner that is not directly face to face. One such instance is when a child victim is testifying about the acts of the defendant. The US Supreme Court has overturned cases wherein state statutes allowed children of a tender age to testify either behind a screen or via closed-circuit television as a blanket rule.[2] The Supreme Court has allowed such procedures in cases only if "necessary to further an important public policy and only where the reliability of the testimony is otherwise assured."[3] In the Maryland case, the Maryland statute allowed a child to testify via closed-circuit television if testifying in the courtroom will result in the child suffering severe emotional distress such that a child cannot reasonably communicate. For example, if Sara, who is six years old, takes the witness stand and is unable to testify against her abuser because the abuser is in the courtroom, Sara may be allowed to testify via closed-circuit television if it can be established that the defendant's presence in the courtroom is the reason she cannot communicate and that she will suffer serious emotional distress from the testimony. If this mechanism of testimony is utilized, the witness will still be subjected to cross-examination, which is another aspect of the confrontation clause.

The right to confront witnesses is tantamount to the concept of a fair trial for the accused. Cross-examination is purported to expose false testimony and bring out the truth in trials. This is the foundational purpose of courts disallowing hearsay testimony because by definition it negates the defendant's ability to confront the person making the statement against him. For example, If Investigator Lockemup takes the witness stand and says that a witness named Chris Tatle said the defendant committed the crime, the defendant would be precluded from confronting Chris Tatle. This would certainly prejudice the defendant and give him no recourse.

The right to confront witnesses can also be limited in certain instances if justice requires. States have enacted certain rules outlining what testimony may be elicited on cross-examination and what information may not. For example, If Chris Tatle takes the witness stand and testifies that he saw the defendant commit the crime, the defense may want to impeach Chris Tatle with the fact that he has a prior felony conviction. The state rule may disallow impeachment of witnesses with certain criminal convictions. For example, if Chris Tatle has a prior conviction for possession of marijuana, the court may disallow the cross-examination about that conviction finding that a conviction for possession of a narcotic has no bearing on the witness's credibility and is therefore irrelevant. While on the other hand, if Chris Tatle's prior conviction was for perjury, the court may find that it is relevant to the credibility of his testimony. States may also prescribe rules for determining that a conviction is too remote in time to be applicable. For example, Chris Tatle's prior conviction may be thirty years old and the court could consider this too remote to adequately represent the witness's current character.

Along with the defendant's right to be present and confront the witnesses against him or her, the government also has the right to conduct a peaceful and safe trial. A defendant can lose his or her right to be present and confront the witnesses against him or her by his or her conduct. This does not mean that

2. *Coy v. Iowa*, 487 US 1012 (1988).

3. *Maryland v. Craig*, 497 US 836 (1990).

the defendant may be excluded from the courtroom after a single outburst or even a few outbursts, but the judge may exclude the defendant from the courtroom following repeated warnings to cease disruptive behavior.[4] The *Allen* Court ruled that the privilege of personally confronting witnesses may be lost by consent or at times even by misconduct. Although courts must indulge every reasonable presumption against the loss of constitutional rights, a defendant can lose his right to be present at trial if, after he has been warned by the judge that he will be removed if he continues his disruptive behavior, he nevertheless insists on conducting himself in a manner so disorderly, disruptive, and disrespectful of the court that his trial cannot be carried on with him in the courtroom. Once lost, the right to be present can, of course, be reclaimed as soon as the defendant is willing to conduct himself consistently with the decorum and respect inherent in the concept of courts and judicial proceedings. The *Allen* Court notes that the defendant can reclaim his right to be present and the judge can allow the defendant to rejoin the trial with assertions of the defendant's good behavior.

The *Allen* Court also outlined other ways to address a defendant's misconduct in a trial. Trial judges who are confronted with disruptive, contumacious, stubbornly defiant defendants must be given sufficient discretion to meet the circumstances of each case. No single formula for maintaining the appropriate courtroom atmosphere will be best in all situations. There are at least three constitutionally permissible ways for a trial judge to handle an obstreperous defendant: (a) bind and gag him, thereby keeping him present; (b) cite him for contempt; and (c) take him out of the courtroom until he promises to conduct himself properly.

The Right to Counsel

The Sixth Amendment to the US Constitution states that "in all criminal prosecutions, the accused shall enjoy the right . . . to have the assistance of counsel for his defense." As discussed earlier, the *right to counsel* attaches much earlier than the trial because the need for counsel arises long before the adversarial proceeding. The right to counsel exists in criminal prosecutions if actual imprisonment is ultimately imposed. This right exists regardless of whether the defendant can afford counsel. In cases of indigent defendants, counsel will be appointed to the defendants. Some jurisdictions have a public defender's office while others have a contract appointment system. No matter the system, the counsel appointed must be competent for the case.

Counsel for the defendant must not have a conflict that would cause prejudice, and counsel must be effective. A claim of ineffective assistance of counsel is a common motion filed by defendants convicted after trial. The defendant can always argue something that counsel should have done differently. The standard for an ineffective assistance of counsel claim is whether the counsel was so ineffective that the outcome of the trial would have been different. This is a difficult standard to make.

4. *Illinois v. Allen*, 397 US 337 (1970).

Criminal defendants may also be appointed experts to assist in the trial of their case, such as medical experts, psychological experts, laboratory testing experts, investigators, and so on. These experts could be appointed to the defendant at no cost if the court finds that they are necessary to aid in the defense.

Along with the right to counsel, criminal defendants have the right to present evidence in their case. The right to a defense and to "have compulsory process for obtaining witnesses in his favor" is guaranteed by the Sixth Amendment to the US Constitution. The US Supreme Court interpreted this further in *Washington v. Texas* by saying that the Sixth Amendment protects the right to offer testimony of witnesses and to compel their attendance, and the right to present the defendant's version of the facts as well as the prosecution's to the jury so that it may decide where the truth lies.

A defendant can always call himself or herself as a witness. The defendant also has the right to remain silent and that silences shall not be the result of comment by the government during the trial. If the defendant testifies, he or she will be subjected to the same cross-examination as any other witness and the same rules of evidence will apply.

The defendant also has the right to subpoena witnesses. This is known as the Compulsory Process Clause. This clause guarantees the defendant subpoena power to obtain witnesses or documents that will aid in his or her defense. The defense may subpoena any witness, including the prosecution witnesses.

The defendant also has the right to have all material and relevant evidence presented. The trial court is the sole determining factor of whether a piece of evidence is admissible during the trial of a case. The court must not exclude a relevant piece of evidence that is crucial for the defense. An exception to this general rule of inclusion is if the exclusion is a sanction for violation of the pretrial discovery rules. For example, if the state files a pretrial motion requesting discovery from the defense and the defense fails to discover evidence or witnesses that the state is entitled to during trial, the defendant can be precluded from offering that testimony.[5]

The Right to Protection from Double Jeopardy

The defendant's protection from *double jeopardy* is grounded in the Fifth Amendment to the US Constitution. The Fifth Amendment states that "no person shall be subject for the same offense, to be twice put in jeopardy." The basic premise of the double jeopardy provision is that a person who has committed a single criminal offense can only be subjected to one punishment for that offense. Whether the defendant's prosecution for a single offense resulted in a conviction or an acquittal is irrelevant; the defendant cannot be prosecuted again for the same offense. This, in essence, prevents the government from trying to convict the defendant again after an acquittal.

The purpose of the double jeopardy clause was to give defendants calm knowing that once they have faced prosecution, they will not have to face the same prosecution again. It prevents the government from getting more information in the first criminal trial and using it against the defendant in subsequent

5. *Taylor v. Illinois*, 484 US 400 (1988)

trials. The chances of conviction could get greater and greater until possibly an innocent man could be convicted.

The double jeopardy clause applies only to criminal prosecutions. Thus, if the defendant is prosecuted in criminal court, the state, or any other party, may also bring a civil case against the defendant for the same act. Likewise, if the defendant has already been held liable in a civil lawsuit for a tort involving criminal conduct, the government may still prosecute the defendant in criminal court. The burdens of proof are quite different in civil and criminal cases. The burden to convict in a criminal action is proof beyond a reasonable doubt, while the burden to prevail in a civil action is by a preponderance of the evidence. This standard is defined as more probable than not. It is a mere tipping of the scales of justice. Some call it a 51 percent burden. By any nickname, it is a long way from beyond a reasonable doubt.

The classic example of the differences in burdens of proof in a criminal versus a civil proceeding is the case of O.J. Simpson. Simpson was acquitted in 1995 of the murder of his ex-wife, Nicole Brown Simpson, and her friend Ronald Goldman. It was one of the most sensationalized criminal trials in history. The trial went on for weeks and was highly publicized. Most Americans tuned in regularly to watch the trial, and many discussions were had about the police action and the defendant's guilt or innocence. Ultimately, the jury found Simpson not guilty. Simpson was also sued by the victims' families for wrongful death, and the civil trial began the following year. In just a few months, that jury found him responsible for the deaths of Nicole Brown Simpson and Ronald Goldman and awarded their families over thirty million dollars in damages. This can be attributed to several factors, the greatest of which is the differences in the burden of proof required in a civil trial and a criminal trial. Since the second trial was civil in nature, there were no double jeopardy concerns.

The double jeopardy clause is an interesting law; in fact, even movies have been made about the nuances of the clause. The key to understanding the double jeopardy clause is to know when it attaches. Jeopardy attaches in a criminal jury trial when the jury is sworn. Jeopardy attaches in a bench trial when the first witness is sworn.

The double jeopardy clause does not apply if the defendant pled guilty to the charges leveled against him or her. When a defendant pleads guilty, he waives certain rights, and double jeopardy is one of them. For example, if Louise pleads guilty to possession of stolen property and then receives a sentence that she was not expecting, Louise may file a motion to set aside her guilty plea. Louise will have the burden of showing that her attorney or the judge accepting the plea failed to inform her of the range of punishment and therefore her plea was not knowing and voluntary, as required for a valid plea. If Louise's plea is set aside, she is back in the criminal system in the same position as before her plea. She can plea again or have a trial on the charges. Double jeopardy will not apply merely because she pled because it hadn't formally attached.

Exceptions to Double Jeopardy

With most rules, there are exceptions, and the double jeopardy clause is no different. There are instances where subsequent prosecutions may occur after jeopardy has attached. Once such exception is when a mistrial occurs. A mistrial occurs when the trial is not completed because of a mistake occurring during the trial process. The question that must be asked is what the mistake was and who caused it. If the defendant makes a motion for mistrial, he is said to have waived the right to complain about a subsequent prosecution. If the government is the moving party for the mistrial and the defendant objects to the mistrial motion, the trial judge must find a "manifest necessity" for granting the mistrial. Manifest necessity has been defined as occurring when a scrupulous exercise of judicial discretion leads to the conclusion that the ends of public justice would not be served by a continuation of the trial.[6] This usually occurs when an event happens that is out of the control of either party—for example, in the instance of the death of the judge, attorney, or juror; the jury cannot reach a verdict and are hung; or a community disaster disrupts the trial. Other examples that have led to findings of manifest necessity for a retrial are instances where the defendant caused the mistrial by his intentional conduct or a scrivener's error in the charging instrument that was not discovered pretrial.

Another exception to the double jeopardy clause that could allow the defendant to be retried for the same offense after jeopardy attaches is known as the dual sovereignty doctrine. This doctrine allows for two different sovereignties to try the same defendant for the same crime. The Supreme Court has upheld the ability of the federal and state governments to prosecute a defendant successively for violating both federal and state laws, even if those laws seem to criminalize the same conduct. The rationale is that where there are two sovereigns, there are two laws and two offenses. This may also apply when the defendant's crime occurs in two states, because they are separate violations of separate laws.

Because the government has only one opportunity to try the defendant for the crime committed, the government must bring all evidence to bear during that trial. It is not a manifest necessity to retry the case against the defendant if a state's witness fails to show for the trial. Therefore, the government needs to have all witnesses and all evidence accounted for before the jury is sworn. If a government witness fails to show up for testimony, it is possible that the judge will continue the case for a reasonable amount of time to allow the government an opportunity to locate the witness. However, courts and juries will lose patience quickly in this circumstance and could hold it against the government's case.

If the government is not successful in prosecution of the case and the defendant is acquitted, the government cannot appeal. This is the end of the prosecution for this charge by this sovereignty against this defendant. This is why the prosecutor may request pretrial rulings on evidentiary issues from the trial

6. *Illinois v. Somerville*, 410 US 458 (1973).

judge. If the government is dissatisfied by a pretrial ruling, the government may appeal that ruling to a higher court pretrial. When this occurs, the trial is stayed and continued until the ruling is passed down from the appellate court. This is the prosecutors' only remedy for an adverse legal ruling, yet it comes with a high standard of proof for the government. The government must show that the judge abused his discretion in the ruling. This is a very high standard because judges are given wide latitude on evidentiary rulings. Also, there is no guarantee that a judge would allow a pretrial hearing or make a pretrial ruling. If the judge conducts evidentiary hearings after the jury has been sworn, the prosecution may not appeal the rulings.

> The state is preparing to try a case of child sexual abuse wherein the victim is the stepdaughter of the defendant. The victim alleges that the defendant began molesting her at the age of six, when her mother and he began dating. She alleges that it continued until she was sixteen years old when she finally reported to a school counselor what had been happening. The victim's mother was a drug abuser and left the victim and the boyfriend when the victim was ten. The victim hasn't had any contact with her mother since then. When the victim was fifteen, she and the defendant moved to the jurisdiction. The indictment in the case alleges that the defendant committed several different sex acts while in the jurisdiction over the last year and a half. The prosecutor files an Other Bad Acts Motion asking to discuss, in the trial of this case, the other acts that occurred between the defendant and the victim from age six to fifteen in another jurisdiction. The parties have a pretrial hearing on the motion and the judge rules that the other bad act testimony is not allowed. The prosecution appeals the ruling believing that the jury needs to hear that this started when the victim was younger and continued until she reported. Since the jury has not been sworn, the government has the ability to appeal this judge's ruling and the case will be continued awaiting the appellant court's ruling on the issue. This is one of the few ways the government can appeal a ruling in a criminal case.

If the prosecution is successful and the defendant is convicted, the defendant has the right to appeal. If the defendant is successful on appeal, his or her case can be retried and is not barred by double jeopardy because by appealing the conviction, the defendant is said to have waived the right to claim jeopardy. The defendant must be tried for the same offense. The government may not charge a greater offense merely because the defendant's appeal was successful. For example, in the first trial, the defendant is charged with murder, but the jury convicts him of a lesser included offense of manslaughter. The defendant appeals the manslaughter conviction and is successful. The state cannot get another try for a conviction of murder. The defendant can only be retried for manslaughter because it is believed that the jury has acquitted him on the original charge of murder; therefore, jeopardy attached to the charge of murder.

The double jeopardy clause generally does not prevent a defendant from receiving a higher sentence after a second prosecution. If the defendant successfully appeals his conviction and it is overturned, this will result in a second trial. If the defendant is convicted at the second trial, the judge or jury can give the defendant a higher sentence than he received in the first trial for the same charge. This may seem unfair and vindictive, but remember that in states where juries sentence offenders, it is a whole new group of people with different thoughts on punishment. This could result in stiffer punishment for the defendant.

Although the double jeopardy clause does not prevent a defendant from receiving a higher sentence, the equal protection clause could. The Equal Protection Clause prevents the trial judge from imposing a higher sentence on reconnection absent a showing of additional facts that would support the greater sentence. Otherwise, there is a threat of judicial vindictiveness, which could deter defendants from appealing convictions. This is to be distinguished if the appeal is granted simply because of a mistake in sentencing. For example, the defendant was tried and convicted of shooting into an occupied vehicle. The trial judge gave the defendant a sentence of eight years. The defendant appeals the conviction. On appeal, the higher court finds no reversible error in the trial phase of the proceeding. The appellate court does find the sentence to be illegal because the state law provides for a minimum sentence on the charge of shooting into an occupied vehicle of ten years. The higher court could send the case back to the lower court and order the court to resentence the defendant in accordance with the law. In that case, the defendant would receive a higher sentence after appeal.

A defendant can also be convicted of two crimes that involve one set of facts. A single act may violate multiple statutes proscribing a criminal offense as long as the offenses have different elements. For example, a defendant may be convicted of burglary and larceny or of theft of property and being in possession of stolen property. This is also the case when the defendant commits a substantive criminal offense and a conspiracy to commit that offense. An agreement or meeting of the minds is an essential element for a conspiracy charge, which is a separate and distinct element from the substantive crime. Therefore, a defendant can be charged with both the conspiracy and the crime committed without a violation of the double jeopardy clause.

The Right against Entrapment

Individuals have the right to not be entrapped into a criminal offense by the government. **Entrapment** is a defense to a criminal case and not necessarily grounded in constitutional law, as the other rights discussed above. Entrapment is the "conception and planning of an offense by an offender, and his procurement of its commission by one who would not have perpetrated it except for the trickery, persuasion or fraud of the officer." The *Sorrells* Court stated that "society is at war with the criminal classes, and the courts have uniformly held that in waging this warfare the forces of prevention and detection may use traps, decoys and deception to obtain evidence of the commission of the crime." The *Sorrells* Court concluded "the fact that the government agents merely afforded opportunities or facilities for the commission of the offense does not constitute entrapment.

In *Sherman v. United States*, Sherman met the government informant at a doctor's office where both Sherman and the government informant were being treated for a narcotics addiction. After some time, the informant befriended Sherman and asked him where narcotics could be purchased. Sherman seemed reluctant to purchase narcotics for the informant, but eventually Sherman began purchasing and sharing narcotics with the informant. The informant informed government agents he was working with, and Sherman was arrested. Sherman asserted an entrapment defense at trial but was convicted. Sherman appealed the conviction, and his case was overturned. The *Sherman* Court held that the defense of entrapment is established as a matter of law in a prosecution for unlawful sales of narcotics where the undisputed testimony of the prosecution's witnesses shows that these sales, made to a government informer, were brought about by the informer's persistent solicitation in the face of obvious reluctance on the part of the defendant, whom the informer believed to be undergoing a cure for narcotics addiction, and by the informer's appeals to sympathy based on mutual experiences with narcotics addiction and tales of his suffering. Moreover, the informer not only procured a source of narcotics but apparently also induced the defendant to return to the habit. They went on to say entrapment occurs only when the criminal conduct is the product of the creative activity of law enforcement officials—that is, when the criminal design originates with the officials of the government and they implant in the mind of an innocent person the disposition to commit the alleged offense and induce its commission in order that they may prosecute; on the other hand, the fact that government agents merely afford opportunities or facilities for the commission of the offense does not constitute entrapment.

This defense would not be afforded to a criminal defendant who is readily available to commit a criminal offense without much persuasion. For example, Catherine is arrested for possession of cocaine. The law enforcement officer making the arrest asks if she would be willing to work as a police informant to gain favor on the possession of narcotics charge. She agrees and tells the law enforcement officer that she can purchase cocaine from three different individuals. The law enforcement officer places a hidden recording device on Catherine and she makes a purchase of cocaine from Mike. The recording shows that she drives up at Mike's house and he is on the front porch. She asks Mike for fifty dollars worth of cocaine. Mike goes inside his home and returns with a small bag of cocaine. She gives him the money and he gives her the cocaine. She drives away and meets the law enforcement officer at the predetermined location. She turns over the cocaine to the law enforcement officer. The law enforcement officer later obtains a warrant for Mike's arrest for sale of narcotics. Mike asserts an entrapment defense at trial and is not successful. The facts indicate that Mike was predisposed to sell narcotics and all Catherine needed to do was to ask for the narcotics. There was no undue inducement by a government agent to persuade Mike to commit a criminal act, therefore no entrapment.

Consider another example. Catherine is working as a government informant and says that she can sell narcotics to Phillip. The government agents provide Catherine with an amount of cocaine for her to make a sell to Phillip. Catherine, while wearing a hidden recording device, drives to Phillip's house. Phillip is in the yard with several other individuals. Catherine says to Phillip, "Do you still need some of that blow?" Wherein Phillip answers "yes." Catherine exchanges a quantity of cocaine for money with Phillip and leaves. She meets the law enforcement officer at a predetermined location and turns over the money. Phillip is later arrested and asserts an entrapment defense at trial. Phillip's defense states that Phillip would not be in possession of cocaine but for the government agent supplying it to him. Phillip is unsuccessful. Phillip's defense would need to make a showing that Phillip was not predisposed to possess cocaine, which is impossible under these facts.

Another example of the use of an entrapment defense is the case of *Jacobson v. United States*. The defendant had ordered and received magazines containing images of nude preteen and teenage boys. At the time of Jacobson's orders, there was no state or federal law against ordering or possessing such images. Then, Congress passed the Child Protection Act of 1984, which criminalized the receipt through the mails of sexually explicit depictions of children. US postal inspectors found Jacobson's name on the bookstore mailing list, and, as a result, the postal service sought to explore Jacobson's willingness to place a mail order that would violate the new law. The postal inspectors (federal agents) mailed Jacobson letters from three fictitious organizations purported to sell such materials. Each of the letters discussed (a) protection and promotion of sexual freedom and freedom of choice, and (b) funding of lobbying efforts by catalog sales. Jacobson responded to the letters by answering questionnaires and expressing interest in the organizations' goals. Twenty-six months later, federal agents mailed Jacobson an advertisement for photographs of young boys engaging in sex. Jacobson placed an order for the illegal material, but the federal agents did not fill the order. The postal service then posed as another organization with concerns about government censorship and suppressions of freedoms and offered sales of pornographic materials. Jacobson ordered and received from this fictitious organization, through the mail, a pornographic magazine depicting young boys engaged in various sexual activities. Jacobson was arrested. A search of his home revealed the magazines bought from the bookstore and the materials sent by the government during its investigation but revealed no other materials indicating that the farmer collected or was actively interested in child pornography. At Jacobson's trial, he asserted an entrapment defense. Jacobson was not successful with the entrapment defense and convicted of the charges. He appealed his conviction. The US Supreme Court stated that the fact that officers or employees of the government merely afford opportunities or facilities for the commission of an offense does not defeat the prosecution for the offense because artifice and stratagem may be employed to catch those engaged in criminal enterprises.

However, government agents may not originate a criminal design, implant in an innocent person's mind the disposition to commit a criminal act, and then induce the commission of the crime so that the government may prosecute. The government may not play on the weaknesses of an innocent party and beguile the party into committing crimes that the party otherwise would not have attempted. Law enforcement officials go too far when they implant in the mind of an innocent person the disposition to commit an alleged offense and induce its commission in order that they may prosecute. When the government's quest for convictions leads to the apprehension of an otherwise law-abiding citizen who, if left to the citizen's own devices, likely would never have run afoul of the law, the courts should intervene.

The practice test for whether a defendant was entrapped to commit the criminal offense is focused on the predisposition of the defendant to commit the act charged. The entrapment defense would only apply if the accused has no criminal predisposition to commit the crime but did so due to the inducement by the government. The predisposition of the defendant must exist "pre" (before) the crime. The defendant's mere inclination to engage in the criminal conduct will not be adequate to show predisposition to commit the crime. The government's involvement in the inducement is also examined. If the government's involvement is long term and heavily weighted toward a goal, such as in Jacobson, the greater the likelihood that the defendant was entrapped.

Another situation that could arise with the use of a police agent is the use of an agent or informant to form a conspiracy with the defendant. The same entrapment analysis applies if the crime is coupled with a second charge of conspiracy. The courts must still look at the predisposition of the defendant to determine whether there has been entrapment. For example, in *United States v. Russell*, an undercover agent posed as a manufacturer of narcotics and offered to supply the one ingredient that Russell needed to manufacture a drug. Russell was convicted and appealed to the US Supreme Court. The Supreme Court found that there was no entrapment because Russell was predisposed to the criminal activity. The court stated as fact that officers or employees of the government merely afford opportunities or facilities for the commission of the offense. This does not defeat the prosecution nor will the mere fact of deceit defeat a prosecution, for there are circumstances when the use of deceit is the only practicable law enforcement technique available. It is only when the government's deception actually implants the criminal design in the mind of the defendant that the defense of entrapment comes into play.

The Victims' Rights at an Adversarial Proceeding

Victims of crime have certain rights in an adversarial proceeding. These rights are not founded in the constitution or even in case law, but they are established by rules established by federal and state government. There are also crimes that are considered "victimless crimes" because there is no named victim. Examples of these crimes are drug violations, and violations of child pornography and sex offender registration laws. These crimes and other like crimes affect society as a whole and are prosecuted by the government on behalf of the community. Even though there aren't specific crime victims' rights enumerated in the constitution, the US Supreme Court routinely discusses the balancing of the defendant's rights against the victim's or societal rights.

Victim Rights

See a listing of core **victims' rights** at this website.

Read at: https://victimconnect.org/learn/victim-rights/

Rules to Remember

Below is a list of rules to remember from this chapter.

- The US Supreme Court has identified three purposes for the right to a speedy trial: it prevents excessive incarceration, (b) it minimizes anxiety experienced by the accused as a result of the publicized accusation, and (c) it prevents damage to the defendant's case resulting from too much delay.
- Criminal defendants charged with a crime that has a potential punishment of greater than six months' imprisonment have a right to a jury trial.
- Criminal defendants can waive the right to a jury trial, but the prosecution must also agree.
- The courts have four ways that they can minimize the effect of pretrial publicity on criminal trial: (a) voir dire, (b) change of venue, (c) sequestration of the jury, and (d) gag orders.
- The criminal defendant's right to a jury trial is not absolute and can be lost by the behavior of the defendant.
- Exceptions to a defendant's right to confront witnesses can (a) occur when a witness testifies via closed-circuit television or (b) occur when hearsay statements are allowable in the trial.
- The right to counsel applies to cases where imprisonment is actually imposed rather than merely being a possibility.
- The right to counsel can also give criminal defendants the right to other assistance at trial, such as an investigator or expert witness.
- Defendants can be prosecuted for the same act as long as the prosecution is in a different sovereignty.
- Entrapment is a defense to a criminal action wherein the defendant accuses the government of making him or her do the crime. To be successful, defendants must show that they were not

predisposed to commit the crime.

- Victims of crimes have many rights at trial, but those rights are not constitutional in nature and must be balanced against the defendant's rights.

End of Chapter Comprehension and Application

Directions: Use what you have learned in this chapter to help you respond completely and correctly to each question or prompt below.

1. What is the defendant's right to a speedy trial? When does the right attach? What must the defendant show to prevail on a motion for speedy trial?
2. The defendant is charged with possession of cocaine and makes bond while he awaits trial. The case is continued for a year because the lab testing the cocaine is backed up. When the case goes to trial, the defendant complains that his rights to a speedy trial were violated. The judge denies his motion and ultimately the defendant is convicted. He begins serving a two-year sentence and appeals his case alleging that his rights to a speedy trial were violated. Will he prevail? Why or why not?
3. Does the right to an impartial jury apply to all defendants charged with a criminal offense? Why or why not?
4. Give a factual example of how a defendant charged with a traffic ticket could get a jury trial.
5. Can a defendant waive the right to a jury? Does this alone mean that his or her case will be tried before a jury?
6. Under what circumstances would a defendant want to waive a jury trial? Under what circumstances would the government want to waive a jury trial?
7. In what ways could pretrial publicity hurt the prosecution of a case? Give a factual example.
8. Describe the four ways that courts can minimize the effect of pretrial publicity on trials.
9. Of the options in the above question, which do you think is the most effective and why?
10. What was the Court's rationale in In re Oliver?
11. The defendant is charged with possession of child pornography. Prior to the trial of his case, the prosecution files a motion to close the courtroom because of the sensitive nature of the evidence that will be presented in the trial. The prosecution argues that the photographs and videos, which are the basis of the charge, will be presented to the jury and these images are not appropriate for the public at large to view. Should the judge close the courtroom? Why or why not? Is there anything else that the prosecutor's motion should include?
12. Can all codefendants be tried in a single trial? Why or why not?
13. Do you think criminal defendants should be able to confront all witnesses against them? Why or why not?
14. Under what circumstances can criminal defendants represent themselves? Do you believe that

criminal defendants who cannot afford an attorney should get appointed an attorney, whether the defendant wants an attorney or not?

15. What do you think about a defendant losing his or her ability to attend his or her own trial because of behavior? List three actions you believe, if done by the defendant, would warrant taking away the right to be present.
16. Explain how the double jeopardy clause applies to criminal defendants.
17. If a defendant is charged with kidnapping, and the kidnapping began in one state and continued across many state lines, where could the defendant be charged for the single act of kidnapping?
18. What is the test used by the courts to determine whether entrapment has occurred? Give a factual example of a defendant being entrapped.
19. What rights do victims have a trial?
20. Do you think the defendants' rights discussed in this chapter affect victims' rights? If so, in what ways?

References

United States v. Ewell, 383 U.S. 116 (1966), https://supreme.justia.com/cases/federal/us/383/116/
Doggett v. United States, 505 U.S. 647 (1992), https://supreme.justia.com/cases/federal/us/505/647/
Baker v. Wingo, 407 U.S. 514 (1972), https://supreme.justia.com/cases/federal/us/407/514/
Duncan v. Louisiana, 391 US 145 (1968), https://supreme.justia.com/cases/federal/us/391/145/
Ludwig v. Massachusetts, 427 U.S. 618 (1976), https://supreme.justia.com/cases/federal/us/427/618/
Ramos v. Louisiana, 140 S. Ct. 1390 (2020), https://www.lexisnexis.com/community/casebrief/p/casebrief-ramos-v-louisiana
Nebraska Press Association v. Stewart, 427 U.S. 539, (1976), https://supreme.justia.com/cases/federal/us/427/539/
In re Oliver, 333 U.S. 257 (1948), https://supreme.justia.com/cases/federal/us/333/257/
Sorrells v. United States, 287 U.S. 435 (1932), https://supreme.justia.com/cases/federal/us/287/435/
Sherman v. United States, 356 U.S. 369 (1958), https://supreme.justia.com/cases/federal/us/356/369/
Jacobson v. United States, 503 U.S. 540 (1992), https://supreme.justia.com/cases/federal/us/503/540/
United States v. Russell, 411 U.S. 423 (1973), https://supreme.justia.com/cases/federal/us/411/423/

Chapter 10

Posttrial Proceedings

Introduction: What Happens after a Defendant Is Convicted

This chapter will discuss the defendant's rights after conviction and what happens at a sentencing hearing, and give an overview of the ways a defendant could overturn a conviction.

Chapter Objectives

In this chapter students will learn:

- What the defendant's rights are at the sentencing hearing
- What the victim's rights are at a sentencing hearing
- The general procedure for a sentencing hearing
- What constitutes cruel and unusual punishment under the Eighth Amendment
- How a convicted defendant can appeal
- What happens on appeal if the defendant is indigent
- What collateral attacks can be made on the conviction
- What a writ of habeas corpus is

Key Terms

Key terms and professional terminology that are used in this chapter include:

- **Mandatory sentencing enhancements**
- **Cruel and unusual punishment**
- **Bifurcated proceeding**

- **Aggravating factors**
- **Direct appeal versus discretionary appeal**
- **Prosecutorial misconduct**
- **Indigency**
- **Habeas corpus**

The Sentencing Event

The sentencing stage is often the last stage in the criminal justice system for the defendant. This stage occurs after the criminal defendant has been convicted, by either a guilty plea or a finding of guilt by a judge or jury. In most states, the judge is the person who sentences. In the minority are states allowing juries to sentence the defendants only after a jury trial. In 2000 only, Virginia and Kentucky had such a law.

There are exceptions for capital murder cases, cases involving the death penalty, also. In those cases, there is a bifurcated trial. This means that there are two separate proceedings, one to determine the guilt of the defendant and the second to determine the sentence to be imposed. All states allow for the jury to determine whether the death penalty will be imposed. As of 2017, Alabama became the last state to abolish judicial override. Jury override occurred when the jury would recommend a sentence of life without the possibility of parole, and the judge would override that sentence and sentence the defendant to death. Now, in all fifty states, the jury verdict as to sentencing is the sentence the judge must impose. In a case involving the death penalty, the sentencing hearing can be formal and complex. After all, the ultimate punishment is at issue.

The sentencing hearing can occur directly after the finding of guilt or at a later time. Usually, the sentencing occurs later and at a separate sentencing hearing. This is because the court may not know any of the facts or circumstances of the case or have any information about the defendant's criminal history. The court needs these important pieces of information to ensure a fair sentence. These things are usually complied in a presentence investigative report. The report may include such things as the defendant's family history, employment history, and criminal history; the details of the current crime committed; any substance abuse or mental health history; and an optional statement by the defendant. The court reviews all this information in determining the appropriate sentence. Knowing as much information as possible before imposing sentence gives the court comfort. The defendant can waive the presentence investigative report, but the court may still require one.

There are circumstances, however, where sentencing can occur immediately. Some of those circumstances are when the defendant is convicted of a misdemeanor or minor offense, when the defendant and the state have reached a plea agreement to include an agreement on sentence, or when the defendant requests immediate sentencing.

1. When the defendant is convicted of a misdemeanor or minor offense, the court may sentence the defendant directly after conviction. These sentences usually involve a form of probation. The

probationary sentence can be either supervised or unsupervised. If the sentence is unsupervised, the defendant does not check in with a probation officer and is supervised, basically, by the community as a whole, meaning that if the defendant commits a new offense, the government could move to revoke the defendant's probation. This doesn't always occur, because the officer arresting the defendant for the new offense may not know that the defendant is on probation for another offense. If the probationary period is supervised, the defendant will be checking in with an assigned probation officer. This may be weekly or monthly, depending on the circumstances. The judge may give the probation officer the discretion to decide how intensely the defendant will be supervised. The defendant may also have conditions of his or her probation. Those conditions could include things such as attending substance abuse classes, obtaining a GED (general educational development) certificate, or performing community service. Supervised probation will usually require that the defendant submit to a regular drug test. This could be upon check-in with the probation officer or randomly at the request of the probation officer. There could also be fees attached to the supervision. This could be a fee paid directly to the probation officer at each check-in (supervision fee) or a drug test fee paid at each drug test. The probationer will also be expected to pay the costs of court regularly during the probationary period. These costs could include the administrative costs of court, any fines accessed by the judge, and the recoupment of attorney fees. Even indigent defendants, who are appointed counsel, are expected to repay those attorney fees to the court.

2. When the defendant and the state have reached a plea agreement, it usually involves a term of sentencing. Even with an agreement between the parties, the judge must ratify the agreement. If the judge feels that the agreement is not just, the judge can go higher or lower with the sentence. Of course, at the time of the plea, the court must instruct the defendant that the agreement is not binding on the court and the court can go higher or lower if it so chooses. If the court does not advise the defendant that the sentence could change, the plea could be set aside as involuntary. If the judge considers the sentencing conditions just, the judge will usually sentence the defendant immediately after the plea. In some cases, the judge may move all cases directly to a sentencing docket, as a matter of efficiency. For example, if a judge has twenty cases set to plea, the judge may not have the time to also sentence twenty cases that same day.
3. The court may immediately sentence the defendant after plea, at the request of the defendant. This usually occurs when the defendant has more than one charge and may be already doing time on a prior charge. If a defendant is incarcerated in a prison system, it may be difficult for him or her to participate in programs offered by the prison system if he or she has a pending charge. The prison system will not want to allow the defendant to start an intensive drug treatment program knowing that the defendant may have to be transported back to the state court to address pending charges. This causes many defendants to request early disposal of newer charges. The defendants can plead guilty, waive the presentence investigation, and request the judge sentence immediately, so they can begin the sentence. Usually, the sentences will run

concurrently, so that defendants do not serve any extra time for the new charge, depending on the length of the original sentence.

Options for Sentencing

Several different sentencing options may be available for judges. The judge may impose a sentence of incarceration. In that case, the defendant can be given a determinative term in days, weeks, months, or years. The judge may sentence the defendant to a term of probation. This probationary term may be supervised or unsupervised or come with certain conditions that must be met to remain on probation. The judge may impose a split sentence to include a term of incarceration followed by a term of probation. The amount of discretion that the judge has depends on the jurisdiction. Some states give the sentencing court wide latitude to sentence the defendant however the judge sees fit. Other jurisdictions give judges a range of punishment for each class of offense—for example, a defendant committing a burglary of a home may have a range of punishment between one and ten years, whereas a defendant committing an armed robbery may have a sentencing range of ten years to life. As you can see, the latter gives judges a wide range of discretion in sentencing the defendant.

Some states have **mandatory enhancements of sentences** wherein if a defendant has a certain number of prior felony offenses, the defendant's mandatory minimum sentence is increased. For example, a defendant convicted of burglary may have a sentence of one year and a day to ten years. If a defendant with one prior felony commits the same burglary, his sentence may be enhanced to two to twenty years. If a defendant with two prior felonies commits the same burglary, his sentence may be enhanced to ten years to life. If a defendant with three prior felonies commits the same burglary, his sentence may be ten years to life. Depending on the jurisdiction, enhancements may be added for other things such as selling narcotics near a school, possessing or using a firearm during the commission of the crime, or targeting a certain race while committing the crime.

Keep in mind that the sentence the judge imposes is not usually the sentence that is served. Each state has a parole board that determines the appropriate time for parole of each incarcerated defendant. This is calculated on many different factors, such as type of crime committed, length of the sentence, behavior while incarcerated, recommendations for or against early release, and others. Nonviolent offenders have the greatest chance for early parole and are often released upon serving only a fraction of their sentences. Many states and the US federal government have enacted truth in sentencing laws, which are aimed at abolishing the need for a parole board because the incarcerated defendant will serve the term of years ordered by the judge. This is a public policy to give both the public at large and the criminal defendants an amount of certainty in the amount of time that will be served upon incarceration.

The federal system and most state criminal courts have enacted sentencing guideline acts. These are statistically created worksheets that are calculated for each offender's case. The worksheet may include things such as the type of crime committed, the number of cases being sentenced at the same time, the number of prior felony offenses the defendant has, the amount of misdemeanor offenses the defendant has, whether the defendant served any time of incarceration on previous convictions, whether the defendant got his or her probation or parole revoked on prior cases, whether the defendant used a firearm during the commission of the crime, whether there was injury to the victim, whether the monetary loss was great, and many other factors. Each defendant is given a score, and that score correlates to an amount of time that the defendant should be ordered to serve. This can be a set term of years or a sentencing range for the sentencing judge to follow. Some states make these sentencing guidelines mandatory for the judge to follow, while it is voluntary in other states. In the states where the guidelines are mandatory, there are usually additional rules allowing for either party to file for exceptions to be taken from the guideline range of punishment. Attorneys may file certain aggravating or mitigating factors to persuade the judge not to follow the guideline sheets and argue their respective positions.

> In the state of South Calihoma, the defendant committed an armed robbery in Smallville and was given a sentence of thirty-five years. Also in the state of South Calihoma, another defendant committed a similar armed robbery and received a twelve-year sentence. The state of South Calihoma began reviewing the sentences for similar crimes across the state and determined that different judges had different ideas of a reasonable punishment. Therefore, the state of South Calihoma enacted laws setting sentences based on a sentencing guideline computation based on several factors, such as the offender's criminal history and types of prior crimes committed. The sentencing guideline sheets increased the punishments in Big City but lowered the average punishment in Smallville. Judges in both jurisdictions were unhappy because they lost the discretion they believed they were due. What do you think about sentencing guideline sheets?

The Defendant's Rights at Sentencing

Once convicted, the criminal defendant has several constitutional rights at sentencing. These rights include:

- The right to be free from double jeopardy.
- The defendant has the right to counsel.
- The defendant has the Eighth Amendment right to be free from cruel and unusual punishment.
- The defendant had the right to participate in the sentencing process.
- The defendant has the right to know the prior convictions the government intends to use as enhancement or any other enhancement factors.
- The defendant has the right to be advised of the right to appeal.
- In death penalty cases, the defendant has the right to have the jury pronounce sentence.

The Right to Be Free from Double Jeopardy

A lot of the same rights afforded to the defendant at trial carry over into the sentencing hearing. Double jeopardy was discussed in depth in a previous chapter but is especially applicable to the sentencing hearing. Remember that the defendant's protection from double jeopardy is grounded in the Fifth Amendment to the US Constitution. The Fifth Amendment states that "no person shall be subject for the same offense, to be twice put in jeopardy." The sentencing of the criminal defendant is really what puts him or her in jeopardy. Consider this: The defendant is charged with two counts of burglary in the first degree. One count alleges that the defendant entered the dwelling house of another with the intent to commit a crime therein while armed with a deadly weapon or dangerous weapon. The second count of burglary in the first degree alleges that the defendant entered unlawfully into the dwelling house of another to commit a crime therein, and while effectuating entry or flight there from, caused injury to another person present. This charges the defendant with the same crime twice but in alternate ways. A prosecutor may elect to charge in the alternative if proof is weaker on one count, allowing the jury to convict on either or both charges. In this example, the defendant is convicted after trial by the jury of both counts of burglary in the first degree. At the sentencing event, the judge will need to vacate one count because the defendant can only be sentenced to one alternative of the same crime.

The Defendant Has the Right to Counsel

The criminal defendant has the same right to counsel as discussed in a previous chapter about the defendant's right to counsel at trial, regardless of the defendant's ability hire an attorney. Often it is the same attorney who has represented the defendant at trial who represents the defendant at the sentencing hearing. However, if the attorney withdraws or the defendant fires his attorney after conviction, the defendant will need new representation. The criminal defendant may also be appointed additional assistance at sentencing if he or she cannot afford it. A defendant also has the right to represent himself at a sentencing hearing, just as in trial. The court must confirm that the defendant's waiver of counsel was knowing and voluntary.

In cases wherein the defendant is looking at the possibility of death, the court may appoint stand-in counsel or a mitigation expert for the defendant. A mitigation expert is someone who, through specialized training or experience, can offer consulting to a criminal defendant to develop effective themes and strategies for presentation of mitigation evidence. The mitigation expert may perform a psychological examination of the criminal defendant, conduct interviews with the defendant's family and friends, obtain prior records of the defendant or other individuals involved in the case, or provide statistical reports about the application of the death penalty.

The Defendant Has the Eighth Amendment Right to Be Free from Cruel and Unusual Punishment

The Eighth Amendment to the US Constitution possesses a clause providing for the criminal defendant to be free from **cruel and unusual punishment**. This clause has been the subject of much interpretation by the US Supreme Court because it is a clause that can be interpreted subjectively. The basis of the court's decisions has been to hold sentences unconstitutional if they are cruel and unusual, impose imprisonment only for indigent defendants, or impose a greater sentence after appeal of the case.

Cruel and Unusual

The US Supreme Court addressed this issue in *Miller v. Alabama*. Evan Miller was fourteen years old at the time of his crime. Miller had by then been in and out of foster care because his mother suffered from alcoholism and drug addiction and his stepfather abused him. Miller, too, regularly used drugs and alcohol, and he had attempted suicide four times, the first when he was six years old. One night in 2003, Miller was at home with a friend, Colby Smith, when a neighbor, Cole Cannon, came to make a drug deal with Miller's mother. The two boys followed Cannon back to his trailer, where all three smoked marijuana and played drinking games. When Cannon passed out, Miller stole his wallet, splitting about $300 with Smith. Miller then tried to put the wallet back in Cannon's pocket, but Cannon woke up and grabbed Miller by the throat. Smith hit Cannon repeatedly with a nearby baseball bat. Miller placed a sheet over Cannon's head, told him "I am God, I've come to take your life," and delivered one more blow. The boys then retreated to Miller's trailer, but soon decided to return to Cannon's to cover up evidence of their crime. Once there, they lit two fires. Cannon eventually died from his injuries and smoke inhalation. A jury found Miller guilty and imposed a minimum sentence of life without the possibility of parole for the capital murder offense. The Alabama Court of Criminal Appeals affirmed, holding that Miller's sentence was not overly harsh when compared to his crime. The US Supreme Court took the Miller case and another similar case from Arkansas for review. They held that a mandatory life without parole for a juvenile precluded consideration of his chronological age and its hallmark features—among them, immaturity, impetuosity, and failure to appreciate risks and consequences. It prevented taking into account the family and home environment surrounding him—and from which he could not usually extricate himself, no matter how brutal or dysfunctional. It neglected the circumstances of the homicide offense, including the extent of his participation in the conduct and the way familial and peer pressures may have affected him. Indeed, it ignored that he might have been charged and convicted of a lesser offense if not for incompetencies associated with youth—for example, his inability to deal with police officers or prosecutors (including on a plea agreement) and his incapacity to assist his own attorneys. The Eighth Amendment forbade a sentencing scheme that mandated life in prison without possibility of parole for juvenile offenders.

Impose Imprisonment Only for Indigent Defendants

This violation usually occurs when a criminal defendant is imprisoned solely because of his or her inability to pay a fine or costs of court. The court cannot hold this indigent defendant in jail simply because he or she is indigent. This could also occur when alternatives to jail time exist but are costly. Indigent prisoners would not be able to take advantage of the alternative simply because of their inability to pay, wherein defendants with resources could be released from incarceration because of their ability to pay. For example, Indigent Inge is arrested for a drug possession charge. Rich Ralph is also arrested on a drug possession charge. The jurisdiction in which they are arrested has a drug court program allowing defendants to leave jail and be placed in a rehab, but only if the defendant can pay for the costs of the rehab. Rich Ralph is released from jail to the rehab facility because he has the ability to pay. Indigent Inge remains incarcerated in jail because he does not have the ability to pay for the rehab. This is a violation of the Eighth and Fourteenth Amendments.

Greater Sentence after Appeal of the Case

This is sometimes called the government's revenge. The government is not allowed to retaliate against a criminal defendant who is successful on appeal by increasing the charges or punishment after appeal. This does not mean the defendant cannot get a higher sentence or an additional charge(s) on appeal, but it cannot be vindictive. Each case must be viewed on a case-by-case basis. For example, a defendant appeals a fourteen-year sentence and is successful because he alleges his attorney was ineffective in the sentencing phase of the trial. The sentence is overturned and the case is sent back to the original trial court to be resentenced. The case has the same prosecutor, same judge, same facts, only different defense counsel. The judge gives the defendant twenty-four years on his resentencing. This is a violation of the Eight Amendment.

The Eighth Amendment has been debated many times regarding the imposition of the death penalty. The court has consistently ruled that capital punishment itself is not a violation of the Eighth Amendment but that some applications of the death penalty are "cruel and unusual." For example, the court has ruled that execution of people with intellectual disabilities is unconstitutionally cruel and unusual, as is the death penalty for people who were under age eighteen at the time of their crime. The court has also ruled that certain methods of execution were cruel and unusual—for example, the hanging of an extremely overweight person, which may result in decapitation.

The US Supreme Court has found that the Eighth Amendment does not have a proportionality aspect to the cruel and unusual clause. In *Harmelin v. Michigan*, an inmate claimed that his sentence was cruel and unusual because it was disproportionate to the crime and the sentencing judge was statutorily required to impose it. The court held that the Eighth Amendment contained no proportionality guarantee. In so holding, the court rejected its prior decision of *Solem v. Helm*. The court's prior assumption that cruel and unusual included disproportionate punishments was erroneous because, while severe, mandatory penalties might be cruel but they were not unusual in the constitutional sense, having been employed in various forms throughout the nation's history. The clause disabled the legislature from authorizing particular forms or modes of punishment and, specifically, cruel methods that were not customarily employed. The court found that what was cruel and unusual was to be determined without reference to the particular offense. A sentence that was not otherwise cruel and unusual did not become so simply because it was mandatory.

The Defendant Has the Right to Participate in the Sentencing Process

In the very early days of American criminal law, the defendants did not have the right to participate in a sentencing hearing. If the accused was convicted, he or she was given a sentence and that was the end of the story. As the country evolved, the courts have found it important that the defendant be present at the sentencing hearing and have the opportunity for involvement in that hearing. This gives criminal defendants rights similar to those available to him or her at trial—the right to subpoena witnesses, the right to give testimony, and the right to make an argument for a particular sentence to the judge or jury.

The defendant also has the right to a timely sentencing event. A convicted defendant has the same Sixth Amendment right to speedy sentencing as he or she has to a speedy trial.

The Defendant Has the Right to Be Advised of the Right to Appeal

There is no constitutional right to discretionary appeal, but most states have enacted statutes that give defendants a right to be given notice of the option for appeal.

In Death Penalty Cases, The Right to Have the Jury Pronounce Sentence

Death penalty cases involve a **bifurcated proceeding** wherein after the jury convicts the defendant, the jury has a secondary phase to receive evidence concerning punishment. The evidence presented at the sentencing phase is not necessarily evidence that would be admissible in the first stage of the trial. For example, a family member may be called as a witness in the sentencing phase to discuss the life of the defendant and the hardships the defendant suffered. This would not necessarily be relevant in the guilt phase of the trial. Also, the victim's family may be able to express all the ways the victim's death has affected their lives and why they are seeking certain punishment. These are known as aggravating and mitigating factors. **Aggravating factors** are often required by the state law to enhance the punishment to the death penalty. For example, a murder may have occurred, but to be eligible for the death penalty, two or more aggravating factors must have been present. Each state is free to establish what these aggravating factors are and how many are required. For example, in the state of Georgia, state law lists aggravating factors to elevate murder to a capital (death penalty) offense. See the textbox below for the most current 2022 Georgia Code.

2022 Georgia Code

Title 17: Criminal Procedure

Chapter 10: Sentence and Punishment

Article 2: Death Penalty Generally

Section 17-10-30: Procedure for Imposition of Death Penalty Generally

Read at: https://law.justia.com/codes/georgia/2022/title-17/chapter-10/article-2/section-17-10-30/

The government will call witnesses to prove one or more of these aggravating factors and argue its position for the death penalty.

The defendant has the right to be present and cross-examine the witnesses called by the government. The defendant also has the right to provide evidence of mitigating factors. Mitigating factors are also known as extenuating circumstances surrounding the commission of the crime of which the defendant has been convicted. Mitigating factors can be any factor that reduces the culpability of the defendant. These can be a history of mental illness, a previous trauma suffered by the defendant, a handicap that the defendant possesses, the absence of a criminal history, adversities the defendant has faced in his or her lifetime, or the age of the defendant. The mitigating factor can also be a factor surrounding the facts of the crime committed—for example, if the defendant had a codefendant, and the codefendant took more of a leadership role in the murder, or the defendant somehow showed mercy during the crime. The list of mitigating factors is unlimited. The defense witnesses can vary from calling the defendant's mother to beg for his or her life to a hired mitigation expert spouting statistics about the defendant's circumstance.

The Victim's Rights at Sentencing

Crime victims also have rights at a sentencing hearing. Crime victims have the right to be present at a sentencing hearing. The sentencing event may be postponed for a reasonable amount of time to give the victim notice and the opportunity to be present. The crime victim also has the right to speak at a sentencing hearing. This is often called the victim's impact statement. This statement can be in writing directly to the court or verbally at the sentencing hearing or both. Many judges give victims or victims' families wide latitude to speak, present evidence, or bring others to speak on their behalf.

The federal criminal court system has the Crime Victims' Rights Act[1]. A crime victim has the following rights:

1. The right to be reasonably protected from the accused.
2. The right to reasonable, accurate, and timely notice of any public court proceeding, or any parole proceeding, involving the crime or of any release or escape of the accused.
3. The right not to be excluded from any such public court proceeding, unless the court, after receiving clear and convincing evidence, determines that testimony by the victim would be materially altered if the victim heard other testimony at that proceeding.
4. The right to be reasonably heard at any public proceeding in the district court involving release, plea, sentencing, or any parole proceeding.
5. The reasonable right to confer with the attorney for the Government in the case.
6. The right to full and timely restitution as provided in law.
7. The right to proceedings free from unreasonable delay.
8. The right to be treated with fairness and with respect for the victim's dignity and privacy.
9. The right to be informed in a timely manner of any plea bargain or deferred prosecution agreement.
10. The right to be informed of the rights under this section and the services described in section 503(c) of the Victims' Rights and Restitution Act of 1990 (42 U.S.C. 10607(c)) and provided contact information for the Office of the Victims' Rights Ombudsman of the Department of Justice.

Crime victims also have the right to recoup a reasonable amount of restitution from the defendant for the crime committed. Restitution is monetary in nature for losses due to injury, property damages, lost wages, incidental expenses, psychological care, and any other expense related to the crime committed against them. Also, a victim's representatives may collect the restitution if the victim is unable. For example, a family may be awarded funeral expenses to be paid for by the defendant for the murder of their loved one.

Unfortunately, the reality of the situation is that many defendants are not in a position to pay restitution to victims and certainly cannot make the victim whole with payment of restitution, especially if the defendant will be incarcerated for a lengthy amount of time and has no assets. In these circumstances, there may be crime victim's compensations funds set up in the particular stage that will reimburse victims for a portion of their loss. These reimbursements are rarely the full amount but may offset the victim's losses.

1. United States Government, "Crime Victims' Rights Act," United States Code, United States Government.

The Defendant's Right to Appeal

An appeal is the process by which a convicted defendant can seek recourse from a higher court in hopes of setting aside the decision of the lower court. All types of criminal cases may be appealed—felony, misdemeanor, traffic offenses, and even city ordinances. Trials are very complicated proceedings and there is lots of room for errors by all parties involved. The defendant may complain about any number of things that occurred wrongfully during the trial and appeal those issues.

No Constitutional Right to Appeal

Although the criminal court system is set up with appellate courts to ensure defendants' rights are upheld, there is no constitutional right to appeal. The US Supreme Court in *McKane v. Durston* states that an appeal from a judgment of conviction is not a matter of absolute right, independent of constitutional or statutory provisions allowing such appeal. A review by an appellate court of the final judgment in a criminal case, however grave the offense of which the accused is convicted, was not at common law and is not now a necessary element of due process of law. It is wholly within the discretion of the state to allow or not to allow such a review.

It is the state legislature that enacts the rules for appellate procedure for each state and Congress for the federal criminal justice system. The appellate process is not founded in common law or constitutional law. In fact, most state courts have enacted laws giving convicted defendants at least one appeal. This is known as a **direct appeal**. This means that the appellate court must hear the appeal and does not have the ability to deny it outright.

Another type of appeal is called a **discretionary appeal**. This is an appeal filed in which the higher appellate court can decide to hear the appeal or not to hear the appeal. The US Supreme Court is a court of discretionary appeal.

The Appellate Process

An appeal of a state court decision proceeds to the state appellate court, and an appeal of a federal decision proceeds to a federal appellate court. It is also possible to appeal municipal court convictions that arise within city courts on misdemeanors, and traffic and ordinance violations. Municipal appeals are handled within the state criminal justice system according to the statue of each state. For example, a state statute may read that municipal appeals rise to the state circuit court for a trial de novo. A trial de novo means a trial anew. This means that the trial will be had as if there was no previous trial. This is important because the municipal courts are not courts of record, meaning that there is no court reporter or recording device to evidence the occurrences in the first trial. Therefore, the appellate trial will begin again with the swearing of witnesses, the taking of testimony, and the entry of evidence. If the witnesses or evidence are unavailable, the defendant may be found not guilty in the second trial. As part of the appeal process, again according to the state statute giving the right to appeal, the defendant can request a bench trial or a jury trial. The circuit court will make rulings as in any other more serious cases tried before the bench. If a jury demand has been made, the jury will render the verdict as in all other cases and will not know that the case has been tried before. This same process will occur for any misdemeanor or less serious offense appealed from a court without a record.

When cases are appealed from courts of record, there is evidence of what happened in the first trial and therefore no need to begin the trial again. In this case, the appellate courts review the record of the previous proceeding when accessing the defendant's appeal. The common issues that are appealed are (a) ineffective trial counsel, (b) prosecutorial misconduct, (c) improper judicial rulings, and (d) insufficiency of evidence.

Ineffective Trial Counsel

Notably, most appeals and postconviction relief requests center around complaints of trial counsel's actions. Defendants believe that the trial counsel should have argued harder, called more witnesses, objected more strongly to the prosecution's evidence, advised the defendant differently, and so on. This is especially true when the defendant is indigent and the trial counsel was appointed. The appellate courts must sort out these issues from the record and determine whether the trial counsel acted effectively and within the standards of the profession. The appellate court will review the entire record, not just the trial proceedings. This includes pretrial hearings, motions filed, and subpoenas issued. The defense attorney needs to have adequately prepared the case for trial and documented that representation in the court record. The following are common ways a criminal defense attorney could be ineffective:

1. **Failing to communicate with the defendant.** This occurs when a criminal defense attorney does not meet with, call, or otherwise communicate with the criminal defendant. It is especially easy to prove that there was a failure to communicate if the criminal defendant is incarcerated because the jail should have a record of visits, calls, and letters. Objective reasonableness will be applied, meaning if the attorney communicated once a month, this may be sufficient although the criminal defendant does not think so.
2. **Making decisions in the criminal case without consulting the defendant.** The criminal defendant is the sole decision-maker. The criminal defense attorney is available to provide advice to the criminal defendant, but the defendant will be the final decision-maker on all issues related to the case. This is why it is important for the criminal defense attorney or judge to have the defendant respond on the record, when possible, that he is making certain decisions. If this is not possible, then the criminal defense attorney needs to have certain forms drafted for defendants to sign agreeing that he or she is making the final decision.

Olivia is on trial for the murder of her newborn baby. She has a criminal history of drug sales and misdemeanor assault. During the trial, the state offers evidence that Olivia brought the unresponsive baby to the emergency room. Olivia stated that the baby had fallen off the bed while co-sleeping. The state offers testimony from an expert witness, the medical doctor who examined the baby. The expert witness testified that the baby had a skull fracture consistent with a high-speed automobile crash. The expert witness testified that the baby had petechiae of the eyes, which are tiny spots of bleeding under the eyelids that occurs when a baby is shaken roughly and the blood vessels rupture. The expert witness further testified that the baby had eight other broken but healing fractures on its appendages. The expert witness testified that in his expert opinion the baby was subjected to child abuse and died as a result of the abuse. Olivia's counsel advises Olivia it is in her best interest to testify and explain what happened just before the baby was brought to the emergency room. The attorney believes that Olivia will be soft spoken and demur in her testimony and the jury may feel sorry for her loss of a baby. Olivia takes the witness stand and does well under direct examination. However, when the state's prosecutor cross-examines her, she gets irritated and angry, and begins shouting at the prosecutor. The prosecutor is able to bring up Olivia's priors for distribution of drugs and misdemeanor assault. The jury convicts Olivia of murder. Olivia complains that her trial counsel was ineffective. She alleges that he did not counsel her on the pitfalls of testifying and that she would have never taken the witness stand but for her attorney telling her she had to tell her side. What should her attorney have done to protect himself in this situation?

Prosecutorial Misconduct

Another common complaint on appeal by a criminal defendant is **prosecutorial misconduct**. The prosecutor is the adversary and often the focus of the criminal defendant's animosity for the trial process. The prosecutor is also a professional bound by oath to seek the truth. However, prosecutors can also make mistakes, both unintentional and intentional. The question is whether the prosecutor's actions were within the bounds of the defendant's due process rights. The most common complaint against prosecutors is withholding evidence. Prosecutors have the duty to turn over any exculpatory evidence, evidence that would tend to make the defendant look not guilty. When a prosecutor tampers with evidence or withholds evidence, it is a reversible offense. Other areas of potential prosecutorial misconduct are witness tampering, juror tampering, discrimination in jury selection, and improper comments to the jury.

Christina is a new state attorney and is trying her first child sexual abuse case. She has met with the child victim multiple times and has formed an attachment with the victim. She is disgusted with the allegations of sexual abuse and believes that the defendant should rot in prison for what he has done to this innocent child. During the trial, the child victim testifies and is subjected to cross-examination and gets extremely upset during that process. The defendant declines to take the witness stand. In closing argument, Christina argues that the child was brave enough to take the witness stand and tell what happened, but the defendant was not. The defense attorney objects that the state is improperly commenting on the defendant's constitutional right to silence and demands a mistrial. The judge instructs the jury to disregard the prosecutor's statement and allows the trial to continue. The jury convicts the defendant, and the defendant appeals. The appellate court finds that the prosecutor's comments violated the defendant's rights and overturns the conviction. Do you think this is the right outcome?

Improper Judicial Rulings

Improper judicial rulings are also frequently cited as issues in appeals in criminal cases. Judges make rulings on evidentiary issues, make objections, and give instructions to the jury. Each one of these responsibilities comes with great latitude of discretion. Pretrial issues give the parties time to research the issue and present each side to the court—complete with case law (precedent) on the issue—and make a persuasive argument for or against the issue. The judge takes time to listen and react to the presentation at the pretrial hearing. The judge may also defer ruling until a later time to give him or her time to independently research the issue or consult with colleagues. Therefore, when the judge issues his or her pretrial ruling, it has been well pondered. If the defendant gets an unfavorable ruling, he or she may raise that issue on appeal.

It is important to note that this is one of the few instances in which the government has the opportunity to appeal a ruling of the trial court. If the government gets an unfavorable ruling on appeal, the government may appeal the issue to a higher court and stay the trial waiting on the appellate ruling. The double jeopardy clause prevents the government from appealing a judge's ruling at trial or after the conclusion of the case.

Issues that arise during trial carry a little more time pressure. An attorney may make an offer of proof with a witness on the stand, and the judge must rule on the issue immediately. Attorneys also routinely object during a witness's testimony from the witness stand. These rulings must also be made immediately so that the trial may proceed in a timely manner. This means that a judge must rely on his training and experience in ruling. A judge may interpret the law relative to a particular set of facts based on his understanding of precedent. There are also those cases of first impression, wherein the judge must make a decision without relying on the comfort of a higher courts' previous ruling on the same issue. If the defendant gets an unfavorable ruling on an objecting during trial, he or she could raise that issue on appeal.

Judges are also responsible for instructing the jury on the law and the facts that apply to the case. The judge may have time to work on these instructions pretrial or during the trial based on what the judge knows about the case. There will inevitably be issues that arise during the trial that cause a deviation in the instructions. For example, a set of facts may develop leaving an opportunity for a lesser included instruction for a lesser charge. The parties will surely argue about whether the lesser included charge is warranted; ultimately, the judge will decide to give the instruction or not. There may be other instructions that are requested by both sides such as a flight instruction, an other bad act instruction, a self-defense instruction, or others. If the defendant does not get a favorable ruling, he or she could raise this issue on appeal.

Judicial mistakes that are nonconstitutional in nature, such as admitting a piece of evidence or testimony that should have been suppressed, are subjected to the harmless error rule. A harmless error is a mistake made at the trial level that did not affect the outcome of the case. This is a mistake that can be made by either party or the judge. These nonconstitutional errors have nonconstitutional consequences.

Eric Rain is on trial for capital murder. The state presents evidence that he beat his six-year-old son to death. The law in the jurisdiction states that a person commits capital murder if he commits an intentional murder and the victim is less than twelve years old at the time of the murder. Capital murder carries a sentence of death or life without the possibility of parole. At the conclusion of the case, the attorneys submit jury instructions to the judge for review. The defense submits a requested jury instruction for a lesser included offense of murder. Murder carries a punishment of incarceration for ten years to life. The judge refuses the lesser included instruction, stating that because the murder is capital due to the age of the child victim, there is no possibility that the jury could return a verdict for the lesser included offense because there is no evidence presented to show the child is greater than twelve years old. The judges's ruling will more than likely be sustained on appeal.

Steve Bivens is on trial for distribution of a controlled substance. The state intends to present testimony from a police informant who will say that she was working for the drug task force and purchased cocaine from Steve while wearing a recording device. The recording is hard to hear, as there is a lot of background noise due to the loud rap music Steve was playing during the transaction. It was also dark in the room, making it difficult to clearly identify Steve in the video. The state has filed an other bad acts motion and is requesting to prove Steve's other two drug distribution cases (from four and six months prior) to this same jury. The state intends to call the same confidential informant and play the videos from those transactions (which are much better quality). The state alleges that the other bad acts will show Steve's pattern of conduct for selling cocaine. Steve's defense attorney argues that allowing the state to show the other bad acts will inflame the jury and only show Steve's bad character as a drug dealer. The defense attorney urges the judge to disallow the state from using other acts and to make the state try this one distribution case on the merits of this case alone. The judge allows the state to show the two other drug distribution videos and the jury convicts Steve of distribution of a controlled substance in less than ten minutes. Steve appeals. Steve could be successful depending on what the precedent in that jurisdiction is for allowing other act evidence.

Insufficiency of Evidence

A standard complaint for appeal purposes is that there was insufficient evidence in the government's case to convict the defendant of the charge. This is a difficult appeal ground to prevail on. The natural argument for the government, especially in a jury trial, is that the jury must have thought there was sufficient evidence because they returned a verdict of guilt. The insufficiency of evidence ground goes hand and hand with a claim of newly discovered evidence. Many criminal defendants claim that their convictions should be set aside because there is newly discovered evidence. A classic example of this ground is the modernization of DNA testing.

Louise is on trial for stealing a car from a small, local, buy here, pay here car dealership. She was seen in the stolen vehicle by two people the day it was stolen. The video surveillance from the car lot is poor quality but does show an individual that fits Louise's height and build breaking into the building to get the key and then driving off in the car. The next day, the police found the car parked a few blocks from Louise's apartment. They fingerprinted the vehicle and Louise's prints were inside. Several months go by while Louise awaits trial on her case. The prosecution learns that Louise's defense is that she test-drove the vehicle a few days before it was taken and that explains her fingerprints inside the vehicle. Louise's attorney also tells the prosecutor that the witnesses who saw her in the vehicle must be mistaken about the day and that they saw her on the day of the test drive. The prosecutor sends the investigator back to the car lot and asks employees if they remember Louise test-driving the car. Only one employee is still employed at the lot and cannot remember whether Louise drove the car or not. The car lot does not keep records of test drives past ninety days. Despite Louise's defense, the prosecutor convicts Louise of stealing the car based on the evidence presented. Louise is sentenced to ten years in prison due to her previous criminal history. Louise files an appeal citing discovery of new evidence. She attaches a statement from one of the state's witnesses who says that she is not sure what day she saw Louise driving the vehicle. The witness said that she only said it was that day and time because she wanted to please the officer. Now that Louise is convicted, she feels bad that she did not stand her ground and say she wasn't sure. This is newly discovered evidence that may afford the defendant a new trial.

Indigency and the Appellate Process

A defendant who is **indigent** still has the right to appeal. If the defendant cannot afford appellant counsel, counsel will be appointed. This is the same Sixth Amendment guarantee that gives defendants the right to counsel at trial. The trial transcript is a necessary part of the appeal. The appellant and counsel need a record to review to examine whether there were constitutional violations. Trial transcripts can cost several hundred dollars, if not thousands, depending on the length of the trial. The court reporter is the one who is usually paid for the time to takes to type the transcript and transcribe it into a readable form. If a criminal defendant is indigent, the defendant has the right to a free trial transcript.

Probation and Parole Revocation

If a defendant is given a probationary sentence and then violates the terms of his or her probation, the probationary sentence can be revoked and incarceration imposed. The defendant is entitled to a revocation hearing before being revoked. The standard of proof to revoke a defendant's sentence is that the judge is reasonably satisfied that the defendant has violated the terms of his or her probation. This is a fairly low standard compared with other standards in the criminal courts system.

A defendant also may be given an early release of sentence by being paroled. This is generally done by hearing by a parole board. If released on parole, the defendant will be given a parole officer and certain requirements of parole. These requirements are meant to help the defendant readjust to living in society as opposed to prison. If a criminal defendant cannot conform to the rules and conditions of parole, his or her parole can be revoked and he or she can be sent back to prison. This would occur only after a parole revocation hearing.

Habeas Corpus

Habeas corpus translated from Latin means "show me the body." It is a historical remedy created by English common law courts to prevent individuals from being detained unlawfully. This writ prevented the proverbial "lock him up and throw away the key." It is used as a last resort for prisoners who have exhausted all other remedies available to him or her in the criminal justice system.

What Is It?

The "Great Writ" of habeas corpus is a fundamental right in the constitution that protects against unlawful and indefinite imprisonment. The writ makes no determination of whether the individual is guilty or not guilty but rather whether the individual is being held unlawfully. This could be for any number of reasons, such as violations of constitutional rights or typography mistakes in a charging instrument.

What is the procedure?

To file for habeas corpus relief, the person who is the subject of the habeas corpus petition must be in custody. This petition can be filed by an incarcerated individual or an attorney representing the incarcerated individual. It should be filed in the jurisdiction in which the person is being detained. It can also be filed in a federal jurisdiction concerning a state detention.

What Remedies Does the Writ Offer?

A writ of habeas corpus can empower a judge to release an individual wrongfully detained if the evidence warrants an unlawful detention. The judge need not make any determinations of whether the defendant committed a criminal act. For example, a detainee may file a writ of habeas corpus alleging that his right to speedy trial have been violated in a case where the government has delayed prosecution, yet the individual remains detained. There is no discussion in the writ as to whether the defendant committed the crime charged, but rather that the government is taking too long in reaching the trial in the matter.

Depending on what the issues are, the judge could release the defendant and order him to appear to face the charges when the government is ready for trial or dismiss the charges altogether.

If an individual who has been convicted of a crime and is incarcerated files a writ of habeas corpus, the judge could grant any number of relief options to the defendant. For example, the judge could reduce the defendant's sentence length; immediately release the defendant from prison; or transfer the defendant to incarceration in a less restrictive environment, such as a work release program or community corrections department.

Right to Counsel?

The criminal defendant is entitled to an attorney on a direct appeal or an appeal of right. A criminal defendant is not entitled to counsel on a discretionary appeal. A writ of habeas corpus is akin to a discretionary appeal, therefore there is no Sixth Amendment right to counsel. This means that petitioners often file these writs on their own and without the assistance of an attorney. Sometimes, they employ the assistance of so-called jail house attorneys, who are other inmates who may have filed the same thing at an earlier date.

One common postconviction relief petition is an allegation of ineffective assistance of counsel. Many states have rules of criminal procedure setting out the procedures forfeiting such a complaint and the requirements for a proper filing. For example, the petition may need to be filed within a one year or other statute of limitation. There could be other requirements, such as the issue of ineffective assistance of counsel cannot have been addressed on appeal prior.

To prove ineffective assistance, a defendant must show that their trial lawyer's performance fell below an "objective standard of reasonableness" and "a reasonable probability that, but for counsel's unprofessional errors, the result of the proceeding would have been different." This is a high standard to meet. Even if the attorney's actions or lack of actions fell below an objective standard of reasonableness, the attorney's actions or lack of actions could have resulted in a different outcome. This question is sometimes answered by the strength of the state's case.

Benjamin Paris was convicted of multiple sexual offenses involving his minor children. Three of his children testified against him as victims and witnesses. A forensic scientist testified that the defendant's DNA was found inside the vagina of a ten-year-old victim. The investigator testified that the defendant confessed to the crimes shortly after arrest. The jury convicted the defendant. The defendant files a habeas corpus petition alleging that his attorney was ineffective. The allegations are that the defendant's counsel only met with him twice before the trial and did not subpoena any witnesses. In response, the defense attorney stated that the defendant told him that he did molest his children and the investigator coerced him into the confession. The defense attorney stated that the defendant did not provide him any contact information for the witnesses he wanted to subpoena. Therefore, he could not subpoena the witnesses. Even if the court found that the attorney should have made a greater effort to locate witnesses, it would be hard to establish that the extra witnesses would have changed the outcome of the trial. Both prongs: the trial counsel must have been ineffective and that ineffectiveness must have effected the outcome of the case, must be met to overturn a conviction on a complaint of ineffective assistance of counsel claim.

The Government's Right to Appeal

The government has a very limited right to appeal. Because of double jeopardy, as discussed previously, the government cannot appeal a not-guilty finding. The government can appeal pretrial rulings if the court gives pretrial rulings. However, if the court declines to make a pretrial rulings and jeopardy attaches, appeal is no longer available to the government.

Rules to Remember

Below is a list of rules to remember from this chapter.

- After conviction, the trial judge sentences criminal defendants in most states.
- A judge may have wide discretion in imposing a sentence of a term of years for probation or incarceration.
- A criminal defendant does not usually serve the entire length of the incarceration sentence; many defendants are given early release.
- A criminal defendant has many rights at sentencing, including the right to be free from double jeopardy, the right to counsel, the Eighth Amendment right to be free from cruel and unusual punishment, the right to participate in the sentencing process, the right to know the prior convictions the government intends to use as enhancement or any other enhancement factors,

and the right to be advised of the right to appeal.

- In death penalty cases, the criminal defendant has the right to have the jury pronounce sentence.
- Crime victims have the right to be present and speak at the criminal defendant's sentencing.
- There is no constitutional right to a discretionary appeal; however, many state statues give criminal defendants this right.
- Common issues raised during appeal are ineffective trial counsel, prosecutorial misconduct, improper judicial rulings, and insufficiency of evidence.
- An indigent criminal defendant will be given counsel for direct appeals.
- An indigent criminal defendant will be provided a transcript of his or her trial proceeding for use on appeal.
- A writ of habeas corpus is used as a last resort for incarcerated criminal defendants to attack a conviction.
- The government only has the right to appeal pretrial rulings.

End of Chapter Comprehension and Application

Directions: Use what you have learned in this chapter to help you respond completely and correctly to each question or prompt below.

1. What is jury override and why do you think it was abolished?
2. Under what circumstances would a judge sentence a defendant immediately upon conviction?
3. What are sentencing guideline worksheets? What is their purpose?
4. What do you think about the sentencing guidelines' limit on the judge's discretion?
5. The defendant is convicted of two counts of capital murder of the same victim. One count is because the victim was a child. The second one is because the defendant was committing a burglary when the child was killed. Can the defendant be given two separate sentences for these convictions? Why or why not?
6. At what postconviction proceedings does a defendant have the right to counsel?
7. At what postconviction proceedings does a defendant not have a right to counsel? What do you think about this?
8. The Eighth Amendment's cruel and unusual clause protects defendants from cruel and unusual punishments. Give three examples of punishments that would be considered cruel and unusual.
9. What is the difference between the defendant's and the victim's rights at sentencing? What do you think about this difference?
10. What are the defendant's rights to appeal?
11. What must a defendant show to prevail on an ineffective assistance of counsel claim?
12. Give three examples of prosecutorial misconduct.
13. How can a judge cause a mistrial? Give an example.

14. What is an indigent defendant entitled to on appeal?
15. What is the standard of review for a probation revocation hearing? What are your thoughts about this standard?
16. What is a writ of habeas corpus?
17. Who can file a habeas corpus petition?
18. What remedies are available with a writ of habeas corpus?
19. When can the government appeal an issue to an appellate court? Give an example.
20. Do defendants have greater, lesser, or equal rights on appeal than at trial? Explain your answer.

References

Miller v. Alabama, 567 U.S. 460 (2012), https://supreme.justia.com/cases/federal/us/567/460/
Harmelin v. Michigan, 501 U.S. 957 (1991), https://supreme.justia.com/cases/federal/us/501/957/
Solem v. Helm, 463 U.S. 277, 77 L. Ed. 2d 637 (1983), https://supreme.justia.com/cases/federal/us/463/277/
18 U.S.C. § 3771, Rights of Victims, US Department of Justice, accessed July 5, 2023, https://www.justice.gov/enrd/rights-victims
McKane v. Durston, 153 U.S. 684 (1894), https://supreme.justia.com/cases/federal/us/153/684/
Strickland v. Washington, 466 U.S. 668 (1984), https://supreme.justia.com/cases/federal/us/466/668/

Printed by Libri Plureos GmbH in Hamburg,
Germany